THE MESSAGE
AND THE BOOK

THE MESSAGE
AND THE BOOK

Sacred Texts of the World's Religions

John Bowker

Atlantic Books
London

First published in hardback in Great Britain in 2011 by Atlantic Books, an imprint of Atlantic Books Ltd.

10 9 8 7 6 5 4 3 2 1

A CIP catalogue record for this book is available from the British Library.

Atlantic Books Edition ISBN: 978 1 84887 811 2
Callisto Edition ISBN: 978 0 85740 001 7

Printed in Great Britain by the MPG Books Group

Atlantic Books
An Imprint of Atlantic Books Ltd
Ormond House
26–27 Boswell Street
London
WC1N 3JZ

www.atlantic-books.co.uk

CONTENTS

INTRODUCTION

No one has read all the sacred texts of the world; nor will anyone ever do so. There are simply too many for any individual to read them all. As this book makes clear, there are at least 100,000 of them, perhaps a quarter of a million, maybe even more.

SACRED AND PROFANE

Why is the number uncertain? Mainly because it depends on what counts as a 'sacred text', and that in turn depends on what the word 'sacred' means. It is easy enough to go to a Latin dictionary and find out that the word *sacrum* refers to something dedicated to the gods, or even something set apart for the gods in order that they may destroy it. But the original meaning of a word in one language does not tell us what that word has become when it has moved house and taken up residence in another language.

Even so, it may give us a clue. Thus the word 'sacred' may no longer mean 'something dedicated to the gods', but it does often imply that something has been set apart to be revered or respected for particular qualities or associations. The square at Lord's cricket ground is spoken of as 'sacred turf', not because it has been dedicated to the gods, but because it is associated with the highest levels of the game and with the long history of Test Matches, not least against the Australians.

The distinction between 'sacred' and 'profane' in human life and history is so profound that Emile Durkheim (1858–1917), who is regarded by many as 'the father of social science', took it to be the essence of religion. As he wrote in *The Elementary Forms of the Religious Life* (1912, transl. 1961, pp. 52, 62):

> All known religious beliefs, whether simple or complex, present one common characteristic: they presuppose a classification of all things, real and ideal, of which men think, into two classes or

opposed groups, generally designated by two distinct terms which are translated well enough by the words *profane* and *sacred* . . . A religion is a unified system of beliefs and practices relative to sacred things, that is to say, things set apart and forbidden.

To call a text 'sacred', therefore, implies that it is different in some way from other more ordinary texts. But in what way – or rather, in what ways, since there is no single or simple criterion of distinction or difference?

REVELATION AND TEACHING

The most obvious way in which a text might be called sacred lies in the claim that it does not come from a human author, or at least not from a human author alone. Many texts are believed to come from God (or from some equivalent external source), either because God has written them or because he has inspired people to speak or write them. The ways in which God is believed to have done this are extremely varied, as this book makes clear. What, at least, they have in common is the belief that a text is sacred if it is Revelation and if it is inspired. Bible (p. 25), Quran (p. 125) and Vedas (p. 168) are Revelation in that sense, but they are very different from each other. To the question, 'Who or what is revealed?', this book is the beginning of an answer.

By no means all the texts regarded as sacred are in the category of Revelation. A large number of texts are revered and set apart because they contain teaching that leads to Enlightenment. The sacred texts of Buddhists or of Jains, for example, are not revealed by God, but they are set apart and distinguished because in the case of Buddhists they contain the Teaching of the Buddha, the one who has himself attained Enlightenment and can therefore show the way, or because in the case of Jains they contain the Teaching of 'the Ford-makers', the Tirthankaras, who can therefore be trusted as guides.

So how do we know which are the texts of Revelation or of Teaching? Where Revelation is concerned, it will already be obvious that texts cannot be picked out as revealed on the ground that they contain some agreed and obvious characteristic. Texts do not come into the world stamped with a seal saying 'revealed', 'sacred' or 'inspired'. To say that a text is 'sacred' is a human judgement.

There are many reasons why that judgement has been made in the past about particular texts, whether of Revelation or of Teaching. Often such judgements relate to origin and content – they are made, that is, on the basis of how a text is believed to have come into being, or on the basis of what it contains. For Buddhists, for example, a basic test is whether the text in question helps the person using it to attain the goal (e.g., p. 240).

Fundamental, however, to that judgement is the recognition or acceptance that some particular texts or group of texts have authority. The word 'authority' is derived from the Latin *auctoritas* which in turn is related to *auctor*, 'author'. By having authority, sacred texts may become the author (or at least joint-author) of the stories that people tell through their lives and histories. Sacred texts challenge people, and they offer them warrants and justification for what they think, say and do. The appeal to a sacred text for warrant and justification may be direct and literal, or it may be mediated through interpretation and exegesis, but in either case it is believed that the words should guide or control or inspire the lives of those who read or hear them. The words are then translated into the lives of individuals and into the organisation of families and societies.

SACRED TEXTS AND THEIR READERS

Because sacred texts have authority, people turn to them for an immense variety of reasons, ranging from a direct encounter with God or an immediate experience of Enlightenment, to a need for reassurance, guidance or inspiration. Some may go for far more elementary reasons, to predict the future, for example, or to find a wife.

People also turn to texts in extremely varied ways and with very different expectations. As a result, it is possible for several people to read the same sacred text but find in it entirely different and often conflicting meanings. It is exactly as William Blake observed in 'The Everlasting Gospel':

> The vision of Christ that thou dost see
> Is my vision's greatest enemy.
> Thine is the friend of all mankind;
> Mine speaks in parables to the blind . . .
> Both read the bible day and night;
> But thou read'st black where I read white.

The consequence is not only disagreement, but such contest and anger that it leads to religious wars. The point is there is no single 'meaning' of a text waiting to be found and accepted by all people, and that is true despite the way in which authority figures in religions often attempt to impose an official 'meaning' on a text. In fact, and in contrast to that, texts offer rich opportunities of meaning and interpretation.

There are, of course, limits of possibility set by the text itself – not *all* meanings are possible! Nevertheless, the experience of reading or hearing a sacred text is a two-way interaction: the text offers to readers or listeners challenge and opportunity, but readers and listeners discern in the text the meanings that connect with their own experience and biography – not necessarily in an isolated way, since the hearing and readings of texts often take place in communities.

The fundamental question (and it is indeed the question of fundamentalism in the religious understanding of sacred texts) is whether the text *dictates* its meaning to the reader, or whether the reader *discerns* within the text meanings that have authority but are not necessarily fixed or certain. Dictation theories of meaning allow the text to move from page to person in a direct way, as though the unchanging meaning of the text is already contained within it and can therefore be applied directly to any circumstance or person without the intervention of much, if any, interpretation. To give an example: in 1988 the *Philadelphia Inquirer* reported that the three Strode children (Matthew, six, Pepper, seven, and Duffey, eleven) had been suspended from their school for preaching in the playground. They were suspended (according to the report in the *Inquirer*, 4 September 1988, p. 19a), 'for hurling biblical invective – including references to "whoremongers", "fornicators", and "adulterers" – at their teachers . . . "I never called anybody anything," said Duffey of his preaching. "I just quoted the verse, 'Marriage is honourable in all and the bed undefiled, but whoremongers and adulterers God will judge,' and I guess they took that personally."'

In contrast to the dictation of meaning is the discernment of meaning in what is known as 'hermeneutics' (the shared discipline of interpreting and understanding texts). The 'hermeneutics of opportunity' emphasises that no text has a single, unequivocal 'meaning': the text still has authority, but its possible meanings have to be discerned; those meanings may be contested, and certainly they may change and develop in the course of time, or even in the course of a single lifetime.

It is obvious, therefore, that the interaction between texts and readers is extremely complicated. Not surprisingly, it has given rise to an academic discipline known by such names as 'reader-response criticism', but even the practitioners of that criticism acknowledge its complexity. To give only one example, Suleiman wrote (p. 6):

> Audience-oriented criticism is not one field but many, not a single
> widely trodden path but a multiplicity of crisscrossing, often
> divergent tracks that cover a vast area of the critical landscape in
> a pattern whose complexity dismays the brave and confounds the
> faint of heart.

So the meaning of sacred texts, whether of Revelation or of Teaching, is not immutably fixed or agreed. The meanings are created with great diversity in the lives of those who hear or read them.

SACRED BY ASSOCIATION

In both cases, Revelation and Teaching, other texts then come to be regarded as *sacred by association*: they are a kind of extension of an original Revelation or Teaching and they derive their sacredness from that association. Going back to the distinction between 'sacred' and 'profane', they are more on the side of the sacred because of their association with the original Revelation or Teaching, even though it is usually made abundantly clear that they are not to be confused with it.

Once again, the ways are very varied in which that association is made. It might be, for example, by way of commentary (e.g., *dharmashastra*, p. 180), application (such as Hadith, p. 137, or papal encyclicals, p. 75), or extension. In the latter case, where texts that have come to be accepted as Revelation or Teaching are extended by further texts, there are often claims that those further texts actually belong to Revelation (e.g., the relationship between *smriti* and *shruti*, p. 175) or to Teaching (e.g., the extension to the Buddha's Teaching in Mahayana Buddhism, p. 250).

Such claims may then be rejected by others and this may well produce radical disagreement in a particular religion (e.g., the status of books in the Apocrypha in Christianity, p. 31, or the status of Mahayana sutras in Theravada Buddhism).

But even if the boundaries are blurred or disputed, it is obvious that sacred texts are not confined to Revelation or to Teaching: many texts are held to be 'sacred by association' far beyond the limits of Revelation and Teaching. Examples are the lives of men and women who exhibit the goals of the religion in question (e.g., saints, gurus, teachers), rules of life (e.g., monastic rules, p. 89ff., 243), guidance on the meaning and practice of meditation (e.g., p. 270ff.), chants and hymns (e.g., pp. 77, 161, 168, 198).

SACRED AND SACROSANCT

In the above examples, it is easy to see such texts are 'sacred by association'. There are yet other texts to which people go because they have authority and which are regarded, if not as sacred, then certainly as sacrosanct: in particular, their authority and guidance cannot be contested.

Among the many examples of sacrosanct texts are those which define societies politically, as, for example, in the various Acts of Toleration in England which extended the range of those who can participate in society. The sacrosanct nature of texts that define society can be seen above all in Constitutions. Thus, the 'final court of appeal' in the United States is the Supreme Court, which interprets the Constitution. The Constitution is sacrosanct because although it can be amended, it cannot be ignored or disregarded.

It may be thought that even if Constitutions are sacrosanct they can hardly be regarded as sacred because they have little to do with religion. In fact many Constitutions are derived from religious attitudes and beliefs, and are very closely connected to religions, often by way of affirmation, sometimes by denial. Thus Article 6 of the American Constitution, reflecting a strong desire not to replicate the European wars of religion, lays down that 'no religious Test shall ever be required as a Qualification to any Office or public Trust under the United States.' The First Amendment then added, 'Congress shall make no law respecting an establishment of religion, or prohibiting the free exercise thereof.'

Constitutions as sacrosanct texts are important for religious believers because they define the place of religion in society, and that will be of major consequence, both for religious believers and for the nature of the society in question. To give an example: when Ceylon ceased to be a British colony in 1948 and became once more Sri Lanka (in 1972), it was offered Dominion status. Buddhists objected to this being incorporated in the new Constitution on the grounds that it recognised the Queen as head of the Commonwealth countries. How could one called *Defensor fidei* (p. 66) defend two faiths at once? In the 1978 Constitution, therefore, Buddhism (Buddha Sasana) is given explicit status in the state. Section 3.10 states that 'every person is entitled to freedom of thought, conscience and religion', but that is in the context of section 2.9:

> The Republic of Sri Lanka shall give to Buddhism the foremost
> place and accordingly it shall be the duty of the State to protect and
> further the Buddha Sasana.

In India, to take another example, a deliberate attempt was made to create 'India as a secular state', to quote the title of the book by D. E. Smith, in which he wrote (p. 6):

> The underlying assumption of this concept is simply that religion
> and the state function in two basically different areas of human
> activity, each with its own objectives and methods. It is not the
> function of the state to promote, regulate, direct, or otherwise
> interfere in religion. Similarly, political power is outside the scope

of religion's legitimate aims. The democratic state derives its
authority from a secular source ('the consent of the governed') and
is not subordinate to ecclesiastical power.

But that distinction between 'religion and the state' cannot be achieved in India, and this is due to religious reasons as even the brief account in this book of *dharma* (p. 179) will make clear. Many Indians have a strong sense of Hindutva, the distinctive quality of Indian traditions and achievements, in which they take immense pride. The way in which Hindutva is expressed in political parties like RSS (Rashtriya Svayamsavak Sangh) or BJP (Bharatiya Janata Party) makes the distinction between the religious and the political impossible (on the political implications of Hindutva, see my *Beliefs that Changed the World*, p. 122). Not surprisingly, the Indian Constitution recognises that Indian religions have a special status. Section 3.25.1 states that 'all persons are equally entitled to freedom of conscience and the right freely to profess, practise and propagate religion.' However, section 3.25.2 (b) affirms that nothing in 3.25.1 shall prevent the state from making any law 'providing for social welfare and reform or the throwing open of Hindu religious institutions of a public character to all classes and sections of Hindus'; and Hindus are then defined so as to include 'persons professing the Sikh, Jaina or Buddhist religion'.

That is very different from the Constitution of Pakistan, 1973, which, having stated (2.120) that 'every citizen shall have the right to profess, practise and propagate his religion', also states (9.227.1):

> All existing laws shall be brought in conformity with the
> Injunctions of Islam as laid down in the Holy Quran and
> Sunnah . . . , and no law shall be enacted which is repugnant to
> such Injunctions.

Those examples make clear some of the differing ways in which religions are related to the legal construction of society, and why people go to Constitutions for authority and guidance (for a further example, from Russia, see p. 72). Sacrosanct texts of that kind greatly extend the range of 'sacred texts'. In this book, however, it is possible to look only at the more obvious sacred texts, those that have just been described as existing on two levels: those that are primary and foundational, and those others that are built on the foundations and are secondary, but are regarded as sacred because of their association with the primary texts.

CANONS AND CANONICAL TEXTS

Even the distinction between primary and secondary texts has to be made with caution because, as we have seen, the difference between them is blurred: it is not always agreed in particular religions where the line of distinction is to be drawn. For that reason, attempts have been made in many religions to define the primary and foundational texts, and perhaps even to draw up lists of them. That is why the foundational sacred texts in a particular religion are often gathered into a recognised collection.

The most usual word for a collection of that kind is 'Canon'. The word originated in the Jewish and Christian traditions but is now commonly used for collections of sacred texts in other religions. The word 'canon' comes from the Greek κανων. That word is linked to the Hebrew word קנה meaning 'a stalk' or 'a reed' which was of particular use as 'a measuring rod'. In Greek κανων came to mean a straight stick or rod used especially to measure lengths, but it was then applied metaphorically to the rules and standards by which things can be judged. It thus came to mean a norm or rule of behaviour.

In the early Christian Church (or more accurately Churches) there was much diversity of belief and practice, with many different and often competing interpretations of the nature and work of Jesus as Christ. It took centuries for the Canon of Scripture to be agreed (p. 51f.), but once it was established it and its contents became the standard against which the competing differences could be measured in order to separate the true from the false.

Putting the point more generally, canonical texts are those which communities of believers have established in the past and which subsequent generations accept as having authority. A Canon, therefore, is an authorised or accepted collection of sacred texts, as, for example, in 'the Buddhist Canon' (p. 236f.).

It is often linked to the word 'Scripture', meaning religions that are written down, as in 'the Jewish Canon of Scripture', but that conjunction may be confusing if it implies that canonical texts are printed or at least 'written down' (as the Latin *scripto*, 'I write', might imply). A vast number of sacred texts were originally passed on by word of mouth, and a great many still are. In times before the increase in literacy and the invention of printing (centuries earlier in China than in the West), oral transmission was paramount (e.g., the Mishnah in Judaism, p. 33, or storytelling in India, p. 183). In those circumstances, the learning of texts was of supreme importance, as indeed it still may be: for an example, see p. 125 for the high value given to the learning of the Quran, even by those who do not understand Arabic.

DRAMA, MUSIC AND ART

There are other reasons for not identifying 'sacred texts' with Scripture that go far beyond the importance of their transmission by word of mouth. Sacred texts are also dramatic: they are performed. Examples of this are the Mystery and Passion Plays in England, or Kathakali performances in India (p. 196).

Nor are sacred texts transmitted through dramatic performance alone. They are carried into life and awareness especially by music (for examples see pp. 220, 293). An obvious way in which it happens is when the words from a sacred text (or words derived from a sacred text) are sung or chanted. Examples are the Cantor in Judaism, Gregorian chants or oratorios, ranging from Bach to Pärt, in Christianity – people sing the hymns of the Wesley brothers (p. 79) more often than they read their books.

The importance of music in relation to sacred texts is equally obvious in India, where sound expressed in and through mantras (p. 168) precedes the imperfections of language. But language in association with music comes into its own for Hindus and Sikhs in the singing of devotional hymns known as *kirtan(a)*.

To give an example: Chaitanya (*c.*1485–1533) was the founder of one of the most important movements devoted to Krishna (it is familiar outside India in the form known as ISKCON with Chaitanya's chant 'Hare Krishna, Hare Krishna, Krishna, Krishna, Hare, Hare, Hare Rama, Hare Rama, Hare, Hare'). When he died his teaching and practice were continued by followers known as Goswamis, but Chaitanya did not write any sacred texts to guide or control them. Instead he introduced the intense chanting of Krishna's name accompanied by dance to the *kartal* (two circular brass discs) and *pakhavaj* (a two-sided tambourine). The dancing and chanting of the sacred name took him and those who followed him into the presence of God. *Chaitanya Bhagavata* begins with a prayer of devotion (1.1):

> These two [Chaitanya and his companion Nityanda], with
> long arms extending to their knees, glow as with gold: it is they
> who brought into being the practice of *sankirtan* . . . To them,
> protectors of *yugadharma*, I offer myself – to them the incarnate
> manifestation of the grace of God.

Drama and music are important ways in which sacred texts are carried and conveyed through time. So also is art. In relation to sacred texts, the fundamental art is that of calligraphy. Before the invention of printing all texts had to be copied and written by hand: they were literally 'manu-scripts'.

Those texts that were regarded as sacred were usually treated with great reverence. They were often written in ways that clearly recognised the status of the texts in question.

In India, for example, the general word for 'worship' is *puja*. Among Jains, therefore, the veneration of sacred texts is known as *shastra-* (p. 180) or *jñana-* (p. 191) *puja*. It was the responsibility of senior Jain ascetics, known as *Bhattaraka* ('learned persons'), to maintain the library of sacred texts in each temple and to commission from wealthy donors the gift of new copies in as fine a style as the donors could afford. John Guy has summarised the importance of this in the creation and preservation of Jain texts (p. 92):

> The commissioning of a copy of a Jain text was seen as a meritorious act. It was customary for a lay owner to commission a text to be copied and illustrated for presentation to the donor's spiritual teacher. These in turn would be presented to the monk's temple library. Over the centuries the libraries were recipients of great quantities of these texts, which were employed in the instruction of monks and nuns. The study of the sacred texts (*svadhyaya*) was an important monastic activity, and the libraries fulfilled an important function in making texts available for both study and ritual use . . . In becoming the guardians of sacred literature, the libraries also became the guardians of an important painting tradition.

The integration of text and art is most obvious in the art of China and Japan because texts are often included as part of the finished work of art. As I put it in *The Sacred Neuron* (pp. 65f):

> It is obvious – literally obvious – that empty spaces in Chinese paintings are filled with writing and seals: the first three seals indicate the two names of the artist and some quintessential idea that belongs to the picture; the writing is usually the poetry that is part also of the picture, so much so that the calligraphy is often in the same style as the painting . . . It is because painting and poetry are two ways of saying the same thing that in China poetry is known as the host who issues the invitation and painting is known as the guest.

This was taken even further in Zen calligraphy where 'the way of the pen' (*bokuseki*) is a disciplined way in which to enter the Buddha-nature itself. As I put it in *The Oxford Dictionary of World Religions* (p. 189), 'Zen calligraphy eliminates the gap between subject and object if it is undertaken in the appropriate way and without hesitation: you become what you paint, because you were not other than that in the first place.'

The reference to painting points to an entirely different way in which the work of a scribe might be enhanced: decorations and small paintings might be added to the manuscript. Miniature painting flourished in the whole family of Indian religions, and it began in the illumination of manuscripts – particularly among Buddhists in East India until the thirteenth century, and among Hindus and Muslims under the Mughal/Mogul emperors.

That desire to make the manuscript of a sacred text as worthy of its subject matter as possible is found also outside India. In Europe, for example, it led to the production of illuminated manuscripts of great beauty. In times of widespread illiteracy such pictures, whether in texts or in the stained glass of church windows, were helpful in teaching the faith. But they were equally powerful in evoking an emotional and religious response. That is a point made strongly by Michelle Brown in her introduction to the Folio Society edition of *The Holkham Bible* (pp. 9f.):

> To view it merely as a religious picture book, designed to help
> instruct an illiterate audience in the basics of Bible stories, is to
> miss the point of the work that marks a radical shift in modes of
> communication. It is to mistake an early *Flash Gordon* comic strip
> for George Lucas's *Star Wars* epic. For during the early fourteenth
> century, when the book was made, artists and spiritual directors
> were taking art into spheres as innovative as film would prove to be
> seven centuries later ... Art, like music, can provide an immediacy
> and profundity of access to the senses and to emotional response.

The integration of calligraphy and art, whether in Asia or in Europe, meant that the illumination of a manuscript could in itself become an act of worship. That is almost inevitable in India since those who practise any of the traditional sixty-four arts or crafts acknowledge that their skill is received from Brahma or Vishvakarma and return the gift to the One who bestows it. Stella Kramisch has summarised the way in which an artist or craftsman working on a sacred text (in this case Veda) mediates between heaven and earth (p. 59):

He is linked in a straight line with the fountainhead, sum total of
consciousness, knowledge and inspiration. Its immediate presence
in the actual moment of his work is guaranteed by the unbroken
line of sages and craftsmen who have transmitted his particular
craft to him. He carries it, forms it, and makes it available to
the community that shares in Tradition, each according to his
particular place and station in life. Tradition embraces the life of
the whole community. Thus, the craftsman is involved with his
own people more deeply than by common interests or a sphere of
cooperative living. Tradition thus is not only an oral transmission
of information and beliefs from ancestors to posterity, but also an
inherited culture. It is a body of doctrine and discipline, put forth
and revealed in the words of the Veda.

The creation of a sacred text as an object of worship was not possible for Jews
and Muslims, or at least it was not possible in the same straightforward way.
That is because Jews and Muslims were told in no uncertain terms that they
should never worship God through any image or idol. The version of the Ten
Commandments in *Exodus* 20 begins (1–5):

> Then God spoke all these words: I am the Lord your God, who
> brought you out of the land of Egypt, out of the house of slavery;
> you shall have no other gods before me. You shall not make for
> yourself an idol, whether in the form of anything that is in heaven
> above, or that is in the water under the earth. You shall not bow
> down to them or worship them.

That did not prevent the illumination of manuscripts (since a forbidden
'made' idol would have to be in three dimensions), but it did preclude any
veneration of the Book (cf. Sikhs and *Guru Granth Sahib*, p. 221). In contrast,
therefore, Jews honour their sacred text, Torah, by the way in which it is kept
in the Synagogue. The scrolls of Torah are kept in the Ark (*aron haqodesh*)
which is decorated with as much artistic skill as possible. The ornaments,
however, are designed to honour the *gift* of God: they cannot be an object of
worship in themselves.

   The prohibition against anything that might suggest or lead to the worship
of an idol was powerfully reinforced in the Quran, since Muhammad lived in
a community where idolatry was common. Muslims are forbidden to produce
anything that might seem to be an image of God – or indeed of anything that God

alone creates. Both Muslim and alBukhari (p. 140) record a tradition (*hadith*, p. 137) of Muhammad saying, 'Those who make figures will be punished on the Day of Resurrection, for they will be told, "Put life into what you have created."' There is indeed a *hadith qudsi* (a tradition that records the direct word of God, p. 139) saying, 'Who does greater wrong than those who seek to create the like of what I create? Let them create an atom! Let them create a grain of barley!'

That did not prevent Muslims giving honour to their sacred text, the Quran, since for them the Quran is the absolute and uncorrupted Word of God (see further, p. 125). They did so by making calligraphy the highest of all human arts. Islamic calligraphy was developed in many different styles, and it appears not just on written pages but on buildings as well. In his introduction to Islamic calligraphy, Yasin Safadi wrote (p. 31):

> One of the many sayings on calligraphy which are attributed to the Prophet Muhammad is 'Good writing makes the truth stand out.' It is not surprising, therefore, that calligraphy has been patronised and encouraged at the highest level throughout its history, becoming the most important visible factor that relates the Muslims to each other, and manifesting itself in all branches of Islamic art . . . The Quran, which is the word of God and touches every aspect of Muslim life, has always been an object of devotion and the focus for the artistic genius of Islam. This not only elevated calligraphy to the level of a sacramental art, but made the many hundreds of exquisite Quran copies which were produced the best documentary evidence of the art itself.

SACRED TEXTS IN TRANSLATION

This Introduction began with the observation that no individual can read all the sacred texts of the world because there are too many of them. That becomes even more obvious when one remembers that sacred texts continue to appear. The focus of this book has been on sacred texts that come from the past and are recognised in long-established religions, but new religions have appeared in prolific numbers during the last two centuries, and many of them have their own sacred texts. Mormons, for example, have *The Book of Mormon*, followers of Sun Myung Moon in the Family Federation for World Peace and Unification have *Divine Principle*. Of the fifty-seven religions and cults included in Ankerberg and Weldon's *Encyclopedia of Cults and New Religions*, thirty-six have their own revealed teachings and sacred texts, while others have their own idiosyncratic interpretation of the sacred texts of the religion from which they are derived. It would take another book as long as this to describe them all.

But even if one is interested in reading only a few of the many sacred texts, there remains a further problem: they are written in far too many different languages for any individual to learn. This might not matter too much except that the languages of these texts are often so highly valued and revered that they have come to be regarded as sacred in their own right. Sacred languages like Hebrew, Latin, Arabic or Sanskrit create communities with shared beliefs and values of such a powerful kind that they transcend the limitations of time and geography. In his breathtaking study of the history and spread of languages, Nicholas Ostler pioneers what he calls 'the study of *language dynamics*' or of diachronic sociolinguistics (p. 558). The jargon may be offputting, but the work is of paramount importance:

> It is an approach, previously little explored, to understanding
> human societies: how language, in all its evolving variety, organises
> not just the human mind but also the large groups of human minds
> that constitute themselves into societies, which communicate and
> interact, as well as think and act.

The fact, however, remains that no matter how important the languages are, no one can learn them all. So we have to read most texts in translation. But no translation, we are often told, can ever adequately represent the original text. As the familiar Italian saying has it, *Traduttore traditore*, translators are traitors. The endeavour to translate is always frustrated because there is no single, original meaning to be found and then transferred into another language: there are only the possibilities of meaning, some of which may be more probable than others, but none of which can be exclusively exact. All translations are interpretations and are always open to correction.

That is true, but it does not make translations worthless. In fact the world owes to translators an immense debt of gratitude. They are the true pioneers of globalisation since without their work we would remain isolated from each other and diminished. However approximate translations may be, it is possible to enter through them into the new and other worlds created by far-ranging explorations of the human spirit and imagination, and preserved now in sacred texts.

Through these sacred texts, therefore, there can be a conversation with the past that entirely transforms the present – and that can happen even in translation. To give an example: Hugh Kenner in *The Pound Era* analysed the way in which Ezra Pound's engagement with Chinese poetry transformed the nature of poetry itself. He pointed out how much Pound relied on Mathews' *Chinese–English Dictionary* and on Karlgren's painstaking attempt to supply a word-by-word representation of Chinese words in English (for an example, see p. 296). It enabled Pound, not to translate the Chinese, but to write his own poetry in which he endeavoured to catch the atmosphere (*feng*) of the original. Kenner wrote (p. 521):

> We are deep in the whispering forest of all traditional poetries . . . , where the very words to which millions of minds respond have helped form the minds that respond to them. You and I and Ezra Pound are attending to them for the first time, with Mathews' and Karlgren's help. Follow Pound, put 'East Wind' for your title, write
>
> > Soft wind of the vale
> > that brings the turning rain,
>
> and you stir the whispers of a different forest, the one in which English sensibilities have learned to feel that 'vale' is less topographical than 'valley' . . . ; where moreover soft winds when they blow through very short lines of verse animate a lyric tradition so nearly anonymous that it is rather an air in the mind than a cluster of examples . . . For no more than a Christian can disassociate lying down by still waters from the Good Shepherd, can a Chinese be expected to isolate *feng*, the wind, in these Odes, from generations of moral commentary. There is no way to translate all this.

The first marks, cut with consistency into clay or scratched on oracle bones in China, cannot be deciphered as though we can know what they 'mean', and the same is true of all those many subsequent words written or printed in texts. We can nevertheless respond to them and we may on occasion be moved by them into such a transformed awareness that we are led into the creation of our own new meaning. We can indeed discover truth. And that is the invitation of the sacred texts of the world:

Deliberated marks
cut first in clay
then penned oblique and cursive
to convey
the enigma of intelligence:
communication from a mind
otherwise extinct and gone,
a letter from the lost, unsigned
and open to interpretation.

And yet . . .
one touch enough
to startle sleepiness
from a half open eye into a rough
intelligence: moved by meaning
perhaps even not meant: but see!
a sharp alert, a resurrection life,
idiosyncracy.

It is now our turn to hear the whispers of those different forests and to touch for ourselves the texts of time. This book is offered as an introduction to make that experience possible.

USING THIS BOOK

BIBLIOGRAPHY AND TRANSLATIONS

The Bibliography on pp. 358–88 consists mainly of translations into English of the texts described or mentioned in this book. There are excellent translations into other languages (particularly in the case of European languages into German, French or Spanish), but to have included those would have doubled the length of the Bibliography for each language.

The Bibliography also includes the details of other books mentioned or quoted. For that reason they are referred to in the text as briefly as possible, usually with the name of the author and the page reference. So, for example, Chari's *Philosophy and Theistic Mysticism of the Alvars* is referred to simply as Chari (p. 2): the publication details are in the Bibliography. Similarly, many translations in this book are my own, but translations made by others are indicated by name with details in the Bibliography. The translation of the Bible is that of the New Revised Standard Version.

To save space and to avoid lengthy and repetitive footnotes, the books in the Bibliography have been numbered. At the end of each section, the list of bibliography numbers will take the reader to the relevant translations/books.

In addition to the translations listed in the Bibliography (in which in any case there is no space to include all that have been made), it is important to remember that many texts are translated in the various Series of Translations listed on p. 358. Again for reasons of space, it is impossible to repeat in the Bibliography the texts that have been translated in those Series. However, an index to them can usually be found on the Internet. Particularly important and useful is the Internet Sacred Texts Archive which contains more than 1,700 texts. It is worth remembering also that translations of many individual texts can be found on the Internet.

In the space available it was not possible to provide a history of the many different religions whose texts are described in this book, although an attempt has been made to indicate the context in which the different texts came into being. A more connected history of the major religions (together with their characteristic beliefs) will be found in my *Beliefs That Changed the World* (London: Quercus, 2007), and *God: A Brief History* (London: Dorling Kindersley, 2002). For further information on the people and beliefs mentioned in this book, see my *Oxford Dictionary of World Religions* (Oxford: Oxford University Press, 1997).

It is important to remember that in older books Chinese words and titles are transliterated according to the Wade-Giles system. This was replaced during the last century by the Pinyin system followed in this book. It means that some (often familiar) titles now appear differently – for example, *Tao-te Ching* is now *Daode jing*; *Chuang-tzu* is now *Zhuangzi*. There is a list of corresponding terms and titles in my *Oxford Dictionary of World Religions*.

My thanks go to Wayne Davies and Quercus Publishing for permission to quote and make use of material from *Beliefs That Changed the World*, and to Jonathan Metcalf and Dorling Kindersley for permission to quote and make use of material from *God: A Brief History* and *The Complete Bible Handbook*. I am grateful to them for their generous support.

A major part of this book was written by Margaret my wife. She is in a real sense the co-author of it, and without her it could not have been written. For that and for so much else, my thanks. I am grateful also to Antony Cheetham and to my agent, Felicity Bryan, who first brought this book into being. My thanks go as well to Ted Hardingham and Sarah Brunning for their practical help without which I would have had to stop writing long ago. I owe a major debt of gratitude to Timothy Ratcliffe for his help, and to Dr J. F. Coakley who corrected parts of the book in its early stages with his usual meticulous and erudite attention to detail. My thanks go also to Helen Gray for her careful copyediting, and to Richard Milbank, Sarah Norman and Sachna Hanspal of Atlantic Books for their work on what proved to be a complicated project.

1
JUDAISM

JUDAISM TEXTS: KEY DATES

BCE

c.2000 The ancestors including Abraham

c.1500–c.150 Biblical period

c.1300/1250 Exodus from Egypt

c.1220–c.1020 Settlement in Canaan; Judges

c.1030–1010 Saul

c.1010–c.970 David

c.970–931 Solomon

c.965 Building of 1st Temple

931–722/1 Northern Kingdom

931–587/6 SouthernKingdom

931–587/6 The Prophets

740 ➡ Isaiah

c.735 Micah

627 ➡ Jeremiah

c.600 Habakkuk

587/6 Fall of Jerusalem

587/6–538 The Exile

538 Cyrus restores exiles to Jerusalem

520 Zechariah

c.500 Building of 2nd Temple

c.450 Torah gains recognition

3rd–1st cent. Greek translations incl.
  Septuagint/LXX

167–164 Maccabean/Hasmonean Revolt

164–63 Hasmonean dynasty

1st cent.BCE–70CE Dead Sea Scrolls

37BCE–44CE The Herods

CE

66–70 1st Jewish revolt against Romans

1st cent. ➡ Piyyutim

c.1st or 2nd cent. Amida

132–135 2nd Jewish revolt against Romans

135 Destruction of Jerusalem

c.138–c.217 Judah haNasi

early 3rd cent. ➡ Mishnah & Tosefta assembled

by end of 3rd cent. Canon agreed

8th/9th cent. Halakot Gedolot/Pesukot

c.1075–1141 Judah haLevi, Songs of Zion

1135/8–1204 Maimonides

c.1170–1180 Mishneh Torah

1194–1270 Nahmanides

1240–1305 Moses de Leon

13th cent. ➡ Qabbalah becomes prominent

end 13th cent. Zohar compiled

1488–1575 Joseph Caro

1530–1572 Moses Isserles

1534–1572 Isaac Luria

1564 Shulhan Aruch

late 16th cent. HaMappah

1700 ➡ The Hasidim

1873 Reform Judaism

1948 State of Israel

Previous page: The Scroll of Torah (Sefer Torah) mounted on wooden staves known as *atse hayyim*, 'trees of life'.

THE BIBLE

THE ORIGINS OF THE JEWISH PEOPLE

The Jews are a people who believe that they have been called into a covenant with God in order to show how life with God should be lived. They believe that they have been called to do this, not selfishly for their own benefit, but on behalf of the whole world, so that all can learn to recognise who and what God is: 'The day is coming when ten men from nations of every language will take hold of the cloak of a Jew, saying, "Let us go with you, for we have heard that God is with you"' (*Zechariah* 8.23).

This means that the fundamental conviction in Jewish life is the belief that God is uniquely God. That may seem a strange way to put it, but nothing like as strange as it would have seemed during the Biblical period (very roughly 1500–150 BCE) when the Jewish people and faith were being formed. It was a world in which there were many gods, from Baalim (the owners of the land and its fruits) to gods associated with particular places, to gods living in a heavenly court under the supervision of a high God who would send them to perform particular tasks on earth: the world was alive with the sound of deities and of the prayers and sacrifices being offered to them.

In contrast (and often in fierce competition) with all that, the Jews came to realise that in the case of God, there can only be who or what God is. The most profound statement of Jewish faith is found in *Deuteronomy* 6.4, known from its opening word in Hebrew as the Shema': 'Hear, O Israel, the Lord your God the Lord is One.'

How did that happen? How did it come about that some semi-nomadic tribes – who remembered that their ancestors had been 'wandering Aramaeans' who had been taken into slavery in Egypt (*Deuteronomy* 26.5ff.) – became the people of God? How did a loose alliance of related families, a kinship group known from the name of one of the ancestors as Bene Jacob (the sons of Jacob), become the Jewish people who worship 'no other god but God'?

JEWISH SCRIPTURE: TANAKH

The many books and writings gathered in Jewish Scripture answer those questions in many different ways. The sacred texts in Jewish Scripture were written and collected over a period of more than a thousand years. They were called *HaSefarim*, 'The Books', translated into Greek as *ta biblia*, hence the English word 'Bible'. Other names are *Sifre haKodesh*, 'The Holy Books', or *Kitve haKodesh*, 'The Holy Writings'.

Another more common name, Tanakh, is made up from the initial letters of the three major divisions in the Jewish Bible:

◆ *Torah*: These are the first five books associated with Moses and often called *Chumash* ('five'), hence from the Greek *pente*, 'five', the Pentateuch. The word *torah* is often translated as 'law', not least because the first five books contain many laws. But the word also has a much wider meaning and can indeed refer to the whole of the Jewish Bible. In particular it also means 'guidance' or 'instruction'. Thus the first five books – with names taken from the first word of each, *Bereshith* (*Genesis*), *Shemoth* (*Exodus*), *Vayikra* (*Leviticus*), *Bemidhbar* (*Numbers*) and *Debarim* (*Deuteronomy*) – contain very much more than Law, not least because they carry the story of God's nature and purpose back to creation itself.

◆ *Nevi'im*: Prophets. These are works that give voice to the meaning of God's work in history: the Former Prophets are the historical Books, the Latter Prophets are the books gathering oracles of Isaiah, Jeremiah and Ezekiel, and also of The Twelve (Minor Prophets), Hosea, Joel, Amos, Obadiah, Jonah, Micah, Nahum, Habakkuk, Zephaniah, Haggai, Zechariah and Malachi.

◆ *Ketuvim*: Writings. These are mainly later books of a diverse kind: they include historical Books (*Ruth, Chronicles, Esther, Ezra* and *Nehemiah*), *Daniel* (combining historical reference with apocalyptic interpretation of the present and future), liturgical poetry (*Psalms* and *Lamentations*), Love Poetry (*Song of Songs*) and Books of Wisdom (*Proverbs, Job* and *Qoheleth/ Ecclesiastes*).

Tanakh tells the story of how members of the kinship group Bene Jacob settled in an area on the east Mediterranean coast known as Canaan. It came eventually to be known as Judaea from which they were called Judaeans, hence Jews. At a time of famine in about the thirteenth century BCE, some members of the kinship group migrated to Egypt where they became slave labourers.

Eventually one of their number, Moses, led them out of Egypt in a miraculous escape known as the Exodus, commemorated now in the Passover feast. Moses believed that he in turn was led by God whose name and nature had not previously been known to them. The name is revealed as YHWH, a name too sacred and holy to be pronounced: to this day Orthodox Jews do not attempt to pronounce it but simply say HaShem, 'the Name'. Others conventionally write Yahweh, translating it as 'the Lord'.

Under Yahweh, Moses led the people through the wilderness for forty years of testing, during which time Moses received commandments directly from God on Mount Sinai. These commandments become the terms and conditions which the people must keep as they enter into a Covenant of agreement with God: God offers peace and prosperity on condition that people keep to the terms laid down, a point strongly made in *Deuteronomy* (11.26–8):

> See, I am setting before you today a blessing and a curse: the
> blessing, if you obey the commandments of the Lord your God that
> I am commanding you today; and the curse, if you do not obey the
> commandments of the Lord your God, but turn from the way that I
> am commanding you today, to follow other gods that you have not
> known.

God also promises that they will have a land in which to live, the Promised Land of Canaan. The historical Books tell the story of how the Land was conquered. One of them, *Joshua*, also tells in chapter 24 how the members of the kinship group returning from Egypt took an oath with those who had remained in or on the edges of Canaan that together they will now serve Yahweh. As a consequence of this reunion, the tribes began to share with each other their memories, traditions, myths and customs until eventually they were woven together in Torah and the historical Books.

For a long time, however, the Bene Jacob continued as a loose coalition with each part of the kinship group having its own leaders (known as Judges, some of whose stories are gathered in the book of that name), and with an expectation that if one member of the group was threatened, some at least of the others would help. With the arrival of the Philistines on the Mediterranean coast, the threat became common and continuous, and David, having captured Jerusalem as a new and neutral capital, introduced kingship as a way of uniting the whole group. The story of how he achieved this is told in the Books of *Samuel* and *I Kings*.

The following period under kings was ended by the capture of Jerusalem by the Babylonians in 587 BCE. Most of the Jews were taken into captivity in the Exile. The Persian ruler Cyrus restored the exiles to Jerusalem in 536 BCE after which there followed 400 years of reconstruction until a family known as the Hasmoneans or Maccabees led a successful revolt from 167 to 164 BCE against the rulers of the day (the Seleucids). That led to the setting up of an independent kingdom, and this brings to an end the Biblical period.

Throughout most of the period from David onward, the Prophets spoke for God on the ways in which kings and people behaved. It was they who kept the conditions of the Covenant alive: if Yahweh is to keep his side of the bargain, humans cannot be evil, tyrannical and unjust. If they are, then Biblical history shows how God reacts in anger, and the Prophets remind people of this in no uncertain terms. In general, therefore, people know what God has done for them, and how in consequence they should live, as one of the Prophets, Micah, reminds them (*Micah* 6.3–8):

> O my people, what have I done to you? In what have I wearied
> you? Answer me! For I brought you up from the land of Egypt, and
> redeemed you from the house of slavery . . . that you may know
> the saving acts of the Lord. With what, then, shall I come before
> the Lord, and bow myself before God on high? Shall I come before
> him with burnt offerings, with calves a year old? Will the Lord be
> pleased with thousands of rams, with ten thousands of rivers of oil?
> Shall I give my firstborn for my transgression, the fruit of my body
> for the sin of my soul? He has told you, O mortal, what is good;
> He has told you, O mortal, what is good: and what does the Lord
> require of you but to do justice, and love kindness, and to walk
> humbly with your God?

📖 BIBLIOGRAPHY NUMBERS 18

There are so many translations of the Bible and of its individual Books that it is not possible to list them in a bibliography. There is a helpful survey of translations in Metzger, and there is an extensive bibliography to the Books and content of the Bible in Bowker, *The Complete Bible Handbook*. Note also *The Cambridge History of the Bible*: see Ackroyd, Lampe, Greenslade.

TANAKH

HISTORY AND REVELATION

The Bible has traditionally been called 'the Word of God'. It is the foundation of Jewish life and belief. That 'Word', however, is expressed in many different ways – as can be seen, for example, in Psalm 119 where each of its twenty-two sections (one for each letter of the Hebrew alphabet) is made up of eight verses: in each section there is a celebration of God's Word using different but related terms (119.161–8):

> Princes persecute me without cause, but my heart stands in awe of
>   your *words*.
> I rejoice at your *utterance* like one who finds great spoil.
> I hate and abhor falsehood, but I love your *law*.
> Seven times a day I praise you for your righteous *ordinances*.
> Great peace have those who love your *law*; nothing can make them
>   stumble.
> I hope for your salvation, O Lord, and I fulfil your *commandments*.
> My soul keeps your *decrees*; I love them exceedingly.
> I keep your *precepts* and decrees, for all my ways are before you.

INSPIRATION AND PROPHECY

As 'the Word of God', the Bible has been described as 'inspired' by God and as 'the revelation' of his nature and purpose. It is, however, far from clear what exactly 'inspiration' meant in practice to those who brought the Bible into being, either when they began to collect the material together, or when they decided what to include. Even earlier than that, the many people who wrote or spoke the words now collected in the books of Tanakh have left few traces of what this meant to them in their own experience. They have not recorded how they felt themselves to be related to God when they spoke or wrote as they did. They did, however, recognise that there were distinct ways in which God becomes known through human agents – as, for example, in *Numbers* 12.6–8:

> Hear my words: When there are prophets among you, I the Lord
> make myself known to them in visions; I speak to them in dreams.
> Not so with my servant Moses; he is entrusted with all my house.
> With him I speak face-to-face – clearly, not in riddles; and he
> beholds the form of the Lord.

Although, therefore, they did not write or say much about their experience, there is no doubt at all about the urgency of their involvement with God. It is often expressed in the Psalms, and the oracles of the prophets frequently begin with the words, *koh amar Adonai*, 'Thus says the Lord.' One among them, Jeremiah (mid-seventh–mid-sixth century BCE), felt that God had betrayed and abandoned him (15.18): 'Why is my pain unceasing, my wound incurable, refusing to be healed? Truly, you are to me like a deceitful brook, like waters that fail.' At times he would have given anything for a quiet life by ceasing to be a prophet, but he could not do so (20.9):

> If I say, 'I will not mention him, or speak any more in his name',
> then within me there is something like a burning fire shut up in my
> bones; I am weary with holding it in, and I cannot.

In general, however, people, whether prophets or not, were rarely so explicit. On the other hand, what is certainly clear is that the people were transformed through successive generations from a kinship group of loosely related families to the people known as the Jews. They had no doubt that this transformation had been brought about by God – often against their own stubborn resistance. The dramatic events of their history and their fundamental acceptance of the Covenant meant that the words contained in Tanakh came into being in the context of God whose character, authority and purpose were being established for them beyond doubt.

HISTORY AND NARRATIVE

As a result, the people began to write and pray and tell stories in entirely new ways. For example, where other nations around them were content to write Annals (i.e., an annual record of what has happened in any one particular year), they discerned a connected story unfolding the authority and purpose of God. Moreover, they did not hesitate to record in graphic detail occasions when individuals or the whole people had broken the conditions of the Covenant and had gone wrong.

That was true even of David, the great king who was anointed by God: in the underlying Hebrew (*mashiach*, 'anointed one') he was the messiah, the forerunner of the final Messiah who will establish God's Kingdom on earth. But the account in *2 Samuel* 11 does not gloss over the way in which David sent Uriah to his death because he lusted after Uriah's wife, Bathsheba; and it records with searching power the way in which the Prophet Nathan denounced him (12.1–15).

Tanakh, therefore, is unique in the honesty with which it records the way in which the people went through a long process of learning, not least through their mistakes. Again and again, later parts of Tanakh correct what has come to be recognised as inadequate or wrong in an earlier part. What is remarkable is the fact that they did not discard or erase what they came later to recognise as wrong. Attention was drawn to this in my *The Complete Bible Handbook* (p. 7), making the point that parents understand this process very well. They too seek to evoke from their children a curiosity and delight in the world, and to teach them an ethic not to do wrong and not to hurt others. In that process of learning and of growing up, they treasure every effort of their children, at every stage of the process, and they do not discard even the earliest attempts to write a poem or to sing a song. So although home videos and tape recordings may not be great art, they are precious as a record, and parents wish to keep them.

In the same way the children of Israel treasured their early attempts to write of their process of understanding God. And so they preserved these, even though later parts of the Bible often contradict earlier parts. The Bible is thus the result of a maturing process, as the descendants of Jacob gained understanding of how to live in accordance with God's will.

To give only one example of this process of correction and change: Tanakh as a whole grapples with the problem of explaining why God allows some people – even just and God-fearing people – to suffer, while others prosper, even if they are wicked and God-defying. At first it was said that suffering is a punishment for sin, and that if the apparently good are suffering it must be because they *have* sinned but they have concealed their sins. That early answer, which is common in the Psalms, is summarised in the saying, 'Where you see suffering, there you see sin.' But that explanation is open to the objection that it is obviously not true. Even the most casual observation of life makes it apparent that the wicked do not get cut off, and that the ruthless frequently prosper. The question was unavoidable (and it is asked and answered in different ways in the later parts of Tanakh): why is this so?

The answers given in books like *Job* or *Habakkuk* contradict the earlier and classic answer.* And that is extensively true: Tanakh contains corrections and contradictions of one part by others, and it contains mistakes that have been corrected in later times – for example, about the relation between the sun and the earth.

This means that claims, which are still made, that the Bible must be inerrant because it comes from God and God can hardly make mistakes, are completely misguided because they misrepresent what the Bible reveals of itself. Yes, it is a consequence of God becoming known in a unique way of immense consequence for human life – a way, in Biblical language, of judgement, redemption and salvation. But the nature and meaning of God become known through real people and actual events of history as those people acknowledge their mistakes and the justified anger of God, but also keep faith with what they have received from the past by applying it to the present in order to transform the future – exactly as the Prophet Habakkuk put it (3.2,17–19):

> O Lord, I have heard of your renown,
> and I stand in awe, O Lord, of your work.
> In our own time revive it;
> in wrath may you remember mercy . . .
> Though the fig tree does not blossom,
> and no fruit is on the vines;
> though the produce of the olive fails
> and the fields yield no food;
> though the flock is cut off from the fold
> and there is no herd in the stalls,
> yet I will rejoice in the Lord;
> I will exult in the God of my salvation.
> God, the Lord, is my strength;
> he makes my feet like the feet of a deer,
> and makes me tread upon the heights.

---

* For a full account, see my *Problems of Suffering*.

TANAKH

Canon and Translations

The learning process through which the Bene Jacob became the Jews was a long one. It produced many texts, and these were so precious as a record of the purpose and providence of God that they began to be collected as 'sacred texts'.

Eventually some texts were gathered into the collection or Canon known as Tanakh, the Holy Books. But the process of deciding which texts were 'canonical' was also a long one lasting for many centuries, although most of it was recognised by the time of the Dead Sea Scrolls (first century BCE–70 CE) since all the Books of Tanakh appear among the Scrolls except Esther.

The foundation lay in Torah since this was believed to have come directly from God, and, even before the Exile, Torah was recognised as the Word of God. The Prophets, *Nevi'im*, were gathered in the period between the end of the Exile and the Hasmonean revolt, and were believed to be the work of the Holy Spirit mediated through inspired humans.

The gathering of the Writings, *Ketuvim*, was a longer and less certain process because it was disputed whether some books belonged to Tanakh or not. The status of those books that were eventually included in Tanakh (*Proverbs, Ecclesiastes, The Song of Songs* and *Esther*) was still being debated in the second and third centuries CE. In contrast, *Ben Sira* (*Ecclesiasticus*) was originally regarded as canonical, but it was formally excluded in the second century (Tosefta *Yadaim* 2.13). The Canon was finally agreed by the end of the third century. The Books that were in the end rejected are known as *Sefarim Chitsonim*, 'the outside books'.

When Christianity came into being it regarded itself as the continuation and completion of all that God had intended in his original Covenant with the Jewish people. Jesus was believed to be the promised Messiah (pp. 49ff.) or, in Greek, Christos – hence Jesus Christ. Originally Christians were Jews, and Christianity was only one among many interpretations at the time of how the Covenant life with

God should be lived. Tanakh was therefore their Bible. Eventually they referred to the texts in Tanakh as the Old Covenant (or Testament) and their own 'sacred texts' as the New Testament.

The Christian Canon of Scripture, however, is not identical with the Jewish Canon, nor are the Canons of the different Churches in Christianity identical with each other – i.e., the books they contain mainly overlap but the lists are not exactly the same. The Orthodox Churches have ten additional books together with some extensions to *Daniel*, and the Roman Catholic Church adds even more, often attaching them to the relevant or appropriate books in Tanakh. In Protestant Churches those additional texts may be found in the Apocrypha (from the Greek meaning 'hidden' or 'secret') where they are regarded as instructive but not as Canonical.

TRANSLATIONS: TARGUMS

How did this uncertainty about the Canon come about? It came about because the first translations of the Hebrew text were made when the Jewish Canon had not yet been decided, and the early (third–first centuries BCE) Greek translation, the Septuagint, included books and parts of books that were not in the end included in the Jewish Canon. Those who translated the Septuagint into Latin believed mistakenly that those additional parts belonged to the Canon, though others disagreed – hence the disagreements among different Christian Churches about the contents of what they call the Old Testament (see further below).

For Jews the language of God's revelation is Hebrew, but after the Exile they lived in increasing numbers in the Mediterranean world where people mainly spoke Greek or Latin in addition to their own local languages. Thus Jews often spoke Greek and many of them in Palestine/Judaea spoke Aramaic: some later parts of the Bible are written in Aramaic.

If, therefore, ordinary people were to understand the Bible, it would have to be translated. In Synagogues, Torah was always read in its original language, Hebrew, but an interpreter, a *methurgeman*, would then give in Aramaic a version of the reading. These Aramaic interpretations are known as Targums.

Since the original and sacred text had already been read, the Targums (as we know from examples that have survived in printed form) did not have to give a literal or word-for-word translation. They include a brief explanation of what the text means, and they are thus of immense importance in understanding what the Bible meant to Jews in this early period. Here, for example, a Targum explains what the word 'us' means in *Genesis* 1.26 ('And God said, "Let us make man/Adam in our image"'). The explanation was important because Christians in the early Church were claiming that when God said, 'Let *us*' he must have been talking to the Son and the Holy Spirit, thus demonstrating the Trinity at the time of creation. The Targums, therefore, had to suggest as a different meaning that God was talking to the angels, as in this example (for translations of other Targum interpretations of *Genesis*, see my *The Targums and Rabbinic Literature*):

> And God said to the angels who minister before him and who were created on the second day of the creation of the world, 'Let us make Adam in our image . . .'

TRANSLATIONS: THE SEPTUAGINT

Translations into Greek were even more important because so many Jews lived in the Diaspora (the dispersion of Jews from Spain to India), many parts of which were Greek-speaking. The major translation was made (according to tradition) in the third century BCE by seventy-two or seventy scholars: for that reason it is known from the Latin as the Septuagint, often written as LXX. This translation differs from the Hebrew text in many ways – for example, by changing the order of the books and abolishing the threefold categories of *Torah*, *Nevi'im* and *Ketuvim*, and by its inclusion of *Sefarim Chitsonim*, the 'outside books'.

In the early centuries, Christians regarded the LXX as the authentic and inspired text of Scripture, and they therefore regarded what Jews called *Sefarim Chitsonim* as Canonical. When Jerome translated the Bible into Latin in the fourth century, he went back to the original Hebrew, but the authority of the additional texts was not forgotten. When in about the sixth century all the books were collected into a single Bible (known as *editio vulgata*, hence the Vulgate), Jerome's version was the basis, but the Old Latin translations of the additional or Apocryphal Books were added to it, thus ensuring that they became part of the Canon for Roman Catholics – in contrast to Jews and Protestants. At the Council of Trent (p. 118) a Decree was issued in the fourth session, listing 'the sacred books so that no doubt may remain as to which books are recognised by the Council'. It then added:

> If anyone does not accept all these books in their entirety, with all their parts, as they are being read in the Catholic Church and are contained in the ancient Latin Vulgate edition, as sacred and canonical, and knowingly and deliberately rejects the aforesaid traditions, let him be anathema.

BIBLIOGRAPHY NUMBERS 136, 702, 716

INTERPRETATION
OF TORAH

MISHNAH AND TALMUDS; *SHULHAN ARUCH*

In the third century, Rabbi Simlai made a calculation that Torah contains 613 commandments: 365 prohibitions (corresponding to the days in the year) and 248 positive commands (corresponding to the parts of the human body). The calculation was disputed for centuries because it is hard to decide what exactly counts as a law, but now it is widely accepted.

The 613 commandments, *Taryag Mitzvot*, are the foundation of Jewish life because they are the gift from God that enables the Jews to keep their side of the Covenant with God (on behalf of, but in distinction from, other peoples) and therefore to prosper (*Leviticus* 18.1–5):

> The Lord spoke to Moses, saying: 'Speak to the people of Israel and
> say to them: I am the Lord your God. You shall not do as they do
> in the land of Egypt, where you lived, and you shall not do as they
> do in the land of Canaan, to which I am bringing you. You shall
> not follow their statutes. My ordinances you shall observe and my
> statutes you shall keep, following them: I am the Lord your God.
> You shall keep my statutes and my ordinances; by doing so one
> shall live: I am the Lord.'

An immediate problem, however, is that the commandments were given in brief form in days long before the world of mass communication, globalisation and advanced technology. How can the commandments from such a different world in the past be applied in the present?

Many of the texts held in highest value by the Jews emerged to deal with that question. Those texts cannot be sacred texts in the same sense as Tanakh, but they are certainly sacred by association, because they are showing the practical meaning of Torah in constantly changing worlds.

To give an example: in Torah (e.g., *Exodus* 16.23–9, 20.8–11, 31.12–14; *Deuteronomy* 5.12–15) Jews are commanded to keep the Sabbath day holy and to rest from work, as God rested on the seventh day after the completion of creation. The text, however, does not define what counts as 'work': what can or cannot be done on the Sabbath day? It is not permitted to light a fire, but is it permitted to switch on an electric light?

All the laws raise practical questions of that kind, so to answer them scholars and teachers began to build up huge traditions of interpretation and exegesis which amounted in effect to 'case law'. Eventually, it was said that the laws defining what can and cannot be done on the Sabbath day were like a mountain hanging from a hair.

THE RABBIS

The scholars and teachers were originally known as Hakhamim, the Wise, but later they were known as the Rabbis. They built up traditions of interpretation and passed them on to their pupils orally from generation to generation (the early generations of Rabbis were known as Tannaim, 'those who repeat' what they have learnt). Often they could be in dispute and disagreement over particular interpretations, but collectively this tradition became known as *Torah shebe'al peh*, 'Torah according to word of mouth'. This tradition, transmitted orally and memorised, came to have almost the same authority as the original Torah until it was believed that it too had been revealed to Moses on Sinai (see, for example, *B.Berakoth* 5a).

After the defeat of the Jewish Revolt against the Romans in 70 CE (and even more after the defeat of the second Revolt in 135, when Jerusalem was renamed Aelia Capitolina and the site of the temple was ploughed with salt), Judaism had to be reconstructed so that it could be lived and practised without Jerusalem and its Temple. An important part of this reconstruction was to gather together *Torah shebe'al peh* into a single collection.

MISHNAH AND TALMUDS

The reconstruction resulted in R. Judah haNasi at the beginning of the third century assembling the Mishnah ('teaching' or 'instruction'), a collection of laws organised in six Orders, Zeraim ('Seeds'), Mo'ed ('Appointed Season'), Nashim ('Women'), Nezikin ('Damages'), Kodashim ('Holy Things'), Tohorot ('Cleanliness'). The six Orders then contain Tractates, sixty-three in all.

The Mishnah became the foundation of the Jewish understanding of Torah, but even so there was much more material than the Mishnah could contain. A supplementary collection known as Tosefta ('addition') was made, which is about four times as long as the Mishnah. The Mishnah, however, remained the basic authority. But questions about the meaning and application of particular laws did not cease, so the work of answering those practical questions continued on the basis of the Mishnah in the two major centres of the Jewish population, the land of Israel (Eretz Israel) and Mesopotamia (especially in Babylon).

This work of continuing commentary is known as Gemara, and when it too grew vast in size it was organised into two works known as Talmuds. The one created in Eretz Israel (i.e., Palestine) is known as the Palestinian Talmud or Jerushalmi, and the one created in Babylon is known as Babli. References are thus made to either J. or B., followed by the name of the Tractate. The pages in the Babylonian Talmud are printed uniformly in every edition so that they are referred to by page number, followed by 'a' for the first side and 'b' for the reverse. Thus the reference to R. Simlai's calculation of the number of laws (above) is B.M.23b, i.e., Babli Makkot p. 23 reverse side.

Talmud Babli is a vast work of many volumes, but even so it did not answer all questions. The leading experts, known as Geonim (from *gaon*, 'excellence'), gave replies to questions known as Responsa, and the Responsa literature itself grew immense. As a result attempts were made to write summaries of the important laws and their application. *Halakot Pesukot* ('Decided Laws', eighth century) was followed by *Halakot Gedolot* ('Great Laws', ninth century) which listed the 613 Commandments and made use of Talmud Jerushalmi in explaining their meaning and how they should be kept.

This was revised by Moses Maimonides (twelfth century) in *Sefer haMitzvot*, 'The Book of Laws', but his revision was challenged by Nahmanides (Ramban, 1194–1270) who defended *Halakot Gedolot*. Among the many disagreements between Maimonides and Nahmanides, Nahmanides claimed that the Jews are positively commanded to possess the land of Israel, whereas Maimonides did not include that as a command at all even though he revered greatly Jerusalem and the Holy Land.

Maimonides' *Sefer haMitzvot* turned out to be the first and introductory volume of a far more ambitious work, his attempt to synthesise and codify the whole of Jewish law in an accessible system. This work became known as *Mishneh Torah*, 'The Second Torah', a monumental achievement that gave rise to the saying, 'From Moses to Moses [Maimonides], there was none like Moses.' Even so, some disliked it because Maimonides seemed to be laying down his own interpretation as final and decisive without citing alternatives.

His code, therefore, was succeeded by other codes, especially that of Joseph

THE TWO PURPOSES
OF TORAH

In *Moreh Nebuchim* 3.27 (*The Guide for the Perplexed*, see page 37), the twelfth-century scholar Maimonides described the two purposes of Torah:

THERE ARE TWO MAIN purposes of Torah, the well-being of the soul and the well-being of the body. The well-being of the soul is brought about by true beliefs and opinions being communicated to people according to their capacity to receive them, and therefore some are given in simple language, others allegorically . . . The well-being of the body is brought about by careful oversight of the relationships in which we live with each other. This is achieved in two ways: first by eradicating violence from among us by ensuring that people do not act simply as they wish or desire or even can, but act rather in ways that contribute to the good welfare of all; and second, by teaching all people what moral behaviour is in order to produce a good society . . . The true Torah [like God from whom it comes] is One and beside it there is no other Torah. Its purpose, as I have written, is to establish among us the two forms of perfection. It aims, firstly, to establish the best mutual relations among us by eradicating injustice and by inspiring the finest thoughts and feelings . . . It aims, secondly, to educate us in faith and to develop true and correct beliefs when the intellect is sufficiently developed.

Caro's *Shulhan Aruch*, 'The Prepared Table', 1564. *Shulhan Aruch*, however, summarised the law as it was understood and practised by Spanish and Mediterranean Jews known as the Sefardi. It was therefore given supplementary annotations by Moses Isserles to include the Law as followed by the European Jews, the Ashkenazi. Isserles called his work *HaMappah*, 'The Tablecloth', since it now covered the practice of Jewish life. It appears in a shortened version called *Kitzur Shulhan Aruch*. On his tombstone are carved the words, 'From Moses [Maimonides] to Moses [Isserles] there has arisen no one like Moses.'

📖 BIBLIOGRAPHY NUMBERS 343, 625, 669, 929, 952

MAIMONIDES

Mishneh Torah

Maimonides (1135–1204, known as Rambam from the initials Rabbi Moses ben Maimon) was born in Spain, but when the Muslim Almohades began to persecute non-Muslims, he and his family fled to Morocco in 1158. In 1165 he went briefly to the Holy Land before settling in Fostat (Old Cairo) in Egypt where he practised medicine and became court physician.

Maimonides was a man of extraordinary intellectual ability with a fluent command of both Hebrew and Arabic. He was a master of the current Aristotelian philosophy, and he wrote one of his best-known works in 1190, *Dalilat alHariain* or (in its more usual Hebrew title) *Moreh Nebuchim*, 'the Guide for the Perplexed', in order to show that Aristotelian philosophy was not in conflict with Tanakh – provided that one remembers the language of Tanakh is adapted to the levels of understanding of which ordinary people are capable (cf., 'skill-in-means' in Mahayana Buddhism, p. 251). He relied on a principle established long before his time, 'Torah speaks in the language of human beings' (see p. 40).

Maimonides, in his 'Commentary on the Mishnah' (*Siraj*, published in 1168), made an early and pioneering attempt to help ordinary people to understand and keep the laws. In it he included his attempt to summarise the non-negotiable constituents of Jewish faith, 'The Thirteen Principles of Faith' (*Ikkarim*, 'Roots', see p. 38) that are still printed in Jewish Prayer Books (e.g., in Singer and Hertz, pp. 89ff.).

His work of trying to help all Jews to understand and live their faith culminated in *Mishneh Torah* ('Repetition of' or 'Second Torah'). He wrote 'so that the entire Torah [written and oral] might become systematically known to all . . . , consisting of statements clear and convincing that have appeared from the time of Moses to the present, so that all rules shall be accessible to young and old.' So, for example, in answer to questions about

THE THIRTEEN
PRINCIPLES OF FAITH

1. I believe with perfect faith that the Creator, blessed be his name, is the Author and Guide of everything that has been created, and that he alone has made, does make, and will make all things.
2. I believe with perfect faith that the Creator, blessed be his name, is a Unity, and that there is no unity in any manner like his, and that he alone is our God, who was, is, and will be.
3. I believe with perfect faith that the Creator, blessed be his name, is not a body, and that he is free from all the accidents of matter, and that he has not any form whatsoever.
4. I believe with perfect faith that the Creator, blessed be his name, is the first and the last.
5. I believe with perfect faith that to the Creator, blessed be his name, and to him alone it is right to pray, and that it is not right to pray to any being besides him.
6. I believe with perfect faith that all the words of the prophets are true.
7. I believe with perfect faith that the prophecy of Moses our teacher, peace be upon him, was true, and that he was the chief of the prophets, both of those that preceded and of those that followed him.
8. I believe with perfect faith that the whole Law, now in our possession, is the same that was given to Moses our teacher, peace be upon him.
9. I believe with perfect faith that this Law will not be changed, and that there will never be any other law from the Creator, blessed be his name.
10. I believe with perfect faith that the Creator, blessed be his name, knows every deed of the children of men, and all their thoughts, as it is said, it is he that fashions the hearts of them all, that gives heed to all their deeds.
11. I believe with perfect faith that the Creator, blessed be his name, rewards those that keep his commandments, and punishes those that transgress them.
12. I believe with perfect faith in the coming of the Messiah, and, though he tarry, I will wait daily for his coming.
13. I believe with perfect faith that there will be a resurrection of the dead at the time when it shall please the Creator, blessed be his name, and exalted be the remembrance of him for ever and ever.

what work can and cannot be done on the Sabbath, his 'Laws Concerning the Sabbath' begins (*Mishneh Torah*, III.1, trans. Gandz and Klein):

> Abstension from work on the seventh day of the week is a positive commandment, for Scripture says, 'But on the seventh day you shall rest' [*Exodus* 23.12] . . . As for actions which are in themselves permissible on the Sabbath but which may or may not result in prohibited work being done at the same time, the rule is that such actions are permissible as long as the resulting work is not intended beforehand. Thus one may move a couch, a chair, a bench, or a similar piece of furniture on the Sabbath, provided that he does not intend to dig a furrow in the ground while doing so. Consequently, if the article does indeed dig a furrow in the ground, this need cause him no concern, for he did not intend this result. Similarly, one may walk on grass on the Sabbath, provided that he does not intend to uproot any of it. Consequently, if some grass is uprooted this need cause him no concern . . . If, however, one's action results in the doing of prohibited work which is a necessary consequence of the original action, he is liable, even though he did not intend that the prohibited work should ensue. For it is known in advance that the prohibited work cannot fail to result from the intended action. For example, if one requires a bird's head for use as a child's plaything, and cuts it off on the Sabbath, he is liable, even though the actual slaughtering of the bird was not the ultimate motive. For it is a known fact that it is impossible for a living creature to go on living after its head has been cut off, and that death is bound to ensue. The same rule applies in all similar cases.

The great achievement of Maimonides was to make Judaism credible and liveable at a time of great threats, whether from sceptical philosophy or from persecuting Muslims. Yet, for all his achievement, other Jews felt that he had conceded too much ground to reason at the expense of revelation, and he was condemned by some as a heretic. The Maimonidean controversy continued until his books were burned by the Christian Dominicans in 1232.

BIBLIOGRAPHY NUMBERS 406, 625

QABBALAH

ZOHAR

Maimonides explored ways in which to make the meaning of Tanakh and the application of Torah possible for all Jewish people. He did this in part by emphasising that Torah is 'written in the language of ordinary people' (*B. Berakot* 31b), in order to help them to understand, but that metaphors should not be taken literally. When Tanakh says that God is wise or strong, it cannot mean that God is wise or strong in the way that humans are, only that these words point to a wisdom and strength far beyond human comprehension (cf., Aquinas on analogy, p. 108).

If, however, God is always greater than any words or descriptions that we or the Bible use (*Deus semper maior* in the Latin phrase much used in Christianity: see p. 119), how can we say or even know anything about the nature of God? A tradition known as Qabbalah (often transcribed as Kabbalah) developed among the Jews as an answer to that question – and because the question was asked also by Christians, Qabbalah was taken into Christianity as well.

The word *qabbalah* means 'tradition', and although works of Qabbalah became prominent from the thirteenth century onward, the claim was made that the tradition of its teaching was handed down from the earliest rabbinic times. Indeed, since the claim was also made that Qabbalah reveals the true meaning of Tanakh, it was believed to go back to the origin of Tanakh itself.

Basically, Qabbalah accepts that 'what God is', the aseity of God, cannot be known. How, then, can God be known at all, and how can God make contact with a universe so utterly different from himself? Qabbalah answers those questions. It accepts (see my book *God: A Brief History*, pp. 216f.) that the underived and independent nature of God is indeed unknowable, and it is called En Sof ('without limit'), the implication being that God is beyond human comprehension. But, according to Qabbalah, ten manifestations come from the unknowable source like ten rivers from the same spring. The water in the spring supplies the rivers, but the water in the rivers is not identical with it since each river is a different route to the sea. So the water in each river came from the spring, and for that reason it can be said that the spring reaches the sea, and yet the spring water remains unique and different.

The 'rivers' or emanations are known as the Sefirot, ten manifestations derived from God. They are ten in number because they correspond to the ten words in Genesis through which God created all things:

- The first to emerge is the Keter (crown), the willingness of God to extend effect from the En Sof, the unknowable essence.

- The next are Chochmah (Hokmah) and Binah, wisdom and discrimination, the will to create, not as an abstract proposition but in detail and in particular. But even these are too close to the divine essence for people to approach, let alone comprehend.

- From these, therefore, emanate Chesed (love), Gevurah or Din (power and judgement), and from these Tiferet, Netzach and Hod (beauty, majesty and splendour, exactly those features which give to many their first realisation that God exists).

- These merge into Yesod, the foundation of all creation, culminating in Malkhut, sovereignty, through which God acts to govern the world.

The beliefs of Qabbalah were then constructed into a symbolic imagination of the way in which the whole of creation is related to God. The resulting 'map' is extremely complicated and difficult to understand, so that schools and traditions of Qabbalah require long and committed study. The Bible is then read as a code through which the hidden meanings of Qabbalah become clear.

It would, however, be wrong to think that Qabbalah is nothing more than the solution to the intellectual puzzle of how God and human beings can come into contact or relationship with each other if God is indeed En Sof, 'unknowable'. Qabbalah creates a profound imagination of the universe which enables its adherents to fight evil and draw close to God. The powers of the Sefirot (the 'rivers' or emanations) become resources for those who are open to them in understanding and faith.

LATER QABBALAH

In later Qabbalah (particularly in the work of Isaac Luria, 1534–72) that theme of conflict against evil was developed further: the purpose of human life is to engage in God's work of repairing the world. The work of repair is known as *tikkun.* Through it, human beings make themselves and the worlds they inhabit 'receptacles', ready to receive into themselves the presence of God. The Hebrew word *berakah* means 'a blessing', but it was regarded in Qabbalah as a synonym of *beyrakah*, 'a pool' or 'a receptacle'. Those who have made themselves worthy receptacles are filled with God's blessing.

It was believed that the work of repair, the purpose of human life, was originally the responsibility of Adam. After his failure, the Jews were called by God to do this work of repair on behalf of the world. Jewish history is therefore seen as a story of that struggle and of the part that each individual plays in it. Torah, and living within the boundary of Torah, enables this work of repair to continue, and if connection with God is maintained through the Sefirot, the coming of the Messiah is brought nearer.

The many Schools of Qabbalah produced a correspondingly large number of sacred texts: note, for example, R. Joseph Gikatilla's *Sha'are Orah*, 'Gates of Light', with an excellent translation by Weinstein, or Cordovero's *Or Ne'erav*, translated by Robinson. Of them all, the most highly regarded is *Zohar*, 'Book of Splendour', from the word 'brightness' in *Daniel* 12.3. The main part of it was written by Moses de Leon towards the end of the thirteenth century as a commentary on the Pentateuch. There were, however, several other contributors. The commentary is presented as the work of Rabbi Simeon bar Yohai (second century CE) and his son, R. Eleazar, with the help of figures such as Sava ('Old Man') and Yenuka ('Child') who reveal heavenly secrets.

Zohar is an anthology rather than a single work. To the original three volumes, a fourth was added, containing other Qabbalistic works. A fifth volume, *Zohar Chadash*, 'New Zohar', was added later, containing parts of the original *Zohar* that were not included in the original editions. The whole has become, along with Tanakh and Talmud, one of the most sacred texts in Judaism.

According to *Zohar* 'the body is a cumbersome garment that falls off at death, thus leaving those who are enlightened to rise into heavenly light'. Qabbalah acts like a physician, not of the body but of the soul: 'If a physician has no medicine that he can usefully give to the body, he can still give medicine for the patient's soul.' R. Simeon is reported in *Zohar* to have said, 'Come and see: everything has its secret wisdom.'

📖 BIBLIOGRAPHY NUMBERS 496, 514, 781, 1051

LITURGY AND PRAYER

AMIDA AND PIYYUTIM

Prayer, or Tefillah, is deeply embedded in Tanakh which, in addition to the many prayers in the Psalms (*Tehillim*), quotes more than a hundred actual prayers. After the destruction of the Temple (70/135 CE), synagogues became supremely important in gathering and sustaining Jewish communities. In particular, they produced liturgies and rituals that could take the place of those no longer possible in the Temple.

This led, from about the eighth century onwards, to the production of common forms of synagogue prayer in a Prayer Book known as *seder tefillot*, or more commonly as *Siddur* or *Mahzor* ('cycle' of the annual festivals and observances).

There has never been a single agreed Prayer Book. The Ashkenazi (European) and Sefardi (Spanish and Mediterranean) Jews developed their own traditions and Prayer Books, as also have the major divisions in Judaism since the nineteenth century, Orthodox, Reform (or Liberal), Conservative and Reconstructionist. Nevertheless they share much in common, above all one of the oldest and most treasured synagogue prayers known as Amida. It has been claimed that parts of this are pre-Christian, but Reif, in his brilliant study *Judaism and Hebrew Prayer* has issued a warning (p. 60):

> There is . . . no convincing evidence that even the earliest known
> text of the *'amidah* itself predates the destruction of the Temple
> and only on the basis of intelligent and informed speculation
> can it be argued that some of the introductory and concluding
> benedictions were in existence as such at that time.

Amida means 'standing', and the prayer is so called because it is recited standing with one's feet together. In the Talmud it is also called simply *HaTefillah, 'the*

Prayer'. Another early name is *Shemoneh Esreh*, Eighteen, since there were originally eighteen Blessings or petitions addressed to God. A nineteenth was added, probably in the first or second century CE, known as *Birkat haMinim*, a prayer that God will destroy the enemies of Israel, but the number eighteen was retained in the name of the prayer.

The Amida is a central element of prayer in synagogue services. It has three Blessings at the beginning and three at the end, which remain substantially the same, but the thirteen Blessings in the middle change according to the occasion or festival at which the Amida is said. The Amida begins and ends in this way:

> Blessed are you, O Lord our God and God of our fathers, God of Abraham, God of Isaac, and God of Jacob, the great, the mighty and revered God, God far beyond, generous in gifts of kindness and goodness, the One who possesses all things, remembers the faithful love of our fathers, and who out of love rescues the generations that succeed them: King, helper, saviour and shield, blessed are you, O Lord, the shield of Abraham.

> You, O Lord, are powerful for ever, giving life to the dead: you are mighty to save. You sustain the living with generous love, you give life to the dead with great mercy, you support the falling, heal the sick, set the prisoner free and keep faith with those who sleep in the dust.

> Who is like you possessor of mighty acts, who can resemble you, O King, who brings the dead to life as the source of salvation?

> You are holy and your name is holy and holy beings praise you every day. Blessed are you, O Lord, the holy God.

> O Lord our God, accept your people Israel and their prayer. Restore the worship to your holy house and receive in gracious love the fire-offerings of Israel and their prayer, and may the worship of your people Israel be ever acceptable to you.

> We give thanks to you that you are the Lord our God and the God of our fathers for ever and ever. You are the Rock of our life, the Shield of our salvation from generation to generation. We give thanks to you and proclaim your praise for our lives that are held in your hand, and for our souls that are kept in your care, and for your marvels that are with us each day, and for your wonders and

your generous gifts that are with us at all times, in the evening, in the morning and during the day. You are all goodness because your mercy never fails, all merciful because your generous love never fails: we put our trust in you now and for ever.

For all these things your Name, our King, will be blessed and honoured continually now and for ever. Every living thing will give you thanks and praise your name in truth, O Lord God, for you have saved us and given us your help. Blessed are you, O Lord, your Name is goodness itself and to you it is right to offer praise.

Grant peace, welfare, blessing, grace, generous love and mercy to us and to all your people Israel. Bless us, our Father, all of us together, with the light of your countenance, for by the light of your countenance you have given to us, O Lord our God, the Word [Torah] of life, generous love and righteousness and blessing and mercies and life and peace. And may it seem good in your sight to bless your people Israel at all times and in every hour with your peace. Blessed are you, O Lord, blessing your people Israel with peace.

LITURGICAL POETRY: PIYYUTIM

The Synagogue services also produced liturgical poems and hymns known as *piyyutim*, the earliest of which go back to at least the first century CE. They were introduced to give variation in the services and to give expression to appropriate emotions.

Their nature has been summarised by Carmi (1981, p. 61):

> In Palestine under Byzantine rule, an entirely new kind of formal poetry developed, named *piyut*, which served for liturgical purposes. In this tradition, highly formalised poetic cycles were composed for the Sabbaths and holidays. Basically these were complex cycles of strophic poems with rigid norms for a variety of formal devices assigned separately to each part of the cycle. Most of the poems were stringed on an acrostic of the 22 letters of the Hebrew alphabet (sometimes incomplete or containing the name of the poet).

Many of the *piyyutim* are treated as sacred texts because of their association with the Synagogue liturgy and therefore also with Tanakh. They had the effect of producing in every generation Hebrew poets of immense power and skill. By association, many of their other poems are held in the same high regard. This is especially true of Judah haLevi (*c.*1075–1141), whose 'Songs of Zion' are treasured down to the present day. As Carmi put it (p. 107), 'No Hebrew poet since the Psalmists had sung the praises of the Holy Land with such passion.' Three of his poems are translated in my collected poems, *Before the Ending of the Day*, including this lament over Zion:

> Does your care and your questioning cease
> For the fate of your captives, O Zion?
> For those who seek after your peace
> And the remnant distraught from your flock?
>
> Let 'Shalom' be the cry and the word:
> From the east, from the west, from the south,
> From the north let this greeting be heard –
> And 'Peace' from my captive desire.
>
> My tears I will shed like the rain
> On Hermon, like dew at the dawn:
> I long for their falling again
> On your hills, O land of my love.
>
> But a wolf in distress is my voice
> When I think of your sorrow and grief.
> Instead as your lute I'll rejoice
> When I dream of the exiles' return.

📖 BIBLIOGRAPHY NUMBERS 423, 507, 775, 879, 889, 991, 1045

2

CHRISTIANITY

CHRISTIANITY TEXTS: KEY DATES

c.*5BCE–c.33CE* Jesus
c.*62–5* Death of Paul
c.*69–c.155/6* Polycarp
late 2nd cent. Muratorian Canon
2nd/3rd cent. NT Canon formed
325 Council of Nicaea
337 Constantine died
c.*339–97* Ambrose
c.*345–420* Jerome
354–430 Augustine
c.*360–c.430* John Cassian
4th cent. Cappadocian Fathers, Basil
451 Council of Chalcedon
c.*480–c.550* Benedict
5th cent. Pseudo-Dionysius
c.*540–615* Columbanus
6th cent. Vulgate
6th cent. Romanos
7th cent. Caedmon
c.*800* *Book of Kells*
c.*1172–1221* Dominic
1181/2–1226 Francis
1225–74 Thomas Aquinas
1265–1321 Dante Alighieri
c.*1330–84* John Wyclif
1440 Gutenberg printing press
1466–1536 Erasmus
1483–1546 Martin Luther
1487–1569 Miles Coverdale

1489–1556 Thomas Cranmer
c.*1491–1556* Ignatius
c.*1494–1536* William Tyndale
1509–64 John Calvin
1515–82 Teresa of Avila
1517 Luther, *Ninety-five Theses*
1526/34/35 Tyndale New Testament
1530/40 Augsburg Confession
1534 Act of Supremacy
1536/59 Calvin, *Institutes*
1536, 1561 Helvetic Confessions
1537 Matthew's Bible
1539/40 The Great Bible
1542–91 John of the Cross
1545–63 Council of Trent
1549, 1552 Edward VI Prayer Books
1559/63 Foxe's *Book of Martyrs*
1560 Geneva Bible
1568 Bishops' Bible
1582/1609 Douai-Reims translation
1604 Hampton Court conference
1608–74 John Milton
1611 King James Version (AV)
1648 The Westminster Confession
1662 Book of Common Prayer
1703–91 John Wesley
18th cent. *Philokalia*
1869–70 Vatican I
1962–5 Vatican II

Previous page: The Crucifixion. Salvador Dali was inspired to paint his 'Christ of Saint John of the Cross' when he saw in Avila a small drawing by John of the Cross whose poem, 'Living Flame', is translated on p. 121.

THE NEW TESTAMENT
Jesus and the Canon

The early Christians were for the most part Jews, so their sacred text was the Jewish Bible (Tanakh) so far as that had been determined (on the formation of the Jewish Canon, see p. 29). They were, however, Jews who believed that Jesus was the promised Messiah, or in Greek *ho Christos*, hence Jesus Christ.

Why did they believe that? Basically it was because of the powerful and dramatic things that he said and did. They were revolutionary, though not in a political sense. As I have pointed out in *Beliefs That Changed the World* (p. 37), Jesus was not leading a revolution against the Roman occupation of Palestine/Judaea. He was seeking to establish a different kind of kingdom: that of God. He believed that the final completion of that kingdom lies in the future, but there are signs that it is already coming into being: the signs were evident in the way in which Jesus healed people and pronounced that their sins had been forgiven. This work of God was completely unconditional. It did not depend on keeping the law or on having the right ideas about God. For Jesus, openness to God in faith and love is fundamental. He made it clear that this is possible as much for non-Jews as for Jews, but it is not a condition of God's works of healing and forgiveness.

There were other healers and teachers at the time, particularly in Galilee, but Jesus was entirely different in the way in which he acted and taught with a complete independence. He claimed that what he said and did came to him directly from God. What was astonishing (and to some disturbing) was the way Jesus made real in the world things that only God can do: only God, in the belief of that time, could heal the sick, forgive sins and establish God's kingdom on earth.

Jesus did not deny that only God can do those things. That is why he never claimed to be doing or saying these remarkable things out of his own ability or strength. He always said that they came to him from God whom he called

Father. The name they gave to that power was, in Greek, *dunamis* – it appears in English words like 'dynamite' and 'dynamic'.

What is particularly remarkable is that even the strongest enemies of Jesus (who thought that no human should act like Jesus, as though he was 'God on earth') could not deny that something extraordinary was happening in and through the person of Jesus: they simply said that he must be doing it through the power of the devil, Beelzebub, in order to seduce Jews from their true obedience to God.

So the first followers of Jesus, who witnessed his healing of body, mind and spirit, thought that they were seeing God in action. Or, as it is put with sharp brevity in *John* 14.9, 'Jesus said to Philip, " . . . Whoever has seen me has seen the Father."'

The problem for those who opposed Jesus was not simply what he said and did, but the fact that he was doing it in a way that was completely independent of the accepted understandings of what the Covenant life with God should be. There were at that time many different understandings, but that of Jesus was a highly individual interpretation, and it often called the requirements of Torah into question. That meant, in those days, that he was threatening the Temple and its authority, because that is where officially the final decisions were supposed to be made about legitimate or illegitimate teaching.

As a result, Jesus was brought in for examination before the High Priest, but when he remained silent he was clearly refusing to accept that authority – for which the penalty, according to *Deuteronomy* 17.8–13, must be execution. He was handed over to the Roman authorities as a 'disturber of the peace' – a disturber of the *pax Romana* of the Empire in that province. He was executed as the Romans executed other criminals and rebels, and he died on a cross.

The fundamental question, therefore, is how and why the followers of Jesus (those who believed that they had met God in Galilee) continued to believe that this executed criminal was indeed 'the Christ'. The answer is that although they knew beyond doubt that he had died on the Cross, they knew with equal certainty that he was alive after death. At first they could hardly believe it, and yet they found it to be true – not least because they found that the *dunamis* of God (the consequence and effect of God) that they had experienced in his company was still dramatically at work among them.

Not surprisingly, they began to gather accounts of what Jesus had said and done as they took this Gospel (i.e., 'good news') into the world. They also began to write letters and instructions to each other on what these earth-shaking events might mean and on how, in consequence, they should live. For an example from the opening of one such letter, see box on p. 51.

A MESSAGE OF
NEW BIRTH

The opening words of a New Testament Letter:

BLESSED BE THE GOD and Father of our Lord Jesus Christ! By his great mercy he has given us a new birth into a living hope through the resurrection of Jesus Christ from the dead, and into an inheritance that is imperishable, undefiled, and unfading, kept in heaven for you, who are being protected by the power of God through faith for a salvation ready to be revealed in the last time. In this you rejoice, even if now for a little while you have had to suffer various trials, so that the genuineness of your faith – being more precious than gold that, though perishable, is tested by fire – may be found to result in praise and glory and honour when Jesus Christ is revealed. Although you have not seen him, you love him; and even though you do not see him now, you believe in him and rejoice with an indescribable and glorious joy, for you are receiving the outcome of your faith, the salvation of your souls. (*1 Peter* 1.3-9)

THE CANON OF THE NEW TESTAMENT

The writings of the disciples were gradually collected into the work now known as the New Testament (or Covenant), 'new', that is, in relation to the original or Old Testament which, for Christians, did not cease to be the Bible.

Many writings were produced in the early centuries of which several were claimed to be the words of Jesus or to have come from one of his followers. Those claims needed to be tested, and a process of selection therefore became necessary.

Some could be discarded because they were making Jesus into an advocate of beliefs of an eccentric kind (i.e., beliefs 'far removed from the centre' of Christian tradition; for a description of the main discarded texts, see Hennecke). Some, for example, turned Jesus into a Gnostic. Gnosticism (from Greek *gnosis*, 'knowledge') is a name given to related but diverse religions in the early centuries, which regarded the world as imperfect and corrupt. If humans are to escape, they must be taught the knowledge (Gnosis) needed in order to do so. Gnostics claimed that Jesus was an emissary from God who offered that Gnosis and who was himself not truly human and thus did not get involved in an evil world.

Texts of that kind could be rejected as a 'hijacking' of Jesus into an alien philosophy. Deciding which texts should be *included* proved to be a harder and longer process. The earliest list of books identical with the present New Testament occurs in Athanasius' *Festal Epistle*, in 367, calling those texts 'the springs of salvation'.

The basic texts, however, were agreed much earlier. The Four Gospels and the Letters (Epistles) of Paul had been accepted as 'sacred' (i.e., as having authority in the Churches) by the early second century. Some texts now in the New Testament were regarded for much longer as doubtful (*Hebrews, Jude, James, 2 Peter, 2* and *3 John, Revelation*), while others not now in the New Testament were accepted for a while by at least some Churches. Examples are *Epistle of Barnabas, Shepherd of Hermas, Apocalypse of Peter* – that Apocalypse is in one of the earliest lists of Canonical books, the Muratorian Canon (late second century), though it says, 'some of us do not want it read in church'.

There were no agreed criteria for deciding which books should be included or excluded. There was, for example, no appeal to inspiration, although *2 Timothy* 3.16 reminds its readers 'how from childhood you have known the sacred writings that are able to instruct you for salvation through faith in Christ Jesus: all Scripture is inspired [God-breathed] by God and is useful for teaching'. At that time Scripture meant Tanakh, and in any case the words may mean 'every Scripture inspired by God is also . . .'

In either case there is no appeal to inspiration as a guide in selecting texts that might be regarded as sacred or authoritative for Christians. One of the criteria, however, was that a text should have a connection with someone who had been a follower and perhaps an eyewitness of Jesus. That criterion was of great importance in the forming of the Gospels.

BIBLIOGRAPHY NUMBERS 443, 444

The Bibliography to the New Testament and to its individual books is vast. For an initial guide, see Bowker, *The Complete Bible Handbook*.

THE NEW TESTAMENT

THE GOSPELS

When Jesus was alive, he called some men to be particularly close associates and followers. They were the Twelve Apostles (from Greek *apostolos*, 'one who has been sent'). Two of them, Peter and Judas, denied and betrayed Jesus when he was brought before the Temple authorities, but Peter recognised his fault, whereas the betrayal by Judas led to the crucifixion, and Judas is reported (*Matthew* 27.3–5) to have hanged himself. As a result, one of the first acts of the eleven Apostles after the death and resurrection of Jesus was to find a replacement for Judas among the Twelve; and Matthias was chosen.

What governed the choice of a replacement was a requirement that the person had been a companion and eyewitness of Jesus (*Acts* 1.21–2):

> One of the men who have accompanied us throughout the time
> that the Lord Jesus went in and out among us, beginning from the
> baptism of John until the day when he was taken up from us – one
> of these must become a witness with us to his resurrection.

That connection with Jesus became supremely important as faith in the risen Christ began to spread rapidly in the Mediterranean world – the movement was first called 'Christianity' in Antioch (*Acts* 11.26). The expansion of Christianity led to competing interpretations (see, for example, *I Corinthians* 1.11ff.), so that it became urgent to gather records of who Jesus was and of what he had said and done. The results of that process were written down in the Four Gospels, the Gospels according to *Matthew*, *Mark*, *Luke* and *John*.

THE SYNOPTIC GOSPELS

Two of the Gospels (*Matthew* and *Luke*) give traditional accounts of the birth of Jesus, and a third, *John*, offers a prologue in which a profound account is given of the relation of Jesus to God even before his birth. They then follow the same pattern, a record of his life and ministry, leading up to his last days in Jerusalem and culminating in the Crucifixion and Resurrection (though in *Mark* the original Gospel ends with the discovery of the empty tomb but without an account of any Resurrection appearances). This means that the Gospels are in effect (as Martin Kahler has called them) 'Passion narratives with extended introductions'. For part of the Passion according to *John*, see p. 57.

The first three Gospels are closely related to each other in the sense that they often share the same material, though not usually in exactly the same words or necessarily in the same order. For that reason they are known collectively as the Synoptic Gospels because they can be 'looked at together' to see how much material they share. The table on p. 55, for example, shows the three accounts of the words spoken by Jesus over the bread and the cup at the Last Supper.

How the Synoptic Gospels are related to each other is much debated, but the most likely explanation is that *Mark* is the earliest completed Gospel, and that *Matthew* and *Luke* incorporated much of *Mark*, with each of them making use of *Mark* in different ways.

However, *Matthew* and *Luke* sometimes make use of and thus share material that is not in *Mark*, which suggests that they were also using an earlier source that has otherwise not survived. That hypothetical source is known as **Q** (from the German *Quelle*, 'source'). In addition *Matthew* and *Luke* each made use of its own independent and early source (neither of which has otherwise survived). Thus the possible relationship between the Synoptics can be seen in simplified form in figure 1 (see also my *The Complete Bible Handbook*, p. 302).

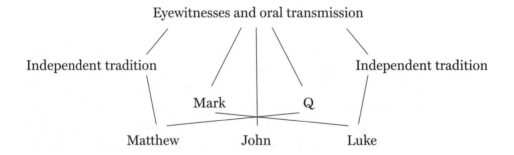

SYNOPTIC GOSPEL ACCOUNTS
OF THE LAST SUPPER

Matthew 26.26–9	*Mark* 14.22–5	*Luke* 22.15–20
		He said to them, 'I have eagerly desired to eat this Passover with you before I suffer; for I tell you, I will not eat it until it is fulfilled in the kingdom of God.' Then he took a cup, and after giving thanks he said, 'Take this and divide it among yourselves; for I tell you that from now on I will not drink of the fruit of the vine until the kingdom of God comes.'
While they were eating, Jesus took a loaf of bread, and after blessing it he broke it, gave it to the disciples, and said, 'Take, eat; this is my body.'	While they were eating, he took a loaf of bread, and after blessing it he broke it, gave it to them and said, 'Take; this is my body.'	Then he took a loaf of bread, and when he had given thanks, he broke it and gave it to them, saying, 'This is my body, which is given for you. Do this in remembrance of me.'
Then he took a cup, and after giving thanks he gave it to them, saying, 'Drink from it, all of you; for this is my blood of the covenant, which is poured out for many for the forgiveness of sins.' 'I tell you, I will never again drink of this fruit of the vine until that day when I drink it new with you in my Father's kingdom.'	Then he took a cup, and after giving thanks he gave it to them, and all of them drank from it. He said to them, 'This is my blood of the covenant, which is poured out for many.' 'Truly I tell you, I will never again drink of the fruit of the vine until that day when I drink it new in the kingdom of God.'	And he did the same with the cup after supper, saying, 'This cup that is poured out for you is the new covenant in my blood.'

EYEWITNESSES AND THE GOSPELS

The Gospel according to John, often called *The Fourth Gospel*, follows the same pattern as the Synoptics, and the author may have known at least one of them. It contains, however, episodes and details that do not appear in the Synoptics, and some have concluded that *John* was written long after the time of Jesus. Nevertheless, *John* is the only Gospel that claims not simply to be based on eyewitness accounts, but to have been written by an eyewitness (*John* 21.20, 24–5):

> Peter turned and saw the disciple whom Jesus loved following
> them; he was the one who had reclined next to Jesus at the supper
> and had said, 'Lord, who is it that is going to betray you?' . . . This is
> the disciple who is testifying to these things and has written them,
> and we know that his testimony is true. But there are also many
> other things that Jesus did; if every one of them were written down,
> I suppose that the world itself could not contain the books that
> would be written.

John extends the narrative style of the Synoptics in reflections that resemble a profound meditation on the nature and meaning of Jesus: many of them read as though they are a consequence of prayer. But that does not make *John* a speculative reconstruction detached from history, as some have claimed. It is only because the history has, so to speak, happened – and has been experienced as happening – that the reflection becomes a part of the testimony or witness to those events.

In forming the Gospels, therefore, it is clear that the writers were relying on eyewitnesses just as the replacement for Judas had to be someone who had been an eyewitness. The First Letter of John (*I John*, perhaps written by the same person as *John*) begins:

> We declare to you what was from the beginning, what we have
> heard, what we have seen with our eyes, what we have looked at
> and touched with our hands, concerning the word of life – this life
> was revealed, and we have seen it and testified to it, and declare to
> you the eternal life that was with the Father and was revealed to us.

In contrast, therefore, to a widespread assumption that the Gospels cannot be trusted to give a reliably historical account of Jesus, Richard Bauckham has argued, on the basis of meticulous and detailed work, that the Gospels gave

A Muslim scribe and a painter of miniatures (p. 11) at work, by Jaganath, *c*.1600.

The tools used by Muslim calligraphers. On calligraphy see p. 13; on God's teaching 'by means of the pen', see p. 126.

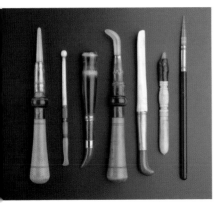

A Sikh at work copying *Guru Granth Sahib*: see pp. 219–22.

A Chinese monk inscribes a sentence from the Diamond Sutra (p. 255) encouraging people not to be attached to anything and to have a heart of compassion.

A Japanese printmaker works at printing from wooden blocks.

Title page of *The Golden Haggadah*. The work contains the story and rituals of the Passover, including Biblical illustrations.

Scenes in *The Golden Haggadah* from *Bereshit* (*Genesis*), starting top right since Hebrew is written from right to left: Adam names the animals; Eve is created from Adam and both are tempted; Cain and Abel offer sacrifice and Cain kills Abel; Noah emerges from the Ark.

A page from Maimonides' *Mishneh Torah*: the title, *Shophetim*, 'Judges', is the last Book (14) of Maimonides' work (see pp. 37–9).

The Babylonian Talmud, showing the page beginning the Tractate Qiddushin (Sanctification): 'The woman is acquired [to be a wife] in three ways…' Babylonian Talmud pages are now printed uniformly (p. 34) with Mishnah and Gemara in the centre surrounded by further commentary.

The title page of a translation of *The Gates of Light* (see p. 42): it shows the Ten Sefirot: see p. 41.

THE CRUCIFIXION
ACCORDING TO JOHN

S O THEY TOOK JESUS; and carrying the cross by himself, he went out to what is called The Place of the Skull, which in Hebrew is called Golgotha. There they crucified him, and with him two others, one on either side, with Jesus between them. Pilate also had an inscription written and put on the cross. It read, 'Jesus of Nazareth, the King of the Jews.' Many of the Jews read this inscription, because the place where Jesus was crucified was near the city; and it was written in Hebrew, in Latin, and in Greek. Then the chief priests of the Jews said to Pilate, 'Do not write, "The King of the Jews", but, "This man said, I am King of the Jews."' Pilate answered, 'What I have written I have written.' When the soldiers had crucified Jesus, they took his clothes and divided them into four parts, one for each soldier. They also took his tunic; now the tunic was seamless, woven in one piece from the top. So they said to one another, 'Let us not tear it, but cast lots for it to see who will get it.' This was to fulfil what the scripture says, 'They divided my clothes among themselves, and for my clothing they cast lots.' And that is what the soldiers did. Meanwhile, standing near the cross of Jesus were his mother, and his mother's sister, Mary the wife of Clopas, and Mary Magdalene. When Jesus saw his mother and the disciple whom he loved standing beside her, he said to his mother, 'Woman, here is your son.' Then he said to the disciple, 'Here is your mother.' And from that hour the disciple took her into his own home. After this, when Jesus knew that all was now finished, he said (in order to fulfil the scripture), 'I am thirsty.' A jar full of sour wine was standing there. So they put a sponge full of the wine on a branch of hyssop and held it to his mouth. When Jesus had received the wine, he said, 'It is finished.' Then he bowed his head and gave up his spirit.

John 19.16–30

special attention and importance to the testimony of disciples who had been eyewitnesses of the ministry of Jesus and of his death and Resurrection. Each Gospel tells the story in its own way and for its own purposes, but the reliance on the early testimony remains. Bauckham therefore summarised his argument by saying (p. 6):

> I shall be arguing in this book that the Gospel texts are much closer to the form in which the eyewitnesses told their stories or passed on their traditions than is commonly envisaged in current scholarship. This is what gives the Gospels their character as testimony. They embody the testimony of the eyewitnesses, not of course without editing and interpretation, but in a way that is substantially faithful to how the eyewitnesses themselves told it, since the Evangelists were in more or less direct contact with eyewitnesses, not removed from them by a long process of anonymous transmission of the traditions.

THE BIBLIOGRAPHY to the New Testament and to its individual books is vast. For an initial guide, see Bowker, *The Complete Bible Handbook*.

THE NEW TESTAMENT

EPISTLES AND OTHER WRITINGS

As well as the Gospels, the New Testament contains an account of the early history of the Church (*Acts of the Apostles*), Epistles/Letters, and a visionary portrayal of the future in the style of Jewish apocalyptic writing (*Revelation*). These texts explore in different ways how Jesus is the one through whom God has fulfilled the promises of the Bible (the Bible of the Jews, later to be called the Old Testament) and has rescued the people from sin and death.

The claim is often made that these sacred texts turned a simple human being, a Galilean teacher and wonder-worker, into a superhuman divine figure sent by God to rescue the world. It is a claim reflected in the title of Philip Pullman's book, *The Good Man Jesus and the Scoundrel Christ* (2010), in which the supposed incompatible contrast is explained on the basis that there were two identical twins. Less absurdly, and more commonly, Paul, the writer of several of the Epistles, is often described as 'the founder of Christianity' who turned a humble Jewish teacher into the dying and rising god of a Greek mystery religion: according to this claim, the earliest portrayal of Jesus (in the Gospels) is of a man remarkable for what he said and did; it was only later that Paul turned him into the Son of God.

JESUS AND GOD

These claims regarding Jesus are often made and widely taken for granted. They are, however, almost exactly the opposite of the truth. The Gospels, as we have seen, rest on extremely early traditions going back to the friends and companions of Jesus, but the earliest *writings* in the New Testament are the Letters of Paul. It is in those earliest writings that the highest titles and descriptions of Jesus in relation to God are to be found. For example, Paul wrote to the Christians in Philippi only about thirty years after the crucifixion, contrasting the obedience of Jesus with the destructive disobedience of Adam in Genesis 3 (*Philippians* 2.5ff):

Let the same mind be in you that was in Christ Jesus, who, though he was in the form of God, did not regard equality with God as something to be exploited [taken advantage of], but emptied himself, taking the form of a slave, being born in human likeness. And being found in human form, he humbled himself and became obedient to the point of death – even death on a cross. Therefore God also highly exalted him and gave him the name that is above every name, so that at the name of Jesus every knee should bend, in heaven and on earth and under the earth, and every tongue should confess that Jesus Christ is Lord, to the glory of God the Father.

At about the same time the following words about Christ Jesus were written to the Christians at Colossae (probably by Paul, though some have questioned this; *Colossians* 1.15–20):

He is the image of the invisible God, the firstborn of all creation; for in him all things in heaven and on earth were created, things visible and invisible, whether thrones or dominions or rulers or powers – all things have been created through him and for him. He himself is before all things, and in him all things hold together. He is the head of the body, the church; he is the beginning, the firstborn from the dead, so that he might come to have first place in everything. For in him all the fullness of God was pleased to dwell, and through him God was pleased to reconcile to himself all things, whether on earth or in heaven, by making peace through the blood of his cross. And you who were once estranged and hostile in mind, doing evil deeds, he has now reconciled in the body of his flesh through death, so as to present you holy and blameless and irreproachable before him – provided that you continue securely established and steadfast in the faith, without shifting from the hope promised by the Gospel that you heard, which has been proclaimed to every creature under heaven. I, Paul, became a servant of this Gospel.

From these and other examples, it is clear that within a few years of the execution of Jesus the early Christians were already associating Jesus with God so closely that the adoration and worship due to God are due also to Jesus. What is so remarkable about this is that the earliest of the texts regarded by Christians as sacred were acknowledging that Jesus is Christ and Lord and yet they went on using his ordinary human name. They knew, therefore, that he was not the invented figure of a Greek mystery religion or of a Gnostic philosophy (p. 52). They knew that he was a man who had lived in Galilee and had died outside Jerusalem, and they went on calling him by his ordinary human name of Jesus.

From the earliest moment, therefore, they believed that Jesus, whom they knew to be human like themselves, had brought God dramatically into the world. He made God wholly and really present in their midst: the healing of body, mind and spirit was the work of God and of no other. Paul then claimed that those who have been baptised have been made a part of Christ, his Body, and that consequently through their involvement in Christ they have overcome death. Like highly valued players, they have been transferred, not from one team to another, but from death to life.

Christians, therefore, are those who are already dead, as Paul wrote to the Christians at Colossae (3.3f.), 'You have died, and your life lies hidden with Christ in God: when Christ who is your life is revealed, then you also will be revealed with him in glory.' That is why Paul repeatedly described Christians as those who are 'in Christ'. Each is like an abandoned child who has been rescued and made safe by being taken into a new home as part of the family, as, for example, in this passage from *2 Corinthians*, 5.14–20:

> The love of Christ urges us on, because we are convinced that one
> has died for all; therefore all have died. And he died for all, so that
> those who live might live no longer for themselves, but for him who
> died and was raised for them. From now on, therefore, we regard
> no one from a human point of view; even though we once knew
> Christ from a human point of view, we know him no longer in that
> way. So if anyone is in Christ, there is a new creation: everything old
> has passed away; see, everything has become new! All this is from
> God, who reconciled us to himself through Christ, and has given us
> the ministry of reconciliation; that is, in Christ God was reconciling
> the world to himself, not counting their trespasses against them,
> and entrusting the message of reconciliation to us. So we are
> ambassadors for Christ, since God is making his appeal through us;
> we entreat you on behalf of Christ, be reconciled to God.

WHY THE NEW TESTAMENT?

The challenge of the sacred texts gathered in the New Testament concerns why they are there at all. What was it that brought them into being? It is easy to see that they are to some extent like other writings in the Mediterranean world.

The Gospels are something like the Lives written of other famous people, the Epistles are something like other Letters of the time, and *Revelation* resembles other works of Jewish apocalyptic. And yet they are completely unlike them. They are a response to a unique person who reached into human lives, turned them around from the frailties and sins which are the common lot of all people, and offered them a new life that will endure through death. No wonder (but it is a wonder unless there had been a unique person who had risen from the dead) Paul could write (*Romans* 8.35–8):

> Who will separate us from the love of Christ? Will hardship, or distress, or persecution, or famine, or nakedness, or peril, or sword? . . . No, in all these things we are more than conquerors through him who loved us. For I am convinced that neither death, nor life, nor angels, nor rulers, nor things present, nor things to come, nor powers, nor height, nor depth, nor anything else in all creation, will be able to separate us from the love of God in Christ Jesus our Lord.

📖 BIBLIOGRAPHY NUMBERS 313, 389

TRANSLATIONS

THE VULGATE, THE AUTHORISED VERSION

The Bible has been translated many times into virtually every language in the world (for a summary, see Metzger). Some of the translations have become 'sacred texts' in their own right: that is to say, they have become not simply a translation, but the equivalent of the sacred text itself. While Latin was the common language of the educated, that was true of Jerome's translation known as the Vulgate. In the English-speaking world, it is particularly true of the Authorised Version, the King James Bible of 1611.

FROM THE SEPTUAGINT TO THE VULGATE

In about 100 BCE, the Jewish Bible (Tanakh, called by Christians the Old Testament) was translated from Hebrew into Greek in the version known as the Septuagint, or LXX (p. 31), but there were other Greek versions as well. So, the LXX was usually the Bible of the New Testament writers but with variations. The LXX remains the Bible text of the Greek Orthodox Church.

Jerome (*c.*345–420) started to translate the LXX into Latin, but he decided that it would be better to go back to the original Hebrew, an initiative that led in due course to the Vulgate. The Vulgate continued as the Bible of the Roman Catholic Church, with translations being made into many other languages. The version into English authorised by the Roman Catholic Church is the Douai–Reims translation (so called from the places where it was made, 1582/1609), though others have been made. During the twentieth century, the faults of the Vulgate and the translations (inevitable, given the time of their origin) came to be recognised, and other translations are now allowed.

Attempts to render the Vulgate into English began much earlier. In the eighth century the Venerable Bede recorded in his *History of the English Church and People* how Caedmon in the seventh century used to sing a version of some parts of the Bible in his own language (Bede 4.24):

He was skilled in composing songs of faith and devotion. When competent people explained a passage of Scripture to him, he could turn it at once into pleasing and stirring poetry in his native English . . . Others later tried to write religious poems in English, but none came near him, because he did not acquire the skill of poetry from human teachers, but rather received it as a free gift from God.

According to Bede, Caedmon sang verses in a style 'truly worthy of God' (4.24):

He sang of the world's creation, of the origin of the human race, and all the history in Genesis. He sang of the exodus of the children of Israel out of Egypt, and of their entry into the Promised Land, along with many other narratives from holy Scripture; he sang of the passion, Resurrection and Ascension of our Lord into heaven, the coming of the Holy Spirit, and the teaching of the Apostles. As well as this, he sang of the terror of the Last Judgement, the horror of the agonies of hell and the joys of the Kingdom of heaven.

FROM WYCLIF TO THE AUTHORISED VERSION

The first translation of the Bible into English is attributed to John Wyclif (Wycliffe, *c*.1330–84) as part of his desire to reform the Church. He believed that the Bible should not be confined to those with a knowledge of Latin (mainly the clergy who thus gained control over the salvation of the laity), but that anyone who could read 'might learn the Gospel in its simplicity'. Wyclif worked with others, and for another century this was the main Bible in English.

Making copies of the Bible by hand was a slow and laborious process even though it led to illuminated manuscripts of stunning beauty: outstanding examples are the Lindisfarne Gospels and *The Book of Kells*, whose 'commanding beauty' was claimed by Sullivan (p. 1) to have 'raised this ancient Irish volume to a position of abiding preeminence amongst the illuminated manuscripts of the world'. The change, therefore, was immense when in 1440 Gutenberg invented a process of printing with the use of movable and changeable type – the Chinese had been printing sacred texts for more than a thousand years, but with the different process of carving woodblocks.

The development of printing was a serious threat to those who wished to control the lives and the beliefs of the laity, especially therefore to the Bishop of

THE GIFT OF LOVE

The translation in the Authorised Version of 1 Corinthians 13.1–12: the word *agape*, love of an unfailing and self-sacrificial kind, is translated as 'charity'.

THOUGH I SPEAK WITH the tongues of men and of angels, and have not charity, I am become as sounding brass, or a tinkling cymbal. And though I have the gift of prophecy, and understand all mysteries, and all knowledge; and though I have all faith, so that I could remove mountains, and have not charity, I am nothing. And though I bestow all my goods to feed the poor, and though I give my body to be burned, and have not charity, it profiteth me nothing. Charity suffereth long, and is kind; charity envieth not; charity vaunteth not itself, is not puffed up, Doth not behave itself unseemly, seeketh not her own, is not easily provoked, thinketh no evil; Rejoiceth not in iniquity, but rejoiceth in the truth; Beareth all things, believeth all things, hopeth all things, endureth all things. Charity never faileth: but whether there be prophecies, they shall fail; whether there be tongues, they shall cease; whether there be knowledge, it shall vanish away. For we know in part, and we prophesy in part. But when that which is perfect is come, then that which is in part shall be done away. When I was a child, I spake as a child, I understood as a child, I thought as a child: but when I became a man, I put away childish things. For now we see through a glass, darkly; but then face to face: now I know in part; but then I shall know even as also I am known. And now abide faith, hope, charity, these three; but the greatest of these is charity.

Rome, known more commonly as the Pope. For those, however, who wished to reform the Church of Rome (including people, like Erasmus, who stayed loyal to it), the printing press was a providential gift – a gift from God. It enabled their programmes of reform to be printed and widely circulated, and it put translations of the Bible into many more hands than would otherwise have been possible. As William Tyndale (*c.*1494–1536) put it to one who thought that the Bible should be kept in the hands of the learned, 'If God spare my life, ere many years I will cause a boy that drives the plough to know more of the scripture than you do.'

Tyndale was spared long enough to complete his great translation. Opposed and threatened in England, he worked in Europe, translating directly from the Greek, not from the Vulgate. He completed the New Testament in 1526, with revisions in 1534 and 1535. In England bishops bought up copies in order to burn them, and Thomas More wrote that it was 'not worthy to be called Christ's testament, but either Tyndale's own testament or the testament of his master Antichrist'.

Tyndale began work on the Old Testament, completing the Pentateuch and *Jonah* by 1531. Those loyal to the Pope continued to try to stop him, and eventually, in 1535, he was arrested near Brussels. He was found guilty of heresy and handed over to the secular authorities for execution. He was strangled and burnt at the stake in 1536.

In England, Henry VIII (once called by the Pope *Fidei Defensor*, 'Defender of the Faith') abolished all Papal power by the Act of Supremacy in 1534. Miles Coverdale brought together a complete English Bible dedicated to Henry VIII, even though it still had to be published on the continent in 1535. The first authorised Bible was produced in 1537, the so-called Matthew Bible. Coverdale revised the Matthew Bible, printed in Paris in 1539 and in England (revised) in 1540, with a Preface by Cranmer. It was known as the Great Bible. The Injunction of 1538 ordered that it should be placed in every church for the instruction of the people in the language they could understand.

The persecution of Protestants under Queen Mary (1553–8) drove many into exile. One of them, William Whittingham, became Pastor of the English Church in Geneva where he produced the Geneva Bible in 1560, dedicated to Elizabeth I. It became the most widely used and popular translation: it is the Bible used by Shakespeare. It was revised in 1568 in a version known as the Bishops' Bible.

When James I became king (1603), the Great Bible and the Bishops' Bible were in competition. A conference at Hampton Court in 1604 proposed that a new translation should be made, incorporating the best of earlier versions, including those of Tyndale and Coverdale. The translation was published in 1611 and is often referred to by that date (though it was in fact revised in

1614). It was never formally 'authorised' by King or Parliament, but it became so universal and so greatly loved that it was eventually labelled 'the Authorised Version' (AV), known also as the King James Version. See the box on p. 65 for an example of its style.

Many subsequent translations have been made. *Brewer's Dictionary of Phrase and Fable* lists eighty-seven well-known English translations. They reflect the vastly increased knowledge of the languages and manuscripts of the Bible, and also the conflicting interpretations of the divided Churches. Take, for example, *Romans* 8.28; the AV translation reads:

> And we know that all things work together for good to them that love God, to them who are called according to his purpose.

In Douai–Reims it is:

> And we know that to them that love God, all things work together unto good, to such as, according to his purpose, are called to be saints.

However, it came to be noticed that in three early Greek manuscripts the word 'God' is the subject of the sentence, and many modern translations make that the meaning (though often drawing attention to the issue in a footnote):

> And we know that in all things God works for the good of those who love him (*New International Version*);

> We are well aware that God works with those who love him, those who have been called in accordance with his purpose, and turns everything to their good (*The New Jerusalem Bible*);

> And we know that God causes all things to work together for good to those who love God (*New American Standard Bible*);

> And in everything, as we know, God co-operates for good with those who love God (*New English Bible*).

These may seem to be small differences, but they have affected profoundly the ways in which Christians have understood suffering and evil in relation to God.

The AV was itself revised in the Revised Version of 1885, but for many the AV remains the paramount version because of the beauty of its language and the familiarity of so many of its phrases, especially in the Psalms. Even so, in *The Book of Common Prayer* the Psalms are included in Coverdale's translation, as in Psalm 23:

> The Lord is my shepherd: therefore can I lack nothing.
> He shall feed me in a green pasture: and lead me forth beside the waters of comfort.
> He shall convert my soul: and bring me forth in the paths of righteousness, for his Name's sake.
> Yea, though I walk through the valley of the shadow of death, I will fear no evil: for thou art with me; thy rod and thy staff comfort me.
> Thou shalt prepare a table before me against them that trouble me: thou hast anointed my head with oil, and my cup shall be full.
> But thy loving-kindness and mercy shall follow me all the days of my life: and I will dwell in the house of the Lord for ever.

BIBLIOGRAPHY NUMBERS 80, 86, 244, 259, 317, 363, 429, 960, 981, 1029

CREEDS AND CONFESSIONS

THE APOSTLES' AND THE NICENE CREEDS; FROM AUGSBURG TO PETER THE GREAT

Attempts to reform the Church were made before the sixteenth century, but it was in that century that the major reformations were summarised collectively as 'the Reformation'. In fact there were many reformations, but a key issue for them all was the translation of the Bible into the vernacular, the languages that people can understand. As Collinson has summarised the point (in McManners, p. 260), 'The first priority was to put the Gospel into the hands of Christians in the form of the Bible in an acceptable translation in their own language.'

The reformations produced not just a single 'reformed Church', but a number of reformed Churches, including Lutheran, Calvinist and Presbyterian. Since they were not altogether in agreement with each other, it became necessary for them to draw up definitions of belief and practice to which members or prospective members must give their assent. Many of these (for some examples, see below) are known as Confessions, following the example of the early Churches in drawing up Creeds.

CREEDS

Creeds are brief statements of fundamental beliefs (from Latin *credo*, 'I believe'). The earliest summaries of belief are found in the New Testament itself, beginning with the simple confession, 'Jesus is Lord' (see *I Corinthians* 12.3, *Philippians* 2.11, *Acts* 8.37 in one form of the text). They came to be associated particularly with the Baptists and were recited by those receiving baptism on entering the Church, as a sign of their commitment.

Originally, the creeds recited at baptism varied from place to place. Any one of these was called *symbolum* ('token' or 'pledge'), a word used in the Roman army meaning 'a password', that is a word that shows who is friend and who is foe, who belongs and who does not.

THE NICENE CREED

I BELIEVE IN ONE GOD, the Father Almighty, maker of heaven and earth, and of all things visible and invisible: and in one Lord Jesus Christ, the only-begotten Son of God, begotten of his Father before all worlds, God of God, Light of Light, very God of very God, begotten, not made, being of one substance with the Father, by whom all things were made: who for us, and for our salvation came down from heaven, and was incarnate by the Holy Ghost of the Virgin Mary, and was made man, and was crucified also for us under Pontius Pilate. He suffered and was buried, and the third day he rose again according to the Scriptures, and ascended into heaven, and sits on the right hand of the Father. And he shall come again with glory to judge both the quick and the dead: whose kingdom shall have no end. And I believe in the Holy Spirit, the Lord and giver of life, who proceeds from the Father and the Son, who with the Father and the Son together is worshipped and glorified, who spoke by the Prophets. And I believe in one Catholic and Apostolic Church. I acknowledge one baptism for the remission of sins. And I look for the resurrection of the dead, and the life of the world to come.

By the fourth century a single Creed was agreed in the Western Church, known as the Apostles' Creed: it was certainly not written by the Apostles but it was thought to represent the traditional faith going back to the original eyewitnesses. It became a basic statement of Christian belief:

I believe in God, the Father Almighty, creator of heaven and earth. I
believe in Jesus Christ, his only Son, Lord. He was conceived by the
power of the Holy Spirit and born of the Virgin Mary. He suffered
under Pontius Pilate, was crucified, died, and was buried. He
descended to the dead. On the third day he rose again. He ascended
into heaven, and is seated at the right hand of the Father. He will come
again to judge the living and the dead. I believe in the Holy Spirit, the
holy Catholic Church, the communion of saints, the forgiveness of
sins, the resurrection of the body, and the life everlasting.

Other creeds followed. Notable among them is the Nicene Creed, so called
because it was believed to have come from a Council of the whole Church,
summoned to meet at Nicaea in 325. That Council did indeed create a Creed
designed to exclude those whose beliefs about Jesus in relation to God were
thought to be inadequate – notably, the followers of Arius.

The longer Creed now known as the Nicene Creed took far longer to produce
and reflects the majority view, excluding others in further disputes. It may
originally have been the baptismal creed of the Church in Constantinople. In its
final form it has become a minimal statement of faith on which (it is hoped) all
Christians can agree (see box on p. 70).

CONFESSIONS

The Confessions of the Reformation Churches are equally fundamental in
defining the faith and practice of their members, and also in excluding those
who differ from them. Notable among them are:

◆ The Augsburg Confession, 1530: it is the work mainly of Melanchthon who
  revised it in 1540; it is a Lutheran statement, hoping for reconciliation among
  believers, and some Calvinist Churches accepted the 1540 version (20):

> Our works cannot reconcile us to God or merit remission of sins
> and grace and justification. This we obtain only by faith, when
> we believe that we are received into grace on account of Christ . . .
> Men are warned that the word *faith* does not signify merely the
> knowledge of an event (the devils and impious men have that),
> but it signifies faith which believes not in an event merely, but also
> in the effect of an event, namely this article, the remission of sins,
> which means that we have through Christ, grace, righteousness and
> remission of sins.

◆ The Helvetic Confessions, 1536 and 1561: they are the work of Swiss reformers expressing the beliefs of Zwingli: the First incorporates some Lutheran beliefs, the Second is more strongly Calvinist.

◆ The Westminster Confession, 1648: it is a Calvinist statement of Presbyterianism drawn up on the authority of the English Parliament as 'a Confession of Faith for the three Kingdoms, according to the Solemn League and Covenant'. It became a definitive statement of Presbyterian doctrine that also has authority for others (e.g., some Baptists):

> The authority of the Holy Scripture . . . depends not on the testimony of any man or Church; but wholly upon God (who is truth itself) the author thereof . . . Our full persuasion and assurance of the infallible truth and Divine authority thereof is from the inward work of the Holy Spirit, bearing witness, by and with the Word, in our hearts . . . The infallible rule of interpretation of Scripture is the Scripture itself.

Other Churches also drew up basic statements of faith and organisation. An example of the latter is 'the Spiritual Regulation of Peter the Great', 1720. It defined how the Orthodox Church in Russia should be organised, thus transforming both the Church itself and its relation to the Imperial government. As Muller has summarised the effect (p. xxv):

> A total of more than three thousand ukases, statutes, charters, treaties, manifestoes, regulations, and other enactments were initiated in Peter's reign. He wrote a great number of them himself and personally supervised the composition of many others. They appeared with increasing frequency in the course of Peter's reign, growing into a formidable body of legislation that touched Russian life – customs, practices, conventions – at many points and affected the church as well as secular institutions . . . The forward course of Petrine ecclesiastical legislation, leading to the enactment of the *Spiritual Regulation,* is thus a part of the entire reform movement.

Texts of this kind are sacred to those who use them, not because they are equal to Scripture but because they are a source of authority derived from Scripture.

📖 BIBLIOGRAPHY NUMBERS 59, 234, 253, 761, 903

COUNCILS

ECUMENICAL COUNCILS, VATICAN I, VATICAN II

The Greek word *oikumene* means 'the whole inhabited world'. In Christian history it has been used in two main ways: first, to describe the Ecumenical Movement, the quest among the different Christian Churches to come into union with each other; second, to describe the Ecumenical Councils (sometimes spelt 'Oecumenical'), the formal occasions when bishops and others assemble to make decisions on issues of doctrine and practice that are binding on all Christians.

The texts from Ecumenical Councils have high authority because they apply the meaning and implications of Scripture to the life of the Church and the lives of individuals, particularly in relation to controversial or disputed issues. We have already met two of these Councils, Nicaea (325, p. 71) and Constantinople (381, p. 71). In the early Church, before the split between the Eastern and Western Churches, there were seven Councils accepted on both sides as Ecumenical.

One of those Councils, that of Chalcedon (451), produced a Definition (see box on p. 74) which has set the terms for 'Christology' ever since (except in some Oriental churches that do not accept this Council). That is to say, it set the boundaries within which must fall any attempt to state how God is wholly present in the person of Jesus Christ without destroying or reducing his humanity.

The Roman Catholic Church has decided that there have been a further fourteen Councils with ecumenical authority, including the Council of Trent (see pp. 118f.). The authority of all twenty-one Councils for Roman Catholics rests on the belief that Councils express the mind of the Church and that the only true Church is that of Rome. In a sense, therefore, the Councils are of greater immediate and practical importance than Scripture, though obviously they are rooted in Scripture and derived from it. This means they take on the role of sacred texts in the way in which they mediate Scripture into the continuing life of the Church. That distinction has been well expressed by Weigel (in Fremantle, p. 11):

THE CONCLUSION OF
THE CHALCEDONIAN
DEFINITION

FOLLOWING THE HOLY FATHERS, we unanimously teach and confess one and the same Son, our Lord Jesus Christ, the same perfect in divinity and perfect in humanity, the same truly God and truly man composed of rational soul and body, the same one in being [*homoousios*, the term used at Nicaea] with the Father as to the divinity and one in being [also *homoousios*] with us as to the humanity, like us in all things but sin [cf. *Hebrews* 4.15]. The same was begotten from the Father before the ages as to the divinity and in the latter days for us and our salvation was born as to his humanity from Mary the Virgin Mother of God. We confess that one and the same Lord Jesus Christ, the only-begotten Son, must be acknowledged in two natures, without confusion or change, without division or separation. The distinction between the natures was never abolished by their union but rather the character proper to each of the two natures was preserved as they came together in one person and one hypostasis. He is not split or divided into two persons, but he is one and the same only-begotten, God the Word, the Lord Jesus Christ, as formerly the prophets and later Jesus Christ himself have taught us about him and has been handed down to us by the Symbol [p. 69] of the Fathers.

All these things, therefore, having been defined by us with every accuracy and care, the holy and ecumenical Synod has decreed that it is unlawful for anyone to put forward, write, compose, invent, or teach to others any other Faith. Those who dare to put forward any other Faith, or to offer or teach or deliver any other Symbol to those wishing to turn to a full knowledge of the truth from Hellenism or from Judaism or indeed from heresy of any kind whatsoever, let those people if they are bishops or clergy be deposed, the bishops from their episcopacy and the clergy from their office. If they are monks or laity, they shall be anathematised.

The Catholic does not say in the first instance, What does the Book say? Rather he asks, What does the teaching Church say? The Church and the Book say the same thing, and since the Book is in a peculiar sense God's Word, he will turn to the Book. However, this is not his ultimate recourse. He has only one ultimate recourse, the Church herself, and the Book is accepted from her hand and with her explanation. The Book is not the proof but only a divine expression in human language of the Church's teaching. Over the Book stands the Church, while according to the Reform conception, over the Church stands the Book.

For Roman Catholics, the authoritative Church teaching is not of course confined to the twenty-one Councils. It is expressed in the pronouncements of the bishops, and above all of the Bishop of Rome, i.e., the Pope. Papal pronouncements come in many forms, but supremely in Constitutions, Bulls (from the Latin *bulla*, 'a seal'), Decrees and Encyclicals. The word 'encyclical' comes from the Greek *en*, 'in', and *kuklos*, 'a circle'. An Encyclical is thus a letter that is meant to be sent round to the whole Church.

VATICAN I AND VATICAN II

The authority of the Pope was greatly enhanced at the First Vatican Council (Vatican I, 1869–70). The Council was cut short, but it still had time to issue the Dogmatic Constitution *Pastor Aeternus* in which it was declared that the Pope, when he speaks *ex cathedra*, is infallible when he defines a doctrine concerning faith or morals:

> We, with the approval of the sacred Council, teach and define: It is a divinely revealed dogma that the Roman Pontiff, when he speaks *ex cathedra*, that is, when, acting in the office of shepherd and teacher of all Christians, he defines, by virtue of his supreme apostolic authority, a doctrine concerning faith or morals to be held by the universal Church, possesses through the divine assistance promised to him in the person of Blessed Peter, the infallibility with which the divine Redeemer willed his Church to be endowed in defining the doctrine concerning faith or morals; and that such definitions of the Roman Pontiff are therefore irreformable of themselves, not because of the consent of the Church.

The Second Vatican Council (Vatican II, 1962–5) made an attempt to set that Definition in the context of the responsibility and work of all the bishops, in what is known as 'collegiality':

> Just as, by the Lord's will, St Peter and the other apostles
> constituted one apostolic college, so in a similar way the Roman
> Pontiff as the successor of Peter, and the bishops as the successors
> of the apostles are joined together . . . Together with its head, the
> Roman Pontiff, and never without this head, the Episcopal order is
> the subject of supreme and full power over the universal Church . . .
> The same collegiate power can be exercised in union with the Pope
> by the bishops living in all parts of the world, provided that the
> head of the college calls them to collegiate action, or at least so
> approves or freely accepts united action of the dispersed bishops,
> that it is made a true collegiate act (*Lumen Gentium* 3.22).

In practice, however, the years since Vatican II have seen increasing centralisation of authority and power in the Pope and the Vatican, and for many this is a necessary reaffirmation of Papal pronouncements acting as 'a sacred text'.

📖 BIBLIOGRAPHY NUMBERS 191, 315, 752, 972

PRAYER AND HYMNS

THE OFFICE, THE BOOK OF COMMON PRAYER, HYMNS, JOHN AND CHARLES WESLEY

The early Christians were mainly Jews and as a result they shared in Jewish prayer and worship. In *Ephesians* 5.19 they are encouraged to be 'filled with the Spirit as you sing psalms and hymns and spiritual songs among yourselves, singing and making melody to the Lord in your hearts, giving thanks to God the Father at all times and for everything in the name of our Lord Jesus Christ'.

When, however, Christians and Jews became separated, Christians could no longer participate in Jewish daily prayer or in Temple sacrifices (the Temple in any case was destroyed in 135). What they could do was to continue the practice of saying prayers at fixed hours. In both Eastern and Western Churches the practice developed of praying in the morning (Mattins and Lauds) and evening (Vespers and Compline) and also at the third, sixth and ninth hours in services known in the West as Terce, Sext and None. The seven fixed times of prayer reflect the commitment of Psalm 119.164, quoted on p. 25.

This practice was incorporated into the monastic Offices (based on the whole Psalter being recited each week) and thus to *Officium Divinum*, the Divine Office, which clergy and professed members of religious Orders in the Roman Catholic Church are obliged to say daily – though since 1971 in a revised form. The word *officium* meant originally 'service' and 'duty', hence 'work done as a matter of obligation'. On that basis, the Divine Office was defined as 'the work of God'.

All this was far more than laypeople could undertake, and although shortened versions were produced, it remained out of reach for most people, not least because it was in Latin and in the early centuries was not printed. This became an issue for the reformers of the Church. Just as they insisted that people should be able to read the Bible in their own language, so also they realised that people should praise and worship God in words they could understand. In the Preface to Henry VIII's Primer, Thomas Cranmer wrote (1545, in Cox, p. 497) on the King's behalf of his 'right great labour and diligence'

> that men may know both what they pray, and also with what words, lest things special good and principal, being inwrapped in the ignorance of the words, should not perfectly come to the mind and to the intelligence of men; or else things being nothing to the purpose, nor very meet to be offered unto God, should have the less effect with God, being the distributor of all gifts.

Reformed Churches produced their own Prayer Books except for those for whom prayer through set words is 'vain repetition': in their view, set words deny the freedom of the Holy Spirit to inspire prayer, since people 'filled with the Spirit' will pray as the Spirit, not as a book, wills. 'Free prayer', perhaps accompanied by 'speaking with tongues', remains for many Christians a mark of the true Church.

Cranmer, however, was one among the majority who realised the power of 'sacred *text*' in the lives of believers. He began the process that led (through the two Prayer Books of Edward VI, 1549 and 1552, and other revisions) to *The Book of Common Prayer* (BCP), authorised in 1662. His influence can be seen especially in the Collects (a cycle of prayers throughout the Christian year, some of which were translated or written by Cranmer himself). Here, for example, is his Collect for Advent Sunday (for text and commentary see Barbee, p. 2):

> Almighty God, give us grace, that we may cast away the works of darkness, and put upon us the armour of light, now in the time of this mortal life (in the which thy son Jesus Christ came to visit us in great humility;) that in the last day when he shall come again in his glorious majesty to judge both the quick and the dead, we may rise to the life immortal, through him who liveth and reigneth with thee and the holy ghost now and ever. Amen.

The BCP draws deeply on Scripture and its language reflects the measured beauty of the AV (p. 67) – the AV was introduced into the 1662 Prayer Book as the version to be read in the Epistles and Gospels at the service of Holy Communion. Cranmer's hope that it would work its way into people's lives was realised: many, for example, were taught to learn by heart the Collects, a practice that has only recently become uncommon.

HYMNS

The early Offices were based on the Psalter, but they included Office hymns. Written in Latin and Greek, they continue to the present day, many of them translated into English and other languages. Despite the widespread use of hymns there was uncertainty about them during the sixteenth-century Reformations. For some it seemed wrong to set hymns alongside Scripture since Scripture is the Word of God. They could at least accept the many ways in which the Psalms were turned into metrical versions, as, for example, in the Scottish Psalter of 1650 (cf., with this, Coverdale's version on p. 68):

> The Lord's my Shepherd, I'll not want;
> He makes me down to lie
> In pastures green; he leadeth me
> The quiet waters by.

For other Reformers, however, with Luther among them, hymns were simply an extension of Scripture into a memorable form. He himself wrote 'Ein feste Burg', translated by Thomas Carlyle as, 'A safe stronghold our God is still, A trusty shield and weapon.' Others, the Moravians in particular, produced hymns that through translation had an influence far beyond Germany.

Among those influenced by the Moravians was John Wesley who, with the help of George Whitefield and his brother Charles, founded the movement within Anglicanism that became eventually the Methodist Church. John Wesley published in 1737 the first hymn book used in an Anglican Church, *A Collection of Psalmes and Hymns*, but it was his brother Charles who wrote memorable and enduring hymns in prolific number (about 6,500). Many are still well known, including 'Hark! The Herald Angels Sing' (originally 'Hark, how all the welkin rings!') and 'Love Divine, all loves excelling, Joy of heaven to earth come down':

> Love Divine, all loves excelling,
> Joy of heaven to earth come down,
> Fix in us thy humble dwelling,
> All thy faithful mercies crown.
> Jesu, thou art all compassion,
> Pure unbounded love thou art;
> Visit us with thy salvation,
> Enter every trembling heart.

Finish, then, thy new creation;
Pure and spotless let us be:
Let us see thy great salvation
Perfectly restored in thee;
Changed from glory into glory,
Till in heav'n we take our place,
Till we cast our crowns before thee,
Lost in wonder, love, and praise.

After the Reformation, the writing of hymns and their use in worship became far more common. This led to the creation of hymns of such power that they have become for many people the 'sacred text' through which their beliefs and their hopes are expressed. Hymns like 'Amazing Grace', 'Guide me, O Thou Great Redeemer', 'Abide with Me' and 'Morning Has Broken' (to take examples from different centuries) have inhabited the popular mind and appear on secular as well as on religious occasions. Ian Bradley began his book, *Abide with Me* (p. xi), with the words: 'Hymns played much the same role in Victorian culture that television and radio soap operas do today.' He also quoted the observation of Susan Tamke (p. 2):

> It seems indisputable that quantatively the effect of hymns on the Victorian public was more profound than the literary works which traditionally have been mined so assiduously by cultural historians. In sheer volume, the writing of hymns far outweighed the writing of poetry ... More important, the people whose lives were affected by hymns far outnumber those who were affected by poetry. Only a small percentage of Victorian society read the Greek or Latin poets, or even the more popular Southey or Wordsworth. But hymns were sung everywhere – on street corners, at secular meetings, in the nursery; as well as in the churches and chapels.

BIBLIOGRAPHY NUMBERS **68, 218, 250, 252**

LITURGY AND EUCHARIST

THE LAST SUPPER; KONTAKIA

The word 'liturgy' comes from two Greek words meaning 'people' and 'work'. In the LXX (the Septuagint, the Greek translation of the Hebrew Bible: see p. 31) it is the word used for the Temple services. In Christianity it is used for official Church services and above all for the commemoration of the Last Supper that Jesus ate in Jerusalem with his disciples before his arrest and crucifixion.

That service of commemoration is known by many names in different parts of the Church, as, for example, the Eucharist (a New Testament word meaning 'thanksgiving'), the Divine Liturgy, the Mass (from *missa/missio*, the 'sending out' with which the service ends), the Holy Communion, the Commemoration of the Lord's Supper.

THE LAST SUPPER

Those many names given to the commemoration of this reflect different understandings of what Jesus did and intended at the Last Supper. It is clear that when Jesus went to Jerusalem for Passover on that last occasion, he knew that his way of living and teaching put his life in danger because of its challenge to the Temple authorities. He made clear that he did not expect to eat with his disciples again on earth, and at the Passover meal he foretold that one of his disciples would betray him.

At the meal he tried to convey to his disciples that although he was about to die, nevertheless he would continue to be with them, so that all they had experienced through him of God's effect and consequence (*dunamis*, dynamic, p. 50) would continue. That seemed such a wild idea that the disciples could not understand what he meant. Jesus therefore put his words into actions of the kind that in those days prophets used to perform when they needed to bring home to people the urgency of their message. It was believed that these actions made some future event certain.

According to the earliest written account of what Jesus said and did (in Paul's *1st Letter to the Corinthians*, 11.24–5), Jesus took bread and said, 'This is my body that is for you: do this in remembrance of me,' and he took a cup containing wine and said, 'This cup is the new covenant in my blood: do this as often as you drink it, in remembrance of me.'

The exact words that Jesus said are uncertain because the Gospels record them with slight differences: see p. 55. Nevertheless, they make it clear that Jesus, knowing what awaited him, created a new Covenant in which the relationship established through him with God in the present will continue in the future 'as often as . . . , as often as' (the words are repeated in *I Corinthians*) they do this in remembrance of him. The Liturgy is the act of commemoration in which for believers the promise of Jesus comes true.

Jesus made that promise of his continuing presence not just for the disciples on that occasion, but, as *Mark* 14.24 puts it, 'for many' (i.e., for an immense multitude). Christians subsequently have found the promise to be true, but Jesus did not explain how it would happen. As a result, there have been many different understandings of what is happening when Christians gather to commemorate Jesus at the Last Supper, ranging from the belief that the bread and wine become the Body and Blood of Christ, to the belief that the bread and wine represent his Body and Blood – hence the many different names referred to above.

THE DIVINE LITURGY

What is common to all the names used is that the repeating of the words and actions of Jesus connects believers, not just to the words of a sacred text, but to the fulfilment of the intention and promise of Jesus, binding them to himself and to each other. That is why the Orthodox Church chose the name 'the Divine Liturgy', emphasising the underlying meaning of the Greek word *leitourgia*. As the introduction to *The Divine Liturgy of Our Father among the Saints* puts it (pp. xf.):

> It is a 'public service' – the meaning of *leitourgia* in Ancient Greek,
> as well as in Modern – in which all the members of the Church are
> the workers. To put it another way: it is not a 'spectator sport' in
> which the Priest, Deacon, Servers and Singers are the players and
> the congregation the audience or viewers . . . Together we proclaim
> our Faith, together we call on God as 'Our Father'. We do not come to
> the Liturgy as isolated individuals; we are there as the limbs, as the
> members of the Body of Christ. We come to hear together the words
> of the Apostles, to listen together to the words of the Lord himself
> in the holy Gospel. And finally, when we approach the Chalice at

PHOS HILARION:
O GLADSOME LIGHT

O GLADSOME LIGHT, O GRACE
Of God the Father's face
The eternal splendour wearing;
Celestial, holy, blest,
Our Saviour Jesus Christ
Joyful in thine appearing.

Now, ere day fadeth quite,
We see the evening light
Our wonted hymn outpouring;
Father of might unknown,
Thee, his incarnate Son,
And Holy Spirit adoring.

To Thee of right belongs
All praise of holy songs,
O Son of God, Lifegiver;
Thee, therefore, O Most High,
The world doth glorify,
And shall exalt forever.

Translation by Robert Bridges (1844–1930)

Communion, we share together in one Bread, we drink from one Cup. By the rules of the Church a Priest may not celebrate the Liturgy alone; there must always be at least one person with him, one person who represents the People of God, whose work the Liturgy is.

In the 'holy communion', 'sacred text' becomes living Word, and it issues, as we have seen, in an outpouring of hymns of thanksgiving and praise. That is as true in the Eastern as in the Western Church. Writing at the end of the fourth century, Basil the Great described as 'ancient' the evening hymn *Phos hilarion*, 'O Gladsome Light', which is still sung at Vespers in the Orthodox Church each day (see box).

In particular, the Orthodox Church developed Kontakia, celebrations in verse of Christian truth chanted to a set form. Once again, the fundamental sacred text, the Bible, is given expression in a memorable and accessible way. Particularly powerful is the way in which the refrain (printed here in italics) is repeated. The Kontakion of Romanos (sixth century) on the crucifixion begins (trans. Lash, p. 155):

> The sword of flame no longer guards the gate of Eden
>   [*Genesis* 3.24],
> for a strange bond came upon it: the wood of the Cross.
> The sting of Death [*I Corinthians* 15.55] and the victory of
>   Hell were nailed to it.
> But you appeared, my Saviour, crying to those in Hell:
> 'Be brought back
>   *again to Paradise.*'
>
> Nailed to the form of the Cross
> as truly a ransom for many [*Mark* 10.45],
> you redeemed us, Christ our God,
> for by your precious blood in love for mankind
> you snatched our souls from death.
> You brought us back with you
>   *again to Paradise.*
>
> All things in heaven and earth rightly rejoice with Adam,
> because he has been called
>   *again to Paradise.*

BIBLIOGRAPHY NUMBERS 558, 579, 814

PRAYER AND
MONASTIC ORDERS

BASIL THE GREAT, DIONYSIUS, *THE PHILOKALIA*

The development of Prayer Books as 'sacred texts' reflects the fact that individuals may pray on their own but they are never alone when they pray. They are always, in Christian understanding, part of the Body of Christ (p. 61). Prayer is the way in which the Holy Spirit within them enables them to cry, 'Abba, Father!' (*Galatians* 4.6). In prayer they turn their lives to seek the face of God, and they support each other in love.

The two together led to the development of monasticism. At first sight, that seems contradictory. The underlying word 'monk' comes from the Greek *monos*, 'alone', and *monachos*, 'solitary', and the earliest forms of 'monasticism' seem to have come from people known as 'anchorites' or 'hermits' who (perhaps in imitation of Jesus who began his ministry with a withdrawal into the desert, *Matthew* 4.1–11, *Luke* 4.1–13) withdrew from the world in order to draw closer to God. But even those early hermits were related to the communities which gave them support and for which they prayed. *Historia Monachorum*, an early account of the beginnings of monasticism, observed at the end of the fourth century (Russell, Prologue 10):

> There is no village or town in Egypt or the Thebaid that is not
> surrounded by hermitages [Greek, *monasterioi*] as though by walls,
> and the people rest secure on the prayers of the monks as if on God.

MONASTIC RULES

The purpose of the Desert was not the absence of people but the presence of God. Gradually, the 'solitaries' were gathered into communities, and at the beginning of the fourth century Pachomius, an Egyptian, began to impose on them a common rule of life. That led to Basil the Great (fourth century) emphasising the importance of life in Community when he responded to questions about monasticism. Those questions and answers were gathered into a work known as *Asceticon*, commonly referred to as 'The Rule of Basil'. An earlier form is known as 'The Short Asceticon'. By the sixth century, *Asceticon* was expanded by the addition of *Regulae Morales* or *Moralia* ('The Moral Rules') and some other works. In this later form the questions and answers are divided into two parts, 'The Longer Rules' (*regulae fusius tractatae*, fifty-five detailed rules) and 'The Shorter Rules' (*regulae brevius tractatae*, 313 applications to particular circumstances). The rules are founded on Basil's belief that the greatest human good is to live in the constant condition of praise and thanksgiving for the gifts of life and creation.

Basil's Rule became the foundation of subsequent Rules governing monastic communities in the Eastern Church, as also in the Western Church through the work of John Cassian (*c.*360–*c.*430) in his *Institutes* and *Conferences*.

Basil was one of a group of Greek thinkers and theologians known as the Cappadocian Fathers. They lie at the root, not just of Christian monasticism but also of the way in which prayer relates to the unknowability of God. He wrote (*de Divinis Nominibus*, 3):

> God is near to all things, but not all things are near to God. We can
> come near to God only with holy prayers and cleansed minds, and
> with our souls prepared for union with God. God is not in space
> so as to be absent from any place, or to move from one place to
> another. To speak of God as omnipresent is a misleading way of
> recognising this all-transcendent and all-embracing infinitude. So
> let us simply press on in prayer always longing for the Divine light
> and blessing. It is as if a chain is hanging down from the heights of
> heaven to this world below, so that when we seize it, first with one
> hand, then with another, we seem to be pulling it down, whereas
> in actual truth we are not pulling it down, we are being ourselves
> carried up to the highest splendour of shining light. Or it is as if
> we, being on a ship, are hanging on to ropes which tie the ship to
> some rocks, and when we pull on the ropes we are not pulling the
> rocks to the ship, we are pulling the ship to the rocks . . . So it is
> that we must begin with prayer before attempting anything, and
> especially before attempting anything in relation to God. We do
> this, not in order to pull down to ourselves what is already near,

both everywhere and nowhere, but to be drawn into the presence of
God, thus being united to God by these prayers and remembrances.

God cannot be known as an object in the universe, nor even in the ways through
which a universe and its constituent parts can be known. In other words, the
aseity of God (what God actually is) lies beyond human knowledge, but it can
nevertheless be approached in prayer. The paradox is that the deeper people
enter into that recognition in prayer, the more they realise that they know
even less than they did when they set out. Gregory of Nyssa, another of the
Cappadocian Fathers, put it like this (*The Life of Moses* 162–3, trans. Malherbe):

> As the mind progresses and, through an ever greater and more
> perfect diligence, comes to apprehend reality, as it approaches
> more nearly to contemplation, it sees more clearly what of the
> divine nature is uncontemplated. For leaving behind everything
> that is observed, not only what sense comprehends but also what
> the intelligence thinks it sees, it keeps on penetrating deeper until
> by the intelligence's yearning for understanding it gains access
> to the invisible and the incomprehensible, and there it sees God.
> This is the true knowledge of what is sought; this is the seeing that
> consists in not seeing, because that which is sought transcends all
> knowledge, being separated on all sides by incomprehensibility as
> by a kind of darkness. Wherefore John the sublime, who penetrated
> into the luminous darkness, says, 'No one has ever seen God'
> [*John* 1.18], thus asserting that knowledge of the divine essence is
> unattainable not only by men but also by every intelligent creature.

DIONYSIUS AND THE PHILOKALIA

This paradox of the unknowability of God who nevertheless *is* known in prayer,
even if only 'through a glass darkly', as Paul put it (*I Corinthians* 13.12), is what
is called in a fifth-century work (*The Mystical Theology*) 'the light of the divine
darkness':

> By an undivided and absolute abandonment of yourself and
> everything, shedding everything and freed from everything, you
> will be uplifted to the light of the divine darkness which transcends
> everything that is.

Those words were thought to have been written by Dionysius the Areopagite (*Acts* 17.34), but since it is now known that that cannot have been the case, the unknown writer is known as Pseudo-Dionysius. His works (see Luibheid and Rorem) became profoundly influential in the Church, both West and East, because he emphasised that the unknowability of God is not a barrier to prayer but an invitation to it. Prayer then also becomes a way of understanding what humans may become in their recognition of the unknowability of God.

In the Eastern Church guidance in those ways of prayer produced a large number of texts all of which are rooted in Scripture. The most highly regarded of these were gathered together in the eighteenth century in a collection known as *Philokalia*. The texts were intended only as a guide, not as a substitute for prayer. To read the texts and then do nothing further about them is to read a menu but then fail to eat the meal. As one of the texts puts it (Hesychios of Sinai, 'On Watchfulness and Holiness', in Palmer, p. 185):

> A donkey going round and round in a mill cannot step out of the circle to which it is tethered; nor can the intellect which is not inwardly chastened advance in the path of holiness. With its inner eyes blinded, it cannot perceive holiness or the radiant light of Jesus. A proud and spirited horse steps out delightedly once the rider is in the saddle. But the delighted intellect delights in the light of the Lord when, free from concepts, it enters into the dawn of spiritual knowledge . . . A traveller setting out on a long, difficult and arduous journey and foreseeing that he may lose his way when he comes back, will put up signs and guideposts along his path in order to make his return simpler. The watchful man, foreseeing this same thing, will use sacred texts to guide him.

📖 BIBLIOGRAPHY NUMBERS 74, 185, 394, 453, 595, 606, 748, 778, 824

MONASTICISM

RULE OF BENEDICT

As monasticism took root in the Church, both East and West, many monastic Rules were written incorporating the work particularly of Augustine and John Cassian. In the Western Church at least thirty Rules (*Regulae*) were written between 400 and 700 CE. Of these, the most important by far was *The Rule of Benedict* which, as Bernard McGinn has put it, 'proved decisive for the future of monasticism' (p. 27):

> The *Rule of Benedict* is the single most important document in the history of western monasticism, and arguably the most significant text from the whole late antique period. During 12 centuries it has been the subject of such intense study and annotation that it may be said to have attained a position that is almost scriptural in the Catholic tradition.

BENEDICT AND THE BENEDICTINES

It 'proved decisive' because it became for about 600 years (550–1150) the basis of monastic life in the Western Church in Europe (with the exception of the Church in Celtic areas: see further p. 93). David Knowles opened his *The Monastic Order in England* with a chapter entitled 'The Rule of Saint Benedict' and with these words (p. 3):

> For some six hundred years . . . in Italy and the countries of Europe north and west of Italy (with the important exception of the Celtic civilisation) monastic life based on the Rule of St Benedict was everywhere the norm and exercised from time to time a paramount influence on the spiritual, intellectual, liturgical and apostolical life of the Western Church. In other words, during these centuries the only type of religious life available in the countries concerned was monastic, and the only monastic code was the Rule of St Benedict.

Benedict (*c.*480–*c.*550) recognised as a young man how far from God the ways of the world were leading him, so he abandoned his studies and in devotion to God lived as a hermit in a cave at Subiaco, south of Rome. His holiness began to attract others, and after some locals tried to poison him, he moved with a small number of those followers to Monte Cassino. There he wrote his Rule, not, it seems, with any intention to found an Order, but as a father instructing his family. He stated that his purpose was to establish 'a school of the Lord's service' (see box below).

A SCHOOL OF THE LORD'S SERVICE

The prologue to *The Rule of Benedict* concludes with the following words:

WHAT THEREFORE WE MUST do is establish a school of the Lord's service. We hope that in founding it there will be nothing severe, nothing burdensome. But even if, for some good reason, there is something by way of constraint for the correcting of evil habits or for the preservation of mutual love, do not immediately panic and run away from the way of salvation to which the entrance cannot be anything other than narrow. But as we make progress in our life together of faith, with hearts enlarged we shall run forward on the way of God's commandments with a sweetness of love that cannot be put into words. The result will be that never departing from his rule but persisting in his teaching in the monastery until death, we will share through our own suffering [lit., 'patience'] in the sufferings of Christ so that even we may be thought worthy to be partakers of his kingdom. Amen.

Benedict envisaged the daily life of his 'family' falling into three broad areas of activity. The first is *Opus Dei*, God's work, the worship of God particularly in the Divine Office (p. 77). It rests on the belief 'that the Divine Presence is everywhere', but, as chapter 19 says, 'Let us above all [*maxime*] believe this when we are performing the Divine Office [*Opus Dei*].'

The second is *lectio divina*, reading that brings one directly into the presence of God. The texts to be read are those of Scripture, but also of the Fathers of the Church and of monastic writers.

The third is *opus manuum*, work with the hands. As chapter 48 puts it, 'Idleness is the enemy of the soul. For that reason the brothers must be occupied at fixed times in manual labour, and again at other hours in sacred reading [*lectio divina*].'

DOMINICANS AND FRANCISCANS

During the ensuing centuries other Orders were founded based on the Rule of St Benedict (however much it was adapted), notably the Cistercians and the Cluniacs. Some Orders had their own Rules, which to them were equally authoritative, but which had to be different when, for example, the Orders were not committed to being a family in a single place. Notable among these were the Dominicans and the Franciscans.

The Dominicans were founded by Dominic (*c*.1172–1221), a Spaniard whose experience of a wealthy Church in the midst of poverty and religious war led him to believe that the Gospel of Christ must be preached by those who share the poverty of Christ. They became an Order of itinerant preachers. On the basis of the Rule of Augustine they drew up their own Constitution in 1216, revised several times until 1228 when it was agreed that no further alterations could be made. The Constitution begins (Tugwell, p. 456):

> Our Rule commands us to have one heart and one soul in the
> Lord, so it is right that we who live under a single Rule and by a
> single profession should be found uniform in the observance of our
> canonical religion, so that the unity we are to maintain inwardly
> in our hearts will be fostered and expressed by the uniformity
> we observe outwardly in our behaviour. And we shall be able
> to observe this more adequately and fully, and retain it in our
> memories, if what we have to do is stated in writing, if we all have
> the evidence of the written text to tell us how we ought to live.

The Franciscans were founded by Francis (Francesco Bernadone, 1181/2–1226), a man committed to God in such complete dependence and trust that he was necessarily committed to poverty and to the poor. Since God is the completely generous creator from whom everything in creation comes as gift, there is nothing that we can call 'our own'. When others joined him he wrote in 1209 a brief Rule (*Regula Primitiva*), but that Rule, now lost, was then rewritten in 1221 and confirmed by Pope Honorius III in 1223. Of his own writings, 'The Canticle of the Sun' is a celebration of the goodness of God experienced at every moment in a world that is received as gift:

> Most High, all-powerful and good Lord,
> to you belong the praise and the glory and the honour and every
>   blessing.
> To you alone, most High, do they belong
> and no one can worthily even speak your name.
>
> Praise be to you, my Lord, with all your creatures,
> especially through my worthy brother Sun who brings each day.
>
> Praise be to you, my Lord, through brother Fire
> through whom you give light in the dark.
> He is beautiful and cheerful and mighty and strong.
>
> Praise be to you, my Lord, through our sister mother Earth
> who sustain us and guards us and brings forth roots in variety
> with coloured flowers and growth.
>
> Praise be to you, my Lord, through those who forgive out of love for
>   you
> and endure sickness and tribulation.
> Blessed are those who endure in peace,
> for by you, most High, they will be crowned.
>
> Praise be to you, my Lord, through our sister bodily Death,
> from whom no one living can escape:
> woe to those who die in mortal sin,
> blessed are those whom she finds following your most holy will,
> whom the second death cannot harm.
>
> Praise and bless my Lord and give him thanks
> and serve him with great humility.

BIBLIOGRAPHY NUMBERS 85, 301, 341

CHRISTIANITY
OF THE CELTS

COLUMBANUS, PATRICK, *CARMINA GAEDELICA*

When David Knowles (p. 89 above) was describing the dominant role of the Rule of Benedict in the formation of early Western monasticism, he drew attention to 'the important exception' of Celtic civilisation. Although the phrase 'Celtic Christianity' is often used, the word 'Celtic' refers not to a Church but to tribes and people who spoke a related group of languages, but of whom it cannot be said that they shared a common culture. They lived in countries ranging from Central Europe to Ireland, Wales and Scotland. Some of them were part of the Roman Empire so that those Celts became part of Western Christianity. However, by the fifth century, the Romans had withdrawn from the furthest boundaries of the Empire, leaving the Celtic peoples there to continue to develop their own beliefs and customs.

In Irish monasticism there was a strong tendency to go back to the severe austerity and asceticism of the early monks of Egypt. Many Irish monks went to Europe in what was called 'a permanent pilgrimage' (*peregrinatio*) to restore Christian belief and practice to what, in their view, they should be. One of them, Columbanus (d. 615), wrote two Rules, *Regula Monachorum* and *Regula Coenobialis*, which are very different from the Rule of Benedict. Monks followed a regime of silence, prayer and fasting, interrupted only by an evening meal of porridge, vegetables and bread. Penances and punishments for breaches of discipline were severe.

Columbanus based his Rules on what he learned in his own formation at Bangor in Ireland, in what Tomás Ó Fiaich has called 'the most austere branch of Irish monastic training'. He describes it in summary in 'Irish Monks on the Continent' (in Mackey, p. 107):

The daily fare was bread, vegetables and water. The dress was a long white tunic with a coarse hooded outer garment and sandals. The monks assembled frequently in the Church by day and night for the canonical hours . . . Fasting, silence, corporal punishment, reduction of sleep, repeated genuflections and prolonged prayer with outstretched arms were normal forms of mortification to be imposed for breaches of the rule. It was an ascetic yet happy milieu, 'the good Rule of Bangor, upright, divine' in which Columban spent many years of his young manhood . . .

In addition to its own Rules (for further examples, see Ryan, 1973), Irish Christianity developed other forms of text to guard and guide believers. Important among them were Loricae, 'Breastplates' – protection in the spiritual warfare that all have to wage (see, for example, *Ephesians* 6.10–17). The Lorica of St Patrick, often referred to as 'St Patrick's Breastplate', has been described by O'Donoghue as 'one of the most remarkable single expressions of Christian piety and practice' ('St Patrick's Breastplate', in Mackey, pp. 45–63: his translation is on pp. 46–9):

> For my shield this day I call:
>> A mighty power:
>> The Holy Trinity!
>> Affirming threeness,
>> Confessing oneness,
>> In the making of all
>> Through love.

> For my shield this day I call:
>> Christ's power in his coming
>> and in his baptising,
>> Christ's power in his dying
>> on the Cross, his arising
>> from the tomb, his ascending;
>> Christ's power in his coming
>> for a judgement and ending . . .

> For my shield this day I call:
>> Heaven's might,
>> Sun's brightness,

Moon's whiteness,
Fire's glory,
Lightning's swiftness,
Wind's wildness,
Ocean's depth,
Earth's solidity,
Rock's immobility.

To be well armed was necessary in the constant fight against 'the devil and all his works'. Monks stood in icy streams to pray, and they built their tiny shelters in places as far away from the inhabited world as possible, often on remote islands in the Atlantic. The created order is full of threat and danger, in the face of which God's protection is frequently prayed for.

Nevertheless, it *is* the created order, and as with Francis nature comes as a gift from God. The Christian Celts frequently celebrate creation, reading it as a second 'sacred text', the Book of Nature alongside Scripture as the Word of God. Here, for example, is the Welsh poet Thomas Jones (1756–1820) writing of a thrush (in Parry, pp. 332f.):

Lowly bird, beautifully taught,
You enrich and astound us,
We wonder long at your song,
Your artistry and your voice.
In you I see, I believe,
The clear and excellent work of God.
Blessed and glorious is he,
Who shows his virtue in the lowest kind.
How many bright wonders (clear note of loveliness)
Does this world contain?
How many parts, how many mirrors of his finest work
Offer themselves a hundred times to our gaze?
For the book of his art is a speaking light
Of lines abundantly full,
And every day one chapter after another
Comes among us to teach us of him.

Since the Celts lived on the edges of the world, it is not surprising that many of their hymns, chants and prayers were preserved, not in written texts, but in memory passed on from one generation to another. Some of these from Scotland were rescued in the nineteenth century from oblivion by Alexander Carmichael when he wrote many of them down. In 1900, he published the first of what became after his death six volumes with the title *Carmina Gaedelica*. Here too faith is immersed in the world as God's creation even in the smallest detail, as in 'Prayer for Seaweed' and 'Prayer of the Teats' (363, 373):

> Produce of sea to land,
>   Produce of land to sea;
> He who doeth not in time,
>   Scant shall be his share.
>
> Seaweed being cast on shore
>   Bestow, Thou Being of bestowal;
> Fruitfulness being brought to wealth,
>   O Christ, grant me my share!

—— · ——

> Bless, O God, my little cow,
> Bless, O God, my desire;
> Bless Thou my partnership
> And the milking of my hands, O God.
> Bless, O God, each teat,
> Bless, O God, each finger,
> Bless Thou each drop
> That goes into my pitcher, O God!

📖 BIBLIOGRAPHY NUMBERS 181, 186, 232, 617, 757, 825

ACTS OF THE MARTYRS

Polycarp, Dietrich Bonhoeffer

Martyrs are those who bear witness. The Greek word *marturos* means 'a witness'. But the word in Christian history has come to refer to witnesses of a particular kind: those who are persecuted for being Christians and who are put to death because they refuse to abandon the faith.

From earliest times (even in the New Testament itself) martyrs were honoured for exemplifying what it means to keep faith. Accounts of martyrs were written down and widely read, not least because they gave encouragement to others when they too were in danger. Texts of this kind from the early centuries are referred to collectively as Acts of the Martyrs.

In the Roman Empire, Christians were persecuted during the first three centuries when their loyalty to the Empire was questioned or tested. There were intermittent persecutions under many of the Roman emperors, from the time when Nero made Christians scapegoats for the Great Fire in Rome (64 CE) until the reign of Constantine (d.337) who recognised Christianity and became a Christian himself. In Persia, persecutions went on until the seventh century.

The persecutions could be savage, as under Diocletian (245–313), so it is not surprising that those early centuries have been called 'The Age of the Martyrs'. Yet in fact every age has been an age of martyrdom: in the twentieth century it is likely that there were more Christian martyrs than in all the previous centuries put together, even though the exact numbers cannot be known.

The martyrs were far more than exemplary. Their faithfulness suggested they must be close to God, and it was believed that they could continue to help the living by their intercession. Ambrose (c. 339–97), the Bishop of Milan who baptised Augustine (p. 101), wrote:

> In the same way that the sick cannot themselves get to the doctor for
> assistance but have to send a request through others for a visit, so

also when the flesh is frail and the soul is sick with sin, we cannot in our feeble state make our way to the throne of the Great Physician. Therefore we must send our request through the angels who have been given to us as guardians, and we must send our request through the martyrs whose care for us we can rely on through their bodily remains.

The 'bodily remains' became increasingly important as a kind of conduit through which the approach to God might be made. The remains (known as 'relics') were brought from their original graves into churches, some of which were specially built for the purpose. Ambrose brought the bodies of two martyrs, Gervasius and Protasius, into a newly built basilica and placed the remains in a sarcophagus under the altar, which he had originally prepared for himself:

> Thanks be to you, Lord Jesus, because at this time when your Church needs greater protection than ever, you have raised up for us the spirits of the Holy Martyrs: they indeed are the defenders that I long for.

Among the earliest of the Acts of the Martyrs is the account of the martyrdom of Polycarp (c.69–c.155/6). It is recorded in a work known as *The Martyrdom of St Polycarp*. After his arrest, he was taken into the arena. The account continues (9.1–3):

> The proconsul, when Polycarp was brought before him, . . . tried to persuade him to deny the faith. He said, 'Think of your age!', along with other things that were often said on these occasions, including, 'Swear by Caesar's Fortune'; 'Change your mind'; 'Say, Away with the atheists!'
>
> Polycarp, however, looked steadily at the immense crowd of lawless heathen in the arena and pointed to them with his hand. Then with a cry and looking up to heaven he said, 'Away with the atheists!' But the proconsul persisted and said, 'Take the oath and I will set you free: curse Christ!' Polycarp replied, 'Eighty-six years I have served him and he has never let me down; how can I blaspheme against my King who saved me? . . . The fire with which you threaten me burns for an hour and after a while is gone; what you have not considered is the fire of the coming judgement and the eternal punishment that awaits the wicked. So why do you delay? Come on, do what you will.'

Throughout Christian history, people valued texts recording the steadfast faith of the martyrs in order to strengthen their own. In 1559/63, for example, John Foxe produced *Acts and Monuments of Matters Happening in the Church*, usually known as *Foxe's Book of Martyrs*. During the Reformation Catholics and Protestants persecuted each other, including the persecution of Protestants in England by Queen Mary. Foxe's purpose was to strengthen others if they came to the test, as he wrote in the dedication of his work to Queen Elizabeth (Foxe, *The Prefaces*, p. viii):

> For as we see what light and profit cometh to the church, by histories in old times set forth, of the Judges, Kings, Maccabees, and the Acts of the Apostles after Christ's time; so likewise may it redound to no small use in the church, to know the acts of Christ's martyrs now, since the time of the Apostles, besides other manifold examples and experiments of God's great mercies and judgements in preserving his church.

The 'acts of the martyrs' are still written. *Dying We Live*, for example, is a record of martyrs in Nazi Germany, among whom was Dietrich Bonhoeffer. His *Letters and Papers from Prison* (1953) were written during his imprisonment before he was executed by the Nazis. Facing execution, Bonhoeffer struggled to understand how God is real and is present in the nightmare of Nazi Germany (p. 122):

> God is teaching us that we must live as those who can get along very well without him. The God who is with us is the God who forsakes us [*Mark* 15.34]. The God who makes us live in this world without using him as a working hypothesis is the God before whom we are ever standing . . . God allows himself to be edged out of the world and onto the Cross. God is weak and powerless in the world, and that is exactly the way, the only way, in which he can be with us and help us. Matthew 8.17 makes it crystal clear that it is not by his omnipotence that Christ helps us, but by his weakness and suffering.

When the guards came to take him to his execution, a fellow prisoner (Best, p. 166) recalled his last words: 'This is the end – for me the beginning of life.'

BIBLIOGRAPHY NUMBERS 8, 88–9, 124, 340, 767

AUGUSTINE

THE CONFESSIONS

The writings of Augustine (354–430) have been immensely important and influential in Christian history, but among them all *The Confessions* is the most widely read: it will, wrote Henry Chadwick, 'always rank among the greater masterpieces of Western literature'.

In *The Confessions*, Augustine asks how humans, in the brief and often tragic circumstances of life, can approach the immense reality of God. From his own life he looked at the major issues which seem to separate people from God or which seem to call the truth of God into question:

◆ What if they sin? Book 2 begins: 'I intend to bring to mind the wickednesses and the carnal corruptions of my soul, not because I love them but in order that I may love you, my God.' His sins, he felt, ranged from the apparently minor (stealing pears that he did not even want to eat, 2.4) to the dark and burning lusts of adolescence (2.1). Do such sins separate us from God for ever?

◆ What if loved ones die? In 4.4 Augustine recalls his devastation when a friend and fellow student died: 'My heart was black with grief, and everything I looked at was death.' Where is God in that experience?

◆ What if their studies as they grow up lead them away from God? Augustine's mother Monica (spelt by Augustine 'Monnica') was a Christian, but Augustine was drawn towards the Manichaeans for whom, as rigorous dualists, the world is an unending conflict between good and evil (see further Zoroaster, p. 162). Is God unable to overcome the evil and suffering in the world?

◆ What if God seems to have 'lost the plot' in history? How can catastrophes like the fall of Rome to Alaric, or the unending corruptions in society and politics, be reconciled with the goodness and providence of God? Augustine wrote *The City of God* (*de Civitate Dei*) to show how good and evil remain entangled until the final judgement of God (14.28, trans. Bettenson):

> We see then that the two cities were created by two kinds of love:
> the earthly city was created by self-love reaching the point of
> contempt for God, the Heavenly City by the love of God carried as
> far as contempt of self . . . The one city loves its own strength shown
> in its powerful leaders; the other says to its God, 'I will love you, my
> Lord, my strength.'

Augustine came to realise that in the face of all these questions the fundamental issue is that of the human will: what do I truly desire above all else? If it is God, then God is the only answer. That is why Augustine's realisation that Manichaeaism must be false (in supposing that evil is an independent substance or entity, as opposed to being the contingent absence of good) led to him immersing himself in Neoplatonism because Neoplatonists claimed to show how the soul can ascend from its entanglement in this world until it enters into union with that which alone is the Real, the flight of the alone to the Alone.

Yet that too proved inadequate. Augustine had become a proficient orator immersed in the classics of Rome – hence the brilliance and beauty of his Latin. He became professor of rhetoric in Milan where, under the influence of Ambrose, Bishop of Milan, he was converted to Christianity in 386. Now at last he had found his heart's desire, and *The Confessions* is the result.

'Confession' usually means for us 'to make confession/acknowledgement of some fault'. But that is only part of what Augustine was doing in this work. The word 'confession' (*confessio*) also means the acknowledgement of God in celebration and praise. That is exactly where *The Confessions* begins (1.1, 4):

> Great are you, O Lord, and highly to be praised [*Psalm* 47.2].
> Human beings, so small a part of your creation, long to praise
> you . . . You rouse us up to take delight in praising you because
> you have made us for yourself, and our heart is restless until it
> rests in you . . . Most high, wholly good, most powerful, most
> merciful and just, completely hidden and completely present, most
> beautiful, most strong, unmoving and beyond our comprehension,
> unchanging yet changing all things, never new, never old, . . .
> always active, always at rest, gathering all to yourself yet needing
> nothing, supporting and completing and protecting, creating and

AUGUSTINE'S VISION OF GOD

S O WE SAID: 'IF there is anyone in whom the tumult of the flesh has fallen silent, if the images of earth and sea and sky have fallen silent, if even the heavens are silent and the soul itself has fallen silent, . . . if all language and every sign and everything that is transient has fallen silent (for if they could be heard they would be saying with a single voice, We did not make ourselves but He made us who abides for ever), if with those words they then fall silent because they have attuned our ears to Him who made them, then He Himself alone would speak, not through them but through Himself: we would hear His word, not through any tongue of the flesh, nor through the voice of an angel, nor through the sound of thunder, nor through the puzzle of symbolic story, but Him we would hear – Him, Himself, whom we love in all these things – and without those things we would hear simply Him; just as we together reached out and in a flash of the mind hit home on the eternal wisdom that endures beyond all things. And if this could continue and all other visions of such a lesser kind could be withdrawn, then this one alone would so ravish and absorb and embrace in profound joy the one who sees it that his life would be for ever of the quality of that moment of insight for which we had been sighing. And is not this the meaning of the words, "Enter into the joy of your Lord" [Matthew 25.21]?'

(Confessions 9.10.25)

sustaining and bringing to perfection, ever seeking while in need
of nothing . . . And yet in all this, what have I said, my God, my life,
my holy sweetness, or what can anyone say when he speaks of you?
Yet woe to those who, in all the many words they speak, are silent
about you.

In *The Confessions*, Augustine traces how he was led to the praise of God –
even at one moment to feel that he has attained the vision of God. It happened
when he and his mother were leaning on a windowsill in Ostia a few days
before she died. They talked together about their longing for God and were
suddenly caught up into a moment of union with God, a touching, as it were,
of the hem of his garment (*Matthew* 9.20) (see box p. 102).

    The Confessions is a brilliantly written prose-poem in which Augustine
shows how he – and indeed everyone – can move from adolescent delinquency,
through explorations of current theories about the universe and our place
within it, until we arrive at the vision of God. Beyond that *The Confessions*
is even more complex and profound. Certainly it includes 'confession as an
acknowledgement', but it is also a work of thanksgiving for the way in which
Augustine came to recognise the providence of God in his life. He acknowledges
how late he was in recognising God, but then he pours out his thanks for the gift
(*The Confessions* 10.27.38):

> Late have I loved you, Beauty so ancient and so new, so late have
> I loved you! But look! You were within me and I was outside and
> there I searched for you and my ugliness distorted those things of
> beauty that you made. You were with me, but I was not with you.
> Those things were holding me far from you, yet if they had not
> come from you, they could not even exist. You called and cried to
> me to break through my deafness; you sent forth light to shine on
> me in order to banish my blindness; you breathed sweetness upon
> me, and I drew in my breath so that I now long for you. I tasted you
> and now I hunger and thirst for you. You touched me and now I
> burn for your peace.

So *The Confessions* does not end with the vision of Ostia. There
are another three books after that on memory, time and creation, because
the whole work is Augustine's celebration of praise and wonder at the
providence of God. The whole work ends where it began: in praise and
thanksgiving (13.38):

In truth, God, you alone are good, never ceasing to do good . . . You, the Good, needing no other good, are ever at rest since you yourself are your own rest. What human being can give to another human any understanding of this? What angel to another angel? What angel to a human? From you it must be asked, in you it must be sought, at your door we must knock [*Matthew* 7.7–8]. Thus, thus only, is it received, thus it is found, thus the door is opened.

BIBLIOGRAPHY NUMBERS **60, 235**

THOMAS AQUINAS

Summa contra Gentiles, Summa Theologica

When Thomas Aquinas was a student he was called by his fellow students 'the dumb ox'. Less than a hundred years later he was canonised (recognised as a saint on account of his learning) by Pope John XXII and became known as Doctor Angelicus, 'The Angelic Doctor'. He began his greatest work, *Summa Theologica* (or *Theologiae*), with the words (Prologue), 'Because the Doctor [recognised teacher] of catholic truth not only ought to teach the proficient but also it is incumbent on him to instruct beginners, . . . it is our intention in this work to deal with those things which pertain to the Christian religion in a way that is appropriate for the instruction of beginners.' Beginners are soon taken far beyond their first faltering steps, and the work of Aquinas became the foundation of theological understanding and teaching in the Western Church.

His own work came partly from his education and training. He was born in 1225, and in 1230 he was sent to Monte Cassino as a Benedictine oblate. In 1239 he went to the University of Naples where, in 1244, he became a Dominican. The Dominicans (p. 91) were 'the humble servants of preaching' and they became known as the Order of Preachers. From them he learned the importance of trying to reach others with the good news of God, especially through reason and argument.

His work was also formed in the context of a new and larger world, especially in relation to Islam. Crusades had been fought against Muslims in Spain and even more in the Holy Land for over a hundred years, and it was not until 1291, seventeen years after Aquinas died, that the last of the Latin possessions in the Holy Land was lost.

Increasing contact with Muslims, however, had shown how extensive was their commitment, not just to God, but to science and philosophy. Muslims had rescued much of Greek philosophy including many of the works of Aristotle that had survived in Europe but had been neglected. Two Muslim philosophers in particular, ibn Rushd (known in the West as Averroes) and ibn Sina (Avicenna), had used Aristotle to write impressive philosophical accounts of the nature and existence of God. The new knowledge proved exciting, as Chenu, in his detailed guide to the writings of Aquinas, has summarised the point (pp. 290–1):

> Intellectually, at the level of an Arabic civilisation which conveyed the assets of Greek science and philosophy, menace and attraction simultaneously operated at the same pace as this Arabic literature was being discovered and translated . . . Islam was revealing itself no longer as a violent military menace alone but as a civilisation that was superiorly rich. The entrance of Aristotle was opening to Christians, thanks to Islam, a scientific vision of the universe outside the religious imagery of the Bible. The problem facing Christendom was a knot, unique in its kind, and Saint Thomas found himself right in the midst of it.

In the Dominican spirit of rationality and argument, Aquinas wrote *Summa contra Gentiles* over a period from about 1258 to 1263. He wrote it to establish truth that is accessible to reason, surveying in the first three books God, creation and the moral life, arriving in the fourth book at those truths about God 'which even natural reason [*ratio naturalis*] cannot attain' (1.3). His purpose was 'to make manifest that truth which faith confesses and reason explores' (1.9).

That purpose was made more extensive and more systematic in *Summa Theologica*, written between 1265 and 1272. This massive and comprehensive work is written in the style of argument prevailing at the time among the Schoolmen (teachers in the Schools of which the universities of Paris and Oxford were pre-eminent) – hence its description as Scholastic. The text is made up of Parts, Prima (First, I), Secunda (Second, II) and Tertia (Third, III), with Secunda itself being divided into two parts, Prima Secundae and Secunda Secundae. Each Part contains questions (Q) with a number of specific Articles pertaining to each question. The Articles take particular relevant issues ('whether such-and-such is the case?'), state Objections to the underlying proposition, followed by a general answer and by specific replies to each objection. References to *Summa Theologica* reflect that structure. Thus, Ia-IIae means 'the first part of the second Part', with subsequent numbers referring to Questions, Articles, Objections and replies to (ad) the objections.

Thus to give an abbreviated example in which the detailed answer is omitted, Question 12 in Part 1 asks in its first Article 'Whether any created intellect can see the essence of God' (1a.12.1):

Objection 1. It seems that no created intellect can see the essence of God, ... as Chrysostom has written ..., and as Dionysius [pp. 87f.] has written, 'There is neither sense, nor image, nor opinion, nor reason, nor knowledge of God.'

Objection 2. Further, everything infinite is in itself unknown. But God is infinite, and therefore in himself is unknown.

Objection 3. Further, the created intellect can know only existing things ... Now God is not some *thing* existing, ... therefore God cannot be known by us ...

To the contrary [in general], it is written, 'We shall see God as God is' (*1 John* 3.2).

I answer that all things are indeed knowable according to the way in which they are actualised, but God is pure act without unrealised potentiality mixed in, so God is in himself supremely knowable ... Hence it must be granted absolutely that the blessed see the essence of God.

Reply to Objection 1. Both Chrysostom and Dionysius wrote also of the vision of perfect comprehension.

Reply to Objection 2. The infinity of matter not made perfect in form [of some kind] is unknown in itself, since all knowledge is attained through form. However, the infinity of the form not limited by matter is in itself supremely known. God is infinite in that way, and not in the first way.

Reply to Objection 3. God is not said to be 'not existing' as if God did not exist at all, but only because God exists above all that exists, since God is his own being. So it does not follow that God cannot be known at all, but rather that God transcends all [human] knowledge, from which it follows that he is not comprehended by it.

Aquinas believed that human reason can know *that* God is (and in Ia.2.3 he offered five arguments pointing in that direction), but *what* God is can be known only if God reveals it. Aquinas thus accepted that what God is (the aseity of God) cannot be known. He wrote (Ia.1.7 ad 1): 'Concerning God we are not able to know what he is'; or again (Ia Prologue to Q.3): 'Concerning God we are not able to know what he is, but only what he is not.' We can say that God is not round because God cannot be known in the way that objects in a universe are known, by picking out the attributes they have (what belongs to them and makes them what they are). That is so because God is not an object among other objects in a universe: God as Creator is the unproduced Producer of all that is. So God does not *have* attributes in the way that a Christmas tree might or might not have decorations attached to it. Rather, he *is* his attributes – i.e., everything that God is, is what God is.

But in fact we do talk about God as though God has attributes. We (and the Bible) say that God is wise, merciful, loving and so on. Aquinas therefore argued that we do so only by analogy: on the basis of what we know about human wisdom, mercy, love and so on, we can say that God, as he has become known to us through such acts as creation and redemption, does act wisely, mercifully, lovingly and so on, but not exactly as we in our limited way understand wisdom, mercy and love among ourselves.

God is thus present and yet lies beyond the limits of time and space as the Good in which we find our final and complete blessedness and bliss [*beatitudo*]. In *Summa contra Gentiles*, Aquinas wrote (3.61–2):

> The intellectual soul is created on the boundary between time and
> eternity . . . The way in which it acts to come into conjunction with
> those higher things that are above time, participates in eternity . . .
> From this it follows that those who reach the ultimate bliss in the
> divine vision cannot ever lose it.

On that basis we can enter into a relationship with God of adoration and praise, often expressed by Aquinas in words that are still sung, as in this example celebrating the Eucharistic presence of Christ:

> Of the glorious Body telling,
> O my tongue, its mysteries sing,
> And the Blood, all price excelling,
> Which the world's eternal King,
> In a noble womb once dwelling,
> Shed for this world's ransoming . . .
>
> Therefore we, before him bending,
> This great Sacrament revere;
> Types and shadows have their ending,
> For the newer rite is here;
> Faith, our outward sense befriending,
> Makes the inward vision clear.

📖 BIBLIOGRAPHY NUMBERS **39**, 914–15

POETRY

DANTE AND OTHERS

In the year that Aquinas died (1274), a boy nearly nine years old went to a children's party. He saw a girl there, about a year younger than himself, and fell instantly in love. The boy was Dante Alighieri, the girl was Beatrice. Of that first sight of Beatrice, Dante wrote twenty years later, in *La Vita Nuova* (2):

> She came into my presence at about the beginning of her ninth
> year when I was almost 10. She appeared dressed in a most noble
> colour, a rich and yet delicate red, tied and adorned in a style
> well-suited to her tender age. In an instant that vital urgency which
> dwells at the inner heart of our being made me tremble so violently
> that I felt it in every pulse, and it cried out, 'Behold, a God stronger
> than I has come to rule over me' ... And speaking to my sight it
> said, 'Now has your bliss [*beatitudo*] become manifest.'

It was almost another ten years before Beatrice spoke to him again, but he never forgot the impact of that stunning moment when he discovered that beauty and love lie at the heart of life and indeed of all things. It led him to write, first *La Vita Nuova* in memory of Beatrice, and then his supreme poem of the Christian vision of God, *La Divina Commedia*, 'The Divine Comedy', a 'text' so highly regarded that it has been called 'the fifth Gospel'.

The poem is in three parts, Inferno (Hell), Purgatorio (Purgatory) and Paradiso (Paradise). It begins with Dante on the journey that all people have to make through life to death and beyond – but with different outcomes depending on how the journey is made. Dante begins in 'the dark wood' of human ignorance and error. 'Inferno' 1 begins (trans. by Sissons):

Half way along the road we have to go,
I found myself obscured in a great forest,
Bewildered, and I knew I had lost the way.

He is met by Virgil (70–19 BCE), the famed author of *Aeneid*, who offers to guide Dante as far as he can. Virgil represents the best vision and guidance that humans can achieve on their own in philosophy, art and poetry. Many, however, do not follow even those elementary guides, and Virgil shows Dante those who are held in the twenty-four circles of Hell because they have become trapped in 'capital' sins. Those sins are often called 'the deadly sins', but they come from the head, or in Latin *caput* (hence the name 'capital sins'). They are actions and attitudes that are fundamentally good (as, for example, hunger or desire), but they become destructive and sinful when they take control of human life in the form of greed or lust.

Virgil then leads Dante on to the terraces and ledges of the mountain of Purgatory, where people are still in the condition of fault, but it is now fault that is being dealt with – i.e., purged 'in the fire which refines them' ('Purgatorio' 26.148). Virgil brings Dante to the edge of Paradise, but he (human guidance) cannot take him further.

He is replaced by Beatrice because she had been to Dante the first 'God-bearer', the first manifestation of the goodness of God made visible in beauty. Beatrice is thus an example of other 'God-bearers' who carry God into our midst: the Church, the Virgin Mary, even Christ himself. She brings him into Paradise where the light of God, which can be glimpsed on earth but which is obscured by human fault, shines with unqualified glory ('Paradiso' 1.1):

The glory of him who moves everything
Penetrates the universe and shines
In one part more and, in another, less.

The bliss that Dante had glimpsed in Beatrice is now made complete – in a way that is summarised in my *God: A Brief History* (pp. 271–2): 'In this light made manifest in love, humans find their complete and unending joy: all the anticipations that come to them in moments of love, beauty, goodness and truth become a final and unending condition of their being, for in Paradise they are in union with God.' Dante knew that this vision could not be put into words. But he ended with a brilliant glimpse of all those hints of love gathered into the Being of God (33.85–7):

> I saw gathered there in the depths of it,
> Bound up by love into a single volume,
> All the leaves scattered through the universe.

That essential nature of God is one of constant and consequential love (necessarily, therefore, a Trinity: three circles of deep light, in Dante's image), far beyond description though it is (33.121–6):

> O how my speech falls short, how faint it is
> For my conception! And for what I saw
> It is not enough to say that I say little.
>
> O eternal light, existing in yourself alone,
> Alone knowing yourself; and who, known to yourself
> And knowing, love and smile upon yourself!

Dante knew, finally and for ever, that he too is caught up in that love (33.142–5):

> At this point high imagination failed;
> But already my desire and my will
> Were being turned like a wheel, all at one speed,
>
> By the love which moves the sun and the other stars.

An entirely different epic is John Milton's (1608–74) *Paradise Lost* and *Paradise Regained*, telling of the Fall of Man (*Genesis* 2–3) and its consequences. The epic ends (12.645–9) with the expulsion of Adam and Eve because of their disobedience:

> Some natural tears they dropped, but wiped them soon;
> The world was all before them, where to choose
> Their place of rest, and Providence their guide:
> They hand in hand with wand'ring steps and slow,
> Through Eden took their solitary way.

The epic begins with Milton's prayer that he may understand what brought about this punishment, and how, therefore, God's justice can be reconciled with his mercy and love (1.1–6a, 19–26):

Of man's first disobedience, and the fruit
Of that forbidden tree, whose mortal taste
Brought death into the world, and all our woe,
With loss of Eden, till one greater Man
Restore us, and regain the blissful seat,
Sing Heav'nly Muse . . .
Instruct me, for thou know'st; thou from the first
Wast present, and with mighty wings outspread
Dove-like sat'st brooding on the vast abyss
And mad'st it pregnant: what in me is dark
Illumine, what is low raise and support;
That to the height of this great argument
I may assert Eternal Providence,
And justify the ways of God to men.

Dante and Milton are a reminder of the way in which poems become for Christians 'sacred texts' because they give expression to Christian faith in such a powerful way. R. S. Thomas (1913–2000), himself a poet, once observed (*Autobiographies*, p. 104) that 'there is nothing more important than the relationship between man and God, nor anything more difficult than establishing that relationship.' Poets, he argued, are those who can explore that relationship (1963, p. 9):

The mystic fails to mediate God adequately insofar as he is not
a poet. The poet . . . shows his spiritual concern and his spiritual
nature through the medium of language, the supreme symbol.

That has been true in many languages, but particularly in English where so many poems have moved into liturgy as hymns. Particularly well known are those poems of George Herbert (1593–1633) that are sung as hymns ('King of Glory, King of Peace, I will love Thee'; 'Let all the world in every corner sing, My God and King'; 'Teach me my God and King, in all things Thee to see'). The process has continued down to the present. Eleanor Farjeon (1881–1965), for example, was asked by her friend Percy Dearmer (1867–1936) to provide a hymn for his collection *Songs of Praise* (1926), so she adapted one of her poems and produced:

Morning has broken,
Like the first morning,
Blackbird has spoken

Like the first bird;
Praise for the singing,
Praise for the morning,
Praise for them springing
Fresh from the Word.

Sweet the rain's new fall,
Sunlit from heaven,
Like the first dewfall
On the first grass;
Praise for the sweetness,
Of the wet garden,
Sprung in completeness
Where his feet pass.

Mine is the sunlight,
Mine is the morning,
Born of the one light
Eden saw play;
Praise with elation,
Praise every morning,
God's re-creation
Of the new day.

Commenting on the relationship between poetry and sacred texts, James Trott began his anthology of Christian poetry with these words (pp. 15, 17):

> It comes as a shock to those of us who have undergone secular educations to discover the vast majority of poets writing and being published in English have been Christians . . . The glory of God may have been diminished by sectarian motives at various times and in various hearts, but the 'channel' of the stream was always faith – and a good deep channel it remained, even in the worst of times. There was an unbroken succession of men and women praising God – to which we belong.

📖 BIBLIOGRAPHY NUMBERS 260, 293, 946–7, 956, 979

THE REFORMATIONS

LUTHER, CALVIN

'The Reformation' is associated particularly with the sixteenth century but reformations of the Church have happened periodically throughout its history. The way in which the Church in the West came to be organised in a hierarchy, with the Bishop of Rome, the Pope, at its head, often gave rise to clashes of interest with nation-states and their rulers. The way in which its officers – the clergy, the religious and the bishops – were often seen to be extravagant, promiscuous and living lives at odds with what Christianity professed, gave rise to discontent.

There were serious questions also about the teaching of the Christian Church – for example, about whether the bread and wine of the Last Supper become the actual body of Christ at the Mass, whether the Virgin Mary and the Saints have a role in intercession greater than that of others and even as great as that of Christ, or whether laypeople should be allowed to read the Bible for themselves in a language they could understand (p. 64).

Such things were debated in universities, but those questions and grievances were being raised far more widely within the Church, and some had even felt compelled to stand outside it, as did, for example, in the Middle Ages the Waldensians, the Hussites and the Lollards.

The protests gained particular force when the printing press made the Bible available for many to read in their own language, for the Bible seemed to say little or nothing about Pope, bishops, sacraments or the structures of the Church as they were being experienced in Europe at the end of the fifteenth century. The protests developed into 'the Reformation' when cries for reform were not accepted by the papacy, and its supporters were called Protestants as a result. The voices of protest, however, were varied and were not always in agreement with each other, so that 'the Reformation' is a collective name for what were in fact several different reformations including those that were attempted in the Church of Rome.

LUTHER

The reformations of the sixteenth century took their lead initially from Martin Luther (1483–1546). He was an Augustinian monk and professor of theology who came to believe that natural reason is extremely limited in what it can achieve in relation to God, and that 'to aim at a perfect comprehension [of God] is dangerous work in which we stumble, fall and break our necks . . . We look with the blind eyes of moles on the majesty of God' (*Table Talk*, 118).

Instead we must rely on what God has revealed, on Scripture alone (*sola scriptura*). Luther therefore translated the New Testament into German so that people could have direct access to the word of God. There they will find that God has acted to save us, not because we deserve it through acts of merit, but simply and solely because God wills us to do so. We cannot deserve to be saved: it is done by grace alone (*sola gratia*) to which the only response has to be one of faith (*sola fide*). Faith is not a matter of bargaining or negotiation: faith is complete and absolute trust from which love flows as from a surging spring (*quellende Liebe*). This is strongly emphasised in his *Short Catechism* (1530), as in his explanation of the first article of the Creed:

> 'I believe in God the Father Almighty, Maker of heaven and earth.'
> What does that mean?
> *Answer.* I believe that God has created me, and all other creatures,
> and has given me, and preserves for me, body and soul, eyes, ears,
> and all my limbs, my reason and all my senses; and that daily he
> bestows on me clothes and shoes, meat and drink, house and home,
> wife and child, fields and cattle, and all my goods, and supplies
> in abundance all needs and necessities of my body and life, and
> protects me from all perils, and guards and defends me from all
> evil. And this he does out of pure fatherly and Divine goodness and
> mercy, without any merit or worthiness in me; for all which I am
> bound to thank him and praise him, and, moreover, to serve and
> obey him. This is a faithful saying.

Luther realised that the Church, particularly insofar as it had become a money-making business, had moved far from the kind of Church that is described in the New Testament. His first protest focused on the way in which the Church made a great deal of its money from the sale of Indulgences.

Indulgences rest on a belief that those who sin, even once their sin is forgiven, must suffer deserved penalties, not least after death. The penalties might be paid for in Purgatory, but better still they might be removed by the purchase of Indulgences.

It was believed that Christ, Mary and the Saints have built up a vast treasury of merit on which the Church can draw in order that the penalties, both of the living and of the dead, might be cancelled. This benefit could be bought through the purchase of Indulgences. It was the widespread sale of Indulgences, particularly in Germany by Johann Tetzel, that was the focus of Luther's first protest, since it made the Church 'a cult of the living in the service of the dead':

> So soon as coin in coffer rings
> The soul from Purgatory springs.

In 1517 Luther is said to have nailed to a church door in Wittenberg ninety-five theses criticising Indulgences. They can hardly be said to be 'a sacred text' because very few people have read them (some are translated in Hillerbrand, pp. 51f.), but they represent a critical point in the developing protests against Rome. In the often quoted words of Luther, 'Here I stand, I can do no other.' His anger against Tetzel he recalled in 1541 (*Wider Hans Worst*, Hillerbrand, p. 45):

> To speak about the real cause for the 'Lutheran scandal': at first
> I let everything continue in its course. Then it was reported to
> me, however, that Tetzel was preaching some cruel and terrible
> propositions, such as the following:
>
>> He had grace and power from the Pope to offer forgiveness
>> even if someone had slept with the Holy Virgin Mary, the
>> Mother of God, as long as a contribution would be put into
>> the coffer.

CALVIN

Luther himself did not write texts that have become authoritative, but that is not the case with another reformer, John/Jean Calvin (1509–64). Calvin's *Institutes of the Christian Religion* (first published in 1536, but with several revisions until 1559) was the first systematic presentation of the beliefs of Christians who were protesting (i.e., Protestants) against the errors of Rome. It expounds the clauses of the Apostles' Creed (pp. 70f.) and is the foundation of the Reformed Churches.

Calvin agreed with Aquinas that there is a natural knowledge of God (1.3.1, trans. Allen):

We lay it down as a position not to be controverted, that the human
mind, even by natural instinct, possesses some sense of a Deity . . .
Now, since there has never been a country or family, from the
beginning of the world, totally destitute of religion, it is a tacit
confession, that some sense of the Divinity is inscribed on every
heart.

Creation reveals the wisdom of God as much to ordinary people as to scientists
(1.5.1–2). But what status does that 'natural knowledge' have in throwing light
on what is necessary for salvation? Calvin thought that it gave as much light as
a single flash of lightning gives light to a traveller in a coach on a pitch-black
night.

How then can God be known as the One who alone can deliver us from sin?
Only through Scripture:

Though the light which presents itself to all eyes, both in heaven
and in earth, is more than sufficient to deprive the ingratitude of
men of every excuse, since God, in order to involve all mankind
in the same guilt, sets before them all, without exception, an
exhibition of his majesty, delineated in the creatures, – yet we need
another and better assistance, properly to direct us to the Creator
of the world. Therefore he hath not unnecessarily added the light
of his word, to make himself known unto salvation . . . For, as
persons who are old, or whose eyes are by any means become dim,
if you show them the most beautiful book, though they perceive
something written, but can scarcely read two words together, yet,
by the assistance of spectacles, will begin to read distinctly, – so the
Scripture, collecting in our minds the otherwise confused notions
of deity, dispels the darkness, and gives us a clear view of the true
God . . . The Scripture discovers God to us as the Creator of the
world, and declares what sentiments we should form of him, that
we may not be seeking after a deity in a labyrinth of uncertainty.

BIBLIOGRAPHY NUMBERS 76–8, 176, 450, 611, 719

THE REFORMATIONS

TRENT, JOHN OF THE CROSS, IGNATIUS

There were many within the Church of Rome who recognised the need for reformation but who made an attempt at reform within the Church itself. In the fifteenth century Erasmus (*c*.1466–1536), known as 'the wisest man in Christendom', had pointed out with sharp brilliance the grievous failings of the Church, but he had hoped that the Church might reform itself.

Moves in that direction were made at the Council of Trent which met in three distinct periods, 1545–7 (sessions 1–8), 1551–2 (sessions 9–14) and 1562–3 (sessions 15–25). Trent is regarded by Roman Catholics as the nineteenth Ecumenical Council (p. 73) since in their view the Church of Rome is the universal and Catholic Church with other Churches being in different degrees of imperfection. As it was put in the Decree of the Second Vatican Council (Vatican II, 1962–5), *Unitatis Redintegratio*, 1964, 3:

> The separated Churches and Communities as such, though we
> believe them to be deficient in some respects, are by no means
> deprived of significance and importance in the mystery of
> salvation. For the Spirit does not decline to use them as means
> of salvation – means which derive their efficacy from the very
> fullness of grace and truth entrusted to the Catholic Church . . .
> For it is only through Christ's Catholic Church, which is the
> all-embracing means of salvation, that the fullness of the means
> of salvation can be enjoyed.

At Trent there was a real desire to hold the Church together, but in the end it reaffirmed Indulgences, Purgatory and the veneration of saints – exactly the aspects to which Luther had objected since they seemed to turn God into the manager of a supermarket of salvation.

There were, however, other ways to bring reform and renewal to the Church. Among them was the reform, or else the founding, of Religious Orders, both of which produced their own sacred texts.

IGNATIUS

One of those who sought to live more completely and faithfully in the presence of God was a Spaniard called Ignatius (1491–1556). He wrote in a letter in 1545 (*Monumenta Ignatiana*, I, p. 339):

> I reckon that those who abandon themselves to enter into their
> Creator and Lord will experience an unwavering attentiveness and
> consolation in feeling how our eternal Good is present in all things,
> bringing them into being and keeping them therein by his infinite
> being and presence; and that for those whose love for Christ is
> unreserved, all things help them, first to gain merit, and then to
> unite them in total love with their Creator and Lord.

Ignatius began life as a soldier, passionate about fighting and women. A serious wound, however, led to a long convalescence during which he read a Life of Christ and the Lives of Francis and Dominic, all of which moved him profoundly. The way in which he discerned an entirely different feeling within himself became a fundamental part of Ignatian prayer, the discernment of what God is doing in the soul.

Ignatius dedicated himself to fight thenceforth under the banner or Standard of God, not under that of Satan. At Manresa he saw a vision that gave direction to his life. A small group gathered round him, and together they formed Compania de Jesus, the Society of Jesus (the Jesuits), recognised by the Pope in 1540.

Ignatius wrote down what he had learned in his vision in the book that eventually became *The Spiritual Exercises*. The Exercises are a guided programme of prayer under a Director who helps the participant to discern the work and purpose of God in the soul. Ignatius knew that God is always greater (*Deus semper maior*) than anything we can know or understand, but we can begin to know something of God, especially through God's incarnation in Christ. So the participant in *The Exercises* is encouraged to enter imaginatively into scenes of the Gospels, thus making a direct connection between Scripture and the life of the believer. *The Exercises* are divided into four Weeks: the first week reflects on sin and its consequences; the second focuses on the life of Christ with reflection on the 'Two Standards'; the third week enters into the Passion of Christ; the fourth leads to the Resurrection. Its Foundation is that humans are created to praise, reverence and serve God who wills to share life with them for ever.

TERESA AND JOHN OF THE CROSS

Among those who sought to reform the Church from within was Teresa of Avila in Spain. She had become a Carmelite in 1535, but had found the Order and discipline far too lax. Encouraged by visionary experiences of God, she introduced the Carmelite Reform called 'discalced' (i.e., 'not wearing shoes', either literally or in the form of sandals). In 1562, in the spirit of reform, she founded the convent of St Joseph at Avila.

She was opposed by those who resisted change, but she found support from John of the Cross. He had joined the Carmelites in 1563, but, like Teresa, he was dismayed by the laxity in the Order. He was close to leaving when Teresa persuaded him to help her in the work of reform. He did so, but he too was opposed by those of the Calced Carmelites who resisted change. He was imprisoned and eventually banished, but it was in prison that he began to write 'such fresh, vibrant poetry that he is hailed as one of the greatest poets Spain has ever produced' (Farina, in Kavanaugh, p. 10).

Among his poems, three are of particular importance because he wrote extensive commentaries on them that have become classic texts of guidance for those who seek seriously to unite themselves with God, and especially for those who find themselves in 'the dark night of the soul' (the title of one of his works, below). The 'Dark Night' is not a kind of depression. It is a realisation of the apparent absence of God who previously has seemed to be a real presence. To persist in the darkness is to find it is the only way in which God can bring us from our immature ideas about God to the reality of God. As Iain Matthew has put it (p. 83):

> If the living God, and not our image of God, is to fill the emptiness
> of the human spirit, even that image – the closest we have got to
> God himself – may need dismantling . . . When John later had
> time to relate this experience in prison, he perceived it as 'a loving
> mother of the grace of God, undoing him to recreate him.'

John wrote his commentaries on three of his own poems: *The Spiritual Canticle* on the long poem 'Cantico Espiritual'; *The Ascent of Mount Carmel* and *The Dark Night of the Soul* on 'Noche Oscura'; and *The Living Flame* on 'Llama de Amor Viva', 'songs of the soul in loving union with God' (trans. Flower, p. 18):

Flame, living flame, compelling,
yet tender past all telling,
reaching the secret centre of my soul!
Since now evasion's over,
finish your work, my Lover,
break the last thread, wound me and make me whole!

Burn that is for my healing!
Wound of delight past feeling!
Ah, gentle hand whose touch is a caress,
foretaste of heaven conveying
and every debt repaying:
killing, you give me life for death's distress.

O lamps of fire bright-burning,
with splendid brilliance, turning
deep caverns of my soul to pools of light!
Once shadowed, dim, unknowing,
now their strange new-found glowing
gives warmth and radiance for my Love's delight.

Ah! gentle and so loving
you wake within me, proving
that you are there in secret and alone;
your fragrant breathing stills me,
your grace, your glory fills me
so tenderly your love becomes my own.

BIBLIOGRAPHY NUMBERS 247, 488, 492, 509, 676, 687, 893, 953

بِسْمِ اللّٰهِ الرَّحْمٰنِ الرَّحِيمِ

الْحَمْدُ لِلّٰهِ رَبِّ الْعَالَمِينَ ۝ الرَّحْمٰنِ

الرَّحِيمِ ۝ مَالِكِ يَوْمِ الدِّينِ

إِيَّاكَ نَعْبُدُ وَإِيَّاكَ نَسْتَعِينُ

اهْدِنَا الصِّرَاطَ الْمُسْتَقِيمَ

صِرَاطَ الَّذِينَ أَنْعَمْتَ عَلَيْهِمْ غَيْرِ

الْمَغْضُوبِ عَلَيْهِمْ وَلَا الضَّالِّينَ

3

ISLAM

ISLAM TEXTS: KEY DATES

570–632 Muhammad
622 Hijra from Mecca to Medina, 1st year of Muslim calendar
632 Final sermon
632–4 Abu Bakr 1st caliph
634–44 Umar 2nd caliph
642–728 Hasan of Basra
644–56 Uthman 3rd caliph
656 Ali 4th caliph
658 Beginning of Sunni/Shia divide
699/700–767 Abu Hanifa ➔ Hanafites
c.704–768 ibn Ishaq, *Sirat Rasul Allah*
699–767 Abu Hanifa
c.713–801 Rabia alAdawiya
c.716–795 Malik b. Anas ➔ Malikites
d.737 atTabrizi *Mishkat alMasabih*
767–820 asShafii ➔ Shafiites
780–855 Ahmad ibn Hanbal ➔ Hanbalites
d.834 ibn Hisham
d.870 alBukhari
d.875 Muslim
d.875 Abu Dawud
d.886 ibn Maja
d.892 atTirmidhi
d.915 anNasai

c.950–1013 alBaqillani
972 Founding of alAzhar, Cairo
1058–1111 alGhazali, *Tahafut alFalasifa, Munqidh min adDalal, Ihya 'Ulum udDin*
1100 ➔ Sufi orders founded
1077–1166 Abd alQadir Jilani ➔ Qadiriyya
c.1141–1236 Khwajah Mu'in adDin Hasan ➔ Chishtiyya
c.1184–1296 Sa'di, *Gulistan*
1197–1258 Abu 'lHasan ashShadhili ➔ Shadhiliyya
1207–73 Rumi, *Mathnawi, Divan-i-Shams-i-Tabrizi*
d.1221 Najm adDin Kubra ➔ Kubrawiyya
d.c.1229 Attar, *Mantiq atTayr*
d.1277 anNawawi, *Forty Hadith*
1317–89 Khwaja Baha adDin Muhammad Naqshband ➔ Naqshbandi
d.1389 Hafiz
1414–92 Jami, *Diwan*
d.1431 Shah Nimat Allah ➔ Nimatullahi
1542–1605 Akbar
1563–1625 Shaykh Ahmad Sirhindi
1703–62 Shah Wali Allah, *Hujjat Allah alBaligha*

Previous page: The Opening Sura, alFatiha, of the Quran. The Sura is translated on p. 136.

THE QURAN

MUHAMMAD THE PROPHET

When the teaching stops the learning begins for many Muslim children. In Muslim communities in all parts of the world children after school may join a different kind of class in order to learn by heart the sacred text of Islam, the Quran. The text is in Arabic, a language that the children are unlikely to understand, but the recitation of the language has its own intrinsic value since it brings a blessing, *baraka*, from God.

The task of memorisation is formidable since there are 6,236 verses in the Quran. Not everyone can accomplish it, but anyone who does so is known and honoured in the community as Hafiz, 'guardian' of the text.

So what is the Quran, and why do Muslims hold it in such high regard? In Muslim belief, the Quran is the collection of words transmitted by God through the agency of the angel Jibril/Jibra'il (Gabriel) to the Prophet Muhammad who recited or proclaimed them to the people around him. The Mother of the Book (*umm alKitab*) is with God in Heaven, so that Arabic is not simply one language among many: it is the language through which God chose to reveal his Word. That is the reason why it is not only learned and recited, but also cannot be translated. Versions in other languages are at best interpretations: they cannot *be* the Word of God.

The word Quran is related to the Arabic word *qara'a*, 'he read' or 'he recited'. According to Muslims, Muhammad was illiterate so he could not have read texts in order to compose the Quran. Indeed, Muhammad did not compose the Quran at all – or, in other words, he is not the author of a book called 'the Quran'. Muhammad received the Quran from God through the agency of Jibril, and the very first words that he received begin with the command, *Iqra*, 'recite', derived from that same word *qara'a* (96.1–5: references to the Quran are by 'chapter and verse', i.e., Sura and Ayat: see further p. 136):

Recite in the name of your Lord who created – created man from a
drop. Recite! and your Lord is most generous – he who taught by
means of the pen, taught man what he did not know.

So who was Muhammad and how did he come to be a prophet? He was born in
Mecca in Arabia in 570. When he was young he had an experience of two figures
who 'opened his chest and stirred their hands inside', an experience perhaps
referred to in Quran 94:

Did we not cut open your chest and remove from you your burden
which twisted your back, and returned to you your memory of it?
So, surely, with every difficulty there is relief – surely, with every
difficulty there is relief. So, when you are free, still labour hard, and
to your Lord direct your desire.

It was the first of a number of experiences that led Muhammad to seek a better
understanding of God. At the time the Meccans worshipped many gods and
goddesses, in particular three known as alLat, alUzza and Manat – denounced
in 53.19–23 (see further, p. 135). Muhammad, however, was already beginning
to feel that God (*the* God or, in Arabic, Allah) must be much greater than the
human construction of idols.

He was encouraged in this instinct by his uncle, Zayid ibn Amr, who had
already joined a group of people called Hanifs. They were so profoundly
influenced by the Jews in Arabia (with their insistence that there is only One
God) that they called themselves 'followers of the religion of Abraham'. Like his
uncle, Muhammad began to go alone to a cave on Mount Hira to search for God
away from the many varieties of religion and idolatry. It was in that cave that he
felt Jibril pressing in urgency on him (ibn Ishaq, *Sirat Rasul Allah*):

The angel came while I was sleeping with a cloth on which there
was some writing. The angel said, 'Recite.' I answered, 'I am not one
of those who recite.' Then he took me and pressed upon me until
it was unbearable; then he let me go and said: 'Recite.' I said, 'I am
not one of those who recite.' So he took me and pressed upon me
a second time until it was unbearable; then he let me go and said:
'Recite.' I said, 'I am not one of those who recite.' So he took me and
pressed upon me a third time until it was unbearable, so I said,
'What then shall I recite?' I said this only to save myself from him
in case he did the same to me again. Then he let me go and said:

'Recite in the name of your Lord who created – created man from a drop . . . ' [96 above].

Aisha, a favourite among his wives, later recalled (alBukhari 1.1.3):

> Then the apostle of God returned with it, with his heart trembling, and went into Khadija [his first wife] and said, 'Hide [or 'wrap'] me, hide me!' So she hid him until the awe left him. Then he said to Khadija (telling her what had happened): 'I am terrified for my life.' Khadija answered: 'No, by God! God will not bring you to disgrace, for you bind together the ties of relationship, you carry the burdens of the weak, you earn what you earn to give to the destitute, you welcome the guest and you help where there is genuine distress.'

Muhammad was not altogether reassured and he thought that he had gone mad (*majnun*, which means 'possessed by the jinn of the desert') or, if not that, then at least that he had become one of the other possessed creatures who were not uncommon in Arabia, a *kahin*, a *sahir*, or a *sha'ir*. Those were people who went into ecstatic states and gave what they claimed to be messages from God. In the end Khadija reassured him. She advised him to wait and see what transpired – 'After all,' she added, 'perhaps you did see something.' 'Yes,' he answered, 'I really did.'

Muhammad knew with complete conviction and beyond doubt that if God is actually God, then that is what God is, Allah, the One who is God. There cannot be any division or diminution of what God is: there cannot be other gods or the division of one god from another. The only absolute and true reality is God, Allah, the One who is God, the unproduced Producer of all that is:

> Say: He is God, alone [literally, *ahad*, 'one'], God the absolute.
> He does not beget, he is not begotten,
> And there is none in any way equal to him (s.112).

That is the Sura in the Quran (*alIkhlas*) known as the Sura of Unity. It is believed that Muslims who say that Sura with complete conviction and sincerity will find that all their sins fall from them as leaves fall from a tree in autumn.

Muhammad's life and message became a working out of the implications of that fundamental vision: all creation and every aspect of life are received from the One who alone is the Creator and who can have no rival or competitor. This means that for all people every detail of their lives, everything that they do or say or think, is received from God and returns to God for judgement after death. Every word and action must bear witness that 'there is no God but God'.

The dominant theme of the Quran is therefore praise and thanksgiving to God who creates and sustains everything in existence and who has placed upon human beings special responsibilities in the world. God has repeatedly sent prophets to call people to remember God at all times and to enter into the condition of safety in obedience to God, which is the meaning of *islam*. The Quran lays out what should be the true life-way (*din*, often translated as 'religion', but that is misleading unless it is remembered that, in Islam, religion embraces the whole of life). The Quran lays down many details of life in family and society, and of how Muslims should relate to non-Muslims. All this is the guidance of God, and the extent to which people put it into effect is weighed up on the Day of Judgement: the consequences in heaven or in hell are described in detail, as in this passage (25.10–16):

> Blessed is He who if He wills can give you better than that [the world of the unbelievers], with gardens beneath which rivers flow, and He can give you palaces for a dwelling.
>
> But they deny the Hour [of Judgement]. Yet we have prepared for those who deny the Hour a blazing fire.
>
> When it sees them from a far-off place, they will hear its fury and its groaning.
>
> And when, bound together, they are thrown into a confined place within it, they will plead for destruction there and then.
>
> That day do not lay claim to one destruction, lay claim to destruction constantly repeated.
>
> Say: Is that best, or is it the everlasting Garden promised to the righteous? For them that is a reward as it is their goal. For them there will be in it what they have wished for and they will dwell there for ever. It is a promise to be prayed for from your Lord.

None of this is gathered in the Quran in a systematic or thematic way. It is therefore difficult to read the Quran as a connected text from beginning to end. An extremely helpful guide for those unfamiliar with the Quran is Cragg's *Readings in the Qur'an* (250).

📖 BIBLIOGRAPHY NUMBERS **783**

THE QURAN

REVELATION, THE PEOPLE OF THE BOOK

After the encounter in the Cave, there was a period known as the Fatra ('gap') when Muhammad received no further revelations. After that the Quran was revealed piece by piece throughout the rest of his life.

The revelations were recognised at once as being utterly different from the ordinary words of his everyday life. In Muslim belief, the Quran is eternal and uncreated, and there is nothing else like it. The Quran itself challenges those who at the time thought that it was Muhammad's own composition to produce something like it – and some tried but patently failed. When alBaqillani (c.950–1013) wrote a work on 'the inimitability of the Quran', he told his readers to look at the pre-Islamic poetry of Arabia and to see how rough and crude it is in comparison.

Not only did the Quran sound different, but Muhammad often looked different when he was receiving it. In the Traditions (*ahadith*: on the status of Hadith in Islam, see pp. 137f.) there are many descriptions. These are examples taken from the Collections of Muslim and alBukhari:

◆ 'Over the apostle of God was a garment with which he was covered [hence the cloak and perhaps the translation 'wrap' in the account of the experience in the Cave on pp. 126f.]; then Safwan ibn Yala put his hand under, and saw that the apostle of Allah was red in the face, and that he was snoring.'

◆ 'Aisha [his wife] said: "I saw him when revelation came down on him, when the day was extremely cold, then it left him, and his forehead was dripping with sweat."'

◆ 'Zaid ibn Thabit said: "God sent down [*nazala*, 'he sent down' is the common word for 'he revealed', and the noun *tanzil* is the usual word for 'revelation'] on his apostle, when his leg was resting on mine, and the weight was so great on me, I feared my leg would be crushed."'

◆ 'Harith b. Hisham asked the apostle of God: "How does revelation come to you?" He answered: "Sometimes it comes to me like the clanging of a bell, and that is heaviest upon me; then it leaves me and I remember from what he said; and sometimes the angel comes to meet me resembling a man and speaks to me, and I remember what he says.'"

◆ 'Ubadah b. asSamit said: "When the revelation came down on him, the Prophet was like one overwhelmed with grief and his face changed. According to one report he hung down his head and his companions did the same.'"

THE PEOPLE OF THE BOOK

At the time of Muhammad, there were many Jews and Christians in Arabia (mainly as refugees from different kinds and occasions of persecution), and Muhammad certainly had contact with them. He believed that Jews and Christians would recognise him as a prophet like their own, proclaiming the same message of the unity and sovereignty of God, of the ways in which people should behave, and of the account that all must render on the Last Day of Judgement. In the event, some did become his followers, but mainly for political and strategic reasons. They could not accept the proposition that he was a prophet like their own, since from their point of view the direct inspiration of prophets belonged to particular periods of their own history in the past.

That, however, did not affect the Muslim belief that Muhammad is the last of the prophets through whom God has revealed his word. The same Revelation has been sent to the Jews through such prophets as Musa (Moses), to Christians through 'Isa (Jesus), and through various prophets to other peoples. Those who have received Revelation have a special status in Islam, being known as Ahl alKitab, 'the people of the Book'. According to Muslims, the Revelation entrusted to the prophets is identical since the Mother of the Book (*umm alKitab*) is with God in heaven, but it is related to the particular language and circumstances of the prophets and their people who are receiving the Revelation. Thus the Quran makes reference to people and events that are specific and contingent to the time and circumstances of Muhammad, but the message is eternal and unchanging.

It is obvious, however, that the Bible, Jewish or Christian, does not resemble the Quran. Where the Quran includes accounts of Biblical figures such as Ibrahim (Abraham) or 'Isa (Jesus), they are not the accounts given in Tanakh or the New Testament, but rather the interpretations given in the Targums or (in the case of Christianity) the stories told of Jesus in apocryphal Gospels to show that he was not genuinely human but only an appearance.

This sometimes has dramatic consequences. For example, *Genesis* 11.31

states that Terah and his son Abram (as he was then known) left their home in Mesopotamia, specifically the town of Ur of the Chaldeans. This was the beginning of Abram's great journey around the Fertile Crescent to settle in the land that became Palestine/Judaea.

However, the town of Ur was destroyed and completely disappeared until archaeologists rediscovered it in the nineteenth and twentieth centuries. The Targum interpreters (for Targums, see p. 30) were left with a puzzle when they encountered this sentence: 'They went out together from Ur of the Chaldeans' (*Genesis* 11.31). They had no idea that Ur was a place, so they took it to be the Hebrew word *ur* which looks the same and which happens to mean 'a fire'. The interpreters therefore took the sentence to be saying that Terah and Abram 'had escaped from the fire of the Chaldeans'.

But what was the fire? It was taken to be the fire that was worshipped in Mesopotamia (the Zoroastrians from that area have important rituals involving fire). At the same time, it was also understood as the fire into which those idolaters cast any who refused to worship with them. The escape from the fire of the Chaldeans could then be seen as the refusal of Abraham to participate in idolatry, and also as his rescue by God from the penalty of being burnt alive. Many stories were then told of how all this had happened, and these stories became the model for other Jews to resist persecution even if it meant martyrdom, and to continue to worship the One and only God. Not surprisingly, those stories appear in the Targums as they interpret the Hebrew text taking Ur to be the word *ur*, meaning 'fire'.

It is clear, therefore, that the Targums rest on a mistake since they simply did not know that Ur was a place. The Quran, however, repeats the interpretation of the Targums since that of course was what the Jews in Arabia understood Scripture to mean. Quran 21.52/51–71, for example, records the argument of Ibrahim/Abraham with the idolaters in a way that foreshadows the argument of Muhammad with the idolaters of Mecca. The idolaters condemn Ibrahim to be burnt to death, but God defends him: 'We said, "O fire, be cool and a place of safety for Ibrahim."'

Examples of this kind raised profound questions of contingency – that is, of the relation between the eternal Quran and the particular historical circumstances in which it has been revealed and which the Quran mentions. Muslims, however, are unlikely to ask these questions because for them the differences between Quran and earlier Scriptures have arisen, not because of the history of interpretation, but because Jews and Christians have corrupted the Revelation entrusted to them: they have done so by confusing the message from God with additional material such as stories about their prophets, histories and letters, with the result that the pure and uncorrupted Word of God is to be found only in the Quran. For that reason Muhammad is called 'the Seal of the Prophets'.

Sura 17 ends with the praise of God whose name is Rahman (the Merciful, one of the ninety-nine Beautiful Names of God to be found in the Quran) for his gift of the Quran:

In truth we sent down [*anzilnahu*, i.e., we revealed, hence *tanzil*, 'revelation'] and in truth it came down, and we sent you for nothing except good news and warnings.

It is a Quran that we have divided up in order that you may recite it to people at intervals: we have revealed it in stages.

Say: Whether you believe in it or you do not believe in it, surely those who were given knowledge beforehand when it was recited to them fell to the ground in humble prostration.

And they say, 'Glory to our Lord, for the promise of our Lord has been fulfilled.'

They fall to the ground weeping and it increases their humility.

Say: Call on God or call on Rahman or call by whatever name, for His are the most beautiful names. And do not speak your Prayer [*salat*] loudly nor speak it too softly, but seek a way between the two.

Say: Praise be to God who does not beget a son and does not have any partner in His kingdom, and does not have any need of one to protect Him from contempt. So magnify Him for His magnificence.

BIBLIOGRAPHY NUMBERS **783**

THE QURAN

THE MUSHAF

The Quran was not necessarily written down when it was first delivered, though some people made notes. It was committed to memory by Muhammad and by others of his followers. After the death of Muhammad it continued to be recited from memory, and some individuals were recognised as Quran memorisers and reciters (*qurra'*).

COLLECTING THE QURAN

As time went by, however, and as Muslims were engaged in wars to defend or extend their territory, the original reciters began to die or to be killed in battle. The decision was therefore made to gather the memorised recitations into a single collection. Ibn Hajar (IX, p. 9) recorded the account given by Zaid b.Thabit of how this happened:

> Zaid said: 'Abu Bakr [the first Caliph or successor after the death of Muhammad] summoned me when those died who were killed in the Yamama campaigns. Abu Bakr said: "Umar has told me that death has struck grievously at the *qurra'* in the Yamama campaigns, and I fear that it will strike them grievously also in other campaigns so that much of the Quran will disappear. I believe therefore that you should give orders for the Quran to be collected." Abu Bakr said that he replied to Umar, "How can we do something that the Prophet did not do himself?" Umar answered, "Despite that, it is a good thing to do"... Abu Bakr went on: "Zaid, you are young and bright and we have heard nothing said against you. You used to record for the Prophet the revelations, so go and look for the Quran and gather it together." By God! If they had told me to move a mountain it could not

have been a weightier burden than that . . . I therefore went and looked for the Quran, gathering it together from palm-leaves, flat stones and people's memories. I found the last verses of the Sura called atTawba [9, "Repentance"], from "There has now come to you" [9.129/8] to the end, in the possession of Abu Khuzaima alAnsari, having failed to find it with anyone else.' The pages that Zaid prepared in this way were kept by Abu Bakr. When he died they were passed on to Umar who passed them on when he died to his daughter Hafsa.

From this and other accounts it is clear that Muhammad had not collected the Quran, although there are references to his ordering that parts of it should be written down. For the early Muslims, therefore, it was important to make it clear that the collection of the Quran was undertaken by his closest Companions (including Zaid and the first four Caliphs) or by his family, including his widows Aisha, Hafsa and Umm Salama.

Collecting the Quran was not a straightforward process, and various questions arose that preoccupied the early Muslim communities for years. For example:

◆ How could they be sure that all the Quran had been collected?

◆ Was it possible that Muhammad had forgotten part of what had been revealed to him? The Quran itself states that God himself might cause something to be forgotten: 'We do not cause one of our verses to be replaced [*ma nansakh min ayatin*] or cause it to be forgotten without bringing a better than it, or its like' (2.100/106; cf., 17.86/84, 87.6f.).

◆ As the Quran was collected, it was found that there were variant versions and readings, some of which remain known to this day: what should the status of these variant readings be?

◆ How should the Quran be pronounced? There were many different dialects of Arabic at the time, as there still are, and some of those different pronunciations affect the meaning of the text. In the end it was decided to adopt the pronunciation of Muhammad's own family group in Mecca, the Quraysh, and even to this day reciters of the Quran learn this particular pronunciation in recital known as *tajwid*.

Equally searching questions were raised about the consistency of the Quran: what should the Muslim community do when one verse in the Quran seems to contradict another, or when the practice of the community is at variance with what the Quran seems to command?

REPLACEMENT AND ABROGATION

Questions of that kind raised profound issues about the status and authority of the Quran as the uncreated and eternal Word of God. Not surprisingly, they led to vast and complicated discussions in the years after Muhammad's death. They are focused on the concept of *naskh*, or *alnasikh wa almansukh*, the word that appears in the quotation from 2.100 above. It is usually translated as 'abrogation', but it means in practice something more like 'suppression' or 'replacement'.

In the end it was decided that God allowed three kinds of *naskh*:

1   The suppression of *both* a ruling (*hukm*) *and* its wording, so that it no longer appears in the Quran at all. Thus the denouncement of the three Meccan goddesses (53.19f., p. 126) originally included the verse, 'These are the high-flying cranes whose intercession is to be hoped for'; and clearly Muhammad was holding out a hand of reconciliation to the Meccans in the early days of their opposition to him. Jibril told him that Satan had whispered these words in his ear and they were excluded from the Quran: these are the original 'Satanic Verses'.

2   The suppression of one ruling by another ruling with the retention of the words – it is this that comes closest to the abrogation of an earlier ruling by a later. There is thus a sequence of four verses on intoxicants (such as alcohol) moving from disapproval to prohibition: the last of these abrogates the others. Or again, the early approval of God-fearing Jews, Christians and Sabians in 2.59/62 is abrogated in 3.85/91, just as the command in 2.186/190 to fight only defensive wars and not to be aggressive is abrogated in 9.5 which commands Muslims to kill the Mushriks (for the meaning of Mushrik see p. 140) wherever they find them.

3   The suppression of the words with the retention of the ruling: the penalty for adultery in 24.2 is a beating with 100 strokes. Nevertheless, in practice, as early as the time of Umar, the second Caliph, the penalty was stoning to death: Umar was entirely clear that it was not in the Quran, but he claimed that he was simply following the practice of Muhammad and Abu Bakr. In this case, the words are not in the Quran, but the ruling has been retained in practice.

SURAS IN THE QURAN

Eventually a uniform text of the Quran was agreed, and this text is known as the Mushaf. It is arranged into 114 'chapters' called Suras. Each Sura has its own name, as with atTawba mentioned above. It is then divided into verses known as *ayat* (which means in general a sign that points to God), but the divisions are not uniform in all editions – hence the references with two numbers, as, for example, 3.85/91.

The Suras follow, not the chronological order in which passages were revealed, but the order of length from longest to shortest (though there are slight exceptions to this). An obvious exception is that the Quran opens with a short Sura, alFatiha, 'The Opener' (see box). It is then said whether they were revealed in Mecca (the earlier part of Muhammad's work as a Prophet) or in Medina (the later part), but that is only a rough guide: much work was done by Muslims to try to identify the occasions when particular parts of the Quran were revealed.

alFATIHA: THE OPENING SURA OF THE QURAN

IN THE NAME OF God, the merciful Lord of mercy.

Praise be to God, the Lord of all being,

The merciful Lord of mercy,

Sovereign of the Day of Judgement:

You alone do we serve and to You alone we come for help:

Guide us in the straight path,

The path of those on whom You have bestowed favour,

Not of those against whom is the wrath,

Nor of those who are straying in error.

📖 BIBLIOGRAPHY NUMBERS **329**

HADITH

THE SIX SOUND COLLECTIONS

The Quran is the non-negotiable foundation of Muslim life. It does not, however, deal with every situation that might arise, so careful methods of acceptable exegesis were developed in order to move from Quran to the changing conditions of life. The main methods are *ijma* (consensus), *qiyas* (analogy), *ra'y* (well-considered and informed opinion), *ijtihad* (application) and *istihsan* (preference); for a fuller discussion of these, see Hasan (cf., the development among the Jews of *Torah shebe'alpeh*, p. 33).

SUNNA AND HADITH

The earliest people to apply Quran to life were Muhammad himself and his Companions. Traditions of what they said and how they acted (and also of what they did not say, i.e., their silences) were collected as *ahadith* (sing. *hadith*, 'narration', known collectively as Hadith). Hadith records the Sunna (lit., 'custom') of Muhammad so that Hadith, on the foundation of Quran, becomes the guide to Muslim life.

For that reason the number of claimed *ahadith* increased rapidly. As they were being collected, a fundamental issue was how to distinguish the authentic traditions from the doubtful or even invented ones. It was recognised that a tradition might, for example, be invented in order to support a particular doctrinal or political opinion. That was a real possibility after the split between Sunni and Shia Muslims, the latter saying that only the descendants of Muhammad should have succeeded him as Caliphs, of whom the first was Ali (hence their name *shi'at 'Ali*, 'party of Ali'; Sunnis are those who follow the Sunna of the Prophet).

Muslims therefore recognised that claimed *ahadith* might not be genuine. Apart from those that had been invented and were clearly false (known as *maudu'*), others might contain mistakes that had been incurred in the course of transmission from generation to generation, or again others might have been misremembered. As a result, Muslims made an immense effort to classify *ahadith* by content (*matn*) and by the process of transmission in order to establish those that could be accepted as genuine (known as Sahih, 'sound') or at least as reliable (Hasan, 'fair'). Eventually all the *ahadith* were classified in two groups, Accepted (*maqbul*) and Rejected (*mardud*). The immensely detailed study of Hadith involved in all this is known as *'ilm alHadith*, the Science of Hadith.

THE AUTHENTICITY AND CLASSIFICATION OF HADITH

The first and major task was to establish (so far as it could be done) the chain of people who were reported to have transmitted each tradition. The chain is known as *isnad*. Ideally the *isnad* would start with Muhammad, and then each link of the *isnad* down to the time of the collector would be made up of reliable people – and especially in the early stages of the *isnad* of those who were closely linked to Muhammad. Immense journeys were made to verify whether claims that 'x heard this from y' could be substantiated: did it happen that x and y actually met?

The importance of the *isnad* explains why in Collections of Hadith each tradition is prefaced with a statement of its *isnad*. Thus to give a typical example (relevant to issues concerning recitation of the Quran, p. 134), alBukhari 50.29.3 reads:

> Sulaiman b.Harb told us [*hadathna*]: 'Shu'ba told us from Amr
> b.Murra from Ibrahim from Masruq who said: Abd Allah [ibn
> Masud, a renowned reciter of Quran] was brought to mind in the
> presence of Abd Allah b.Amr who said: That man has been dear to
> me since I heard the Apostle of God (may God bless him and give
> him peace) say: Learn the recitation of the Quran from four people:
> from Abd Allah ibn Masud whom he mentioned first, Salim the
> freedman of Abu Hudhayfah, Ubayy b.Kab and Muadh b.Jabal. I
> do not remember whether he mentioned Ubayy or Muadh first.'

To be accepted in Islamic law as an authoritative source of legal ruling, a *hadith* must meet five conditions: an unbroken chain or *isnad* of transmitters; proof of the trustworthiness of the transmitters; and of their good memory; coherence of a *hadith* with others; no incidental defect. The strongest *ahadith*, known as alHadith alMutawatir, must then satisfy a further four criteria concerning the number and nature of the transmitters: at least four different transmitters in each generation; who cannot have colluded in fraud; comparability of the transmitters; whose imagination can be checked.

Ahadith which nearly, but not quite, match the four criteria of alHadith alMutawatir are known as alHadith alAhad, and they are classified according to the ways in which they fall short. There are many categories into which a *hadith* might be put, each of which reflects a different way in which the *isnad* falls short. The diagram below gives three examples where in a generation there is a record of, not four, but three, two or one transmitters.

AlHadith alAhad are also placed in categories according to the way in which an *isnad* is related to Muhammad. In the examples in Figure 1, the classification depends on whether the chain of transmitters goes back to the Prophet, or just to one of his Companions, or only to a successor of one of the Companions.

On the basis of those and many other considerations alHadith alAhad are classified as Strong (*Sahih*), Fair (*Hasan*) or Weak (*Da'if*). The Weak are also categorised and classified in detail, but only the Strong and the Fair, not the Weak, can be used as an authority in the forming of Islamic law. In this diagram an illustration is offered of that process of Hadith transmission from the Prophet to legal rulings.

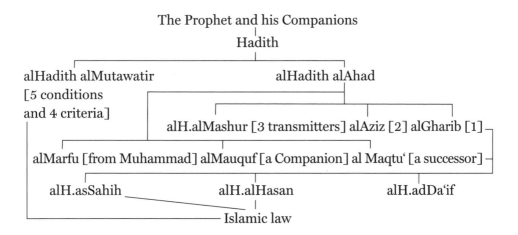

In the classification of Hadith there is another important distinction. Muslims were clear from the outset that Hadith must not be confused with Quran. Nevertheless, some *ahadith* are closer to the Quran than others in the sense that some record Muhammad's report of what God had said to him. These *ahadith* are called collectively Hadith Qudsi ('sacred') in distinction from Hadith Sharif ('noble'). Many different collections of these were made (see, e.g., Ibrahim). This *hadith* is an example relevant to the condemnation of *mushriks* (loosely 'polytheists', those who associate anything with God as though equal to God):

> From Abu Huraira who said: the Apostle of God (may God
> bless him and give him peace) said: God (may he be blessed and
> glorified) said: I am the totally self-sufficient among those claimed
> to be equal – far beyond the claimed associates. Whoever performs
> an act for the sake of one associated with me as well as for me, he
> will have it rejected along with the one associated with me.

THE SIX 'SOUND' COLLECTIONS

The huge effort devoted to *'ilm alHadith* led eventually (300 years after the death of Muhammad) to 'the six canonical collections' of the Sunni Muslims known as *Sihah Sitta* or *alKutub asSittah*, 'the six books'. These are the six Sahih (Sound) collections of Hadith (of which the first two have the highest reputation), gathered by:

1 Abu Abdullah Muhammad who was born at Bukhara and is therefore known as alBukhari: *Sahih alBukhari* is a collection of 2,602 carefully scrutinised *ahadith*, though the total with repetition is over 9,000.

2 Abu 'lHusain Muslim b.alHajjaj alNisapuri, known usually as Muslim: his collection is known as *alMusnad asSahih* with the title abbreviated to *Sahih*.

3 Abu Abdur Rahman Ahmad b.Shuaib b.Ali b.Sinan b.Bahr alKhurasani anNasa'i, known usually as Nasa'i: his collection is known as *asSunan alMujtaba*.

4 Abu Dawud Sulaiman: his collection is known as *Sunan* (the title *Sunan*, the plural of *sunna*, means that the book has been organised according to topics requiring legal definition).

5 Muhammad b.'Isa atTirmidhi: his collection is known as *asSunan* (also called *alJami*).

6 Abu Abdullah Muhammad b.Yazid arRabi, known usually as ibn Maja: his collection is known as *Sunan* (he was not concerned to identify weak traditions, so that some later scholars argued that it should not be included in the Six Books).

There are many other collections of Hadith. Important among the earlier ones are those of Malik b.Anas, *Kitab alMuwatta* (containing opinions and comments as well as *ahadith*) and Ahmad b.Muhammad, *alMusnad* (collecting *ahadith* associated with particular Companions). Among later collections, two of importance in Muslim life are atTabrizi's *Mishkat alMasabih* and anNawawi's *Forty Hadith* – one of several collections with that name since they reflect a particular saying of Muhammad: 'Whoever commits to memory and preserves for my people forty *ahadith* relating to their *din* [the comprehensive lifeway that is Islam] God will raise him on the Day of Resurrection.' anNawawi's *Forty Hadith* begins:

> On the authority of the Commander of the Faithful Abu Hafs Umar ibn alKhattab [the second Caliph], may God be pleased with him, who said: I heard the Messenger of God (the blessings and peace of God be upon him) say:

> > Actions depend [for their worth] on the intention [with which they are performed], and to all people will be reckoned what they intended. Thus whoever has made the Hijrah for God and His messenger, his Hijrah is [reckoned to be intended] for God and His messenger, but whoever has made the Hijrah to achieve some benefit in this world or to take a particular woman in marriage, his Hijrah was for that for which he made it.

> This was transmitted by two imams among the experts in Hadith, Abu Abdullah Muhammad ibn Ismail ibn Ibrahim ibn alMughira ibn Bardizbah alBukhari and Abu 'lHusain Muslim ibn alHallaj ibn Muslim alQushairi anNaisaburi, in their two Sahihs [Sound Collections] which are the soundest of the collected books.

Shi'ite belief and practice rest on the Quran and on many of the same Hadith as do those of the Sunnis, but Shiites have their own Hadith (called *khabar*, pl. *akhbar*, 'news') supporting their own position and interpretations; and they have their own revered texts, particularly 'The Four Books' (*alKutub alArba'*) which, as Jafri has observed (p. 309), 'have the same importance for the Shi'ites as the six canonical collections of Sunni *Hadith* have for the Sunnis'.

📖 BIBLIOGRAPHY NUMBERS 16, 35, 388, 418, 629, 668, 694

SHARIA AND THE LIFE
OF MUHAMMAD

IBN ISHAQ, *SIRAT RASUL ALLAH*

The Quran, Hadith and the Sunna of the Prophet are the foundation of Muslim life. But in themselves they are not organised systematically (although, as we have seen, some collections of Hadith were organised by topics or transmitters). Various attempts were therefore made in different parts of the Muslim world (in Iraq, for example, in Kufa and Basra, or in the Hijaz in Medina and Mecca) to produce more comprehensive accounts of what Muslim law (*fiqh*) requires. The resulting Schools are known as *madhabib*, or in the singular (and collectively) as Madhab ('direction').

SCHOOLS OF SHARIA

The aim of Madhab is to tell Muslims how they should live and to some extent what they should believe, and this is summarised in Sharia, 'the right path' to follow. The word *shari'a* is used to describe the well-worn path followed by camels to a watering-place. Sharia is an idealised, though highly practical, picture of what Muslim life should be, in the sense that it shows how ideally Muslims should live. As Khadduri has put it (pp. 3f.):

> The law of Islam, the shari'a, has the character of a religious
> obligation; at the same time it constitutes a political sanction
> of religion. As a consequence the shari'a has greater practical
> importance to Muslims than the creed ... In Islamic legal theory
> the shari'a is derived from a high divine source, embodying God's
> will and justice. Unlike positive law, it is regarded as the ideal legal
> order; but, like positive law, it mirrors the character of the society
> in which it developed. The idealization of the shari'a as the perfect

legal system was the product of legal speculation which occupied
the minds of jurists for generations.

Not surprisingly, this 'work of generations' produced a vast number of texts
which, because of their direct connection to the Quran, were treated with
profound respect – with a kind of derivative sacredness. The number of texts
was increased even further by the fact that the Schools of Sharia differ from
each other (though the four main Schools are regarded as equally 'orthodox' and
Muslims can move from one to another depending where they live). They differ
mainly because there was no agreement on what are the legitimate methods of
interpretation (on these, see the reference to Hasan on p. 137).

The four main Schools, named after their founders, are those of the Hanafites
(from Abu Hanifa, d.767CE), allowing interpretation to meet changing circumstances, and strong in Turkey, parts of Iraq, Syria, Afghanistan and nearby
states, Pakistan, India and China; the Hanbalites (from Ahmad ibn Hanbal,
d.855), seeking to stay as close to Quran and Hadith as possible, and strong in
Arabia, some of the Gulf States and increasingly in Africa; the Malikites (from
Malik b. Anas, d.795), conservative but allowing consensus, and strong in the
Maghrib (i.e., the northern coastline of Africa from Egypt to Morocco); and
the Shafiites, from asShafii (d.820), relying on Quran and Hadith with strict
rules of exegesis, and strong in South-East Asia. Of asShafii's critical role in the
development of Sharia, Hasan wrote (p. 178):

> asShafii stands at the turning point in the history of Islamic
> jurisprudence. With him begins a new phase of the development
> of legal theory . . . [His] differences from the early schools are of
> fundamental nature and, therefore, he cannot be placed on a par
> with them. The reason for his disagreement with the early schools
> is that by his extensive study of law and debates with the jurists
> of different regions he formulated certain new principles of law
> and strictly followed them. These principles are spread out in his
> writings, especially in *arRisala*.

In *arRisala* he described how the Sunna (the exemplary Way recorded in
Hadith) is related to the Quran (trans. Khadduri, p.180):

> The sunna which the Apostle has laid down on matters for which
> a text is to be found in the Book of God is always in full agreement
> with that text and clarifying on God's behalf a general text; the

MUHAMMAD'S ADDRESS ON HIS LAST PILGRIMAGE TO MECCA

THEN THE APOSTLE OF God went on with his pilgrimage, showing the men the rituals and teaching them the Sunna ['customs'] of their hajj ['pilgrimage'] . . . Having praised God and glorified him, he said: 'Men, listen to what I say. In truth, I do not know whether I will meet you here again after this year. Your lives and your property are haram ['sacrosanct'] until you meet your Lord as this day and this month are haram. In truth you will meet your Lord who will question you concerning your works. I have made this known clearly. Whoever has with him a pledge let him return it to whoever gave him the pledge. All usury [riba] is abolished, but your capital is yours. Do not do wrong and wrong will not be done to you. God has commanded that there is to be no usury, so the usury of Abbas ibn Abd alMuttalib is totally abolished. And all blood shed in the period of ignorance [Jahiliya, the period before the birth of Muhammad] is not to be avenged . . .

In truth, Shaitan [Satan] has given up hope of being worshipped in this land of yours, but if he can be obeyed in anything less than that, he will be satisfied with what you may think unimportant, so be on guard in your way of life [din]. "In truth, postponing a sacred month is an addition to unbelief by which those straying in error are led into unbelief. They make it lawful in one year and forbidden in another year in order to manipulate the number of months that God has forbidden and to make lawful what God has forbidden." [Quran 9.37]. Time has gone according to its process as it was on the day when God created the heavens and the earth. The number of months with God is twelve of which four are *haram* . . .

Men, you have legal rights over your wives and they have legal rights over you. Your right over them is that they should not defile your bed and also that they should not flaunt themselves openly. If they do so, then surely God has allowed you to send them to their own bed and give them a beating but without severity. And if they keep away from these things, food and clothing are theirs with kindness. So give your instructions to women with generosity, for they are with you as your possession having no authority over themselves in anything. In truth you have received them in trust from God, and you take pleasure in them according to the word of God. So, you men, understand my words, for in truth I have told you and I have left with you that by which, if you grasp hold of it, you will never stray into error: it is a clear word, the book of God and the Sunna of his Prophet. Men, hear my word and understand it. Know that every Muslim is a Muslim's brother, and that the Muslims are brothers. It is allowed [*halal*] to take from a brother only what he has given willingly, so do not wrong yourselves. O God, have I not made this known clearly?'

[Apostle's] specification is more explicit than the text. But as for the Sunna which he laid down on matters for which a text is not found in the Book of God, the obligation to accept them rests upon us by virtue of the duty imposed by God to obey the [Prophet's] orders.

THE LIFE OF MUHAMMAD

Just as Hadith are not an organised compendium of Fiqh, so also they are not a connected biography of Muhammad. Accounts of his campaigns (*almaghazi*, and therefore known as the Maghazi books) were gathered early on, but the first major attempt to organise Hadith into a chronological biography was the *Sira* ('Life') of ibn Ishaq – and even that is referred to by other Arabic writers as 'The Book of Campaigns and his Life'.

Muhammad ibn Ishaq was born in 704 (about eighty-five years after the Hijra) and he died in 768. His original *Sira* is known now mainly through the edited version of Ibn Hisham (d.833). Parts of the original are known from other sources (see, for example, Guillaume, *New Light on the Life of Muhammad*).

The way in which Ibn Hisham edited ibn Ishaq has been described by Guillaume as 'impertinent meddling' (p. xli). However, Ibn Hisham's editorial method, according to his own account, was simply to omit anything that does not mention Muhammad, anything about which the Quran says nothing, things that are disgraceful to mention and matters that might cause distress to some people. So despite the editing the substance of ibn Ishaq's work remains. For an example of Ibn Hisham's edited version of the *Sira*, see box, pp. 144–5.

📖 BIBLIOGRAPHY NUMBERS 53, 58, 407, 408, 427, 485, 863

ALGHAZALI

Ihya 'Ulum udDin, Munqidh min adDalal

During the summer of 1095, while men in England, according to
the Anglo-Saxon Chronicle, were lamenting a typical summer in
which the crops had to be abandoned unharvested, preparations
in Europe were being made for those expeditions against the
Muslim empires of the East which are now referred to as the First
Crusade. That same summer in Baghdad, one of the most eminent
teachers among Muslims of the time was preparing to teach a class
of students. His lectures were always well attended, because he
was, as near as could be, an absolute master of his subject – not
simply *fiqh*, jurisprudence, but also philosophy, theology, and
those subjects which would now come within the scope of natural
sciences. So there should have been no complication or worry about
giving this particular lecture. And yet when he stood up to speak
he found that his voice was paralysed: he was completely unable to
speak, and he stood before his class in silence.

These are the words with which I began the section on Islam in my book *The
Religious Imagination and the Sense of God* (p. 192). The 'eminent teacher'
was alGhazali, the famous author of *Tahafut alFalasifa* ('The Refutation
of the Philosophers'), a man so highly esteemed that he came to be known
as *hujjat alIslam*, 'the proof of Islam'. He later wrote an account of what
had happened to him, in a work known as *Munqidh min adDalal*, 'The
Deliverance from Error' (iii.4):

God shrivelled [or 'parched'] my tongue until I was prevented
from giving instruction. So I used to force myself to teach on
a particular day for the benefit of my various pupils, but my

tongue would not utter a single word . . . The doctors despaired.
They said: 'This matter has descended into his heart, from where
the poison has spread into his whole body. There is no possible
treatment except that he be delivered from the anxiety which
overwhelms him.'

The anxiety which overwhelmed him was his realisation, as he tried to give his
lecture on God, that he did not know what he was talking about. He understood
'God' intellectually, but he did not know God.

As a result of this crisis, he made provision for his family and withdrew for
ten years from active involvement in the world. He spent two years in a mosque
in Damascus where he withdrew for long periods into the minaret and locked
himself in.

There he set himself to know God in a real way, and he took as his guide the
Sufis, because Sufis are Muslims who seek direct and personal experience of
God (see further pp. 151–7):

> At last I turned to the way of the Sufis, a way that combines both
> knowledge and action. Its purpose is to remove from oneself
> the faults and defects of character until the heart is stripped
> of everything that separates from God and is constant in the
> remembrance [dhikr] of God's name.

That passage comes from *Munqidh min adDalal*, 3.4. In that work alGhazali
looked back at his life to show how he had come through his crisis and had
reached certainty in God. He described how he explored and tested the ways
in which people arrive at true empirical knowledge, and how he had come to
recognise the limitations of that knowledge in relation to God. He then recorded
how he had struggled to avoid the issue of choice, deciding one day to give up
everything for the sake of God, only to find the next day that worldly desires
pulled him back, until the moment of decision arrived (3.4):

> The love of lesser things kept me chained in my place until the
> herald of faith cried out to me, 'On the way! On the way! The day
> is short and the journey before you is long. Your knowledge and
> action are deceit and self-deception. If you do not prepare now
> for the world to come, when will you prepare? If you do not cut
> through your attachments now, when will you do so?'

He went on to describe the light that dawned in his darkness as a result of his ten-year withdrawal from the world:

> I remained like that for 10 years during the course of which there were shown me things that I cannot adequately put into words. What I learned is that the Sufis are the supreme explorers of the way of God, and that their life is the most admirable, their way the most carefully guarded, and their moral character the most pure. If all those of keenest intellect, the wisest philosophers, the knowledge of the most informed of those concerned with Sharia, combined to improve the beliefs and practices of the Sufis, it would be impossible for them to do so. The Sufis, at rest or in activity, on the outside or within themselves, are given illumination from the light which shines from the Source. There is no other light on the face of the earth [the reference here is to Quran 2.35, a profound verse especially for Sufis on which alGhazali wrote *Mishkat alAnwar*, 'The Niche for Lights'].

Because *Munqidh min adDalal* includes this account of alGhazali's spiritual quest, it has often been compared to Augustine's *Confessions* (pp. 100–4) and indeed Field's translation (of only part of the text with no indication of the omissions) is entitled *The Confessions of Al Ghazzali*, but the purpose of alGhazali was very different from that of Augustine.

On the basis of his immersion in the Sufi way, alGhazali, before he died, returned briefly to active life and writing. He completed the text for which he is most admired, *Ihya 'Ulum udDin*, 'The Revival of the Religious Sciences'. It is a lengthy work divided into 'four quarters', each of which is divided into ten books. The First Quarter, after a review of knowledge, is concerned with the ways in which humans should serve God – the external practices by which they bring themselves into the presence of God and prepare themselves for the life of the world to come. The Second Quarter deals with daily life and ends with a portrayal of Muhammad as the one who exemplifies how that life should be lived. The Third and Fourth Quarters are entitled 'things leading to destruction' and 'things leading to salvation', and together they explore the interior life and the formation of character.

AlGhazali believed that he was living at a time when most of the supposed guides and leaders had been 'lured by iniquity and overcome by Satan'. He therefore began *Ihya* with a statement of purpose (trans. Faris, 1962, pp. 2f.):

Since this is a calamity afflicting religion and a grave crisis overshadowing it, I have therefore deemed it important to engage in the writing of this book; to revive the science of religion, to bring to light the exemplary lives of the departed imams, and to show what branches of knowledge the Prophets and the virtuous fathers regarded as useful . . . I have begun the work with the Book of Knowledge because it is of the utmost importance to determine first of all the knowledge which God has, through His Apostle, ordered the elite to seek. This is shown by the words of the Apostle of God when he said, 'Seeking knowledge is an ordinance obligatory upon every Muslim.' Furthermore, I have begun with the Book of Knowledge in order to distinguish between useful and harmful knowledge, as the Prophet said, 'We seek refuge in God from useless knowledge'; and also to show the deviation of the people of this age from right conduct, their delusion as by a glistening mirage, and their satisfaction with the husks of knowledge rather than the pith.

Throughout this work alGhazali insists that Sharia is the indispensable foundation of Muslim life, but he claims that the Sufis build on that foundation the road that leads directly to God. 'What it means to be a Sufi,' he wrote in *Aiyuha alWalad*, 'is to live unceasingly in union with God and at peace with all people.' So he concluded in *Ihya 'Ulum udDin* 4:

Those who know that what belongs to God is enduring, and that the blessedness of that other life is finer and more permanent than the delights of this life (just as jewels are finer and more lasting than snow) yearn to change this life for the other. No one with a handful of snow would hesitate to change it for jewels and pearls. This world is like snow beneath the sun: it goes on melting until it is completely gone, whereas the life to come is a precious jewel which cannot ever vanish.

BIBLIOGRAPHY NUMBERS 20, 489, 688, 927

SUFIS

Sufis are Muslims who seek to follow Sharia and on that basis to devote themselves completely to God. The origin of the name is uncertain though it is often understood to have come from the Arabic word meaning 'wool' because of the humble clothing they wore. This was in contrast to the splendid lifestyles of many Muslims as the empires of Islam spread rapidly from the Atlantic to China. The Sufis believed that the pleasures of this world are as nothing compared with the delight of serving God:

> Beware of this world with all its deceit: it is like a snake, smooth
> to the touch, but deadly in its poison. This world has in itself no
> particular weight or worth with God. It is so slight that it weighs
> with him less than a pebble or a speck of dust. As the Word ['Isa/
> Jesus] used to say, 'My daily bread is hunger, my emblem is fear,
> my clothing is wool, my mount is my foot, my lantern is the moon,
> my fire is the sun, my food is whatever the earth brings forth for the
> animals and cattle; by nightfall I have acquired nothing, but there
> is no one richer than I.'

That was written by Hasan of Basra (642–728) in a letter to the Caliph, Umar II. Hasan was a key figure in establishing and extending the Sufi way, insisting that true devotion must not be for the sake of gaining heaven or of avoiding hell, but only for the sake of God. Later Sufis called him 'the third master' after Muhammad and Ali, the founder of *'ilm ulqulub*, 'the science of hearts'.

Early Sufis were too committed to God to spend time writing texts, but their teaching (especially their sermons) and their prayers were remembered, and many stories were told about them. Among the most remarkable was Rabia alAdawiya (*c.*713–801) who loved creation as a gift from God. Once when Hasan visited her he found her surrounded by deer and other animals, but when he approached they all ran off. He asked her why. She answered abruptly, 'Because you eat them.' She once prayed:

> O God, whatever you have set aside for me from the things of this world, give to your enemies; and whatever you have set aside for me from the things of the world to come, give to your friends; for you and you alone are more than enough for me.

SUFI ORDERS

Gradually Sufis began to organise themselves in schools or traditions known as *turuq* (sing., *tariqa*, 'way') in order that the teachings and above all the practices of the Sufi way could be preserved and transmitted. The Orders were very different from each other, but each of them traced a chain of transmission going back to Muhammad himself, often through Hasan. The chain is known as *silsilah* and in many Orders it forms an important part of ritual and prayer.

The Orders rapidly multiplied in number until, by the end of the nineteenth century, more than half of all Muslim men were attached to one. Eventually the major Orders subdivided into many smaller groups, particularly as they spread to all parts of the world. Not surprisingly, more emphasis began to be placed on written texts so that the teachings, practices and rituals could be well known. In each of the Orders the founding documents became sacred texts because they are, with Sharia, the guide to God. Their 'sacredness' is derived from the connection through Muhammad to the Quran.

Since there are so many Sufi Orders, it is not surprising that the number of sacred texts is correspondingly large. Here it is possible to indicate only a few of the different kinds of text that were produced in some of the major Orders:

◆ The Qadiriyya were founded by Abd alQadir Jilani (1077–1166) who emphasised the importance of Sharia and of 'sober Sufism', not seeking ecstatic states. God is the presence before whom people can learn to live and from whom each moment of life is then transformed. His major work is *AlGhunya liTalibi Tariq alHaqq* ('That Which Suffices for the Seekers of the Way of Truth').

◆ The Chishtiyya (from Chisht in Afghanistan) were founded by Khwajah Mu'in adDin Hasan (*c*.1141–1236) who stressed the importance of austerity and ascetic poverty, recognising that our good actions come, not from ourselves, but from the teaching of the *pir* (guide) and the prompting of God. The texts

(Right) The ending of *The Gospel according to John* in Codex Sinaiticus, a fourth-century manuscript of the New Testament and part of the Old Testament. The text here begins at ch.21.1b.

(Below left) An illuminated initial from *The Book of Kells* (p. 64), showing the opening of *The Gospel according to Mark*: INI TI UM EVAN GE LII IHU XPI.

(Below right) A page of the Eusebian Canons in *The Book of Kells* in which an attempt is made to show parallels between the Gospels: for modern Synoptic parallels, see p. 55.

Polyglot (Gk, 'many tongues/languages') Bibles gather versions of the Bible in different languages. Walton's Polyglot (with seven languages plus translations) was a key step toward modern Biblical study.

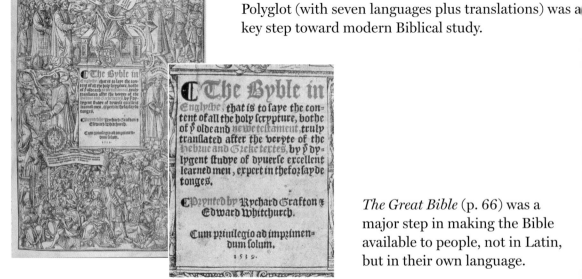

The Great Bible (p. 66) was a major step in making the Bible available to people, not in Latin, but in their own language.

Islamic calligraphy displayed in a wall hanging, with words, embroidered in gold thread, from the Yasin Sura of the Quran (s.36), so called from the abbreviated letters *ya* and *sin* of its opening verse.

This example of Kufic script contains the last two verses of sura 38 ('In truth this is nothing other than a reminder [*dhikr*] to the worlds, and you will know its true message before long'), the title of sura 39 and the invocation, 'In the name of God, the merciful Lord of mercy.'

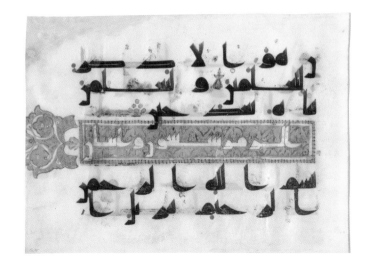

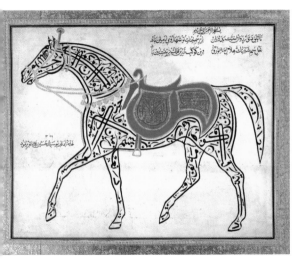

Muslim calligraphers took delight in creating forms of animals and birds (zoomorphic calligraphy) as in this example of a Shi'ite prayer composed by Sayid Husain Ali, 1848.

Shaykh Zadeh's illustration of a poem in *The Diwan of Hafiz* (p. 154),
where Hafiz denounces the hypocritical difference between preaching
and practice in the Mosque.

in this Order are biographies (e.g., *Siyar alAwliya*, 'The Lives of the Friends of God' by Mir Khwurd, fourteenth century), records of teaching sessions and conversations (*Malfuzat*) and letters (*Maktubat*).

◆ The Kubrawiyya were founded by Najm adDin Kubra (d.1221) who was known as 'the Maker of the Friends of God' (*wali tarash*) and who based his teaching on visionary experiences of God. He described these in *Fawa'ih alJamal wa Fawatih alJalal*, 'Scents of Beauty and Anticipations of Majesty', in which he also wrote a guide on the theory and practice of the Sufi way.

◆ The Shadhiliyya were founded by Abu 'lHasan ashShadhili (1197–1258) who wrote, not books, but litanies of prayer (*ahzab*, sing., *hizb*) based on sections of the Quran. These have been widely used by Muslims, including those who do not belong to the Order. They can be found in popular prayer manuals, some parts of which were translated by Constance Padwick in *Muslim Devotions*.

◆ The Naqshbandi were founded by Khwaja Baha adDin Muhammad Naqshband (1317–89) who insisted on people obeying strictly the laws of Sharia. The Order was reorganised by Shaykh Ahmad Sirhindi (1563–1625) who rejected strongly the attempts being made by a Muslim ruler, Akbar, to unify the religions of India. Sirhindi also argued against any Muslim philosophy (especially that of Ibn Arabi) that subverted Quran and Sharia. That work was taken further by Shah Wali Allah (1703–62) whose *Hujjat Allah alBaligha*, seeking to conserve traditional Islam, became a key text for the Order.

◆ The Nimatullahi were founded by Shah Nimat Allah (d.1431) who believed that the Sufi way to God is not limited to elite specialists but is open to people working in the world (he was himself a farmer). He put his teaching into poetry gathered in his *Diwan*.

Shah Nimat Allah was not alone in seeing that Sufi devotion and experience can be best expressed in poetry. It led to the inspiration of the great poets of Persia.

📖 BIBLIOGRAPHY NUMBERS 28, 430, 435, 477, 572, 784, 859, 989

THE POETS OF PERSIA

FARID, SA‘DI, HAFIZ, JAMI, RUMI

The Sufi poetry of Persia was an extraordinary achievement. It has been read and treasured far beyond the borders of Persia and far beyond the boundaries of Islam. It has been said often that the sound and balance of the Persian simply cannot be translated, but attempts at translation have nevertheless made the work of many of these poets a part of the shared spiritual inheritance of the world. In his *Persian Sufi Poetry*, de Brujin shows how they worked within 'a highly formalised artistic tradition', applying 'certain unchangeable rules' (p. 3), and yet also how those constraints set them free to explore the languages of love as the key to understanding the love of God.

Among the many poets who were regarded as guides on the way to God, some are particularly revered:

◆ Farid udDin Attar (twelfth century) is said to have written 114 works corresponding to the number of Suras in the Quran. Nothing like that many have survived, but he was certainly prolific. His opponents accused him of having 'verbal diarrhoea' (*bisyar-guy*), to which he replied that he only wrote much because God had entrusted to him so much truth. His major and enduring work is *Mantiq atTayr*, 'The Conference of the Birds', an ingenious allegory of the Sufi quest for God. It has been made accessible in a superb translation by Darbandi and Davis.

◆ Sa‘di (*c.*1184–1296) worked hard to perfect the writing of Persian so that it might at least reflect the perfect language of Arabic. His *Gulistan* is a prose work containing much of his poetry.

◆ Shams udDin Muhammad Hafiz (d.1389) is admired as the most perfect of the Persian poets. He is called *lisan alghaib*, 'the voice of hidden things', and *tarjuman alasrar*, 'the interpreter of heavenly mysteries'. On his tomb is carved one of his verses:

Old though I am, hold me to yourself
that at the wakening dawn I, young once more
from your warming touch on my cheek
will rise – rise up! Then let my eyes
widen with delight at your beauty.
You are the end, the goal to which we all press on,
you, the One whom, idols dissolved, Hafiz adores:
your face, toward him turned, bids him
from world and life come forth and rise, rise up.

◆ Abd arRahman Jami (1414–92) has been called *Khatam ashShu'ra*, 'the Seal of the Poets' (cf., Muhammad as the Seal of the Prophets, p. 132). He belonged to the Naqshbandi Order (p. 153) and wrote many works and individual poems, some of which are collected in his *Diwan*.

RUMI

Of all the Sufi poets, the best known, at least to the outside world, is Rumi (Jalal udDin Muhammad Balkhi, 1207–73) who succeeded his father in 1231 as a Sufi teacher in Konya in Southern Turkey, an area known, from an earlier occupation, as Rum (Rome), hence his name. During his life he wrote nearly 6,000 shorter poems and two major works, *Mathnawi* and *Divan-i-Shams-i-Tabrizi*. The versions here are taken from Harvey, *Light Upon Light: Inspirations from Rumi*.

By 1244, his fame had spread and people flocked to him for instruction. In that year, he met Shams-i-Tabrizi (Sun of Tabriz), and his life was blown apart. Shams was a famous Sufi who had abandoned books and teachers in order to cling, in utter devotion, to God alone (p. 3):

All theologies are straws His Sun burns to dust;
Knowing takes you to the Threshold, but not through the Door.
Nothing can teach you if you don't unlearn everything
How learned I was, before Revelation made me dumb!

Shams had asked God to send him to someone who would understand and practise this total love, and God sent him to Rumi. Shams arrived in Konya in 1244, and Rumi immediately recognised God in him. Through the person of Shams, he fell in love with God totally and without reserve (p. 181).

Love is here like the blood in my veins and skin
He has annihilated me and filled me only with Him

His fire has penetrated all the atoms of my body
Of 'me' only my name remains; the rest is Him.

Rumi saw God in all aspects of the world as they point beyond themselves to the perfection of God (p. 209):

O incomparable Giver of Life, cut Reason loose at last!
Let it wander grey-eyed from vanity to vanity.
Shatter open my skull, pour in it the wine of madness!
Let me be mad, as mad as You, mad with You, with us.
Beyond the sanity of fools is a burning desert
Where Your Sun is whirling in every atom; drag me there,
Beloved, drag me there, let me roast in Perfection!

Rumi was so immersed in God through Shams that his pupils became jealous and drove Shams away. The experience of absence made Rumi almost lose his mind. But Shams returned, and once more they lived in a communion of love, praying, dancing, chanting together in a union with God (p. 182).

I was snow, I melted in your rays
The earth drank me: mist now, and pure spirit,
I climb back to the Sun.

In 1247, there was a knock at the door. Shams stood up and said, 'It is time. I am going. I am called to my death.' Rumi was grief-stricken, but the parting, he realised, was necessary. He spent the rest of his life trying to share in words with others the ecstasy of that enduring and unending love of God. In addition to his poetry he wrote a prose work of advice on spiritual life, much of it sharp and concise: 'If you look in the mirror and see an ugly face, you are not going to improve matters by smashing the mirror with your fist.'

Rumi summarised his life by saying, 'My religion is to live through love.' He died as the sun set on 17 December 1273. He said, 'My death is my wedding with eternity' (p. 3):

If you are seeking, seek us with joy
For we live in the kingdom of joy.
Do not give your heart to anything else
But to the love of those who are clear joy,
Do not stray into the neighbourhood of despair.

For there are hopes: they are real, they exist –
Do not go in the direction of darkness –
I tell you: suns exist.

BIBLIOGRAPHY NUMBERS 10, 41, 43–9, 57, 159, 262, 420, 440, 503, 632, 807, 822, 845, 885, 920, 1042

4

ZOROASTRIANS
AND PARSIS

ZOROASTRIANS AND PARSIS TEXTS: KEY DATES

BCE

c.*6000 (trad.)* Zarathustra

c.*1700–600* Birth of Zarathustra

c.*1700–600* *Yasna, Gathas*

549–331 Achaemenid/Persian empire

331 Alexander defeats Darius III

331–26 Conquest of Achaemenids

3rd cent. Rise of the Parthians

2nd cent. BCE–224CE Parthian empire

CE

224–642 Sasanian empire

3rd cent. Forming of Zoroastrian 'Canon'; Magi formalise *Avesta*

3rd cent. Development of Zurvan: *Bundahishn, Dadistani Menogi Khrad*

636 Arab Muslim victory at Qadisiya

652 Muslims hold most of Iran; Zoroastrianism no longer official religion

10th cent. Zoroastrians migrate/flee from Iran to Gujarat

18th/19th cent. Parsis (Persians) spread in NW India esp. to Mumbai

Previous page: The Faravahar, a Zoroastrian symbol possibly associated with the *fravashi*, the preexistent soul in its union with Ahura Mazda.

ZARATHUSTRA

GATHAS, YASNA, AVESTA

The dates of Zarathustra (known also as Zoroaster) are uncertain. Greek authors guessed that he might have lived at around 6000 BCE, but more likely dates range from 1200 to 600 BCE. The major sacred text of the Zoroastrians is *Avesta*, possibly meaning 'The Injunction' (of Zarathustra). Only about a quarter of the original has survived, written in two different dialects of an otherwise unknown Iranian language, Old Avestan (closely related linguistically to the language of *Rigveda*, p. 170) and Young Avestan.

Among the Old Avestan texts are seventeen hymns known as *Gathas*. They are thought to have been composed by Zoroaster himself. They are part of a longer text known as *Yasna*. The *Gathas* are *Yasna* 28–34, 43–51, 53. They are by no means easy to understand or translate since they contain words otherwise unknown. Nevertheless, they give some indication of Zoroaster's teaching and belief. He called himself *zaotar*, or priest, and also *manthran* (one who is able to compose or speak a *manthra*; cf. Sanskrit *mantra*, p. 168), and *vaedemna*, one who has insight or knowledge.

According to tradition, Zoroaster was thirty when he saw a vision of Ahura Mazda (the Wise Lord). During a ritual ceremony, he went to fetch water from the river. As he returned in a state of ritual purity, he saw on the bank a shining Being who led Zoroaster into the presence of Ahura Mazda and six other Beings whose light was so intense that he could not see even his own shadow on the ground. They are the Seven Holy Beings possessing sacred power (*spenta*) to create and to help those in need. Zoroaster proclaimed (*Yasna* 43):

> I recognised you, Mazda Ahura, as holy and divine. I saw you as the
> Beginning and the Everlasting when life began. At that time you
> commanded a reward for thoughts, words and deeds that are good,
> and you ordained through your wisdom that the wicked will receive

an evil consequence, and that the good will receive the consequence of their goodness. So it will be until the end of time.

The *Gathas* refer to other visions which gave to Zoroaster his vocation to live in the service of Ahura Mazda ('I know, my Lord, that I was set apart from the beginning to be yours for the performing of this immense work', *Yasna* 44.11) and to teach others ('While I have strength and vigour I will teach people to seek what is right and just', *Yasna* 28.4).

Ahura Mazda is the uncreated source of all creation, the unproduced Producer of all that is, including the other Holy Beings. In that case it would seem obvious that everything in creation should be a manifestation of that complete and eternal goodness of Ahura Mazda. Yet in fact and in experience it is obvious that there is much in the created order that is not good. In a further vision, Zoroaster saw the reason for that experience. He saw Angra Mainyu, the hostile Being, who is also eternal. As the great Adversary of Ahura Mazda he seeks only to defeat and destroy the good (*Yasna* 30.3f.):

> In the beginning the two Beings appeared in conflict with each
> other. They are two, good and evil in thought, word and deed . . .
> From the conflict between them life and not-life were created. In
> the end the worst consequence will be for those who pursue evil,
> and the best consequence will be for those who pursue whatever is
> right and just.

Why, then, did Ahura Mazda bring into being this creation in which the experience of pain and evil is unremitting and universal? In Zoroaster's belief, Ahura Mazda created a perfect universe knowing that Angra Mainyu would be unable to resist the temptation to destroy it – that he would, in other words, 'go about as a roaring lion seeking whom he might destroy'. This means that this creation is a battleground in which Angra Mainyu is drawn into a final conflict that Ahura Mazda knows he will in the end win.

Individuals are a part of this conflict. The battle between good and evil rages in every life, and the teaching and rituals of Zoroastrianism are designed to help individuals in the conflict. This means that Zoroastrianism is a deeply moral religion, not least because the moral struggle which all people experience is not a matter that concerns individuals in isolation. It is a part of the entire cosmic battle between good and evil, in which individuals in their own moral struggle contribute to the final triumph of the good.

During the period of the Parthian empire (second century BCE–third century CE), the magi (the ritual experts who according to *Matthew* appeared at the birth of Jesus) gathered together many of the oral traditions and written texts of the Zoroastrians into a more organised form of *Avesta* and of the alphabet in which it was written.

When the Sasanians from south-west Persia overthrew the Parthians in the third century CE, they created an official version of Zoroastrianism in order to legitimise their rule. This included the transcribing of the official Zoroastrian Canon into twenty-one groups (*nasks*) corresponding to the twenty-one words of the prayer known as Ahunvar, the fundamental prayer taught to every Zoroastrian child:

> Ahura Mazda is the Lord for whom I long, the One who judges
> according to what is right and just, the One who creates deeds of
> good purpose and of life. His is the kingdom, his the power to care
> for those who are humbly committed to him.

The twenty-one *nasks* are then divided into three groups of seven. In the first group are the *Gathas* and other works associated with them; in the second are works of reflection and inquiry; in the third are works containing instructions for rituals and more general laws.

This new form of Zoroastrianism (known as Zurvan from its emphasis on Time as the agent of change and of events in history) produced its own texts that came to be revered as sacred. Notable among them are *Bundahishn* ('Creation', also known as *Zand-Agahih*, 'Knowledge of Zand', Zand being commentary on *Avesta*), and *Dadistani Menogi Khrad*, 'Judgements of the Spirit of Wisdom', a guide to the meaning and practices of Zoroastrianism.

The Muslim invasion of Persia put an end to more than a thousand years of Zoroastrianism in that area, but Zoroastrians survived in India as Parsis, the people from Persia.

📖 BIBLIOGRAPHY NUMBERS 141, 142, 164, 361, 765

In *Zoroastrians*, Mary Boyce observed (p. 230) of the *Gathas*, 'There is no standard translation in any language,' though there are now translations on the Internet. There are some translations of Zoroastrian texts in Sacred Books of the East; otherwise English versions are often translations from other European languages. Note, however, Gershevitch, Insler.

5

INDIA

INDIAN TEXTS: KEY DATES

BCE

c.*2000–1000* Vedas

c.*1000–700* Brahmanas

c.*800–600* Aranyakas

8th cent. → Early Upanishads

c.*600* → Kalpasutras, Dharmasutras, Dharmashastras

c.*500* Yaska

c.*400* → Smartasutras

c.*400* → *Mahabharata* formed

c.*4th cent.* → *Ramayana* formed

c.*2nd cent.?* *Bhagavadgita*

c.*1st cent.*BCE–*2nd cent.*CE Badarayana/Vedavyasa, *Vedanta Sutra*

c.*1st cent.*BCE–*2nd cent.*CE Patanjali, *Yoga Sutras*

CE

c.*100–300* *Manusmriti* compiled

c.*320–c.500* Gupta dynasty, Puranas compiled

6th–9th cent. Alvars: Nammalvar

6th–9th cent. Nayanars: Appar, Campantar, Cuntarar, Manikkavacakar

7th cent. → Practice of Bhakti developed

c.*788–820* Shankara

c.*10th cent.* *Bhagavata Purana*

11th/12th cent. Ramanuja

12th cent. Jayadeva, *Gitagovinda*

12th cent.? *Devi Bhagavata Purana*

15th cent. Kabir, *Bijak*, *Pañcavani*

16th cent. Mirabai

16th cent. Krishnadasa Kaviraja, *Govindalilamrita*

1869–1948 Mahatma Gandhi

1888–1975 Radhakrishnan

Previous page: Durga slaying the demon buffalo, Mahisa, illustrating the power of the Feminine in Indian religion: see p. 203.

THE VEDAS

Indian religion is often referred to as 'Hinduism' and its followers are called 'Hindus'. The names, however, are misleading if they give the impression of a single system of belief. Indian religion is more like a large family of related religions. The different members have much in common. Many of them share basic and fundamental sacred texts, though in the case of India it is important to remember that the early 'texts' are far more likely to have been passed on by oral tradition than in writing or, until recently, in printing (on the importance of oral tradition in India, see further, pp. 183). The different members of the family each have their own histories and they have produced sacred texts of their own. Some members of the family have actually 'left home' and have become separate religions, including Jains, Buddhists and Sikhs.

Even among those who have remained in some relationship with each other, there are many different ways of practice and belief to help people to move towards liberation (*moksha*) from the round of rebirth (*samsara*) – for example, Yoga (p. 177), Tantra (pp. 201ff.) and Bhakti (pp. 191–200). In Indian religions there is a deeply held belief in rebirth or reappearance from one life to another. It may be necessary to be reborn as many as 84,000,000 times before reaching the goal, so the coexistence of different ways to proceed during any particular life makes sense.

The basic texts in Indian religion are known collectively as the Veda (from the word *vid*, 'knowledge'). In Indian belief, the Vedas are *apaurusheya*, 'not made by humans'. They have always existed: they are uncreated and indeed eternal. Where a Christian Gospel (*According to St John*) begins, 'In the beginning was the Word', Indian belief begins further back, 'In the beginning was the Sound'. From the undifferentiated Sound or reverberation all things take form or shape, including the sacred texts – as one of those texts puts it (*Brihadaranyaka Upanishad* 2.4.10; the names and works are explained later):

> As smoke pours forth when a fire is lit from damp wood, so also
> pour forth *Rig Veda, Yajur Veda, Sama Veda, Atharvangirasa,*
> Epics, Puranas, Knowledge [*vidya*], Upanishads, Shlokas, Sutras,
> explanations and commentaries: from this One all these are
> breathed out.

It is still possible to hear the primordial Sound in chants closely connected originally with the ritual and known as mantras, especially AUM (or OM), the primordial Sound and the seed of all other mantras. The Vedas articulate the Sound. They were first discovered (not composed) by Rishis who saw them in their mind's eye (the name itself means 'one who sees') and who heard them. Since the Vedas were heard and not originally written down, and since also they were passed on orally from person to person and were thus heard rather than read, they are known, along with other texts attached to them, as Shruti ('heard').

According to Yaska, a writer (*c.*500 BCE) who was interested in grammar and words, the Rishis had a special gift: when that gift was lost in subsequent generations the Vedas had to be recited, then written down (*Nirukta* 1.20 in Gonda, 1975, p. 33):

> The seers had direct intuitive insight. By oral instructions they
> handed down the hymns to later generations who were destitute
> of this insight. The later generations, declining in [power of] oral
> communication, repeated [compiled] this work, the Veda, and
> the auxiliary Vedic treatises from memory, in order to convey their
> meaning.

Shruti, 'the heard', therefore means in effect 'revelation', the ultimate authority, the infallible source of all truth. Indeed, some Indians regard as members of 'the family' (i.e., as Hindus) only those who accept Veda as revelation – though it is not necessarily *divine* revelation since there are Hindus who believe that Sound articulates and brings into being gods and goddesses along with everything else.

It is not certain when the Vedas were first written down, but it seems likely that it was during the period from 2000 to 1000 BCE. Vedic religion was based on sacrifice and ritual, to which the Vedas are closely related in different ways. Some record hymns and chants used on ritual occasions, others give instructions on what has to be done, while others offer explanations and interpretations of what the sacrifices mean.

The Deities (gods and goddesses) to whom sacrifices are offered are closely related to the world in which people lived at that time, and in particular to the natural phenomena that might help or hinder their survival. Thus Indra, the god of the heavens, commands the powers of nature with which he can help those who approach him through sacrifice. Ushas is praised for bringing the dawn with the light and warmth of the sun, as in *Rig Veda* 7.77 (trans. Panikkar, p. 169):

> Dawn comes shining
>   like a Lady of Light,
> stirring to life all creatures.
>   Now it is time
>   to kindle the Fire.
> The light of Dawn scatters the shadows.
>
> Her faced turned toward
>   this far-flung world,
> she rises, enwrapped in bright garments.
>   Shining with gold,
>   with rays of light bedecked,
> she sends forth the world on its course.

Of particular importance was Agni, the god of fire (cf. Latin *ignis*). Quite apart from the importance of fire in the home (and in India the fire rituals associated with the home are of enduring importance), it is fire, Agni, who carries up in smoke the offerings of sacrifice when they are burned in fire. The first hymn in *Rig Veda* celebrates Agni:

> It is Agni I worship – the performer of ritual, the mediator of the
> sacrifice, the one who bestows blessing. May Agni, worshipped by
> Rishis in the past and now, lead the gods here. Through Agni may
> our wealth be increased day by day with well-being and with many
> heroic sons. O Agni, the sacrifice with its ritual that you embrace
> on every side goes indeed to the gods . . . O Agni, be open to our
> approach as a father is to his son: join us for our well-being.

Vedic texts fall into two main categories: Samhitas ('collections', verses used in ritual and liturgy) and Brahmanas (commentaries mainly in prose, giving the rules for the rituals and explaining their meaning).

There are three main Samhitas, to which a fourth is usually added:

1   *Rig Veda* contains 1,028 hymns (*suktas*) in ten Mandalas or Books: 1–8 are
    associated with particular Rishis; Book 9 contains hymns to Soma; Book 10
    contains hymns addressed to a range of questions, including speculations on
    the origins of the universe, as in 10.29:

>   At that time there was neither non-existence nor existence;
>   neither the worlds below nor the sky beyond. What moved? And
>   where? For whose delight? Was there water unfathomably deep?
>   At that time there was neither death nor immortality, nothing
>   distinguishable between night and day. The One breathed without
>   breath in its own being [aseity]. Beside that nothing existed . . .
>   So who knows, who can tell, whence all this came into being? . . .
>   Where did this creation come from? Perhaps it formed itself or
>   perhaps not. The One who sees it all from the highest heaven, only
>   he knows. Or he does not know.

2   *Yajur Veda* contains short sentences and verses used in ritual: it exists in two
    versions known as the Black and the White.

3   *Sama Veda* is a book of hymns or songs (*saman*) based on *Rig Veda* with
    guidance on how to recite them.

4   *Atharva Veda* contains popular and folk material to help people cope with
    life.

The Brahmanas (manuals and explanations for the brahmans who officiate at
the rituals) are attached to the Vedas, and to many of the Brahmanas are attached
texts known as Aranyakas, ('forest texts', so called because they may have come
from world-renouncers of the kind that produced Jains and Buddhists). The
Aranyakas are mainly reflections on the inner meaning of the rituals, and they
act as a bridge to another large group of texts, the Upanishads: on these, see
pp. 171–4.

Originally, each of the four Vedas had attached to it a Brahmana, Aranyaka
and Upanishad, but not all of these have survived. Together these texts make up
Shruti, revelation, and they are the fundamental texts of Indian religion.

BIBLIOGRAPHY NUMBERS 37, 40, 146, 271, 386, 513, 618, 733, 897,
976

UPANISHADS
AND AGAMAS

The Upanishads are works in prose and poetry that continue the work of the Aranyakas in interpreting and explaining the meaning of the Vedic earlier ritual. One of the earliest Upanishads is actually called *Brihadaranyaka Upanishad*, the Great Aranyaka Upanishad, and a further seven of the early Upanishads are attached to their own Aranyaka, each of which is in turn attached to a Brahmana.

The name Upanishad is usually thought to come from *sad* ('sit down', though also 'destroy' or 'loosen') + *upa* ('near') + *ni* ('devotedly'). If that is so, the name suggests pupils or students sitting near a teacher in order to receive instruction, and the word came to mean any teaching about the true nature of Reality restricted to qualified students – in other words, privileged or esoteric teaching. In contrast, though, Shankara (*c.*788–820, perhaps earlier?), a major philosopher and commentator on the Upanishads, took *sad* in the sense of 'destroy' and understood the name to mean 'that which destroys ignorance'.

Many Upanishads were composed, and they continued to be written until at least the seventeenth century CE. The most authoritative, however, are the early Upanishads, dating from about the 8th century BCE onward. They are considered part of revelation (Veda) and are therefore also known collectively as Vedanta, the end or culmination of the Veda. The later Upanishads are more likely to be classed among the Agamas ('that which has been passed down'): Agamas, as the name suggests, are believed to be extremely ancient, and they comprise the sacred texts of particular groups. There are thus 108 Agamas of the Vaishnavites (followers of the god Vishnu), 28 of the Shaivites (followers of Shiva) and 77 of the Shaktas (devotees of Goddess and her power; these Agamas are also known as Tantras).

There is no universally agreed 'Canon' or list of the early Upanishads. The most widely accepted list is in *Muktika Upanishad* ('Deliverance') which names 108;

Shankara (the major philosopher of Advaita Vedanta: see p. 197) commented on roughly twelve (that number is inexact because there is uncertainty about whether he wrote some of the works attributed to him); S. Radhakrishnan, a President of India (1962–7) and an influential interpreter of Indian thought, translated and commented on eighteen; R. E. Hume translated thirteen. Major early Upanishads are *Aitareya, Brihadaranyaka, Chandogya, Isha, Katha, Kaushitaki, Kena, Mahanarayaniya, Maitri, Mandukya, Prashna, Shvetashtavara, Taittriya.* The exact dates of these are not known, but they come from roughly the eighth century BCE onward.

It is impossible to summarise the contents of the Upanishads because they deal with many topics in an unsystematic way. However, together they established major themes of profound importance in subsequent Indian religion – above all the meaning of Brahman as the supreme and only Reality.

Thus in *Brihadaranyaka Upanishad* (3.9.1) a revered teacher of the time, Yajñavalkya, is asked how many deities there are – there are many in the Vedas alone! He answered that there are 3,306, the number invoked in a hymn addressed to all the gods. His questioner persisted: 'Yes, but how many gods are there?' Yajñavalkya replied, ' Thirty-three.' 'Yes, but how many gods are there?' Yajñavalkya answered, 'Six.' 'Yes, but how many gods are there?' 'Two.' 'Yes, but how many gods are there?' 'One' . . . 'Which is the one God?' 'The Breath. He is Brahman. They call him That [*tat*].'

BRAHMAN AND ATMAN

The word *brahman* means, basically, 'to grow great', 'to increase', 'to strengthen', and may originally have referred to the power generated by sacrifices, rituals and prayers. From its connection with ritual power, *brahman* was applied also to those in charge of it – or, in other words, the brahmans/brahmins. But when the Aranyakas and the Upanishads began to look for the inner meaning of the rituals, they emphasised the quest, not for ritual power, but for insight and knowledge of a kind that will lead people to gain release (*moksha*) from the otherwise unending process of rebirth (*samsara*).

As a result, in *Shatapata Brahmana,* and then in the Upanishads, the word Brahman took on a different meaning. Brahman is the *source* of power, the impersonal, Supreme One that alone truly is, creating, supporting and ruling the entire universe. Through this creating and sustaining power Brahman pervades the whole universe – and some Indians believe that the universe is the 'body' through which Brahman becomes manifest. *Mundaka Upanishad* affirms it in these words (2.1.1–3):

That [Brahman] is Truth. Just as from a blazing fire myriads of sparks with the same nature of fire pour forth, even so, dear friend, innumerable beings are born from the Unchanging, and into the same they return.

Supreme, formless is this Being. He is without and within, unborn, without breath or mind, pure, transcending the highest height.

From him are born life, mind, the senses, wind, light, water and earth that gives support to all.

This means that within humans Brahman is present as *atman*, the inner self or soul. *Atman* is now entangled in the material body and world, and that is why rebirth continues until its true nature as 'not other than Brahman' is recognised and recovered. What the Upanishads offer is the teaching and the insight that will lead to the recognition of what has always been the truth: that 'I' am already (and always have been) nothing other than Brahman: *atman* is identical with Brahman. This is summed up in the Upanishads in the Mahavakyas (Great Sayings of the Upanishads and *Bhagavadgita*), 'You are That' (*tat-tvam-asi*), 'I am Brahman', 'All this is Brahman', 'This Self is Brahman', 'Pure Consciousness is Brahman'.

To say that *atman*, the true inner nature of a human being, is identical with Brahman is to say immediately that *atman* is immortal, since Brahman is the unproduced and pre-existing Producer of everything that is. That is a major change from early Vedic religion when it was believed that there is no substantial or worthwhile life after death. In the Upanishads, in contrast, the obvious point is made that if Brahman cannot die, the human *atman* cannot die either.

But while *atman* remains entangled in the body as *jiva* (the self remaining in ignorance), it is bound to be reborn. The forms in which that rebirth may occur are immensely varied (as much animal, for example, as human). The form of rebirth depends on the way in which a person lives and behaves now. According to the Upanishads, there is a moral law in the universe, known as *karma*, with outcomes as inevitable as the laws of nature: for someone who steps off a roof, the natural law of gravity leads inevitably to a fall. For someone who behaves badly, the law of *karma* leads inevitably to an appropriate rebirth: 'Those who act well in this life will come quickly to a good womb, . . . Those who act wrongly will come to an evil womb' (*Chandogya Up.* 5.10.7).

The wise course, therefore, is to turn away from the compromises of this world and aim instead to return to Brahman. One should do this, according to

Mundaka Upanishad (2.2.3), much as one would take up a bow in order to aim an arrow at a target:

> Take as the bow the great weapon of the Upanishads, fix on it the arrow of pointed concentration, draw it back with the mind focused on the thought of That [Brahman], and, dear friend, hit the target of unalterable Brahman.
>
> The Pranava [the sound AUM] is the bow, *atman* is the arrow, Brahman is said to be that target. Shoot without faltering and like the arrow you will become one with the target.
>
> Know the One alone, the Self, from whom are woven heaven, earth and space, as also the mind and all the vital breaths. Abandon whatever else is said: this is the bridge to Immortality.

 BIBLIOGRAPHY NUMBERS **964**

SUTRAS

Badarayana's *Vedanta Sutra*, Patanjali's *Yoga Sutra*

The words gathered in Shruti ('revelation', p. 168) are the sacred and eternal truth now made manifest in the form of written texts. In addition to Shruti there is an even larger number of texts known as Smriti ('recollection'). They have authority, but their authority is derived from Shruti so to that extent they are secondary. Also, their boundary is fluid in the sense that no final or fixed decision has been made about their number or their content – in contrast to Jewish and Christian decisions about 'the Canon of Scripture' (pp. 29, 51).

The additional works in Smriti include Sutras, Puranas (see further p. 187), Epics (p. 183), the elaborations of Dharma (p. 179), Vedangas ('limbs of the Veda') and Upangas (additional 'limbs'). Vedangas and Upangas deal with most aspects of Indian life, from sacrifice and science to grammar and etymology, including therefore life in family and society. Those who follow the guidance and instructions of Smriti are known as Smartas, i.e., observant 'Hindus'.

The amount of material in Shruti and Smriti is enormous, and efforts were therefore made to condense and summarise at least parts of it. This resulted in the Sutras whose style is so condensed that they are by no means easy to understand, as Bhattacharji has summarised the point (p. 289):

> The extreme anxiety for brevity and condensation of the authors led
> to deleting verbs, pronouns, expletives and all dispensable adverbs
> and adjectives. The result is a terse, pithy, telegraphic language, at
> times almost impossible to decode without commentaries.

Because the Vedangas are written in this condensed Sutra style, they are also known as the Vedanga Sutras. Sutras, however, are not confined to the Vedangas. Of paramount importance among them is *Vedanta Sutra* which became a sacred text in its own right. It is also known as *Brahma Sutra*, attributed by some to Badarayana, by others to Vedavyasa. Its date is uncertain – perhaps some time between the first century BCE and the second century CE.

VEDANTA SUTRA

Vedanta Sutra consists of 555 verses in which an attempt is made to summarise the teaching of the Upanishads:

◆ The aim of human life is *moksha* (liberation from continuing rebirth).

◆ *Moksha* is effected by the direct knowledge of Brahman.

◆ The direct knowledge of Brahman stands alone and does not depend on ritual acts.

Vedanta Sutra was so highly regarded that it came to be included as part of Shruti. Even so, it is, on its own, almost unintelligible because it is so highly condensed. A literal translation of the opening verses gives an indication (1.1.1–4):

> Now therefore the desire to know Brahman.
> Origin of this from which.
> Shruti from being the source.
> That being the result of harmony.

It is obvious that *Vedanta Sutra* cannot be understood without guidance, so it is usually read in conjunction with later commentaries, above all those of the great philosophers Shankara, Ramanuja and Madhva. To give an example, Shankara's commentary on 1.1.1 begins in part:

> The word 'now' [*atha*] implies that the the desire to know
> Brahman [*Brahmajijñasa*] is a consequence of some antecedent
> condition . . . What, then, is the condition that must precede the
> inquiry into the nature of Brahman? The antecedent conditions
> are . . . : the discrimination between what is enduring and what
> is not enduring; complete detachment from the consequences
> of one's actions here and hereafter; attainment of tranquillity
> and self-restraint and the other virtues [listed elsewhere as faith,
> endurance, self-surrender and ability to be dispassionate]; the
> desire for *moksha* . . .

The word 'therefore' [atah] suggests the reason: because the
fire-offering and sacrifices [actions according to Dharma] are
said by the Veda to be impermanent and we are told [Taittiriya
Upanishad 2.1] that 'One who knows Brahman becomes Brahman',
it follows that the desire to know Brahman is the highest possible
aim ... The third word [Brahmajijñasa] indicates that Brahman is
the direct object of inquiry.

YOGA SUTRA

Equally revered among Sutras, but very different again, are the *Yoga Sutras*
of Patanjali (second century CE). Yoga ('yoking', 'joining') is often associated
outside India with techniques, exercises and postures that lead to calmness or
other new states of consciousness, but that is only a small part of Yoga and of no
importance on its own.

The point of Yoga is that it leads to a transformed understanding of the
cosmos and of human nature within it, and on the basis of that transformed
understanding it teaches the ways in which through practice one can attain
extraordinary powers (*siddhi*) and the state known as *samadhi*. The word
samadhi has various meanings, such as concentration, contemplation and
altered consciousness of a trancelike kind. In its strongest and ultimate meaning,
it is a state of complete and blissful stability far beyond the seething turmoil of
ideas and events.

Patanjali summarised existing practices and beliefs of Yoga into a single
and coherent system – and its original title was *Yoga Darshanam*. *Darshana*
means 'looking', and it is the word used for recognised 'viewpoints' or schools of
philosophy. Patanjali linked his system to the *darshana* (philosophy) known as
Samkhya, and for that reason it is also known as Samkhya-Yoga.

Samkhya sees the universe as a consequence of the interaction between
Purusha (the intelligent and conscious Self) and Prakriti (the unconscious
and material Potential of the natural order). In itself, Prakriti rests in a state of
perfect equibrilium. It unfolds or evolves into an 'out of balance' universe only
when Purusha is present to it, thus creating the duality of subject and object.
Purusha remains entangled in Prakriti so long as it forgets its true nature and
regards the mind or body as the true self. The union of the two is compared to
a lame man with good sight (Purusha) being carried on the shoulders of a blind
man with good legs (Prakriti).

The purpose of Yoga is to understand this process and its consequence. It
then offers practical ways that will help to disentangle the true Self, Purusha,

from Prakriti. The major difference between Patanjali and Samkhya is that, whereas Samkhya can understand the process of the universe without God (since the Deities are simply part of the unfolding process), Patanjali believed that God, the supreme Lord (Ishvara), is the inviting teacher leading to the goal.

Yoga Sutra is in three sections (*pada*):

1 *Samadhi Pada*, concentration, giving an overview of how Yoga begins and of where it leads.

2 *Sadhana Pada*, methods, including the Eight Steps of Yoga (2.29–32, 46, 48, 49; 3.1–3):

> The eight implementations [or 'accessories'] of Yoga are *yama* [restraint], *niyama* [observances], *asana* [posture], *pranayama* [breath-control], *pratyahara* [detachment], *dharana* [concentration], *dhyana* [being pure emptiness], *samadhayo* [*samadhi*].
>
> [The restraints are] non-violence [*ahimsa*], truthfulness, honesty, continence and abandoning possessions.
>
> They are the great vow, always applicable and not limited by class, place, time or circumstance.
>
> [The observances are] cleanliness, contentment, austerity, study [repeating *mantra*] and meditation on God . . .
>
> Posture is that state and position which can be sustained easily . . .
>
> From there, detachment from this or that obtains.
>
> When posture is maintained, breath-control is the regulation of breathing in and breathing out . . .
>
> Focus of the mind is concentration.
>
> Holding the understanding there completely is *dhyana*.
>
> That alone, enlightened wholly with its End, its own self gone, becomes the form of the contemplated [*samadhi*].

3 *Vibhuti Pada*, powers, culminating in *Kaivalya* (the condition of complete freedom), sometimes regarded as a distinct fourth section.

📖 BIBLIOGRAPHY NUMBERS 38, 64, 145, 619, 756, 831, 975, 1040

DHARMASUTRAS AND DHARMASHASTRAS

MANUSMRITI

Many Sutras deal, not with Vedanta or Yoga, but with the practical details of everyday life: they summarise what is known as Dharma, the ways in which people should act and behave appropriately. The word 'Dharma' comes from the root *dhr* which underlies words meaning 'support', 'hold', 'sustain' and 'protect'. It is closely related to a word *rta* in early Vedic texts which refers to the way in which the cosmos is sustained by consistent law and order. Dharma is the translation into human life and society of the fundamental and natural way that all things are meant to follow. That is why Indians call their own religion *sanatana dharma*, everlasting Dharma. Dharma can thus be understood as 'appropriate behaviour'.

DHARMA TEXTS

The Dharmasutras and all the other extensive Dharma texts fill in the detail of what the appropriate behaviour is in any of the many different circumstances of life. It thus becomes a guide to what is ethically and morally right.

Dharmasutras are gathered in Kalpa (Action) Sutras which are divided into two main categories, Shrautasutras and Smartasutras (*shrauta* derived from Shruti, *smarta* from Smriti, the two forms of sacred text: see p. 175). Shrautasutras gather instruction on rituals mentioned in the early Vedic texts (for an example, see Ranade), while Smartasutras deal with everyday life. Smartasutras are divided into two categories: Grihyasutras focus on rituals relating to domestic life, including initiation and marriage, and Dharmasutras deal with the basic rules of individual and social life, including instruction on politics, government, criminal law and the like. Kalpasutras are too numerous to list: for a summary of major texts, see Bhattachari, pp. 305–67.

The Dharmasutras were then developed further in works known as Dharmashastras (the numbers vary from eighteen to thirty-six). They resemble Codes of Law and include *Manusmriti* (see below). They in turn were organised more systematically in works known as Dharmanibandhas (see diagram below). Dates are uncertain, but it seems likely that the earliest Kalpasutras were being produced from about 600 BCE onward, with Smartasutras coming from about 400 BCE to 200 CE.

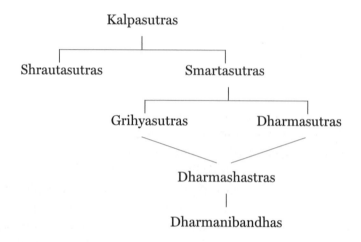

Although texts like the Upanishads are better known outside India, the Dharma texts are of greater practical importance inside India because they provide a detailed map of the right – and rewarded – way to live. The point of the word 'rewarded' is that Dharma is closely linked to *karma* (p. 173), the dispassionate natural law in the moral world that produces outcomes commensurate with good or evil acts. *Karma* is not in itself reward and punishment: it is consequence that cannot be evaded.

GOALS OF LIFE

Dharma texts lay out the ways in which one can be sure that one has acted appropriately, whether as an individual or in the organisation and government of society. In broadest possible terms, Dharma envisages four goals that are worth aiming for in this life – bearing in mind that there may be many other lives yet to come. The four goals are called *purushartha*. The first three (known as *trivarga*) relate to this life, the fourth relates to the goal that lies beyond rebirth. They are:

1 *Dharma* (appropriate behaviour in all circumstances).

2 *Artha* (prosperity).

3 *Kama* (fulfilment of physical and sexual needs).

4 *Moksha* (release, the final goal of all).

Any of the *trivargas* can legitimately be pursued so long as the fourth, *moksha*, is always the final aim, but ideally they should be held in balance, as an early text, *Manusmriti* 2.224, makes clear:

> There are those who say that the highest aim is *dharma* and *artha*, others that it is *kama* and *artha*, others that it is *dharma* alone or *artha* alone, but in truth it lies in the balance of all three.

It is envisaged in Dharma that people will move towards those goals through four stages in their lives: *brahmacarya*, a student receiving instruction; *grihasta*, a householder setting up family, *vanaprastha*, a 'forest-dweller', one who withdraws from the world; and *samnyasin*, one who renounces this life and 'dies a death' before the actual event occurs.

Society is also organised in ways that reflect different levels of work and responsibility. The four social orders or categories (Varnas) are: Brahmans (whose basic responsibilities are to teach and to undertake the rituals); Kshatriyas (originally 'warriors' but subsequently those who exercise *kshatra*, authority and power); Vaishyas (traders, businessmen and farmers); and Shudras (born 'under the feet of Purusha') who are the subordinate servants of others. In addition to the Varnas, there are many castes (*jati*) which are determined by birth, including the Untouchables. Gandhi attempted to integrate them into society by calling them Harijans, the Children of God, but they use for themselves a more realistic name, Dalits, 'the oppressed'.

MANUSMRITI

Among the many Dharma texts, *Manusmriti* is among the most revered and fundamental. The work is attributed to Manu, a legendary figure who is regarded as the progenitor of humanity and ruler of the earth. In *Rig Veda* 10.63.7 he is the first to offer a sacrificial oblation to the gods. It is, however, unlikely that the work comes from a single author. It seems to be a compilation coming from about 100–300 CE (though incorporating much early material), which has been attributed to Manu in order to enhance its authority. It consists of 2,685 verses in *shloka* metre (two linked lines with eight syllables in each) in twelve Books.

Manusmriti covers a wide range of topics, including philosophical reflection. It begins by establishing Dharma in creation itself, making it the foundation of life and society (8.15): 'Dharma when disregarded destroys, when it is obeyed it protects, so Dharma must never be disregarded lest it destroy us.' *Manusmriti* then relates the four Varnas and the four Ashramas to that primordial context. It goes on to deal with the key role of women in family and society ('Wherever women are properly respected the gods are pleased, but wherever that is not so, sacred rituals will not yield good consequence', 3.56), food and diet, the way in which rulers should govern, law of all kinds, and the origins of *jati* (caste).

The treatment of these topics does not unfold in a clear or systematic way, since there are many repetitions (even contradictions) and insertions of fragmentary material. The final book deals with the nature of good and evil acts and their consequences in *karma*, linked as that is to rebirth. So the book ends with an assurance, for those who observe Dharma, of well-being in this world, as also in the world to come of Brahma, the God of creation. *Manusmriti* promises (12.102, 125–6):

> Those who have true knowledge of the Vedas, no matter what their present position in life may be, are ready now to enter into union with Brahman . . .

> Those who recognise the Self in the self in all created beings have an equal attitude to all things and enter into union with Brahman.

> The twice-born who recite these Laws revealed by Manu will always behave appropriately and will attain whatever they desire.

BIBLIOGRAPHY NUMBERS 286, 634, 735, 738–41, 794, 861, 897

THE EPICS

RAMAYANA AND *MAHABHARATA*

Dharma texts summarise and explain how life should be lived, but for millennia the majority of people could not read, and as a result instruction in Dharma was often conveyed either in recitation or in stories.

Storytellers in India are recognised and respected figures because of the paramount importance of the oral transmission of sacred texts. As Coburn has pointed out (p. 445), the Indian practice of transmitting sacred words *orally*, not at first in written form, is 'an ongoing and experientially based feature of the Hindu religious tradition'. Narayan made a detailed study of one such storyteller in Nasik and concluded (pp. 246–7):

> This person [the storyteller] is already seen as a conduit for
> ultimate truths . . . The narrator's own sense of divine inspiration
> can also add to the impact of tales. The folk narratives told are
> listened to not just because they are the insights of a collectivity
> – the folk – but also because they have become linked with vital
> immediacy and power of the teller's presence . . . When disciples
> gather round a religious teller, they listen with an intensity and a
> desire to be edified, not only entertained.

The power of storytelling as the vehicle of Dharma led to the formation of the two great Epics of India, *Ramayana* and *Mahabharata*. They are a part of Smriti known as *iti-ha-asa*, 'so indeed it was'. Itihasa is described in *Chandogya Upanishad* 3.4.1 as the flower which has grown from the root of Veda, and it includes, as well as the Epics, the main Puranas (see pp. 187–9).

RAMAYANA

Ramayana tells the story of Rama, a prince in the northern Kingdom of Ayodhya, who turns out to be much more than a human hero. The Epic story is told in over 24,000 *shloka* couplets in seven Books (*kanda*). It is attributed to Valmiki, a *kushilava* or bardic poet, who is said to have created the *shloka* metre of couplets with eight syllables in each of the two lines. In fact *Ramayana* seems to have come into being over a long period of time, with the text having taken its present form at some time between the fourth and second centuries BCE.

The Books are:

1   *Balakanda* records the birth of four princes and tells how one of them, Rama, wins Sita as his wife: throughout *Ramayana* Sita is portrayed as the ideal woman.

2   *Ayodhyakanda* tells how Rama and his brother Lakshmana are driven into exile in the forest.

3   *Aranyakanda* describes the forest exile where Sita is abducted by the demon king Ravana and taken to Lanka.

4   *Kiskindhakanda* tells how Rama makes an alliance with Sugriva, king of the monkeys, who sends Hanuman in search of Sita.

5   *Sundarakanda* continues the exploits of Hanuman in disrupting Ravana's Kingdom in Lanka before returning to tell Rama where Sita is.

6   *Yuddhakanda* describes Rama's defeat of Ravana and the triumphant return to Ayodhya.

7   *Uttarakanda* ('the last *kanda*') gathers miscellaneous stories relating to Rama and Sita.

Ramayana illustrates the meaning and importance of Dharma, especially in the character of Rama who is the manifestation of God in human form – that is, *avatara*. The word *avatara* means 'descent', and it refers to the many ways in which the reality of God becomes apparent – through an image, for example, or through the carvings on a temple wall, but especially through particular individuals like Rama.

Ramayana is immensely popular in India and far beyond India. It is read and recited everywhere, and most strikingly it is performed in dramas known as *Ram Lilas*. Many new works were composed to retell the story, some of which, like *Ramacaritmanas* ('Lake of the Deeds of Rama') of Tulsidas, have come to be revered at least as much as the original. Macfie (p. vii) called this work 'the Bible of Northern India'.

MAHABHARATA

Mahabharata (*The Great Epic of the Family of Bharata*) is a vast work of about 100,000 *shloka* couplets in eighteen Books. It is attributed to Vyasa, but in its present form it is the result of a process of development coming roughly from a period between 400 BCE and 400 CE.

It has exercised a profound influence on India, not just in the way that it illustrates what Dharma means in everyday life, but also on its art, architecture and literature. It became a TV series in ninety-four episodes and, outside India, Peter Brook made a stage and film version (1989) that was much acclaimed, though not all Indians approved. Pradip Bhattacharya denounced it as a distortion (Boloji.com., 14 November 2004):

> Brook's film is not a portrayal of a titanic clash between the forces
> of good and evil, which is the stuff of the epic . . . Indians do not
> hold dear to their hearts the story of the warring progeny of some
> rustic landlord.

Mahabharata tells the story of a family feud between the Pandavas (sons of Pandu) and the Kauravas (sons of Dhritarashtra). Yudhishtara, eldest son of Pandu, should have become king, but when Duryodhana, the eldest of the Kauravas, refuses to abandon his claim, the Kingdom is divided. When Duryodhana persists in his rejection of Yudhishtara, the two families fight each other in an eighteen-day battle on the battlefield of Kurukshetra.

There are many stories and subplots woven into the narrative, but the central theme of Dharma stands out: 'From Dharma come profit and pleasure; people gain everything by Dharma, because it is Dharma that is the essence and strength of the world' (3.9.30). *Mahabharata* shows what that means in the conflict between Yudhishtara who embodies *dharma* and Duryodhana who embodies the opposite, *adharma*.

The conflict, however, is complex. Woven into the clash between the two opposites is the theme of *karma*, of the working out of consequence derived from events and behaviours in the past, and this certainly affects behaviours and decisions in the present.

So the *Mahabharata* is by no means a straightforward story of the good who do no wrong triumphing over the evil. 'The good' are capable of deceit and lies, and it is recognised that those and various other tricks may well be necessary in order to maintain *dharma* in the face of *adharma*. That kind of 'suspended dharma' is known as *apaddharma* in which during abnormal times the end justifies the means. It follows, as Matilal has put it, that the application of Dharma in *Mahabharata* is flexible and malleable (p. 17):

> The nature of our practical wisdom has a sort of malleability,
> which is comparable to the ever-elusive nature of *dharma*-ethics
> to be found in our [Indian] epic literature. It has been said that
> *dharmasya tatvam nihitam guhayam* ['the truth of dharma
> lies in the dark cave']. It cannot be completely known by us as
> universally fixed. But the acknowledgement of possible flexibility
> does not mean that the fixity and universality of ethical laws will
> be entirely negotiable. Situational constraints may require some
> bending, but by allowing genuine moral sentiments like remorse
> or guilt it makes up for occasional lapses. A moral agent exercises
> his practical wisdom, and also learns from the experiences he
> passes through during his life . . . This is the kind of moral insight
> that can be derived from a scrutiny of the Krishna-ethics in the
> *Mahabharata*.

Dharma, therefore, does not dictate behaviour. Decisions arise from a constant and unending engagement with Dharma in whatever circumstances arise. It is exactly that which sets the scene for a long section of *Mahabharata* known as *Bhagavadgita*, one of the most revered and important of all the sacred texts of India: on this see pp. 190–2.

📖 BIBLIOGRAPHY NUMBERS 149, 622, 790, 793, 959

PURANAS

BHAGAVATA PURANA

The importance of storytelling in India can be seen clearly in the Epics, but it can be seen also in the Puranas. Like the Epics, the Puranas teach and illustrate the meaning of Dharma, but they contain much other material as well. Traditionally a Purana is supposed to deal with five topics:

◆ The origin of a universe (its creation).

◆ The destruction and subsequent re-creation of the universe, exemplifying the Indian belief that each universe goes through four stages (*yuga*) of: a golden age when Dharma is perfectly observed; an age when Dharma declines and Veda has to be written down; an age when Dharma declines even further and few people pay any attention to Veda; and a fourth age, the Kali yuga, when disease, anarchy, warfare and despair dominate – in Indian understanding, we are living now in the Kali yuga; after that the cycle begins again.

◆ Genealogies of the gods and the great ancestors, particularly the Rishis.

◆ The periods of the fourteen Manus, the ancestors of humans (of whom Manu, p. 181, is the first), each of whom rules over an aeon (*manvantara*).

◆ The dynasties of the cosmic (solar and lunar) rulers from whom human kings are descended.

In fact very few of the Puranas deal with all those topics, and in any case they introduce much more material. Many of them, for example, reflect the growing practice of pilgrimage, culminating in the whole of India being regarded as a place of pilgrimage: they tell the stories of when and why particular places became holy, and of the exemplary people who lived there. As Bhardwaj has concluded (p. 58), 'The Puranas are, next to the epic *Mahabharata*, the most important source of our information on places of pilgrimage in India.'

These texts were called *purana* ('ancient'), partly because they were believed to be very old, but partly also because they collect accounts of ancient times. It is possible that they were put together in something like their present form during the period when the Gupta dynasty was ruling in Northern India (*c.*320–*c.*500 CE), but they certainly contain much more ancient material than that. Work continued on them, in terms of editing and making further additions, until about the sixteenth century.

The end result is a collection of texts of huge size: the major Puranas amount to something approaching half a million verses. Traditionally the Puranas are divided into eighteen Great Puranas (Mahapuranas) and eighteen Lesser (Upapuranas), though the lists of the eighteen in each category vary. The eighteen Mahapuranas are then linked in groups of six to the three major gods, the so-called Hindu Trinity:

◆ To Brahma are linked the Puranas *Bhavishya*; *Brahma*; *Brahmanda*; *Brahmavaivarta*; *Markandeya*; *Vamana*.

◆ To Vishnu are linked *Bhagavata*; *Garuda*; *Naradiya*; *Padma*; *Varaha*; *Vishnu*.

◆ To Shiva are linked *Agni*; *Kurma*; *Linga*; *Matsya*; *Shiva*; *Skanda*.

The Puranas, therefore, although they contain much else, are concerned with the central importance of God and the ways in which God becomes manifest and can thus be worshipped. The Puranas played a major part in drawing together the 'family of religions' in India, encouraging coalitions focused on one particular manifestation of God, whether of Shiva and his consorts, or of Vishnu and his *avataras* (appearances on earth to rescue the world when it falls into disorder, of whom Krishna is supremely important). In particular, the Puranas endorsed the home-based rituals and thus made god or goddess possible for ordinary people.

Sometimes a Purana attempts to rank the gods or goddesses according to its own focus of devotion: *Vishnu Purana* 5.34.29, for example, tells how on one occasion Krishna defeated Shiva, thus making Shiva subordinate to Vishnu. But far more commonly the Puranas accept that while there are many forms through which God can be approached and worshipped, they are all ways in which the One who is God (increasingly identified as Narayana) wills to become known. Narayana (originally more associated with Vishnu) is the One who is God from whom all creation and all manifestations of god and goddess come. Through the gods and goddesses as agents of Narayana, the whole process of the universe is kept in being. As *Bhagavata Purana* 8.1 puts it:

Just as rivers come from many sources, yet all become one with the ocean, so all the Vedas, all sacred writings, all truth, though they are different in the way they come into being, all come home to God.

BHAGAVATA PURANA

Of all the Puranas, *Bhagavata Purana* is among the most dearly loved. It celebrates Vishnu and his *avatara* Krishna. It is likely to have been written in about the tenth century CE in the Tamil-speaking area of South India, though it was soon known and revered in North India as well. It was translated into virtually all the many dialects and languages of India, and it became the foundational sacred text for great teachers like Chaitanya.

In its basic structure and content it is clearly derived from *Vishnu Purana*, but it goes much further in the direction of that deep and ecstatic devotion to God which issued in Bhakti. Book 10 gathers together many of the extremely popular stories of Krishna, and in particular his exploits with the *gopis*, the women of Vrindavan who herd the cows and fall in love with Krishna. They have come to symbolise the extreme way in which humans must be devoted to God (Bhakti) and also the extent to which it may be necessary to ignore convention in the service of God.

Equally, they exemplify the anguish, even the despair, that may be involved in the love of God when God seems to have disappeared. This is known as *virahabhakti*, 'absence-bhakti', persistence in the love of God even in the apparent absence of God. It was defined by Hardy (p. 9) as 'devotion in which the sentiment of "separation" is cultivated'. It became a profoundly important theme in the sacred texts of South India (see e.g., p. 195).

Devotion to Krishna and the importance of Bhakti are taken to a supreme height in *Bhagavadgita*.

 BIBLIOGRAPHY NUMBERS 12, 93, 111–15, 428, 779

THE SONG
OF THE LORD

BHAGAVADGITA

Bhagavadgita is a devotional poem of about 700 verses located in eighteen chapters of Book 6 of *Mahabharata*. That rather bleak summary conceals the fact that *Bhagavadgita* is for many Indians – perhaps the majority – the most revered sacred text. In his autobiography Gandhi wrote (p. 27):

> For me the Gita became an infallible guide of conduct. It became
> my dictionary of daily reference. Just as I turned to the English
> dictionary for English words that I did not understand, I turned
> to this dictionary of conduct for a ready solution of all my troubles
> and trials.

The origins of *Bhagavadgita* are uncertain. It seems to have been written at a time (perhaps the second century BCE) when there were many rival ways of 'living appropriately' or, in other words, living according to *sanatana dharma* (p. 179): some of those ways emphasised the importance of ritual action (Karma) and sacrifice, others the way of knowledge (Jñana) and insight, others the way of devotion (Bhakti) to God. Still others felt that the goal could be reached only by separation from the world, and among these the Jains and Buddhists had established new religions: they, along with Samkhya, reduced the importance of God drastically.

Bhagavadgita tries to show how these seemingly incompatible differences can in fact work together in helping people to reach the final goal of *moksha*. It begins with one of those moral dilemmas referred to earlier (p. 186). Arjuna is one of the Pandava brothers who is a warrior in the army of the Pandavas. He is therefore faced with a crisis of conscience because in the army facing him are members of his own family. If he attacks them, he may have to kill them: is that morally right?

He seeks the advice of a friend, Krishna, who is his charioteer. He does not know, however, that Krishna is also the *avatara* (manifestation in human form) of God, Vishnu. *Bhagavadgita* is the record of Krishna's advice and instruction.

Krishna's immediate answer gives three reasons why Arjuna should fight. Since the soul survives the death of the body (2.16–30), it follows that a war justly fought opens the door to heaven (2.32); it is Arjuna's Dharma as a warrior to fight (2.33); if he does not do so, others will accuse him of cowardice (2.34).

In the Indian context of the time no further arguments are really needed. Krishna, however, goes on to point out that there is a far more important goal than the immediate obligation to do one's duty. The goal is *moksha*, freedom and liberation in union with God. To get there, Krishna tells Arjuna, there are three paths or ways (*marga*), known also as *yoga* (the interior effort and purpose needed to reach the goal). They are the ways of:

◆ Action (*karma-marga*): we have already met *karma* as consequence (p. 173), but initially the word *karma* referred to the ritual action of sacrifice and then, by the time of the Brahmanas, it came to mean the power of Brahman brought into effect through the rituals. In *Bhagavadgita*, it is *karma* that sustains the whole universe, including gods and humans, but it must be undertaken for its own sake, not for personal gain:

> All the world is in bondage to the *karman* of action [i.e., to the consequences of *karma*], . . . therefore engage in action for that purpose, disinterestedly' (3.9, trans. van Buitenen).

◆ Knowledge (*jñana-marga*): *jñana* is not 'general knowledge'. It is the particular knowledge that destroys ignorance, exactly as the philosopher Shankara (p. 197) was later to emphasise. It enables people both to understand and to act appropriately without their actions being controlled by calculations of personal profit or loss. This insight or mental attitude is known as *buddhi*, so that *buddhi-yoga* actually combines both *karma* and *jñana*:

> The enlightened who are armed with this singleness of purpose rid themselves of the fruits that follow upon acts, and, set free from the bondage of rebirth, go on to a state of bliss (3.52).

◆ Devotion to God (*bhakti-marga*): God is the One behind all the manifestations of god and goddess whom humans worship. The many forms of manifestation are necessary because people cannot approach, let alone worship, an abstraction. *Bhagavadgita*, however, insists (4.7–8) that God approaches *them* in a 'descent' (*avatara*):

Whenever Dharma declines and *adharma* flourishes, then I take
on existence; for the rescue of the good and the destruction of the
evil, for the sake of establishing Dharma, I am born from age to
age.

Chapter 11 (known as *vishvarupadar anayoga*, 'the yoga of the vision of the universal form') contains a powerful and extraordinary description of the appearance of God in this form (11.53–5):

You have seen this rarely revealed form that is mine: even the
gods always yearn for a glimpse of this form. Thus, as I am and
as you have seen me, I cannot be seen with the aid of the Vedas,
austerities, gifts, and sacrifices. Only through exclusive Bhakti can I
be seen thus, Arjuna, and known as I really am . . .

Because God takes this initiative, all people, irrespective of gender, status or birth, can approach God: 'No servant of mine is lost: even people of low origins, women, Vaishyas, even Shudras reach the highest goal if they rely on me' (9.32).

Bhagavadgita argues that all these three ways of approaching God and of seeking *moksha* (release) are valid. That is why *Bhagavadgita* can be read as an endorsement of all the major ways in India of making progress towards the goal. Its purpose seems to have been a reconciliation, or at least a coexistence, of divergent ideas in order to prevent further schism.

Even so, although it is possible to make progress through any of the three ways, it seems in the end that Bhakti is the highest way. According to tradition, the teaching of the Gita is summed up in a culminating verse (*caramashloka*, 18.66):

Abandon all dharmas and take refuge with me alone. Be not
anxious: I will set you free from all evils.

📖 BIBLIOGRAPHY NUMBERS **92**

THE LOVE OF GOD

GITAGOVINDA

Bhagavadgita emphasises the importance of Bhakti in relation to God. Bhakti (perhaps from a root meaning 'to be loyal', 'to share in') is often translated as 'devotion', and it can be used in that sense of devoted loyalty among humans: *gurubhakti*, for example, is unswerving loyalty to one's guru or teacher, and *vaidhibhakti* is the unquestioning acceptance of his teaching.

Between humans and God, however, Bhakti carries with it a sense of almost ecstatic participation in the reality of God. It is an all-absorbing devotion that carries the devotee (*bhakta*) into a union with God. 'God' in India is brought close to those who seek him through the ways in which that Reality, in itself far beyond words or description, is made manifest. Thus God is, so to speak, made available to those who seek him through such forms of god as Shiva or Vishnu (or his *avataras* like Rama or Krishna) or through the forms of Goddess such as Mahadevi, the Great Mother.

The worship (*darshana*) of any of these may lead beyond itself to union with the One who is God. As the practice of Bhakti established itself in India from about the seventh century CE onward, the consequences of that union overflowed into hymns and poetry of profound and searching beauty. The works of these poets are sacred texts for those who follow in their footsteps.

Bhakti sums up a love for God of such great passion that it is often expressed through the metaphors and descriptions of human love. The poets of Bhakti drew on the long traditions of Indian love poetry in order to express their experience of the love of God. In *Gitagovinda*, for example, the poet describes the love between Radha and Krishna (12.23.10, trans. Mukhopadhyay):

> So the encounter in love began,
> when the shuddering of bodies

hindered firm embrace;
where the joy of contemplating one another
with searching looks
was interrupted by blinkings;
where the mutual sipping
of the honey of each other's lips
was impeded by the utterances
of small love-cries.
Yet even these seeming hindrances
enhanced the delight in love-play . . .
Though entwined in her arms
though crushed by the weight of her breasts
though smitten by her fingernails
though bitten on the lips by her small teeth
though overwhelmed by the thirst of her thighs
his locks seized by her hands
inebriated with the nectar of her lips
he drew immense pleasure from such sweet torments.
Strange indeed are the ways of love!

Gitagovinda was written in the twelfth century by Jayadeva to celebrate the supreme bliss of the union of the soul with God. This is exemplified in the love between Krishna (the *avatara* of Vishnu) and Radha, his favourite among the Gopis, p. 189 (5.11.11–13):

Go quickly, my friend
to the darkened shadowy thicket
in your blue sari.
But first remove
those noisy anklets
that disturb with their jingle
the sport of love.

You, fair one
will shine in radiance
like lightning
with the merit of your accumulated virtues
lying on the bosom of Krishna
he who is dark

with the necklace
as of fluttering white cranes on dark clouds;
in the love-play
Krishna, beneath you.

O lotus-eyed lady,
there on the couch of tender leaves
loosen your garments, untie your girdle
open your loins
for him who gets the delight
of viewing the gem unveiled.

Love, however, is not simply an experience of presence. It is also the painful and often anguished experience of absence. It is the suffering (*dukkha*) people feel when their loved one is absent. This kind of Bhakti is known as *virahabhakti* and it is a common theme, not just in *Gitagovinda*, but in Bhakti poetry in general. Mirabai, a Rajput princess of the sixteenth century who renounced her privileged life, lamented the absence of Krishna in this way (trans. Bowker, 2010, p. 109):

Sharp and piercing is my pain
Through the absence of this night:
When will gently rise again
Shafts of dawning light?
The moonlight – O deceiving foil –
Brings no comfort to my heart;
I wake – again the same turmoil,
Anguished while from you apart:
Lord of mercy, Lord of grace,
    Glimpse me blessings from your face.

Gitagovinda is made up of twenty-four songs. The first two praise Vishnu through Krishna for his appearances on earth as *avatara*, and welcome Krishna as Hari (Hari means 'the tawny one' or 'the destroyer of pain' and is a common way of addressing Krishna). They also tell of Radha's anguish when she sees Krishna 'making love to any maiden without distinction' (2.1), and 'delighting in the embrace of many maidens, eager for rapturous love' (1.3.39).

    The songs are then divided between the themes of absence and separation (3–16), reconciliation and forgiveness (17–21), and union (22–4). The purpose is to awaken exactly the same love of God in those who read or hear the words (12.24.24):

> Let this compassionate song of Jayadeva
> adorn your heart, and let
> this song distil the essence
> of devotion to the feet of Hari
> destroying the several agonies
> of this sinful dark aeon of Kali [the last of the four ages before all is
>   dissolved and destroyed].

Gitagovinda became widely influential, not so much as text but as text in performance. It is the basis particularly for the 'performance of stories in dance' known as Kathakali. In a comparable way it is used in the practice of visualisation – entering through the imagination into the episodes visualised and thus into the union to which they point. In the sixteenth century, for example, Krishnadasa Kaviraja wrote *Govindalilamrita* to show how, after long and careful training, *bhaktas* can experience the love of Radha and Krishna and can thus enter into a comparable union with God (*Govindalilamrita* 1.2f., trans. Delmonico in Lopez, p. 248):

> I surrender in astonishment to Shri Krishna Chaitanya, the
> compassionate one who has cured the world of the madness of
> ignorance and then maddened it again with the nectar of the
> treasure of sacred love for himself. The ultimate goal of spiritual
> development, the loving service of the lotus-like feet of the friend of
> the heart of Radha, though unattainable by Brahma, Ananta [the
> cosmic snake on which Vishnu rests] and others, is achieved only
> through intense longing by those absorbed in his activities in Vraja
> [the pastures where Radha and Krishna met].

It was this yearning for God, seen on earth in Krishna, that brought into being the poets known collectively as the Alvars.

📖 BIBLIOGRAPHY NUMBERS 149, 350, 370, 385, 428, 666

THE LOVE OF GOD

Alvars and Nayanars

From the ninth century onward, philosophers and schools of philosophy worked on Shruti, the sacred texts gathered in Vedanta, to produce coherent understandings of their meaning. Two of particularly lasting importance were Shankara and Ramanuja. Ramanuja's correction (as he saw it) of Shankara led to poems of such profound devotion to God that they became sacred texts.

Shankara (788–820) put forward a philosophy known as Advaita (no duality). In his view, Brahman is the only Reality there is, without any attributes or qualities (*Nirguna Brahman*), and in which therefore no distinctions between subject and object can exist. Indeed, it is not possible to make any positive statement about Brahman. One can say only what Brahman is not (*neti, neti*, 'not this, not this' or, more stubbornly, 'no! no!'). From Brahman come the manifold appearances of the entire cosmos, including gods and goddesses, and including also Sound and Word articulated in sacred texts. In our ignorance, we take the appearances around us to be real, but the only reality is Brahman. It is ignorance that has to be dispelled if we are to attain *moksha*. Shankara summarised his teaching in the sentence: 'Brahman alone is real, the world is appearance, *atman* [the self] is nothing but Brahman.'

Ramanuja (eleventh/twelfth century), who lived in South India, thought that this non-dualism was too extreme. He accepted that Brahman is the only Reality, but in his view the experience of relatedness to God, captured so vividly in Bhakti, is too fundamental to be dissolved in a union of identity with Brahman: relatedness is in the nature of what that Reality is. In other words, Brahman is that which truly is, without distinction (Advaita), but individual selves are also real, dependent on Brahman as a part of what Brahman is. Ramanuja thus qualified Advaita by making Brahman relational in its aseity (in its own nature), and his system is thus known as Vishishtadvaita, qualified non-dualism.

ALVARS

The brief background above is necessary in order to understand how important Ramanuja's interpretation of Vedanta was for the rapid expansion of Bhakti. Where Shankara thought of *moksha* as total absorption into Brahman, Ramanuja saw *moksha* as that final union with God/Vishnu which Bhakti anticipates here on earth. It is a salvation in which selves or souls remain distinct, though always dependent on Vishnu, continuing to be the willing servants of Vishnu in his eternal abode (Vaikuntha).

This personal and devotional understanding of Brahman gave impetus to the Bhakti-marga so powerfully advocated by *Bhagavadgita* and its various extensions (see pp. 204ff.). It inspired the proliferation of Bhakti poets, especially in South India. Among those poets were those known as Alvars ('immersed in God') who flourished from about the sixth to the ninth centuries. They were a group of twelve poets devoted to the Lord Vishnu – i.e., Shri Vaishnavites. To quote the summary of Chari (p. 2):

> They were saints who devoted their entire life to the worship of
> Vishnu as the Supreme Deity. Blessed with spiritual insight and
> intense love for God, they sang the glory of Vishnu and spent their
> active life in the divine service . . . The compositions of the Alvars
> are not merely intended to promote the Bhakti cult, as is commonly
> believed, but they aim at disseminating the knowledge of the
> Vedanta Philosophy [of Ramanuja] among the common people
> through the familiar medium of Tamil.

The poems or hymns of the Alvars are gathered in twenty-four collections known as *prabandhams*. The number of hymns in each of these varies, but the total is reckoned as 4,000, so that the collection is called *Nalayira Divyaprabandham*, 'the 4000 works that capture [*prabandham*] the Supreme Being [*divya*]'. They celebrate God and the many ways in which God becomes known, and they were therefore much used in Vaishnavite ritual and worship.

Among the twelve Alvars, the most revered is Nammalvar ('our immersed in God') who wrote four works so revered and highly regarded that they are known as 'the Tamil Veda' – though some reserve that title for *Tiruvaymoli* alone:

◆ *Tiruviruttam* (*tiru* as a prefix means 'good', 'God-filled', 'divine'; *viruttam* is a form of verse), 100 four-line verses expressing the longing of the soul for God, beginning with his fundamental faith and prayer:

To set us free from ignorance and from evil and pollution in the
body, to save us from endless rebirth, to do this and to give us life,
you, Lord of those who have left death behind, have come down to
earth, taking birth in many wombs and taking many forms: receive,
Lord, my allegiance, made from my heart.

◆ *Tiruvaciriyam* (*aciriyappa* is the metre), seven poems arising from stories
told about God.

◆ *Periya Tiruvandadi* (*periya* means 'great', *andadi* is a style in which the last
word of one verse becomes the first of the next).

◆ *Tiruvaymoli* ('The Divine Word'), 1,102 poems exploring the major themes
of Vishishtadvaita.

NAYANARS

Another equally famous group of Bhakti poets (of roughly the same period as the
Alvars) in South India were the Nayanars ('leaders', 'guides'). They were devoted
to God in the form of Shiva rather than Vishnu and were therefore Shaivites.
However, both Vaishnavites and Shaivites were clear that these manifestations
of God point beyond the characterisations (through which they become known
now) to the One who is God, Brahman beyond description. They both agreed,
in other words, with *Tiruvaymoli* 2.5.9:

He is beyond our knowledge:
He is this and equally he is not this.
He appears in the form that those who urgently seek him need,
And yet that is not his form.

The three major figures among the Nayanars are Campantar (sixth century),
whose name sometimes appears as Sambandar following more closely its
pronunciation, Appar, and Cuntarar (eighth century, also Sundarar). These
three are honoured as *muvar mutalikal*, 'the first three saints', to whom a
fourth was later added, Manikkavacakar (*c.* ninth century), thus making up the
Nalvars, 'the Four'.

Of the hymns of 'the first three saints', 796 are collected in the first seven books
of a work known as *Tevaram*. Later it was also called *Tirumurai*, 'sacred tradition'
or 'sacred text', and it is regarded by Shaivite Tamils as revealed scripture, the
equivalent of the Vedas. Their hymns are the foundation and expression of Bhakti
devotion to Shiva. They are offered as gifts and garlands of worship:

Flowers make fine decoration,
So too does gold.
But if our Lord, the One who dwells invitingly in Arur,
desires any fine decoration for himself,
let us make him the gift, simple heart,
of the fine decoration of Tamil song.

There have to be images and imaginations of God if humans are to love and worship God, but in the end, as this poem of Appar (trans. Peterson, p. 111) makes clear, God lies far beyond words and descriptions – *Deus semper maior*:

You'd like to say:
'Our Lord has long matted hair.
He is the one who shares himself
with the dark-eyed Goddess.
He lives in Kacci Mayanam',
but the Lord is more than this.
There is no one like him,
he isn't any one person,
he doesn't live in any one place,
and you can't compare him
to anything in the world.
If it weren't for his grace,
you would have no eyes to see
his form, his colour and nature,
you wouldn't be able to say:
'This is how he looks;
this is his colour; this is the way he is;
this is God.'

BIBLIOGRAPHY NUMBERS 30, 36, 254, 280, 287, 704, 762, 792, 862, 944, 950

TANTRA

SHRIVIDYA

Tantra is a way of understanding the energies that create and sustain the cosmos, and it is a way also of rituals and practices that relate one's self to those energies particularly by mediating them through one's own body.

Tantra is thus a part of the Indian 'family of religions' (p. 167). It exists partly in its own independent groups of Tantrikas (those who practise Tantra), but has also been taken into other parts of the family. It is as important for at least some Jains and Buddhists as it is among some devotees of Vishnu or Shiva. It is equally important among Shaktas, those who are devoted to Shakta, power and energy in the form of Goddess.

The word *tantra* perhaps comes from a root meaning 'to expand' or 'to spread', possibly therefore implying 'the means by which knowledge is spread'. But more commonly it is understood as 'the strong thread woven on a loom', from *tan* 'to weave' and *tra* 'to protect'. As the fourteenth-century Tibetan Klong-chen rab-'byams-pa put it succinctly (Guenther, p. 158):

> A simile for Tantra is texture: out of the many strands of the weft
> and the warp a piece of cloth is woven. Similarly by different
> explanations one arrives at a single notion. Thus Tantra weaves
> together the threads of belief and practice that will lead to *moksha*.

The sacred texts of Tantra are extremely numerous, often taking the form of a dialogue between Shiva and Shakti his consort. At first sight it may seem strange that there are so many tantric texts, because tantric teaching is not 'on public offer'. It opens the way to the powerful and often destructive energies of the cosmos, so it is passed on by a guru only to those who are capable of receiving it, and they in turn would have to pass through *diksha*, initiation.

Nevertheless, texts were written down. They are known collectively as

Tantra, though they are sometimes referred to as Agama. A particular group of Vaishnavite texts is known as Pañcaratra Samhita (the word used of the Vedas, p. 169). For Tantrikas, revelation has been an unfolding and progressive development: they accept Shruti ('revelation', p. 168) but only as an introductory stage leading to the culmination of truth in Tantra.

Not surprisingly, Tantra has been opposed, and often fiercely denounced, by those who uphold the Vedic way of Dharma. They point to the fact that Tantrikas find cosmic energy in people, objects and activities that to dharma-observant Indians are abhorrent. The Kapalikas ('skull-wearers'), for example, live in cremation areas, covering themselves in the ashes of the dead and using skulls as their cups. Tantrikas of that kind engage in the five 'Ms' (panca-makara), five ritual ingredients (normally avoided) whose first letter is M: Madya, intoxicating liquor; Mamsa, meat; Matsya, fish; Mudra, parched grain; Maithuna, sexual intercourse with prostitutes, women who are menstruating, or the dead. The point is that the same cosmic energy creates and destroys in equal measure, and everywhere connection can be made with it. Consequently, as one Tantra (Jñanasiddhi) puts it, 'By the same acts that cause some to be reborn in hell for a thousand years, the yogin gains eternal salvation.'

Conversely, therefore, early Tantra strongly rejected the tendency in Indian religion to withdraw from the world (e.g., world-renouncers, p. 170) and to regard the body as something from which the self or soul must escape if it is to achieve moksha – soma sema, as the Greeks put it in an entirely different context, 'the body a tomb'. Tantra in contrast sees the body as the vehicle through which the power of the cosmic and divine energy can be activated: it is in and through the body that the intense ecstasy of union with God can be realised.

In human experience, the merest hint of what that ecstatic union might be like lies in the sexual union of a man and a woman. That is why the intensity of that union became in India a controlling metaphor for the union between the soul and God, as we have already seen in Gitagovinda and Bhakti poetry (p. 193). It is why sculptures on Indian temples so often portray Gods and Goddesses in this union (maithuna). In Brihadaranyaka Upanishad (4.3.21) sexual union is used as a metaphor of union with God:

> As a man when in the embrace of the woman he loves knows
> nothing of the outside or inside, so does the person know nothing
> of the outside or inside when in the embrace of the intelligent self
> [atman which is Brahman].

SHAKTI AND SHRIVIDYA

In Tantra, the controlling metaphor became also a matter of ritual practice. Tantra recognises the fundamental conjunction of the female and male in which the female energy, Shakti, is often paramount. From the union between the feminine Shakti (divine energy and power) and the male Lord, the cosmos comes into being: through union of the male worshipper with the divine female energy, the whole process of creation is recapitulated in the body.

In Indian belief, the male gods have various consorts: among those of Shiva, for example, are Parvati, Uma, Devi and Durga, but they are all manifestations of the one Shakti, the source of cosmic creation and energy. What is striking in Tantra is that it is Shakti who gives energy to the gods, not the other way round. An example of that kind of Shakta tantrism is Shrividya (Auspicious Wisdom). It originated in Kashmir and then spread widely, particularly into South India where it developed in different ways.

The name of the Goddess in this cult is Lalita, also known as Shri. But in contrast to Shri of the Shrivaishnavites, she does not become 'auspicious' (*shri*) as a result of her union with Vishnu or any other God. She is auspicious in her own right, and although she is united with Shiva, she is not dependent on him. She has the power to change the created order in any way she wants, and those who worship her do so to bring that power into being for specific needs and occasions.

Shrividya, like other Tantric groups, produced many sacred texts or Tantras, but it is impossible to write a guide or introduction to them. That is partly because they are so numerous, but also because they become sacred not by abstract definition but by a decision on the part of a guru to use them. It is exactly as Brooks has made the point (p. 57f.):

> For a text to gain entry into a lineage's canon, a guru will usually
> claim that its content was either taught previously within the lineage
> or that it reflects lineage belief or practice . . . In contemporary
> Śrividya, all sources bearing the title 'Tantra' are subjected to this
> rather indeterminate test. Thus, a Tantra, may be deemed 'scripture'
> inasmuch as it is agreed to be of divine origin, taught by Śiva or Śakti
> at a certain time to address specific needs, but it may not be deemed
> 'authoritative' in a given lineage because it is either (1) unimportant
> in a given disciple's *sadhana* [discipline] or (2) outside the lineage's
> self-understanding . . . The authority of Scripture is thus determined
> by appealing to criteria of qualification.

BIBLIOGRAPHY NUMBERS 13, 334, 518, 519, 566, 898, 934, 967

THE GITAS

ANUGITA, ISHVARAGITA AND DEVIGITA

The designation of some texts as 'sacred' is extremely fluid in Tantra because all things (and therefore potentially all texts) are vehicles of cosmic energy and power.

For others in India it is possible to identify some texts as being of fundamental authority – as being, in other words, either Shruti itself or the extension of Shruti. *Bhagavadgita* (p. 190) is one such text. But even in that case many other Gitas were composed. The basic form was retained of the Song (Gita) as the direct teaching of the Lord, but the identity of the Lord (and therefore of the teaching) may change.

The best known of these is *Anugita* which is actually a section in *Mahabharata* itself (14.16). *Anugita* is often described as a recapitulation of the Gita because it begins with Arjuna asking Krishna for further instruction. Thus Sharma states (p. 3): 'There can be little doubt that the Anugita sets out to recapitulate the Gita; it may even be described as the Bhagavadgita "recollected in tranquillity".' However, he then points out that the focus of *Anugita* is not on Bhakti but on a better understanding of themes dealt with only briefly in *Bhagavadgita*. It is thus an extension of *Bhagavadgita*, particularly in its claim that Jñana leads to the same consequence as Bhakti.

Another example of the extension of *Bhagavadgita* as a form of instruction is *Ishvaragita* in which it is Shiva not Vishnu who teaches the importance of Bhakti. It makes up the first eleven chapters of the second part of *Kurma Purana* and draws deliberately on *Bhagavadgita*. As Dhavamony points out (p. 91):

> Like the *Bhagavad-Gita*, the *Iśvara-Gita* also proposes
> disinterested activity and explains the deeper meaning of such
> an activity from the point of view of love. In this way, *karma* and
> *bhakti* are fused into one spiritual striving of the soul to obtain the
> true knowledge of God. Detachment or renouncement has value
> only in so far as it includes attachment to Śiva.

MAHADEVI,
THE GREAT GODDESS

In me this whole world is woven in all directions . . .
I am the Lord and the Cosmic Soul; I am myself the Cosmic Body.

I am Brahma, Vishnu, and Rudra, as well as Gauri, Brahmi, and Vaishnavi.

I am the sun and the stars, and I am the Lord of the stars.

I am the various species of beasts and birds, I am also the outcast and thief.

I am the evil doer and the wicked deed; I am the righteous person and the virtuous deed.

I am certainly female and male, and asexual as well.

And whatever thing, anywhere, you see or hear,

that entire thing I pervade, ever abiding inside and outside.

There is nothing at all, moving or unmoving, that is devoid of me;

For if it were, it would be a nonentity, like the son of a barren woman.

Just as a single rope may appear variously as a serpent or wreath,

So also I may appear in the form of the Lord and the like; there is no doubt in this matter.

Devgita 3.12 (trans. C. M. Brown)

A further example of the extension of *Bhagavadgita* is *Devigita*, 'The Song of the Goddess'. This is a sacred text of immense importance to Shaktas (those who worship the divine energy manifested in the form of Goddess) because (as with Lalita in Shrividya) the Goddess is not subordinate to the gods. Rather, it is they who are dependent on her.

Mahadevi is the Great Goddess known as Bhuvaneshvari, the Ruler of the Cosmos. She is the Mother of the World (*jagad-ambika*) who dwells in a paradise known as Manidvipa, the Jewelled Island, where she observes the world and hurries to the rescue of any of her devotees who are in trouble.

The male gods derive their strength from her and without her as the source of Shakti they are impotent. The throne on which she sits is supported by the lifeless bodies of Brahma, Vishnu and two forms of Shiva, Rudra and Ishana, and the seat of the throne is the dead body of another form of Shiva, Sadashiva. The throne is known as *pañca-pretasana*, the seat of the five corpses.

Devigita, like *Anugita*, *Ishvaragita* and *Bhagavadgita* itself, is part of a much longer work, *Devi Bhagavata Purana* (chapters 31–40 of Book 7). It is 507 verses in the roughly 18,000 verses of the Purana. It may come from about the twelfth century CE, but the date is uncertain. *Devigita* is remarkable for the way in which it gives absolute supremacy to Mahadevi Bhuvaneshavari over the male gods. She is Brahman who pervades all things (see box p. 205).

Devigita is closely related to Tantra but only if Tantra does not conflict with Dharma observance. It aligned itself with the Tantric view of the body as the vehicle through which the divine and cosmic energies can be recognised and released. The human body contains within itself a miniature or compressed version of the entire cosmos, and is made up of centres of energy (*cakra*) connected with each other by channels (*nadi*). This anatomy is visualised by the yogin and the energies within are brought to life.

But Brahman as Mahadevi is in essence Goddess, so there is also in *Devi Gita* a strong emphasis on Bhakti (7.11–27). It is through devotion that the nature of Goddess is found to be one's own.

Those who worship Mahadevi are thus brought into contact with the power of the divine, understood as the primordial energy from whom all life and all manifestation are derived. Tantric ritual purifies the body by symbolically destroying it, and then re-creating it as the body of the Goddess through *mantra* (chant) and visualisation. In this state, the power of the Goddess is received and absorbed, and the highest form of *puja* (worship) becomes possible because there is no distinction between the worshipper and the One worshipped. After a detailed description of that *puja*, *Devigita* concludes (10.30–2):

> Whoever in such manner worships the Goddess, the auspicious, world-charming beauty,

For that person nothing is difficult to attain any time, anywhere.
Upon leaving the body, that one most certainly will go to my
Jewelled Island.
Such a person may be recognised as bearing the form of the
Goddess herself. The gods constantly bow before that one.

BIBLIOGRAPHY NUMBERS 281

THE SANTS

KABIR

Shankara (p. 197) had realised that Brahman, the unproduced Producer of all that is, must necessarily lie far beyond the power of human words or imagination to describe. Nirguna Brahman, Brahman without qualities, insists on the logically necessary point that Brahman cannot be described as one might attempt to describe objects in a room.

Yet the prolific and widespread adoration of God in Bhakti made it equally clear that at least something, however inadequate, *can* be said about the qualities or attributes of Brahman – Saguna Brahman, Brahman with attributes. To be known at all, Brahman must manifest itself with some characteristics even if these have to be inferred rather than observed directly. In personified form, Saguna Brahman is Ishvara, God. By extension this creates the forms of God, such as Vishnu (and his *avataras*), Shiva (and his consorts) and Shakti, who are worshipped and adored in Bhakti.

It might seem obvious that in Bhakti the *sagun* emphasis would be inevitable. How can God or Goddess be adored without any characteristics? But in fact there were *nirgun* forms of Bhakti as well. Particularly important among these were the Sants of North India who flourished between the fourtenth and eighteenth centuries.

The word *sant* means 'holy' or 'good'. A Sant, basically, is a holy and dedicated person, but by the fifteenth and sixteenth centuries, the Sants had become organised in schools of training and learning known as *panths*. The Sants did not in any way deny that Brahman, to become known at all, must have some characteristic attributes, nor did they deny that these manifest themselves in the form of Deities who can be approached in worship and devotion, and from whom grace and encouragement can be received. There were therefore many Sants who retained a *sagun* form of worship.

In contrast, however, *nirgun* Sants realised that *all* these many (and often rival) forms of manifestation are provisional and incomplete. The many Deities provide a necessary focus for devotion, but they are, so to speak, a first step, a first point of access to the profound truth of that which is God beyond human words and description.

They then took that insight a stage further. They argued that the provisional manifestations of Brahman in the form of God or Goddess are *equal*: they are all equally provisional, but they are also equal in the way that they point beyond themselves to the One who is 'the God beyond gods'. None of them, therefore, can legitimately claim to be 'better' than the others. Even the claims to revelation in Shruti or in Quran, are expressed in words that necessarily fall short of the aseity of God (whatever it is that God is).

It is not, therefore, the case, as is sometimes said, that the *nirgun* Sants believed that all religions are equally true. They believed, rather, that all claims about God, however helpful they may provisionally be, are equally inadequate. The Sants of *nirgun* Bhakti were clear that the signpost must never be confused with that to which it points.

It follows that devotion to God can be immediate and direct. It does not require any intermediary, not even the *avatara* (incarnation) of God; nor such things as ritual, pilgrimage and sacrifice. The way to God is open to all, including low-caste people and women. All that is needed, according to Namdev (*c.* fourteenth century?), is constant attention to God:

> As a kingfisher stares at a fish,
> As a goldsmith concentrates on the gold while working it,
> As a dissolute man cannot take his eyes off another man's wife,
> As a gambler fixes his eye on the dice before throwing them,
> In that way I look to you, O Ram, I see nothing but you.
> For ever Nam is lost at the feet of God.

Namdev recorded something of his long search for God:

> I sought the truth in Vedic words
> and heard them say 'you shall' and 'you shall not'.
> There is in them no potency for peace:
> they make it seem the power is asked of me.
> I sought the truth in Shruti hoping its words
> would show the form of God, but all its words
> were wrangled, tangled, torn by those
> who lose their way in error and in pride.

Then in Puranas next I sought
the form of God but could not settle there.
I heard men speak of Brahman, but their minds
were set on lust – no path of peace . . .
They glorify in words the Name on high
while down on earth they're snared in ropes of sense.
Lord, here am I, here at last, weary with seeking,
Lord, at your feet I lie: no more the world's glint and fear.
  Nam says: save me, O save me, now and here.

Among the Sants, Kabir is particularly well known and certainly some of his verses became part of a sacred text when they were gathered into the Scripture of the Sikhs, *Adi Granth* (p. 219). His own works, in addition to those gathered in *Adi Granth*, are collected in *Bijak*, the sacred text of the followers of Kabir (Kabir *panth*), and *Pañcavani* in *Kabir-granthavali*.

Kabir lived during the fifteenth century (his exact dates are unknown). He was probably born into a Muslim family, though later sources (sensitive to the Muslim invasions of India) claim that he was born of a Brahman widow and adopted by Muslim parents.

To Kabir, though, it was irrelevant. God can be found everywhere: 'For Banaras go to the east, for Mecca go to the west; but go into your own heart and you will find both Rama and Allah are already there.' It follows that the names of God are all equal in the way they point beyond themselves. He himself often spoke of God as Hari, but he used many other names as well – Ram, Allah, Karim, Rahim (the Merciful One). What matters is to realise the presence of God in the pulse of one's life at every moment (*Kabir-granthavali* 2.177):

They say you must turn to the east to find Hari,
and to the west [i.e., Mecca] to find Allah.
Turn to him in your heart, in the heart of your heart:
that is where he is, Rahim-Ram.
All people who have ever been born
are simply manifest forms of yourself:
Kabir is the child of Allah-Ram:
he is my Guru and my Pir.

The pir in Islam is the spiritual guide, the equivalent of the guru. Kabir knew well that his only guide and guru is God. The most profound human knowledge and most devoted practices always fall short of God, as he wrote (*Kabir-granthavali* 101, trans. Vaudeville, pp. 241ff.):

> Even if you be a Pandit, knowing all scriptures
>   and all sciences and grammars,
> And if you knew all treatises and spells and herb-balms
>   in the end, die you must . . .
>
> And if you be a Yogi, a Yati, a Tapi or a Samnyasi,
>   going on endless pilgrimages –
> With shaven head or plucked hair, a silent One or One with matted
>   locks,
>   in the end, die you must.
>
> Says Kabir, I've thought and pondered,
>   watching the whole world:
>   none has ever escaped –
> So I have taken refuge in You:
>   Free me from that round of birth and death!

When Kabir died, his Hindu and Muslim followers argued whether his corpse should be buried as Muslim or burned as Hindu. As they struggled, so the story goes, they pulled off the shroud covering the body and found nothing but flowers. Half were cremated and half were buried.

BIBLIOGRAPHY NUMBERS 447, 515, 616

6

SIKHS

SIKH TEXTS: KEY DATES

1469–1539 Nanak

c.*1499* Nanak receives commission

c.*1500–33* Travels with Mardana

1479–1574 Guru Amar Das (Guru from 1552)

1539 Death of Guru Nanak

1504–52 Guru Angad (Guru from 1539)

1534–81 Guru Ram Das (Guru from 1574)

1563–1606 Guru Arjan Dev (Guru from 1581)

1595–1644 Guru Hargobind (Guru from 1606)

1601 Guru Arjan Dev completed Golden Temple at Amritsar

1603 Guru Arjan, compiled *Adi Granth*

1604 *Adi Granth* installed at Golden Temple

1621–75 Guru Tegh Bahadur (Guru from 1664)

1630–61 Guru Har Rai (Guru from 1644)

1661–64 Guru Har Krishan

1666–1708 Gobind Rai (Guru Gobind Singh from 1675)

1699 Khalsa inaugurated

1708 *Adi Granth* to replace human Gurus

1734 Bhai Mani Singh compiled *Dasam Granth* from Guru Gobind Singh's writings

1873 Singh Sabha, defence against proselytising

Previous page: The *Guru Granth Sahib* being recited and honoured with the *chaur*, a symbol of authority made, if possible, from the tail hair of a white horse embedded in a silver handle: see p. 221.

GURU NANAK

JAPJI AND *MUL MANTRA*

In about 1499, a young herdsman called Nanak (1469–1539) was bathing in a river, not named in the earliest accounts but later identified as the River Bein in North India. He disappeared beneath the water and was thought to have drowned. But three days later he reappeared and said that he had been in the presence of God. According to an early account (Vir Singh, pp. 16f.), this experience was also one of a commission to go and teach:

> As the Primal Being willed, the devotee was ushered into the
> Divine Presence. Then a cup of *amrit* [the drink of immortality,
> fundamental in Sikh rituals] was given him with the command,
> 'Nanak, this is the cup of Name-adoration. Drink it: . . . I am with
> you, and I bless and exalt you. Whoever remembers you will have
> my favour. Go, rejoice, in my name and teach others to do so . . .
> I have bestowed upon you the gift of my Name. Let this be your
> calling.' Nanak offered his salutations and stood up.

When Nanak returned from the water he spent a further day in silent meditation, after which he spoke the words, 'There is no Hindu, there is no Muslim, so whose path shall I follow? I will follow the path of God: God is neither Hindu nor Muslim and the path which I follow is the path of God.' Those words have been taken to mean, either that in the eyes of God there is no difference between religions, or that no Hindus or Muslims can be found who live their faith wholeheartedly. But in the Sant context at the time when Nanak lived, they are more likely to mean that the Hindu and Muslim characterisations of God fall far short of the aseity of God, the reality of what God is, far beyond human words and imagination. As he put it in his own words (*Japji* 5, trans. Kaur Singh, p. 49):

That One cannot be moulded or made,
Alone immaculate and self-existent.
Those who serve receive honours.
Nanak says, sing of the Treasure of virtues,
Sing, listen, and hold love in the heart
So sorrow is banished, joy ushered in.
Through the Guru comes the sacred Word,
    through the Guru comes the scripture,
    through the Guru, That One is experienced in all.
    The Guru is Shiva, the Guru is Vishnu, the Guru is Brahma,
    the Guru is Parvati, Laxmi and Sarasvati [the Indian Trinity and
        their consorts].
Were I to comprehend, I'd still fail to explain,
    for That One is beyond all telling.
Guru, let me grasp the one thing:
All creatures have one Provider,
    may I not forget this.

That at least is the basis on which Nanak, now a recognised and revered teacher or Guru, established the religion of the Sikhs – the word *sikh* means 'follower' or 'disciple'. Of his inspired poems and hymns (*bani*), 974 were eventually gathered into the sacred text of the Sikhs known as *Adi Granth* and later (and now more commonly) as *Guru Granth Sahib*.

At the head of this collection stands *Japji Sahib* (*Jap*, like *mantra*, is the devout repetition of a name or word; *ji* and *sahib* are words of profound respect): it is recited or chanted daily by Sikhs. Its first line is: *Ikk Oan Kar*, literally, 'One Reality Is'. It begins the *Mul Mantra*, the Mantra that is for Sikhs the most sacred. Indian mantras are chants in which the reality of what they purport to be about is actually contained in a highly compressed form. They are therefore virtually impossible to translate, and *Mul Mantra* is no exception. But an indication of its meaning might be:

One Reality Is
The Name is Truth,
Source and Creator,
without fear,
without hostility,
not subject to time,
unborn, not subject to death,

the grace of the Guru.
Truth before Time,
Truth throughout Time,
Truth now and here,
  Nanak says, unending Truth.

Guru Nanak was born in 1469 in Talwandi near Lahore. Accounts of his life are gathered in *Janamsakhis* ('birth' plus 'stories': their nature and contents are reviewed helpfully by McLeod, 1968, pp. 7–67). For the next twenty-four years after his call he travelled round India, teaching and chanting his *banis* of devoted love, accompanied on a musical instrument, the rebec, by a Muslim companion, Mardana. He wore at this time items of Hindu and Muslim dress to underline the point about God beyond the gods. It is said that he travelled to Mecca and Medina and even as far as Baghdad.

Eventually Guru Nanak settled in Kartarpur, a village in the Punjab on one of the banks of the River Ravi. He gathered a community of men and women around him and established two of the key institutions of Sikh religion, the *sangat* (the congregation in which people recite the praises of the Sovereign Lord) and the *langar* (the hall of community meals and hospitality).

It is clear that Guru Nanak was familiar with, and much affected by, the tradition of Kabir and Ravidas (p. 208). The hymns and poems of both were gathered into *Guru Granth Sahib*, 292 of Kabir and 41 of Ravidas, along with 60 of Namdev. It was even claimed later that Guru Nanak had actually met Kabir, but this seems to be an attempt to exalt Nanak by having Kabir acknowledge Nanak as greater than himself.

As with Kabir and others in the Sant tradition, Nanak believed that God can be directly known: there is no need for intermediaries; nor should one rely on rituals, sacrifices, pilgrimages and the like in order to know God. 'God' is far above all human thought and far beyond words. All that can be spoken is praise (*Japji* 3, trans. Kaur Singh, p. 48):

Filled with might, they sing praise of the Might,
Seeing the signs, they sing praise of the Bounty,
Perceiving the virtues, they sing praise of the Glory.
Some sing praise through high philosophy,
Some sing praise of the power that creates and destroys,
Some sing in awe of the giving and taking of life,
Some sing of the thereness, the utter transcendence,
Some sing of the hereness, the close watch over all . . .
  Says Nanak, the Carefree is ever in bliss.

Since the only proper response is adoration, it is not surprising that *Guru Granth Sahib* is full of praise. *Rahiras*, part of the evening service, opens with that recognition and with praise of the One who brings creation into being with a single word, the One who decides what to make or unmake (trans. Kaur Singh, p. 116):

> That One, ever True Sovereign,
>   true is the praise of that True One.
> That One is, ever will be,
>   and never will that Creator of the world not be.
> Designer of this colourful diversity,
>   Creator of this variegated world,
> You watch over and sustain Your creation,
>   all praise belongs to You.

It is through creation that God is able to be known (*Adi Granth*, p. 4): 'All that he makes is the expression of his Name. There is nothing in any part of creation that is not that self-expression.' This means that God can be encountered and discerned everywhere (*Adi Granth*, p. 25):

> You are the ocean, embracing all, knowing and seeing all.
> How can I, a fish in the ocean, ever perceive the limit of what you
>   are?
> Wherever I look, there you are.
> If I leave you, I gasp and die.

All this Kabir and the Sants would have recognised and understood. Where Guru Nanak differed from Kabir was in accepting responsibility to ensure that his teaching continued. Although there is a Kabir *panth* (community), Kabir did not himself organise it since he recognised the great damage that organised religions can do. Guru Nanak, in contrast, announced in 1539, just before he died, that one of his followers, Lahina, was to be his successor as Guru: he was to be called Angad, 'part of his own body'. From that decision the Sikh religion was ensured.

📖 BIBLIOGRAPHY NUMBERS 412, 413, 504, 505, 963

THE GURUS

ADI GRANTH, GURU GRANTH SAHIB AND *DASAM GRANTH*

The community of Sikhs continued after the death of Guru Nanak under the guidance of a further nine Gurus in succession. Guru Nanak had already gathered a collection of poems and hymns (he was said to have carried them around tucked under his arm). His successors continued and extended the collection. They added their own compositions, signing them with the name Nanak in order to emphasise that they were living and writing in the same spirit.

In 1603, the fifth Guru, Arjan, decided that the growing collection needed to be better organised. By now the Sikh *panth* (community) was increasing rapidly and spreading widely so that a single agreed text was clearly needed. In addition, Pirthi Chand, who had been passed over as Guru when Arjan was appointed, began, with his son Meharban, to compose hymns in the name of Nanak. It therefore became urgent to define and designate the authentic sacred text.

Guru Arjan took Bhai Gurdas into a secluded part of the forest near Amritsar (the site is marked today by a shrine called Ramsar) and together they selected and organised the hymns to be included. The resulting work is *Adi Granth*, 'The First Book'. Guru Arjan completed it with *Mundavani* ('the seal' of the whole work); this, with *Shalok*, a couplet, concludes Evening Prayer:

> In this bowl three things are gathered: truth, peace and
>   contemplation.
> They are saturated with the sweet Name of the Lord by which we
>   are all sustained.
> Those who eat and savour it are set free.
> It must never be discarded: keep it for ever within yourself.
> If we cling to the feet of the Guru the dark ocean can be crossed.
>   Says Nanak: all this vast creation is the work of God.

I do not understand all you have done, nor the way you have made
    me with such powers,
I am unworthy, but you have shown me mercy,
Mercy that pours out such compassion
That I have found the true Friend, the Guru,
    Says Nanak: I live to hear the Name that enlivens body and soul
    with joy.

Adi Granth is usually understood as 'The Primordial Book', but it is also 'first' in relation to *Dasam Granth*, the tenth book, a collection of the hymns of Guru Gobind Singh, the tenth Guru. *Dasam Granth* became a sacred text for Sikhs, though it is not in such frequent use as *Adi Granth*.

The organisation of *Adi Granth* was made, not according to the authorship of the hymns, but according to the musical *rag* involved. A *rag* in Indian music is a scale or combination of notes associated with particular times or occasions. *Adi Granth* is made up of thirty-one different *rags*, with the hymns being allocated to the appropriate *rag*. At the end, though, some hymns are gathered together that do not fit into the general scheme of organisation. This means that in any one of the thirty-one *rags* there will be hymns by a variety of different authors.

That creates a slight complication because, as we have seen, the Gurus all signed their compositions as Nanak. Consequently, Arjan identified them with the word 'Mahalla', followed by the number of each Guru in sequence. *Mahalla* means 'body', indicating that the Gurus have different bodies even though they share the same spirit as Guru Nanak. Bhai Gurdas likened it to one candle being lit from another: the bodies are different but the flame is the same.

Thus 'Mahalla 1' indicates a composition by the first Guru, 'Mahalla 2' by the second, and so on. In addition, a particular hymn may have a title as well as the name of its *rag*. So, to give an example, Rahiras (evening prayer) includes the hymn beginning:

What gate opens the way to you?
What is the nature of your dwelling where you abide and sustain all
    creation?

The reference to this is Sodar Rag Asa Mahalla 1: 'The Gate', in *rag* Asa, written by Guru Nanak. There is, however, a simpler form of reference: *Adi Granth* is printed in a uniform and standard edition of 1,430 pages, so that references can also be given to the page number.

There are, in *Adi Granth*, 5,894 hymns or poems, of which by far the largest number (2,218) are by Guru Arjan. There are 937 hymns by people other than the Gurus. In addition to those by Kabir and Namdev, there are 221 written by Bhaktas (those practising Bhakti) and Sufis (Muslims following a comparable way of devotion: see pp. 151–7).

On 6 October 1708, the tenth Guru, Gobind Singh, decided that he would have no human successor. Instead, he told the Sikh community that the *Adi Granth* would in future be their Guru. The Book was therefore called *Guru Granth Sahib*.

As a result, the Book is treated very much as a living Guru. The shrine in which a copy of *Guru Granth Sahib* is kept is called *gur(u)dwara*, and in it *Guru Granth Sahib* is kept on a decorated throne under a canopy, and it is always raised above those who come to revere it and to consult it. A whisk (*chaur*), a symbol of royal presence, is constantly waved over it to prevent a fly or any other insect alighting on it and perhaps marking it.

Each day at dawn *Guru Granth Sahib* is opened in a ceremony called *prakash karna*, 'making Light manifest'. Those present recite the prayer known as Ardas. *Guru Granth Sahib* is then opened at random and the passage at the top of the left-hand page is read aloud. It becomes the *vak* (word) or *hukam* (wise judgement) for the day.

In the evening, *Guru Granth Sahib* is closed in a ceremony called *sukhasan*, 'resting comfortably'. Ardas is prayed and a further *vak* is chosen. In Ardas the great Sikhs of the past are remembered, and prayer is made for the continuing community. Ardas begins and ends (trans. Kaur Singh, p. 133f.):

> There is One Being, all victory belongs to the Wonderful Guru,
> May the divine Might help us . . .
> Honour of the honourless, Power of the powerless, Shield of the
>   shieldless,
> Our true Parent, *Vaheguru*, the Wonderful Guru!
> We humbly offer our prayers in Your presence.
> May we be free of lust, anger, greed, attachment and pride.
> Overlook our flaws in reading and reciting the sacred text.
> May everyone's actions be fulfilled.
> Join us with the faithful who inspire remembrance of Your Name.
> Says Nanak, may Your Name be ever ascendant.
> And, through Your Will, may everyone in the world fare well.

There are other sacred texts among the Sikhs, including *Dasam Granth*, the *janamsakhis* and even the works of Bhai Gurdas Bhalla because of his loyal and close association with the Gurus of his time. But *Guru Granth Sahib*, as the living Guru, is unique. That is why it is revered with actions and gestures that seem to be identical with worship. But it is not the Book that is being worshipped: it is the Sovereign Lord.

DASAM GRANTH

Dasam Granth is part of the recognised and revered sacred texts of the Sikhs, and it is also called Guru. It is made up of twenty-eight sections including hymns and prayers. Nevertheless, much of its material is very different from *Guru Granth Sahib*, with many epic and legendary stories. For example, Book 3, *Bachitra Natak*, 'Wonderful Drama', tells of Guru Gobind Singh's genealogy and his previous incarnation as an ascetic; Book 4 tells of the exploits of Chandi in a war against the demons. But *Dasam Granth* also supplies the hymns of devotion that Sikhs frequently use including the opening *Japu* of Guru Gobind Singh:

> You have no outward appearance, no *varna* [p. 181], caste or
>   family.
> Your appearance, features or attire cannot be described.
> You are unchanging, self-enlightened and of measureless power –
> This is how you are: supreme among the myriad gods,
> God of gods, King of kings, Ruler of the three worlds, the gods,
>   humans and demons.
> Of you nothing can be said by slightest grass to tallest tree except
>   *Neti, neti* ['not this, not this', p. 197].
> Who can list all your names, O Lord?
> Only by your acts can you be known.

BIBLIOGRAPHY NUMBERS 11, 264, 265, 411, 616, 652–4, 789, 954

7

JAINS

JAIN TEXTS: KEY DATES

BCE

c.850 Parshva, 23rd of the 24 Tirthankaras

599–27 Trad. dates of Mahariva

? Beginning of the divide between Digambaras
and Shvetambaras

CE

c.1st cent. ➡ Emergence of Bhattarakas

2nd–4th cent. Umasvati, *Tattvarthadhigama
Sutra*

453 or 466 3rd *vacana* at Valabhi

Previous page: A *siddhapratima yantra*, a Digambara Jain symbol of the escape from *karma* of a *siddha*, a liberated soul, or Jina: see p. 225.

JAINS

Agamas, Suttas and *Tattvartha Sutra*

Jains are those who follow the way of the Jinas, 'the Conquerors'. The Jinas are twenty-four figures who appear in each world cycle in order to show how to cross the gulf that lies between this world of rebirth (with its accumulation of *karma*) and the attainment of the highest bliss. They are therefore known as the Tirthankaras, 'the Makers of the Ford'. The most recent of these is Mahavira, Great Hero, who lived at roughly the same time as the Buddha. His dates traditionally are 599–27, but he may have lived something like a century later. In Jain belief, therefore, Jain teaching is uncreated and eternal and is simply brought back to life by the Tirthankaras in unending cycles.

In the present cycle, it can be seen that the Jain religion was historically (in about the eighth or seventh centuries BCE) part of the reaction against Vedic beliefs, rituals and sacrifices (as also was Buddhism). Part of that reaction is seen in the world-renouncers who sought the inner meaning of rituals, the forest-dwellers who produced the Aranyakas (p. 170). Collectively, people of this kind were known as *shramanas*, 'those who make an effort', or, in Prakrit, the language of the Jains, *samanas*.

Along with sacrifice and ritual Jains rejected belief in God. If there are deities, they are a part of the cosmos seeking their own release and freedom. That freedom, which humans also seek, is attained by releasing the spiritual self, *jiva*, from its entanglement in the material world. In particular that means disentangling it from the heavy weight of *karma*.

Karma is not the moral law of consequence, as it is elsewhere in India: it is the substantial weight of wrongdoing which permeates those who have acted wrongly. Jains therefore believe that to escape to freedom is to lose the weight of *karma*. The Tirthankaras are those who show how to do this. It requires extreme asceticism with a strong emphasis on *ahimsa*, not killing even the smallest life or possibility of life, and that meant originally not even wearing clothes since the process of making clothes would have involved killing.

Jains produced sacred texts in large numbers. They are known collectively as *agama* and are gathered in *suttas/sutras*. The word 'Agama' means roughly 'that which is received through tradition from acknowledged Teachers', the nearest equivalent to 'scripture'. The Agamas contain the words and teaching of the Tirthankaras, but those words do not originate with the Tirthankaras. They are eternal and uncreated, without any human or even divine origin.

The question of what works belong to the Jain Agama cannot easily be answered – indeed, it is contested among Jains themselves. That has happened because in about the fifth century CE the Jains split into two major groups. The Digambaras ('clothed in air') continued, as the name implies, to wear no clothes, but the Shvetambaras, who migrated south during a famine, began to wear clothes.

Among the issues that have divided them is the question of Scripture. Digambaras believe that the whole scriptural tradition has been lost so that the word *agama* can refer only to the teaching, not to texts; in their view, that teaching can be put into practice with even greater personal commitment since people cannot any longer rely on following words by rote. Even so, there are Digambara texts that are held in high regard, including *Shatkhandagama*, 'Agama of Six Parts', and *Kasayapahuda*, 'Treatise on the Passions', both dealing with *jiva* and its involvement with *karma*.

The Shvetambaras accept that many of the 'ancient' (*purva*) texts have been lost. However, they maintain that their own 'canon' of texts continued to exist precisely because they were not written down: they were recited and thus held in memory and tradition. They record three formal occasions when the texts were recited, and those occasions were actually called *vacana*, 'recitation'. After the third *vacana* at Valabhi (in the fifth century) it was decided to transfer what they believed to be the whole Canon into writing – though the word 'canon' needs to be used with caution because it is not a fixed or agreed collection of texts.

The result is a collection of forty-five texts (*sutras*) divided into five groups – although there is no record of exactly which texts were transferred into writing at Valabhi, so some may come from a later date (for a list of the major works, see Goyal p. 204f.). However, in words perhaps derived from Vedic terminology, the principal texts are the twelve Angas ('limbs'), of which one has been lost, to which are attached twelve Upangas ('subsidiary limbs'). The fourth group is particularly important because it contains texts that form the foundation for anyone embarking on the way of asceticism. They are therefore called *mulasutras*, 'root' or 'foundation' sutras. They are:

◆ *Uttaradhyayana* (Last or Later Chapters).

◆ *Dashavaikalika* (Ten Treatises of the Evening) summarising the correct forms of asceticism.

◆ *Avashyaka* ('obligations') outlining the six obligatory ritual actions.

◆ *Pindaniryukti* and *Oghaniryukti*, usually regarded as a single text, dealing with the behaviour and responsibilities of monks.

TATTVARTHA SUTRA

There remains one text that is held in the highest regard by both Digambaras and Shvetambaras, even though it is not a part of the eternal Word mediated through the Tirthankaras. It is a work written by Umasvati in the second century CE or later, called *Tattvarthadhigama Sutra* ('A Manual for Understanding All That Is'), usually shortened to *Tattvartha Sutra*. It is an attempt to state in Sutra form (i.e., it is extremely condensed and compressed) the main points of Jain belief and practice in religion, ethics and philosophy.

At first sight that may seem to be a self-contradiction, since Jains hold strongly to a belief in *anekanta*, non-absolutism. What this means in practice is that since no one is omniscient, all viewpoints must be approached with respect since they may contain at least a part of the truth. Yet even that is respected in *Tattvartha Sutra* because it begins with the claim that there is more than one way to *moksha* in the context of a priori conditions of truth. The Sutra begins (trans. Tatia, *Tattvartha Sutra*, 1.1–3):

> The enlightened world-view, enlightened knowledge and
> enlightened conduct are the path to liberation.
> To possess the enlightened world-view is to believe in the categories
> of truth.
> The enlightened world-view may arise spontaneously or through
> learning.
> The categories of truth are souls [*jiva*], non-sentient entities, the
> inflow of karmic particles to the soul, binding of the karmic
> particles to the soul, stopping the inflow of karmic particles,
> the falling away of the karmic particles, liberation from worldly
> bondage.

📖 BIBLIOGRAPHY NUMBERS 382, 498, 938, 962

8

BUDDHISM

BUDDHIST TEXTS: KEY DATES

BCE

5th or 4th cent. Siddhartha Gautama, the Buddha

c.4th cent. Assembly at Rajagaha: start of 'Canon'

c.4th cent. Forming of Sangha → Vinaya Pitaka

c.150BCE–100CE Mahayana develops in India

c.100BCE Milindapañha

c.100BCE–7th cent.CE Prajñaparamitavada

CE

78–139 Zhang Heng, *Xijing Fu*

2nd cent. Ashvaghosa, *Buddhacarita*

2nd cent. Nagarjuna, *Madhyamakashastra*

c.3rd cent. *Samdhinirmocana Sutra*

c.3rd cent. → Yogacara

c.300 *Ratnagunasamcayagatha, Ashtasahasrika Sutra*

c.4th cent. Asanga, *5 Books of Maitreya, Yogacarabhumi;* Vasubandhu, *Trimshika, Lankavatara Sutra*

312–85 Dao-an, collected Dhyana texts

406 Kumarajiva translated *Saddharmapundarika*

c.470–c.540 Bodhidharma → Chan/Zen

5th cent. Buddhaghosa, *Visuddhimagga*

538–97 Zhiyi → Tiantai, *Lotus Sutra*

557–640 Dushan → Huayan/Kegon

638–713 Hui-neng, *Platform/Altar Sutra*

732 Split of Northern and Southern Schools

c.750–97 Trisong Detsen, 1st Diffusion in Tibet

767–822 Saicho → Tendai

8th cent. Bodhiruci, ed. *Maharatuakuta*

c.8th cent. *Bardo Thödol*

972 *Dhammapada* block-printed in China

980–1052 Xuedou Chongxian, *Hekiganroku*

1016–1100 Naropa, *Na-ro-chos-drug* (*Chödrug*)

c.1050–1135 Milarepa

1079–1153 Gampopa, *The Jewel Ornament of Liberation*

1183–1260 Wu-men Hui-kai *Mumonkan*

1200–53 Dogen, *Fukanzazengi, Shobogenzo Zuimonki*

1222–82 Nichiren, *Rissho ankoku ron, Kaimokushu, Kanjin Honzonsho*

1290–1364 Bu-ston, *Buddhism in Tibet* organised Kangyur, Tengyur

14th cent. *Anjin ketsujo sho*

Previous page: The Buddha in meditation (p. 231) on a Naga (p. 251).

THE BUDDHA

The First and Final Addresses

Buddhism is the name given to Buddha-dharma or Buddha-sasana, the teaching and tradition of the Buddha. The term 'Buddhism' covers a large number of very diverse ways of belief and practice derived from the teaching of the Buddha. They all produced their own sacred texts, with most of them being traced back by those who use them to the Buddha himself. As a result, the number of sacred texts treasured by the Buddhists is immense.

Siddhartha Gautama (the Sanskrit form of his name: in Pali it is Gotama), who became the Buddha (i.e., 'the Enlightened One'), lived in North India at roughly the same time as Mahavira (p. 225), in either the fifth or fourth century BCE. It was, therefore, at the time when the *shramanas/samanas*, the world-renouncers, were rejecting the Vedic gods, rituals and sacrifices.

Gautama was not originally aware of this. He was a prince brought up in a royal palace by a father who was determined to shield him from anything that might distress him. The time came, however, when Gautama was driven through the Royal Park on successive days. On the first day he saw by the road an old and frail man, on the second a diseased man and on the third a corpse. He realised that all this was waiting to happen to him also. On the fourth day he saw a *shramana*, an ascetic who seemed to be completely tranquil. Gautama decided to seek the same tranquillity, so he left his wife and son, and went into the forest in order to practise asceticism.

His practice was so successful that it did indeed free him from the attractions of this world, but it could not set him free from those examples that he had seen of human frailty and death. He therefore decided to try a 'Middle Way' between extreme luxury and severe asceticism – and Middle Way became a common name for Buddhism. He sat for some days in meditation under a large tree (the tree subsequently was called the Bo or Bodhi Tree, the Tree of Enlightenment), where suddenly he broke through to complete Enlightenment: he saw exactly what the nature of suffering and transience is, how it arises and how it can be transcended. *Dukkha* is usually translated as 'suffering' and it does indeed refer to the various pains of life, mental and physical. But it also embraces the grief, pain and suffering which arise from the fact that everything is transient, that nothing lasts for ever. This was the key to his Enlightenment (*Majjhima Nikaya* 36):

> Thus I saw with the pure deva-eye [the eye of highest insight],
> clear beyond that of ordinary sight, beings dying and being reborn,
> humble and noble, beautiful and ugly, happy and wretched,
> arriving in good or bad states according to their actions ... In
> the second watch of the night I attained this second knowledge.
> Ignorance was scattered, knowledge was born, as it happens for
> those intent on the scattering [of ignorance]. Even so the resulting
> feeling of joy did not distract me. With my mind concentrated,
> pure, free from defilement, open to possibility, ready for
> commitment, I directed my mind to the destruction of desires: I
> knew as it really is: 'This is dukkha'; I knew as it really is: 'This is
> the origin of dukkha'; I knew as it really is: 'This is the cessation
> of dukkha'; I knew as it really is: 'This is the path that leads to the
> cessation of dukkha.' Thus knowing, thus seeing, my mind was
> set free from seeking a sense-directed life; it was set free from
> the delusion of seeking 'to be'; it was set free from the delusion
> arising from ignorance ... I knew that the true life has been lived
> to the limit, there is nothing more to be desired. This is the third
> knowledge that I attained in the last watch of the night.

THE FIRST ADDRESS: THE FOUR NOBLE TRUTHS AND THE NOBLE EIGHTFOLD PATH

His first address, *Dhammacakkapavattana-sutta* ('The Discourse Setting in Motion the Wheel of Dhamma'), was given in the Deer Park at Sarnath, and in it the foundations of the Middle Way are summarised in the Noble Eightfold Path and the Four Noble Truths (*Samyutta Nikaya* 5.420):

> Once the Buddha was living at Isipatana in the Deer Park where
> he addressed five bhikkhus [Sanskrit *bhikshu*; disciplined
> followers usually translated as 'monks']: 'There are two extremes
> to be avoided by those who have renounced the world. What are

they? Everything to do with passion and luxurious living . . . , and
everything to do with torture of the self and useless pain. Avoiding
those two extremes the Tathagata [a title of the Buddha indicating
that he has gone before into complete Truth] has reached the
Enlightenment of the Middle Way: it brings perfect insight and
knowledge, and it leads to peace, higher knowledge, Enlightenment
and Nirvana.

And what is this Middle Way? It is *astangika-marga* [the Noble
Eightfold Path] of right understanding, right thought, right speech,
right action, right living, right effort, right mindfulness, right
concentration [*samadhi*].'

These are the Four Noble Truths (True Realities for the Spiritually Ennobled) of
the human predicament involved in *dukkha*.

This is the true reality of *dukkha*. *Dukkha* is birth, it is old age, it is
sickness, it is death, it is the accompanying grief, sorrow, depression
and despair, physical pain and distress. *Dukkha* is involvement
with unpleasing things, it is failing to get what one desires.

This is the truth of the cause of *dukkha*. It is the desperate desire
– binding one to rebirth, expressed in self-indulgence and lust,
looking for pleasure anywhere it can – for continuing existence, or
even for non-existence.

This is the truth of the cessation of *dukkha*. It is the complete
obliteration of desire, it is abandoning and forsaking and letting go,
it is non-attachment.

This is the truth of the way that leads to the cessation of *dukkha*. It
is to follow the Noble Eightfold Path . . .

All this I recognised, . . . and when I had done so knowledge
flooded through me, insight rose up so that the release of my
understanding cannot be reversed: this is my last existence; now
there is no further reappearance.

'Reappearance' (*punnabbhava*, 're-becoming') is the equivalent of the Indian
understanding of the rebirth of the self many times until *moksha* is attained. But
in Buddhist understanding there is no thing that can escape transience: no thing
lasts for ever. It follows that there is 'no self' (*anatman/anatta*) to be reborn:
there is only a sequence of reappearances brought about by the cause and effect

of *karma* until, by following the Eightfold Path, the sequence is brought to an end in Nirvana. Nirvana is not a place like Heaven: it is a condition of perfect stability where there cannot be any cause and effect. It is the condition already attained by Tathagata, who shares with his followers the way to attain that state – but they have to attain it for themselves: he cannot do it for them. In his last address, therefore, he said (in *Mahaparinibbana Sutta, Digha Nikaya* 2.100):

> Now I am grown old and full of years and my journey is near the end . . . So be lamps to yourselves. Be your own refuge and do not look for any refuge outside yourselves. Hold fast to the Dharma as your lamp . . . And all those who, whether now or after I am dead, are a lamp to themselves and a refuge for themselves, and who hold fast to the Dharma as their lamp and as their refuge, looking for none outside themselves, it is they who will reach the highest height. But they must be eager to learn.

According to the same Sutta (*Digha Nikaya* 2.156), his last words were: 'All conditioned things are of a nature to decay [hence '*dukkha* is inherent in all composite things'], so work out your salvation with commitment.'

📖 BIBLIOGRAPHY NUMBERS 91, 271, 272, 283, 697, 992

SACRED TEXTS OF
BUDDHISTS

The Pali Canon and the Canons
of Tibet, China and Japan

The Buddha was clear that there is no God who brought this universe into being and who exists outside the dimensions of space and time. He accepted that among the many appearances within the universe there are those correctly referred to as gods and goddesses, but they too are appearances seeking to move towards Enlightenment. Nevertheless, they are the kinds of beings with which humans can interact, so that although the Buddha rejected as futile the Vedic rituals and sacrifices, he allowed Buddhists to recognise that there are circumstances when it may be wise to enter into a relationship with deities through praise and prayer. In other words, Buddhism is not an atheistic philosophy as it is sometimes described. On the other hand, it does deny the idea of God as Creator, an unproduced Producer of all that is.

From this it follows that there cannot be a God of that kind who is the author of Scripture as revelation. Nevertheless, there are many texts that Buddhists regard as sacred because they are revelatory of the Buddha's teaching and guidance concerning the way to reach Enlightenment and the cessation of reappearance.

There are in fact several different collections of texts that are believed to convey the Buddha's Dharma or teaching. In these collections, a distinction is made between the words of the Buddha (*buddhavacana*) and the recognised commentaries, but both have authority. As a matter of convenience these collections are usually referred to as Canons, but the different Canons are not identical, and Buddhists refer to them by different names. The collections belong to different lineages, meaning by 'lineages' lines of tradition through which texts and teaching are passed on from one certified teacher to another.

The two major lineage groups are those of Theravada ('teaching of the elders') and Mahayana ('great vehicle'; Mahayana Buddhists call Theravada Hinayana, 'small vehicle'). There are many divergent lineages within Mahayana, and each of all these lineages will have its own designated sacred texts. It follows that the total number of sacred texts in the whole of Buddhism is vast.

The major collections are located geographically, following the origin and spread of Buddhism, beginning in India, going north into Tibet, south and south-east into Sri Lanka and South East Asia (mainly Theravada), and then east into China, Korea and Japan (mainly Mahayana).

THE BUDDHIST 'CANONS'

Little of the Indian Sanskrit Canon has survived in its original language, but much of it was translated into other languages as Buddhism spread, particularly in China and in Tibet when it took root from the seventh century CE onwards. The Tibetan Canon is made up of two parts: one part containing words and texts attributed to the Buddha is known as bKa'-'gyur (pronounced Kangyur), 'Translation of the Word of the Buddha'; the other part is known as bsTan-'gyur (pronounced Tengyur), 'Translation of the Treatises'. bKa'-'gyur contains more than 600 texts attributed to the Buddha in five groups, and bsTan-'gyur contains about 3,626 texts: in its Chinese edition it runs to 224 volumes.

When Buddhists moved from India to Sri Lanka they took with them orally transmitted texts that were first written down (in Pali) in Sri Lanka. The palm-leaf manuscripts were kept in 'three baskets' (*tipitaka/tripitaka*). The baskets are:

◆ Vinaya Pitaka, the Basket of Discipline, referring particularly to *bhikkhus* and *bhikkunis*, monks and nuns: it is in three parts, *Suttavibhanga*, including *Patimokkha* rules for monks (227) and nuns (311), *Khandaka* and *Parivara*.

◆ Abhidhamma Pitaka, the Basket of Further Teachings, clarifying the components of Buddhist analysis in terms of a set of basic interacting processes, changing from moment to moment.

◆ Sutta Pitaka, the Basket of Discourses/Addresses. This Pitaka is made up of five Collections (*nikaya* means 'collection'):

1 *Digha Nikaya*, 34 Long (discourses).

2 *Majjhima Nikaya*, 150 Middle Length (discourses).

3 *Samyutta Nikaya*, 7,762 Connected (discourses).

4 *Anguttara Nikaya*, 9,550 One Upward (discourses), grouped according to the number of items involved.

5 *Khuddaka Nikaya*, Little Texts, 15 texts, some often quoted because they are extremely early, although not all Buddhist Schools accept them as 'canonical'; they include *Dhammapada* (verses on ethical behaviour), *Petavatthu* (on rebirths among the spirits of the departed), *Theragatha* and *Therigatha* (verses celebrating the ways in which early monks and nuns attained Enlightenment), *Jataka* (547 'birth stories' of events in previous lives of the Buddha) and *Buddhavamsa* (Chronicle of the Buddhas on the lives of twenty-four earlier Buddhas).

The Buddhism that reached China was Mahayana. Mahayana Buddhists believe that much of the teaching of the Buddha was not entrusted to the world all at once: as in the distinction between elementary and higher education, the higher levels of teaching were held back until people were ready to receive them. From the Mahayana point of view, the elementary education is found in the Hinayana. The advanced teaching is passed on through (Mahayana) lineages and is expressed especially in Sutras.

The Chinese Canon is known as 'The Great Treasury of Scriptures'. It is also called 'The Triple Treasury', but it was not divided into 'three baskets'. It contains parallels to most of the texts found in the Pali Tripitaka but it adds many more – not just Sutras but also commentaries, histories, biographies and some writings that are not even Buddhist. Chinese lineages are inclined to treat the Treasury more as a library than a canon – not surprisingly, since the number of texts is daunting; the Japanese edition (*Taisho Shinshu Daizokyo*, to which references are given in the form T followed by the volume number) contains 2,184 texts in 55 volumes, and the setting up in China of an official canon is aiming to produce 4,100 texts in 220 volumes.

In Japan the idea of a canon of sacred texts becomes even more complicated, not to say imprecise. Buddhism came to Japan from Korea and China, and for centuries many of the lineage teachers in Japan received their training in China. Nevertheless, they soon gave to the Chinese lineages a distinctive Japanese style and interpretation. They then established and developed lineages of their own with their own individual sacred texts. The process of innovation continues to the present day in what are known as 'new religions', of which there are more than 200 with Buddhist roots. The word 'new' is slightly misleading because some of those with the most influential sacred texts go back to the thirteenth century (as, for example, in the case of Nichiren: see further, pp. 265f.).

It follows that the question of what is to be included in a canon as legitimate and authoritative is not easy. In a sense it is irrelevant, because what matters, according to the Buddha himself, is not external authority but internal recognition of the diagnosis of the physician (as the Buddha styled himself) and the acceptance of his cure. Even so, attempts were made to separate the authentic from the spurious. Traditionally, it is said that Mahakasyapa, a close follower of the Buddha, convened a council in Rajagrha to decide which words came directly from the mouth of the Buddha or from his close associates, but that hardly satisfied the claim of Mahayana Buddhists that some teaching was deliberately held back. In the end a sacred text has to be decided by its efficacy. It was this that controlled the content of texts like the 'lives of the Buddha' when they came to be written.

📖 BIBLIOGRAPHY NUMBERS 627, 945, 992

LIVES OF THE BUDDHA

JATAKAS, *BUDDHACARITA* AND *LALITAVISTARA*

Buddhists are those who find complete truth and safety in the Three Refuges, known as the Three Jewels or the Triple Jewel (*triratna*, Pali *tiratna*):

> I take refuge in the Buddha;
> I take refuge in the Dharma;
> I take refuge in the Sangha.

'I take refuge in the Buddha' means at the very least accepting his teaching as the correct diagnosis of the human predicament and as the only cure. 'Taking refuge in the Buddha' took on an even more extensive meaning as the understanding of the nature of the Buddha developed in Mahayana Buddhism (see p. 250).

The Three Baskets of the Pali Canon are related to the Three Jewels. 'I take refuge in the Buddha' is related to Sutta Pitaka, containing discourses of the Buddha, including some episodes and a little information about his life. The works contained in Sutta Pitaka, however, were not written as biographies of the Buddha.

Lives of the Buddha of a more connected or chronological kind were produced from about 100BCE onward by different schools or traditions, including *Lalita-vistara* of the Sarvastivadins, *Nidanakatha* of the Theravadins and *Mahavastu* of the Lokattaravadins. One of the earliest is Ashvaghosa's *Buddhacarita* from the second century CE. Ashvaghosa was a court poet who wrote 'The Acts of the Buddha' in Sanskrit in the traditional epic (*mahakavya*) style. Of its twenty-eight Books, only thirteen survive in Sanskrit; the remainder appear in Tibetan or Chinese translations. When Conze translated some parts of this (*Buddhist Scriptures*, pp. 34–66), he drew attention to the importance of this work in Buddhist life (p. 34):

> I have concentrated on those scenes of the sacred drama which have
> impressed themselves most forcibly and extensively on the imagination

of the Buddhist community, and which the art of Asia has over and over again depicted in stone, on silk and on canvas. To decide which of these events are credible or 'historical' was none of my functions, and would have been an unwarranted interference with the tradition.

That last sentence draws attention to the fact that none of these Lives is a biography in any modern sense. What matters is not whether an event happened or a discourse was spoken exactly as it is reported, but whether the material is conducive to the attainment of that 'refuge in the Buddha'. The same point was made by Brewster when he made an anthology of passages from the Pali Canon relating to the life of the Buddha (p. xvi):

> I would not wish to give such an emphasis to historical evidence,
> important as it is, which would confuse it with religious values.
> All schools of Buddhism, I believe, would maintain that what is
> important in their religion belongs to personal experience, and
> should be tested by it.

A further difference in these Buddhist Lives of the Buddha is that they do not begin with the birth of that particular Gautama who lived in the fifth or fourth century BCE. Buddhists believe not exactly in rebirth since there is no 'self' being reborn, but rather in long sequences of reappearance in which the karmic consequences of thought and behaviour are worked out. The Lives of the Buddha therefore include accounts of the many previous lives of the Buddha, culminating in his Enlightenment under the Bodhi Tree. Indeed, most of the Lives end at or near that point: they do not usually record details of his later life until his final attainment of Nirvana (p. 233).

JATAKA

The stories of the previous lives of the Buddha are known collectively as Jataka ('birth-story'). Of these Jataka stories, 547 of the best known are collected in *Khuddaka Nikaya* (p. 237). They are written in verse within a prose context, of which only the verse is usually regarded as 'canonical'. Another work, *Nidanakatha*, tells the story down to events after Gautama's Enlightenment, but it begins far back with his first decision to set out on the way that would lead to his sequence of reappearances to become a Buddha. Among the many Jataka stories, particularly famous is the episode of three princes and the hungry tigress (trans. Conze, 1966, pp. 24–6):

The Buddha told the following story to Ananda: Once upon a time, in the remote past, there lived a king, Maharatha by name ... He had three sons ..., Mahapranada, Mahadeva, and Mahasattva. One day as the princes strolled about in a solitary thicket they saw a tigress, surrounded by five cubs, seven days old. Hunger, and thirst had exhausted the tigress, and her body was quite weak ... Mahadeva said: 'She is quite exhausted, overcome by hunger and thirst, scarcely alive and very weak. In this state she cannot possibly catch any prey. And who would sacrifice himself to preserve her life?' ... But Mahasattva thought to himself: 'Now the time has come for me to sacrifice myself! For a long time I have served this putrid body and given it beds and clothes, food and drink, and conveyances of all kinds. Yet it is doomed to perish and fall down, and in the end it will break up and be destroyed. How much better to leave this ungrateful body of one's own accord in good time! It cannot subsist forever, because it is like urine which must come out. To-day I will use it for a sublime deed. Then it will act for me as a boat which helps me to cross the ocean of birth and death ...' So, his heart filled with boundless compassion, Mahasattva asked his brothers to leave him alone for a while, went to the lair of the tigress, hung his cloak on a bamboo, and made the following vow [the vow of a Bodhisattva: see p. 268]:

> For the weal of the world I wish to win enlightenment, incomparably wonderful. From deep compassion I now give away my body, so hard to quit, unshaken in my mind. That enlightenment I shall now gain, in which nothing hurts and nothing harms, and which the Jina's sons have praised ...

The friendly prince then threw himself down in front of the tigress. But she did nothing to him. The Bodhisattva noticed that she was too weak to move. As a merciful man he had taken no sword with him. He therefore cut his throat with a sharp piece of bamboo, and fell down near the tigress. She noticed the Bodhisattva's body all covered with blood, and in no time ate up all the flesh and blood, leaving only the bones.

It was I, Ananda, who at that time and on that occasion was that prince Mahasattva.

📖 BIBLIOGRAPHY NUMBERS 55, 506, 511

THE SANGHA

VINAYA PITAKA, DHAMMAPADA

'I take refuge in the Sangha': to take refuge in the Sangha (Pali Samgha, 'Community') is to enter into a positive relationship with the organised community set up by the Buddha. Those who enter it formally are known as *bhikkhu* and *bhikkhuni* (Pali; Sanskrit *bhikshu/bhikshuni*), conventionally translated as 'monk' and 'nun'. Laypeople (*upasaka/upasika*) enter into an equally positive relationship with the Sangha since they support it with gifts and receive instruction and benefits from it, not least by receiving merit in the karmic process of reappearance. *Bhikkhus* depend on the laity because they are required to possess only two things, the saffron- (earth-) coloured robe and a begging bowl: 'Wherever he goes he is supported by only two things, just as a bird on the wing carries his wings with him.'

The Sangha is the oldest social organisation in existence since it was established roughly 2,500 years ago. It has two main purposes. The first is for the monks and nuns to reach, through freedom of mind (especially through concentrated and calm meditation, *samatha*) and through understanding (especially through insight meditation, *vipassana*), the highest goal of release (*vimutti*) from *dukkha* and from the cycles of reappearance.

The second main purpose is to use that freedom in order to be of service to others, to live, as Vinaya Pitaka 2.22 puts it, 'for the benefit of many, for the happiness of many, out of compassion for the world'.

The ultimate purpose was summed up by the Buddha in these words:

> Bhikkhus, the aim of the disciplined life is not to gain material
> profit, nor is it to win admiration from others, nor is it to practise
> the highest moral behaviour, nor is it to attain the highest single-
> minded concentration. No. The ultimate end of the disciplined life
> is the complete and irreversible liberation of the mind. That is the
> essence. That is the goal.

VINAYA PITAKA

The Rules governing the Sangha are collected in Vinaya Pitaka. It has two main sections, *Suttavibhanga* and *Khandaka*, together with an appendix *Parivara*. *Suttavibhanga* includes the basic rules for monks, 227 in number, and, for nuns, 311. The rules are known as *Patimokkha/Patimoksha* and are recited regularly (at the time of the quarter moon) in an observance known as Uposatha: during this, any breach of the rules is acknowledged. Laypeople associate themselves with this by receiving instruction and perhaps by taking on three more of the Rules or Precepts (see below).

Khandaka is in two parts, *Mahavagga* and *Culavagga*. Both of these are arranged by topics and include episodes of the Buddha's life. They also include accounts of how the Buddha established the Order of nuns. According to Vinaya Pitaka 2.53–6, it was done circumspectly, and by about the fourteenth century it had disappeared in the Theravadin tradition. The admission of nuns requires the presence of a minimum of five nuns so that when that number could no longer be found, no more admissions could be made. Buddhist Orders of women continued in Mahayana Buddhism.

KHUDDAKA NIKAYA: THERIGATHA, THERAGATHA

The major contribution of nuns in early Buddhism has left its mark on the sacred texts. *Therigatha* (522 'Verses of the Elder Nuns') is included, along with the equivalent for monks, *Theragatha*, in *Khuddaka Nikaya* (p. 237). It is clear from this that the nuns reached the highest levels of attainment, but only after profound struggle – as recorded, for example, in *Therigatha* 67–71 (translated by Schelling and Waldman, p. 89; the attainments in the last lines are 'the three knowledges', *tevijja*, attainable by women, of memory of past lives, of seeing the reappearance of others according to their *karma*, and of experiencing Nirvana):

> It's been twenty-five years since I became a nun
> But I'm still restless
> No peace of mind – not even one moment
> (*she snaps her fingers*)
> Every thought's of sex
> I hold out my arms
> Cry out like a madwoman
> Then I go into my cell
> But I heard Dhamma-Dinna preach
> and she taught me impermanence
> I sat down to meditate:

I know I've lived before
My celestial eye has been purified
I see I see other lives past and present
I read other minds present and past
The ear element is purified
I hear I hear I can really hear.

KHUDDAKA NIKAYA: DHAMMAPADA

Khuddaka Nikaya also includes *Dhammapada*, one of the most widely popular of all Buddhist texts, and a reminder that guidance was written for laypeople as well. Laypeople, as part of that dynamic interaction between Sangha and themselves, undertake five of the ten Rules or Precepts to which novice monks commit themselves. They are 'promises to oneself': *ahimsa*, not taking anything not given, no misconduct involving sense-pleasure, no false speech, no loss of self-control through drugs or intoxicants.

The Precepts cover much of life, but more specific guidance than that was needed and it was offered in the Pali verses of *Dhammapada* ('The Path of Dharma'; there is also a longer version in Sanskrit known as *Udanavarga*). It is an anthology of 423 sayings of the Buddha (though not all are specifically Buddhist), divided according to topics into twenty-six chapters including Vigilance (2) and Control of Thought (3): 'Just as an archer steadies his arrow, the wise calm their shifting and unsteady thoughts which are difficult to control and difficult to restrain. Like a fish taken out of water and thrown on the ground, thoughts shake and tremble caught in the domain of Death [Mara]' (3.1–2).

Other chapters collect sayings on such topics as Flowers (4), Folly (5), Old Age (11), Happiness (15), Anger (17) and the Elephant (23, in which the training of oneself is compared to the training and nature of elephants). Some chapters are devoted to more specifically Buddhist topics, including what it takes to attain the Enlightenment of the Buddha (14.179–96):

It is difficult to obtain the human state, difficult to live as a human, difficult to accept Dharma, difficult to reach Enlightenment.

The shunning of all evil, the acquiring of good, the cleansing of the mind, this is what the Buddhas teach.

Patient endurance is the highest form of asceticism. The fully awakened show Nirvana to be the highest goal. Those who oppress others are not world-renouncers, nor are those ascetics who cause grief to others . . .

Those who are in the grip of fear run for refuge to mountains, to forests, to sacred trees and holy shrines.

None of those is a safe refuge, they are not the best refuge. Those who reach refuges of that kind are not delivered from fear.

But those who take refuge in the Buddha, the Dharma and the Sangha grasp with perfect clarity the meaning of the Four Noble Truths.

Dukkha, the origin of Dukkha, the cessation of Dukkha and the Noble Eightfold Path leading to the cessation of Dukkha,

that beyond doubt is a safe refuge, that is the best refuge: those who reach that refuge are freed from all fear.

Dhammapada exists in many versions and translations, since it went everywhere in the Buddhist world. It was one of the earliest books to be block-printed in China in 972 CE.

BIBLIOGRAPHY NUMBERS 285, 945

DHARMA/DHAMMA

Abhidhamma, Visuddhimagga, Milindapañha

'I take refuge in the Dharma': to take refuge in the Dharma is to accept the teaching of the Buddha with complete commitment and confidence. It is to put one's complete trust in the Buddha as the one who, like a physician, understands an illness and prescribes the cure. Too much hesitation postpones what needs to be done (*Majjhima Nikaya* 63):

> Supposing someone says that he will not follow the Buddha's teaching unless the Buddha can first tell him whether the world is eternal or temporal, finite or infinite, whether vitality is identical with the body or something different, whether the Tathagata continues after death or does not do so: that person will die before the Tathagata can answer all those questions. It is as if someone is hit by a poisoned arrow and those around him summon a physician, but the man then says, 'I will not have this arrow pulled out until I know who it is that wounded me – whether he is a warrior, a prince, a householder, or a servant; or what his name is and to what family he belongs; or whether he is tall or short or of medium height.' I tell you in truth, that person will die before he can learn the answer to all those questions.

The Dharma is found extensively in the Suttas (p. 236), and it is then expounded more systematically in other works, not least in response to particular questions. The Buddha's Dharma makes such distinctive claims about the nature of the cosmos and of human beings that questions inevitably arise. It claims, for example, that there is no permanent self or soul. Where other Indians claim *atman* (p. 173), the Buddha claims *anatta/anatman*. All conditioned things are transient, and there is nothing, not even a self or soul, that can escape. Humans, however, have a strong sense of 'being who they are', of continuing to be the same person through the process of time. How can that sense of 'being myself' arise if everything is indeed transient?

According to the Buddha, it happens because humans are 'put together' by the interaction of five constituent properties, the five Skandhas (Pali, *khandha*, 'group'). The five Skandhas are constantly in the process of change but with provisional continuity. They can therefore be identified in the continuing process of change and referred to collectively by name, as, for example, John or Jane. But they do not require, nor do they constitute, a self isolated or immune from the process.

That answer, however, raises many further questions. For example, what are the Skandhas? How do they come into being? How do they continue through time and then dissolve?

The answers to questions such as these are gathered in the third of the Three Baskets, Abhidhamma Pitaka. Lama Anagarika Govinda summarised the importance of Abhidhamma Pitaka with these words (p. 37):

> The Abhidhamma is the totality of the psychological and
> philosophical teachings of Buddhism, the point of departure of all
> Buddhist schools and tendencies of thought. Without a knowledge
> of the Abhidhamma the nature and development of Buddhism
> must ever remain wanting in clearness.

The works in Abhidhamma Pitaka, therefore, analyse the teaching contained in the Suttas. Each of the lineages of Buddhism has its own version of the Abhidhamma Pitaka, but the only early ones to have survived are those of the Sarvastivadins (a lineage in early Buddhism) in Chinese and Tibetan translations, and of the Theravadins (in Pali).

VISUDDHIMAGGA, MILINDAPAÑHA

The work of analysis and understanding was not confined to Abhidhamma Pitaka. Two particular works are highly regarded among Theravada Buddhists. One is *Visuddhimagga* ('The Way of Purification') by Buddhaghosa (fifth century CE). It is a guide to meditation and doctrine with an immensely careful examination of sources in the Pali Canon, raising questions which are then answered in detail.

The second is *Milindapañha* ('The Questions of King Milinda'), a work of such importance to the Burmese that they included it in their Canon. It is written in the form of a dialogue between a monk, Nagasena, and King Menander, a successor of Alexander the Great's conquest of northwest India. Menander is supposed to have been converted by Nagasena, and this work is the record of the arguments that converted him. Central to the dialogue are the issues of self and not-self, and of the nature of the Skandhas, as in this passage when the King asks Nagasena his name:

'I am known as Nagasena, great King, and that is what my fellow monks call me. But although parents give to their children names like Nagasena or Surasena or Virasena or Sihasena, the word "Nagasena" is just a way of picking an appearance out, a practical designation, simply a name. It does not imply a permanent individual.'

. . . Then the King said to Nagasena: 'If there is no permanent individual, who is it that is giving you your robes and food, lodging and medicines? And who is it that makes use of them? Who is it that lives according to Dharma, meditates and reaches Nirvana? Who is it that destroys life, steals, commits sexual misconduct, tells lies and drinks intoxicants [the Five Precepts] . . . If there is no individual person, there can be no merit or demerit, no fruit or consequence of good and evil deeds . . . If your fellow monks call you Nagasena, what then is Nagasena? Is it your hair?'

Nagasena answered, 'No, great King.'

'Or your nails, teeth, skin, or other parts of your body . . . ? Or your feelings or perceptions or impulses or consciousness? . . . Are any of these Nagasena, or all of them taken together, or anything other than they?'

Nagasena answered, 'No, great King.'

'Then for all my asking I find no Nagasena – Nagasena is a mere sound.'

Nagasena answered, 'Great King, how did you come here? On foot or in a vehicle?'

'In a chariot.'

'Then tell me what is the chariot? Is the pole the chariot?'

'No, honoured Sir.'

'Is it the axle, wheels, frame, reins, yoke, spokes, or goad?'

'None of these is the chariot.'

'Then is the chariot something apart from the combination of those things?'

'No, honoured Sir.'

'Then for all my asking I can find no chariot. The word "chariot"

Zain al'Abidin (early sixteenth century) illustrates an episode in *Ramayana* (p. 184) where Hanuman, sent for a healing herb from a Himalayan mountain, brings the whole mountain.

A scene from *Mahabharata* (p. 185) at the outset of *Bhagavadgita* (pp. 190–3) depicting Arjuna with Krishna as his charioteer.

The conflict in *Mahabharata* between the Pandavas and Kauravas illustrating the importance of 'sacred texts' carved in stone: with appropriate rituals they can become imbued with power.

A Tantric diagram of the cakras, the centres of cosmic energy located in the body: see pp. 201–2, 206.

Two examples of yantras used in meditation, especially in Tantra: text, mantra and diagram are united in visualisation, just as male and female (the upward and downward triangles) are united to generate powerful effect.

The Mul Mantra (*mantar*), the first verses of Japji Sahib (trans. pp. 216–17), opens *Guru Granth Sahib* and is recited in daily morning prayer. The script is Gurmukhi ('from the mouth of the Guru'), used for Punjabi in India and much respected by Sikhs.

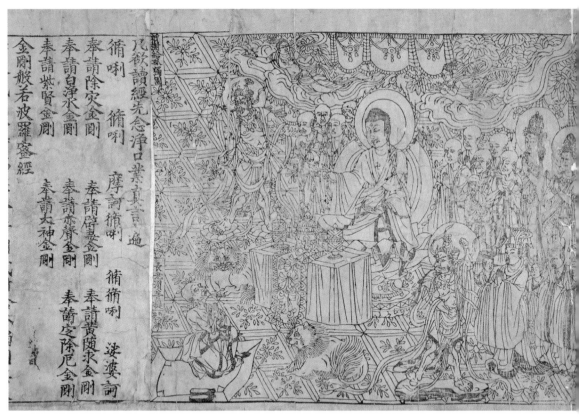

A page from a Prajñaparamita Sutra (pp. 253–5) showing the Buddha teaching Dharma to his ten revered followers.

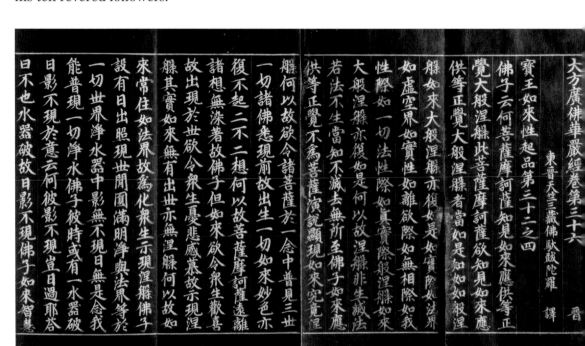

A page from *Avatamsaka Sutra*, a foundation text of Huayan (pp. 261–3).

is a mere sound . . . Surely, great King, what you have said is false! There is no chariot! . . .

The King replied, 'What I have said is not false: when poles, axles, wheels and the rest are put together, the result is called "a chariot". It's a generally understood term, a practical designation.'

'Well said, great King! You know what the word "chariot" designates, and it is exactly the same with me. Because of the aggregated components of the thirty-two parts of the body and the five Skandhas I am known by the generally understood term, the practical designation Nagasena . . .'

The King replied, '. . . Well spoken, Nagasena, well spoken!'

📖 BIBLIOGRAPHY NUMBERS 121, 161, 978

MAHAYANA

Sutras

The movements in Buddhism that came to be known collectively as Mahayana (Great Vehicle) began to emerge in India during the period between 150 BCE and 100 CE. They developed several distinctive beliefs:

◆ In earlier Buddhism, the highest state that can be reached during life is that of *arahat/arahant*, one who has attained the experience of Nirvana and will not reappear on earth or in heaven. That seemed to Mahayana selfish, so they developed the idea of the bodhisattvas, those who could cease to reappear but who choose to continue to perfect Buddhahood through many lives in order to help others still in suffering or distress.

◆ The Trikaya ('Three Bodies') forms, through which the Buddha manifests himself: in the first (Dharmakaya), the Buddha is identical with all that is, the complete and absolute truth of its being; in the second (Sambhogakaya), the Buddhas create splendid heavens and paradises where they appear in celestial forms; in the third (Nirmanakaya), they appear in earthly or physical form.

◆ The Perfection of Wisdom (*prajñaparamita*) leads into the most profound understanding and truth; it is taught not only in Mahayana lineages, but also to bodhisattvas by the Sambhogakaya Buddhas in paradise.

◆ The Buddha-nature (*buddhata*, Jap. *bussho*) is the only reality there is; although there may seem to us in our ignorance to be many different realities, they are not ultimately real: they are simply appearances sustained by the underlying Buddha-nature.

◆ The Buddha can still produce hitherto undisclosed teaching, and Mahayana collected this teaching in Sutras; indeed, followers of Mahayana were identified, not by any particular beliefs or allegiances, but simply by accepting the new Sutras as genuine and authoritative teaching of the Buddha.

It was that last belief which produced a huge increase in the number of sacred texts in Mahayana Buddhism. Traditionalists rejected the new Sutras on the ground that they could not possibly be *Buddha-vacana*, 'the word of the Buddha': self-evidently they were extremely different in style and content from the earlier works in the Pali Canon.

Mahayanists replied with three arguments that the Sutras are genuine 'words of the Buddha':

1 The Buddha cannot cease to exist and therefore is able to communicate teaching through meditation, visions and dreams.

2 A clear line of connection can be traced from early canonical teaching to the elaboration and extension of that teaching in the Sutras.

3 The Buddha deliberately kept back some teaching until people were more developed in the Perfection of Wisdom; some later Mahayana Buddhists thought that he had hidden this teaching in the world of the *nagas*, the snake deities of India who in Buddhism become protectors of Dharma until humans are ready to receive it.

From these arguments, Mahayana developed another characteristic belief which became of widespread importance in explaining why the Buddha's Dharma has taken so many different forms. It is the belief in *upaya-kaushalya*, 'skill in means'. Part of the wisdom of the Buddha was his ability to adapt his teaching to the competence and level of understanding of those particular people to whom he spoke. As parents adapt their teaching to the age of their children, so the Buddha adapts his teaching even to the point of saying something that has later to be corrected. The second chapter of *Lotus Sutra* (see further, p. 264) is entitled *Fang bian*, a Chinese translation of *upaya-kaushalya*. In it, the Buddha states (trans. Kato, pp. 51, 59):

> Ever since I became Buddha, with various reasonings and various parables I have widely discoursed and taught, and by countless tactful methods [*upaya-kaushalya*] have led living beings, causing them to leave all attachments. Wherefore? [Because] the Tathagata is altogether perfect in his tactfulness and Perfection [*paramita*] of Wisdom . . . Therefore I expound the laws by numberless tactful ways and with various reasonings and parabolic expressions. These laws cannot be understood by powers of thought or discrimination; only the buddhas can discern them.

On the basis of those arguments, Mahayana Buddhists produced an extremely large number of Sutras, and thus an extremely large number of sacred texts. The early Sutras fall into four main groups – though some of the most revered Sutras are separate.

◆ *Prajñaparamita*, 'The Perfection of Wisdom', is the earliest collection, on which see p. 253ff.

◆ *Maharatnakuta* ('great' + 'jewel' + 'mountain') in its present form is a collection edited in the eighth century in China by Bodhiruci. Both Tibetan and Chinese sources say that the collection included forty-nine titles, of which only four survive in the original Sanskrit. Five of its Sutras are among the earliest Mahayana texts to have been translated into Chinese, among them the teaching offered to Kashyapa known as *Kashyapaparivarta*. Here, for example, he is taught about bodhisattvas (Stael-Holstein, pp. 17–20):

> Kaśyapa, there are four ways to gain the great treasure of bodhisattvas. What are the four? To take delight in the presence of the Buddha, to absorb the six perfections [*paramita*], to accept teachers of Dharma without envy, to take greatest pleasure in the practice of solitude.
>
> Kaśyapa, there are four aids to help bodhisattvas to overcome evil. What are the four? To keep Enlightenment always in mind, to think no evil of any sentient being, to discern mistaken views, to hold no one in contempt . . .
>
> Kaśyapa, there are four supreme virtues. What are the four? To teach Dharma with a clear mind, to show compassion for people of low status, to transmit the thought of Enlightenment to all beings, to encourage those who are overcome with weariness.

◆ *Mahasamnipata* is a small collection of seventeen diverse sutras in the Chinese Canon, mainly concerned with magic.

◆ *Buddhavatamsaka* survives in two Chinese versions, a mark, perhaps, of its importance when its ideas were developed in the Hua-yan tradition: on this, see further, pp. 260ff.

📖 BIBLIOGRAPHY NUMBERS 197, 459, 526, 623, 899

PERFECTION OF WISDOM

Ashtasahasrika Sutra, the *Diamond-cutter Sutra*, the *Heart Sutra*, and Nagarjuna

The interpretation of Buddhism known as Prajñaparamitavada, the Way of the Perfection of Wisdom, began to appear in India at some time between 100 BCE and 100 CE, and it continued until about the seventh century. This 'Wisdom that has gone to the limit' focuses on the way in which the Buddha discloses the fundamental nature and the *actual* (as opposed to the superficially assumed) reality of all living appearances as they are in themselves.

The key to passing beyond the superficial impressions of reality in the case of living beings is to discern the Buddha-potential within them, the Buddha-nature (*buddhata*) as the only reality there is – insofar as 'real' is an appropriate word. Of course, living beings appear to be different but they are in fact 'devoid of differentiating characteristics'. That cumbersome phrase represents the word *shunyata* (*śunyata*), often, though misleadingly, translated as 'emptiness' or 'the void'.

Earlier Buddhists had accepted the Buddha's insistence that there is no self (*anatta/anatman*, p. 233), in the sense that there is no substantial self or soul which endures through the process of transience and change, or of death. But some of them (mainly an early lineage known as Sarvastivadins) believed that the process of change required a thread of identity to link one moment to another, and they therefore suggested that the human appearance is constituted by an aggregation of constituent properties known as *dharmas*, each with its own inherent nature and reality.

According to Prajñaparamita, that would make each *dharma* the equivalent of a 'self' (since it would have its own character and persistence). In contrast, Prajñaparamita insisted that the understanding of no-self must be driven even deeper in order to realise that there is *nothing* with enduring, individual characteristics. The Sarvastivadins had been wrong to regard the constituent

HRIDAYA SUTRA:
'THE HEART SUTRA'

Homage to the Perfection of Wisdom, the lovely, the holy!
Avalokita, the holy Lord and Bodhisattva, was moving in the deep course of the wisdom which has gone beyond. He looked down from on high, he beheld but five heaps [i.e, Skandhas, p. 247], and he saw that in their own-being they were empty.

Here, O Sariputra, form is *shunyata*, and the very emptiness is form; emptiness does not differ from form, form does not differ from emptiness; whatever is form, that is emptiness, whatever is emptiness, that is form. The same is true of feelings, perceptions, impulses, and consciousness.

Here, O Sariputra, all *dharmas* are marked with emptiness; they are not produced or stopped, not defiled or immaculate, not deficient or complete.

Therefore, O Sariputra, in emptiness there is no form, nor feeling, nor perception, nor impulse, nor consciousness; no eye, ear, nose, tongue, body, mind; no forms, sounds, smells, tastes, touchables or objects of mind; no sight-organ-element, and so forth, until we come to: no mind-consciousness-element; there is no ignorance, no extinction of ignorance, and so forth, until we come to: there is no decay and death, no extinction of decay and death; there is no suffering, no origination, no stopping, no path; there is no cognition, no attainment, and no non-attainment.

Therefore, O Sariputra, it is because of his indifference to any kind of personal attainment that a Bodhisattva, through having relied on the perfection of wisdom, dwells without thought-coverings. In the absence of thought-coverings he has not been made to tremble, he has overcome what can upset, and in the end he attains to Nirvana.

All those who appear as Buddhas in the three periods of time awake fully to the utmost, right and perfect enlightenment because they have relied on the perfection of wisdom.

Therefore one should know the Prajñaparamita as the great spell, the spell of great knowledge, the utmost spell, the unequalled spell, allayer of all suffering, in truth – for what could go wrong? By the Prajñaparamita has this spell been delivered. It runs like this: Gone, Gone, Gone beyond, Gone altogether beyond, O what an awakening, All Hail!

This completes the Heart of Perfect Wisdom.

Hridaya Sutra, translation by Conze, 1966, pp. 162–4

properties in the manifold varieties of appearance as permanent 'building-blocks' or *dharmas*. Beneath the superficiality of appearances everything is equally the same, 'devoid of differentiating characteristics', *shunyata*. Interconnecting all appearance is the same Buddha-nature, but in the end even this is *shunyata*, 'devoid of differentiating characteristics'.

In the end, therefore, one cannot describe the nature of anything except to speak of it as being simply as it is. It is just 'thus' or ' so', *tathata*. The 'thusness' or 'suchness' of something is far beyond words or description: it is simply the way that it is. In later Mahayana understanding, the 'perfecting of Wisdom' is to realise this truth even (or especially) in one's own case since the truth of one's self is *shunyata*; but that means that the truth of one's self is already the Buddha-nature because there is nothing else for it to be.

HRIDAYA SUTRA, 'THE HEART SUTRA'

The perfecting of Wisdom is expressed in many Prajñaparamita Sutras. Of particular importance is *Ratnagunasamcayagatha* and its prose counterpart *Ashtasahasrika Sutra* ('The Perfection of Wisdom in 8,000 Lines'), thought to be the oldest surviving Mahayana text: it was constantly expanded up to about the year 300 CE, so that it eventually formed several works, of which the largest is nearly 100,000 lines long. Two shorter versions were therefore composed: *Vajracchedika Sutra*, 'The Diamond-Cutter Sutra', and the even shorter (one page) *Hridaya Sutra* (see box, p. 254).

NAGARJUNA AND MADHYAMAKA

Like many Sutras, those of Mahayana can be so difficult to understand that they required interpretation in Shastras and commentaries. The major interpreter of Prajñaparamita was Nagarjuna who established the philosophy known as Madhyamaka (the Middle Way, called by Murti 'the central philosophy of Buddhism') – its followers are known as Madhyamikas. They regard Nagarjuna as second only to the Buddha in the power of his insights and teaching, and to them his *Madhyamakashastra* and *Mulamadhyamakakarika* are sacred texts of paramount importance. Here he summarises the implication of *shunyata* (in Garfield's translation, p. 49):

> Everything is real and is not real,
> Both real and not real,
> Neither real nor not real.
> This is Lord Buddha's teaching.

Not dependent on another, peaceful and
Not fabricated by mental fabrication,
Not thought, without distinctions,
That is the character of reality [*tathata*]

Whatever comes into being dependent on another
Is not identical to that thing.
Nor is it different from it.
Therefore it is neither nonexistent in time nor permanent.

By the buddhas, patrons of the world,
This immortal truth is taught:
Without identity, without distinction;
Not nonexistent in time, nor permanent.

📖 BIBLIOGRAPHY NUMBERS 54, 237–42, 439, 620, 683, 696, 774, 966

YOGACARA

LANKAVATARA SUTRA, ASANGA AND VASUBANDHU

Yogacara (*yoga-achara*), 'The Practice of Yoga', assimilated the insights of Prajñaparamita but saw itself as going far beyond them (on the relation between them, see Harris; on Yogacara see Powers). One of its earliest Sutras, *Samdhinirmocana* ('Freeing the Underlying Meaning') calls itself 'the third turning of the Dharma Wheel', the first having been the preaching by the Buddha of the Four Noble Truths (p. 233), the second the Prajñaparamita Sutras.

The basic insistence of Prajñaparamita on *shunyata* was thus correct, but according to Yogacara it stopped too soon: it did not in itself help people to go beyond analysis in order to *realise* its truth. What is needed to do that is to develop, through long practice, focused and concentrated meditation, *samadhi*. Yogacara offers that help, hence its name *yoga-achara*.

That required a far more detailed understanding of what it is that enters into *samadhi*. Yogacarins, therefore, concentrated on answering questions concerning the nature of mind and consciousness in the context of *shunyata*. That extensive analysis of consciousness led to Yogacara also being called Vijñanavada, 'The Way of Consciousness', in which, on the basis of what we can experience, the perceived world is 'only in the mind' (*cittamatra*) or it is 'only a representation' (*vijñapyimatra*), as well as being an empty flow of interacting mind-states.

What is it, then, that enters into *samadhi*? Earlier Buddhists had held that consciousness arises conditioned by the impressions received through the six sense organs (the usual five plus mental awareness arising from the mind (*manas*) counted as one of the 'sensing organs'). Yogacarins believed that this was inadequate because it could not account for the (no-self) continuity of personality, not just through the course of a life, but also through death and into any subsequent reappearance.

They therefore added *alaya-vijñana*, the 'storehouse' or 'receptacle' consciousness (see Schmithausen, Waldron). This is the persistent root and source of the other forms of consciousness. It is not accessible to introspection, but it is affected by all the other aspects of consciousness. Thus when people do good or evil things, the seeds of karmic consequence are stored in *alaya-vijñana*, from where they eventually produce their effect.

The major sacred texts of Yogacara are *Samdhinirmocana Sutra* (mentioned above), *Mahayana-abhidharma Sutra* and, perhaps most highly valued (certainly most widely influential), *Lankavatara Sutra* ('Descent into Lanka'). *Lankavatara Sutra* was developed over a long period (until about 300 CE) as a review of Mahayana teaching in general. Although it is not an exclusively Yogacara work, it nevertheless contains much Yogacara teaching. So, for example, it applies that teaching to Nirvana, pointing out that Nirvana cannot be a 'place', or even a state, outside the truth of *shunyata*. It too is 'devoid of differentiating characteristics' so that it is necessarily indistinguishable from everything else:

> Those who are distressed by the *dukkha* that arises from the
> transient process of reappearance set their desire on Nirvana.
> They do not understand, however, that there is no difference at
> all between reappearance and Nirvana. They mistakenly think
> of Nirvana as the absence of the process of becoming and the
> cessation of the interaction between the senses and what they
> sense. What they have to understand is that all this is the product
> of *alaya-vijñana*.

ASANGA, VASUBANDHU

In terms of commentary and interpretation, the two major Yogacarin figures are Asanga (*c.* fourth century) and his younger brother Vasubandhu. The two brothers are thus regarded as the founders of Yogacara, although in fact Yogacarin texts had been written before their time. Early versions of their lives are in Li Rongxi and Dalia.

According to tradition, Asanga became dissatisfied with the existing Buddhist teaching of his time, and he took himself into the forest for twelve years of meditation. There he was visited by Maitreya, the next Buddha to appear in the future at the end of the current cycle of time. Maitreya dictated to Asanga the five works that became the foundation of Yogacara (and these works may therefore be attributed in bibliographies to Maitreya: they are known collectively as *The Five Books of Maitreya* (on Maitreya, see Sponberg), including *Madhyantavibhaga*, 'Discrimination between the Middle and the Extremes'. In *Uttara Tantra Shastra*, he spoke of the redemptive power of the Buddha-nature for those who aspire to it:

> Even those who mix constantly with associates who do wrong,
> who hate the Buddha, who do the worst of all evils in killing their
> father or mother or an *arhant*, who cause strife in the Sangha,
> they can shed everything like this if they enter wholly into the
> Buddha-nature.

He also wrote a comprehensive work on Yogacara in five extensive sections called *Yogacarabhumi*. It was recognised as a major text and was translated into Chinese and Tibetan. A central chapter (*Tattvartha-patalam*) is concerned with 'knowing what really is'. Willis has stressed the importance of this text (p. ix): 'It directly takes up the central concern of all Buddhist doctrine, namely, the epistemological concern of correctly judging and validating knowledge about reality as it really is.'

Vasubandhu had written important works on Buddhism before his brother persuaded him of the truth of Yogacara. He then devoted himself to works advocating Yogacara, including a commentary on his brother's (or as Yogacarins might prefer to say, Maitreya's) *Madhyantavibhaga*. A work of particularly enduring influence is his *Trimshika*, 'Thirty Verses'. In elliptical form, it lays out the Yogacara understanding of consciousness and summarises his own concern that the eight current understandings of 'what consciousness is' must be dismantled (cf. Matthew on imaginations of God, p. 120). This 'cognitive closure' he called *vijnaptimatra*, arguing that it must be followed by a five-step approach to immediate knowledge or cognition (*jñana*). A translation of *Trimshika* is included in Anacker along with six other works which he arranges 'in a "progressive fashion"' (p. 3), illustrating the characteristic way in which Vasubandhu

> seems interested in introducing concepts only for the dissolving of
> previously-held ones, and these new concepts remove themselves
> later: they are provisional . . . They are makeshift rafts, and once
> they have taken us across a turbulent stream, we do not need to
> carry them on our backs.

📖 BIBLIOGRAPHY NUMBERS 52, 460, 574, 621, 626, 777, 830, 847, 894, 955, 971, 983, 1041

HUAYAN

AVATAMSAKA SUTRA

Kicking off their vermilion slippers among the trays and flagons, they flapped their long flowing sleeves. Their handsome faces, their sumptuous clothes, were radiant with beauty. With their lovely eyes they cast bewitching glances upon the company. One look at them would make one surrender a city. Even if one were as sternly upright as old Liu Hsia-hui or a Buddhist *shramana*, one could not but be captivated.

That passage written by Zhang Heng (78–139, in *Xijing Fu*: see Wright, p. 21) used to be identified as the earliest reference to Buddhism in China. In fact some earlier references have subsequently been found, but together they indicate that Buddhism began to arrive in China from India during the early centuries of the Christian era.

BUDDHISM IN CHINA

This means that Buddhism arrived in China during a time of conflict that lasted from the Han dynasties until the further unification of China during the Tang dynasty (618–906). During that period of incessant rivalry and warfare the Buddhist teaching (of *dukkha* and of the way to the cessation of *dukkha*) made sense in a way that Confucianism and Daoism did not. Furthermore, the Mahayana belief in bodhisattvas who have vowed to offer help to those in suffering or distress offered real comfort in times of crisis.

On the other hand, the early Buddhists had their roots in India, and there was much about those beliefs that was threatening to the Chinese. For example, the Chinese emphasised the importance of the family (see pp. 291–3, 302, 307), but one of the Three Jewels that Buddhists take refuge in is the Sangha with its implication of celibacy. Furthermore, the

Confucian ethic of work to support family and society was contradicted by the expectation that *bhikshus* would not work but would be supported by alms. Perhaps even worse, the Chinese revere their ancestors and they make sure, through offerings and rituals, that the ancestors remain a part of the family. Buddhists introduced the belief that ancestors who have generated bad *karma* may now be an animal, or a frustrated ghost, or in hell.

The Buddhist lineages and Schools therefore adapted their teaching to the new circumstances in China. In that process sacred texts played a major part because of the Mahayana beliefs: (a) that the Buddha is still continuing his teaching; (b) that this teaching is recorded in new Sutras; and (c) that this is entirely to be expected because of the way in which the Buddha teaches through *upaya-kaushalya* ('skill in means': see p. 251).

In the context of those arguments and of Chinese unease about Buddhist teaching, it is not surprising that the number of Chinese Sutras multiplied rapidly (many of them initially translated from Sanskrit), or that the Canon of Chinese Buddhists texts is so vast (p. 237). Nor is it surprising that the Chinese established lineages and Schools of their own. The best known of these are the Four Schools:

◆ Huayan, founded by Dushan (557–640) and taken to Japan as Kegon.

◆ Tiantai, organised by Zhiyi (538–97) and taken to Japan by Saicho (767–822) as Tendai.

◆ Jingtu, Pure Land popularised by Tanluan (476–?560) and taken to Japan as Jodo.

◆ Chan, Meditation Buddhism derived from Bodhidharma (*c.*470–*c.*540) and taken to Japan as Zen.

HUAYAN AND FAZANG

Huayan was brought into an organised and systematic form by Fazang (643–712). The name is derived from the title of the Sanskrit *Avatamsaka Sutra*, 'The Flower Garland Sutra', translated into Chinese as *Huayanjing*. Two parts of *Avatamsaka Sutra* (both of which have survived in Sanskrit), *Dashabhumika Sutra* and *Gandavyuha Sutra* became separate sacred texts in their own right: *Gandavyuha Sutra* has been described (by Suzuki, *Essays*, p. 69) as 'the most imposing monument erected by the Indian mind to the spiritual life of all mankind'.

It describes the journey of a young man, Sudhana, who was sent to discover what it means to be a bodhisattva. Near the end of his journey he is met by Maitreya (the future Buddha, p. 258) who shows him the vast Tower of Vairocana which contains many other towers and palaces. All of them are individual, but they are so deeply interrelated that they 'contain' each other as well as constituting a single entity. Sudhana realises that a *bodhisattva* is already an interconnected part of the suffering that he seeks to alleviate.

That 'interconnectedness' is a fundamental part of the teaching of Huayan and Fazang. Everything belongs to everything else, and anything that affects a part also affects the whole. Fazang illustrated this with two famous images. In the first he constructed a hall lined on all sides and on the floor and ceiling with mirrors. Each mirror reflected others together with their reflections. In the centre he placed a lighted candle. All the mirrors reflected each other in a near infinite array of light.

In the second image, he produced a lion made of gold. The lion had eyes, feet, tail, mane and all the other constituent parts, and yet they were all made of the same substance, gold. From this he showed that all appearance is different in *shi*, but identical in *li*, the underlying Buddha-nature; and this nature is *shunyata*, 'devoid of differentiating characteristics'. In Huayan belief, 'Every living being and every minute thing is significant, because even the tiniest atom contains the whole mystery.'

Fazang thus illustrated the idea that all the constituted appearances (*dharmas*) in the universe arise simultaneously (*dharmadhatu*), and since they have no differentiating characteristics (*shunyata*), it is only humans in their ignorance who distinguish them and give them separate names:

> The lion comes into existence only because of our senses . . . The golden lion is not any *thing*: it is only the *dharmas* of cause and conditioned appearance, coming into momentary being but disappearing in the same moment . . . The 'gold' and the 'lion' come into appearance at the same time fully and completely. As a result the 'gold' and the 'lion' are entirely coherent with each other since neither can impede the other, and if therefore one focuses on the lion, then there is only the lion with no gold involved: the lion is apparent and the gold is hidden – and *vice versa*. If one focuses on both, then both are apparent and both are hidden . . . When one understands the lion and the gold in this way, the two characters are completely annihilated, our involvement with them through the senses does not even begin, and although we seem to see beauty and ugliness, in fact the mind is as motionless as a calm sea. False thoughts are extinguished because there is nothing to bring them

into being. At last it is possible to step free from all that binds and to separate oneself from every impediment, thus cutting oneself off for ever from the causes of *dukkha*. This is called 'entering Nirvana'.

At the time of Fazang, there were many different forms of Buddhism taking root in China, each developing its own lineage and teaching. Fazang attempted to make a systematic classification of these teachings. He claimed that Buddhism developed in five stages:

1   Hinayana, which taught no-self but maintained that *dharmas*, constituents of appearance, are real (p. 253).

2   Early Mahayana of the Perfection of Wisdom.

3   Later Mahayana, which developed the idea of *tathagatagarbha*, the Buddha-nature as the womb from which all appearance takes its origin – hence its interconnectedness.

4   Sudden Awakening, which later became of paramount importance in Chan and Zen.

5   Huayan, which incorporates and completes the provisional and preliminary teaching of the first four.

According to Fazang, *Huayan Sutra* was the first teaching of the Buddha, but it had to be 'put on hold' until people had been prepared for it. The second of the Four Schools (above), Tiantai, agreed that *Huayan Sutra* was the first teaching, but Tiantai maintained that the Buddha had also taught an even more important Sutra on which they based their own teaching.

BIBLIOGRAPHY NUMBERS **61, 472**

TIANTAI

The Threefold Lotus Sutra, Nichiren

Tiantai was brought into being by Zhiyi (538–97). It was named after the mountain, 'Heavenly Terrace' or 'Celestial Platform', where its main centre was based.

The followers of Tiantai accepted that *Huayan Sutra* contains the first teaching of the Buddha, but they did not place it at the pinnacle of his teaching. They regarded it as simply a part of the way in which the Buddha, by his skill-in-means (*upaya-kaushalya*), continued to reveal his more advanced teaching. Tiantai, therefore, gave priority to two other sutras, *Parinirvana Sutra* and *Lotus Sutra*. On the basis of the Mahayana belief in the Three Bodies (Trikaya, p. 250) of the Buddha, they claimed that the Lotus Sutra was first revealed in his Heavenly (Sambhoga) form. Because of the importance of the Lotus Sutra, Tiantai is sometimes known as The Lotus School.

The Lotus Sutra was important not only to Zhiyi. It was a work that was revered as a sacred text far beyond Tiantai, especially in Japan. Although it is referred to as the Lotus Sutra, it is in fact a work with a complicated structure and history. It began as a Sanskrit Sutra, *Saddharmapundarika*, 'The Lotus of the True Law'. It was translated into Chinese several times, but supremely by Kumarajiva in 406, and it is this translation that forms the basis of innumerable commentaries, as well as being the foundation of several new religious movements in Japan.

The Chinese version has three component parts: the central section is 'The Lotus of the True Law', and this is often referred to as 'The Lotus Sutra'. In China, however, the whole work is known as 'The Threefold Lotus Sutra' because it has two smaller parts at the beginning and at the end. At the beginning is 'The Sutra of Innumerable Meanings', a short work emphasising the importance of bodhisattvas and their works: 'As the captain of a ship, the all-competent captain of a ship, they carry all living beings across the ocean of life and death to the safe shore of Nirvana.' At the end is 'The Sutra of Meditation on the Universal

Virtue of the Bodhisattva', which culminates in a summary of the five ways of re-formation:

> The Buddha said to Ananda: 'If there are any in the future worlds
> who put into practice these ways of reformation, know, Ananda,
> that they have put on the garments of self-knowledge, that they will
> be protected and assisted by the Buddhas, and that they will attain
> complete Enlightenment without delay.

NICHIREN

Tiantai was taken to Japan as Tendai by Saicho (767–822). He set up a centre of learning on Mount Hiei where he taught on the basis of the Lotus Sutra that all people have within them the capability of attaining Enlightenment, and that this can be brought into being by bodhisattvas. Some 400 years later, the son of a fisherman, Nichiren (1222–82), arrived at Mount Hiei for training and saw that the Lotus Sutra unifies the Trikaya forms of the Buddha in a single work of compassion, whereas in his view all other forms of Buddhism concentrate on only one Body to the exclusion of the other two.

He therefore claimed that the name and nature of the Buddha are identical with the Lotus Sutra, and that all people can attain the Buddha through the Lotus Sutra. All that is basically necessary is to chant with absolute commitment the Daimoku, the formula *Nam(u) myo ho renge kyo*, 'Honour to the Lotus Sutra'. He encouraged his followers to write this on a small plaque and to make it the object of meditation. For him and for his followers this was enough (Anesaki, pp. 46f.):

> If you want to attain the Buddha without delay, put aside the
> triumph of pride, throw away the armour of resentment, and trust
> yourself to the Dharma of the Daimoku ... When you fall into a
> deep pit and someone lowers a rope to pull you out, will you hesitate
> to grab the rope because you have doubts about the competence
> of the helper? Has not the Buddha said, 'I alone am the one who
> protects, the one who saves?' Here is the strength! Here is the rope!
> Those who hesitate to seize hold of it and to repeat the Daimoku
> will never climb the steep side of Enlightenment ... Our hearts ache
> and our sleeves are soaked with tears until we see face-to-face the
> gentle figure of the One who says to us, 'I am your father'.

In 1253, he set out on a mission to convert the Japanese to this simple faith in the Lotus Sutra. It was a time of unrest and conflict, including attempts by the Mongols to invade in 1274 and 1281. Nichiren attributed the weakness and failure of Japan to the disastrous errors in the teaching of the other Buddhist Schools, and especially of those devoted to the Buddha known as Amida, to whom they chant the (in his view) useless Nembutsu (see p. 268). He launched ferocious attacks against those other Schools and against the central government, particularly in *Rissho ankoku ron*, 'The Establishment of the Legitimate Teaching for the Security of the Country':

> Disaster! Disaster! For the last thirty or forty years many thousands of people have been beguiled and led astray so that they wander about in Buddha Dharma as people without a guide. Is it not inevitable that the powerful spirits should be angry when people wander away from the Dharma? Is it not obvious that evil spirits should see their chance when they observe people abandoning Dharma and giving themselves up to evil deeds? Better by far it is to make every effort to stave off a threatening disaster than to repeat the useless Nembutsu.

Not surprisingly, Nichiren was attacked in turn. He was exiled in 1261, and again from 1271 to 1274 when he wrote *Kaimokushu* ('On Opening the Eyes') and *Kanjin Honzonsho* ('On Contemplating the True Object of Worship'). Nichiren was condemned to death and then miraculously saved when, according to tradition, he was about to be executed by sword, but the sword of the executioner was struck by lightning just as he was about to strike. After his return from exile, Nichiren continued his denunciations of corrupt government and 'false' Buddhism, holding out instead a vision of Japan as the place where the true Dharma of the Buddha would be restored, and from which it would convert the world. He took the name, Nichiren, to express this vision, *nichi* ('the sun' or Japan) + *ren* (the Lotus). Many of his beliefs and attitudes have been continued in a modern version known as Soka Gakkai.

Obviously, there could be no sacred text for Nichiren and his followers apart from the Lotus Sutra, but his own writings are revered as the true interpretation of the Sutra.

📖 BIBLIOGRAPHY NUMBERS 267, 603, 712

PURE LAND

The devotion to Amida that Nichiren despised was certainly very different from his own understanding of Buddhism. It encouraged a devotion that will lead, not to the salvation of Japan, but to salvation in the Pure Land – hence the name given collectively to the many different lineages and movements of this form of 'devotional Buddhism', the Pure Land School.

It flourished particularly in China and Japan, but it has its roots in India where the Pure Land is known (in Sanskrit) as Sukhavati. In China it is known as Jingtu and in Japan as Jodo, names given to this immensely popular school along with Jodo-shin, True Pure Land in Japan.

The Pure Land School accepts the Mahayana belief that there are innumerable spheres ruled over by Buddhas, and it focuses on the one known as Sukhavati, the Blissful Land (sometimes translated as the Western Paradise because of its supposed location). Sukhavati is ruled over by the Buddha known as Amitabha (Sanskrit, Immeasurable Radiance), or in China as Amita, or in Japan as Amida – and also, especially in Tibet, as Amitayus (Infinite Life).

The Pure Land School gained immense popular support because of the simple way in which it offered an assurance of salvation. Following the Trikaya (Three Body, p. 250) understanding of the Buddha, Pure Land believes that after the appearance of the Buddha on earth and the period of true Dharma, the world will decline into increasing chaos and lawlessness – the age known as *mappo* in which we are now living. In that age, Buddhism will disintegrate into rival and conflicting sects, and as a result, according to Pure Land, it will no longer be possible to be certain of reaching Enlightenment.

In those circumstances, there can be no escape unless some dramatic rescue takes place. That is exactly what Pure Land believes has happened. According to tradition (recorded in *Sukhavativyuha*, a basic text discussed below), a *bhikshu* called Dharmakara (in Japanese, Hozo) received instruction so that he became a bodhisattva. He then resolved with forty-eight Vows to establish a Buddha land for the benefit of others. This was the critical eighteenth Vow:

> If I am at the point of Enlightenment, and if then there are any beings in other worlds who have a strong desire for true and perfect Enlightenment, and if, having heard my Name, they turn themselves with loving desire toward me, and if at the time and moment of death I with my whole company do not stand before them to keep them from defeat, let it not be the case, for that reason, that I attain to perfect and complete Enlightenment.

He became the Buddha Amida, and on the basis of that vow, Amida will never turn away any who come to him in perfect faith and trust. That trust is expressed in the simple formula *Namo Amitabhaya Buddha*, 'Honour to Amitabha Buddha'; in China it became *Namo Amituofo* and in Japan *Namu Amida Butsu*. It is known in Japan as the Nembutsu, the 'recollection [or 'invocation'] of the Buddha'.

Since this is 'all that is necessary for salvation', it might seem that Pure Land would have no need of sacred texts. There were, however, many such texts written in order to show how that state of pure trust can be aroused and then attained, and also to encourage people to make that act of faith. Among those many texts, one of great importance is *Sukhavativyuha*. It exists in two forms, the Shorter and the Longer. Both describe Sukhavati in detail, but there is then a difference in emphasis concerning what is necessary in order to get there. The Longer text states that faith and devotion to Amitabha are a *sine qua non*, but it then insists that faith and devotion must be expressed in deeds and actions that deserve the final reward. The Shorter text states that only faith, prayer and devotion are necessary:

> No one can be born in the Pure Land of the Buddha, the Tathagata Amitayus, as a reward or as a consequence of good works done in this life. To the contrary, those who, even as children in a family, hear the name of the Blessed Amitayus, the Tathagata, and who, when they have heard it, keep it in mind – and with focused and concentrated thoughts continue to keep it in mind, . . . will, after their death, be reborn in the paradise of Sukhavati.

Once Pure Land moved to China and Japan virtually all its lineages had their own text or texts. It is thus impossible to list, let alone summarise them.

However, to give an example, *Anjin ketsujo sho*, 'On Attaining the Settled Mind', has been translated by Hirota (in Tanabe, pp. 257–67). Hirota describes the work as 'an influential tract of the Pure Land Buddhist tradition, treasured since the fourteenth century for its incisive exposition of the interrelationships between the person of the nembutsu and Amida Buddha'.

This section considers whether the Nembutsu will count only if it is uttered with perfect understanding, or whether the salvation is such an act of grace on the part of Amida (who has by his vows already accomplished it) that even a 'late death-bed confession' will be recognised. It is Amida who brings us to birth in his presence (trans. Hirota, p. 261):

> The nembutsu utterance of the person in the lowest grade of the lowest level – the utterance at the point of death by one incapable of focusing thoughts on the Buddha – is taught to be possessed of aspiration and practice; know, concerning this, that the person's own aspiration and practice is not at all involved. For it is the aspiration and practice [accomplished] by Bodhisattva Dharmakara over a span of five kalpas [immensely long Buddhist units of time] and billions of years [of practice] that fulfils the aspiration and practice of foolish beings . . .
>
> To grasp the Eighteenth Vow [p. 268] is to grasp the Name. To grasp the Name is to realise that at the very moment Amida Buddha accomplished beforehand the birth [in the Pure Land] of foolish beings – fulfilling the necessary aspiration and practice in their place – he made the birth of sentient beings throughout the cosmos the substance of his Enlightenment. Hence, whenever we who practise the nembutsu hear the Name, we should realise, 'Already my birth has been accomplished! . . . '
>
> It would be a sad thing for people to assume that they will attain birth only if they have accumulated utterances of the Name, believing – even though they say the Name trusting the Primal Vow – that it represents the Buddha's virtue existing apart [from their own birth]. When faith has arisen in us that our birth having been firmly settled is manifested by 'Namu-amida-butsu', then we see that the substance of [Amida's] Buddhahood is itself none other than the practice bringing about our birth. Thus, where there is a single voicing, birth is firmly settled.

📖 BIBLIOGRAPHY NUMBERS **780, 912**

CHAN

Bodhidharma, *The Platform Sutra*

India and China were closely connected, not just through trade, but through the exchange of ideas. The Silk Roads carried much more than silk. In particular, they carried the beliefs and practices of Buddhists to such an extent that Buddhism flourished in China, while gradually (by about the fourteenth century) it virtually disappeared in India.

MEDITATION: DHYANA

From India, Buddhists carried with them the importance of meditation (Sanskrit, *dhyana*; Pali, *jhana*). *Dhyana* is the focused practice of meditation similar to the kind found in Patanjali's *Yoga Sutra* (p. 177), but in addition to that there were many other methods of *dhyana*, not least in Tantra (p. 201). The purposes of *dhyana* are many and varied, but among them is the desire to rescue the mind from the chaotic distractions of the world so that it may be devoted to a wiser purpose. As Kenneth Ch'en has summarised the point (p. 350f.):

> *Dhyana* . . . refers to the religious discipline aimed at tranquilizing the mind and getting the practitioner to devote himself to a quiet introspection into his own inner consciousness. He is made to feel an interest in things above the senses and to discover the presence of a spiritual faculty that bridges the gap between the finite and the infinite. When he is thoroughly disciplined in *dhyana*, he can keep the serenity of mind and cheerfulness of disposition even amid the world of turbulent activity . . . Continuous practice of *dhyana* exercises enables him to attain to the higher ecstatic trances or to the blissful state of equanimity and wisdom.

This is 'the pacification of the mind' (Japanese *daianjin*), and the word *dhyana* refers also to those 'higher states' which are the consequences of meditation of that kind, as, for example, in *samadhi* (p. 177).

The methods and stages of *dhyana* were analysed in great and sophisticated detail – not surprisingly because they are undertaken in 'the imitation of the Buddha' who taught the *dhyanas* as a key aspect of meditation, as an aid to insight. Much of this analysis and practical instruction was written down in Dhyana texts.

Dhyana/jhana was therefore taken into China as one of the key foundations of Buddhist life. As early as the fourth century, Dao-an (312–85) warned that the whole structure of Buddhism in China was in danger of collapsing because so little was known about the theory and practice of *dhyana*, and as a result he devoted much of his life to collecting and collating Dhyana texts. By the sixth century, Seng-chou (d.560) was so adept in the practice of *dhyana* that he was called 'the greatest expert east of the Himalayas'.

CHAN AND ZEN: BODHIDHARMA

All that, however, was only a prelude to the way in which *dhyana* was made completely fundamental in China in a new development of Buddha-dharma. This was the interpretation known as Meditation Buddhism, or, in the Chinese form of *dhyana*, Chan-na or Chan; in Japan it became *zenna* or Zen.

Chan is believed to have arrived in China with Bodhidharma (Japanese Daruma) in 520. Bodhidharma was believed to be the twenty-eighth successor in descent from the Buddha. According to tradition, he travelled from India to China to teach a form of Buddhism that goes back to an occasion when one of the Buddha's disciples, Mahakasyapa, asked him to summarise his teaching. The Buddha responded by lifting up a flower. Mahakasyapa bowed his head in silence for a while, then he looked up and smiled.

That was a transmission of teaching without the use of words, and from this was developed a way of seeking Enlightenment known as 'mind-to-mind transmission' or as 'the transmission of the mind outside the Teaching' (the title of Charles Luk's translation of the lineage successors of Huineng, below). At first Bodhidharma had little success in teaching this, so he settled in Shao-lin monastery and spent the next nine years in 'face to the wall' meditation, known as *biguan*.

He was then joined by Huikye (later he became Bodhidharma's lineage successor) who begged Bodhidharma to teach him. Bodhidharma made no response until one night Huikye stood motionless in a violent snowstorm. Bodhidharma, moved by compassion, asked him what he wanted. Huikye answered by taking a knife, cutting off his arm at the elbow and giving it to

Bodhidharma. He said, 'My mind is not at rest.' Bodhidharma said, 'Bring me your mind and I will give it rest.' Huikye said, 'I have searched for my mind but I cannot find it.' 'There!' said Bodhidharma. 'I have set it completely at rest.'

Chan teaches by transmission 'outside the written texts', through direct contact between pupil and teacher. It is summarised in a short verse attributed to Bodhidharma:

> A special transmission outside the Scriptures,
> not founded upon words and letters:
> by pointing directly into the mind
> it allows us to see [our true] nature and thus to attain the Buddha-
> nature.

On that basis it would seem obvious that Chan would have no sacred texts, and Chan teachers did indeed set fire to texts and chop up images of the Buddha for firewood in order to destroy, in particular pupils, their reliance on external aids. Nevertheless, Chan rapidly built up its own treasury of sacred texts, among which *The Sutra of the Sixth Patriarch*, also known as *The Platform* [or *Altar*] *Sutra*, came to hold a particularly revered place.

HUI-NENG AND THE PLATFORM SUTRA

The sixth patriarch was Hui-neng (638–713). *The Platform Sutra* exists in different versions and has reached its present form through a complicated history. The early sections contain his autobiography. It continues with teaching on Wisdom (*prajña*), a section of questions and answers, and then sections on the meaning and practice of *dhyana*. The central sections deal with how to prepare one's life to arrive at the point where one might make the bodhisattva vow, and on the distinction between gradual and sudden Enlightenment (this was the issue that split Chan in two between those who held that Enlightenment comes at the end of a long process of preparation, and those who held that preparation is important but that Enlightenment may come suddenly at any moment). The Sutra ends with Hui-neng's final instructions:

> When I have departed, do not follow the way of the world in
> weeping. If you receive messages of sympathy from outsiders and
> if you wear mourning you are no followers of mine . . . Stay with
> your own mind and keep attending to your own nature, neither
> changing nor remaining where you are, rising above birth and

death, entrances and exits, right and wrong, staying and leaving . . .
After my departing, stick to this teaching as if I am still alive, for
if you abandon it, you would gain nothing even if I were still with
you.

The teaching of the dharma-successors of Hui-neng was also revered, and
much was gathered in texts (see Luk, 1974). A famous story tells how the first
successor, Huai Rang, converted Ma zu, to the Chan way (trans. Luk, p. 35):

Huai Rang went one day to see Ma zu in his hut where he lived
in seclusion to practise meditation. Huai Rang took a brick to the
door of the hut and rubbed the brick, but Ma zu paid no attention.
After a long while, Ma zu asked, 'What are you doing?' Huai Rang
replied, 'I am a rubbing a brick to make a mirror.' Ma zu said, 'How
can you make a mirror by a rubbing a brick?' The Master said, 'If
a mirror cannot be made by rubbing a brick, how can one become
a Buddha by sitting in meditation?' Ma zu then rose from his seat
and asked the Master, 'What should one do then?' The Master said,
'If the cart drawn by an ox does not move, is it correct to whip the
ox or the cart?' He further asked, 'Do you want to sit in meditation
or to be a sitting Buddha? If you want to sit in meditation,
meditation is neither sitting nor lying. If you want to be a sitting
Buddha, Buddha is not motionless; moreover (even its opposite),
motion should be neither accepted nor rejected. If you sit (to
become a) Buddha, you will simply kill him. If you cling to sitting
you will never realise the Dharma.'
Upon hearing these words Ma zu awakened (to the teaching),
bowed down and asked Huai Rang, 'How should I use my mind
to agree with the samadhi beyond form?' The Master replied,
'Your study of the Mind Dharma is like sowing seeds and my
expounding of its essentials is like the rain. Since your potentiality
agrees with the Dharma, you should perceive the truth.' Ma zu
asked, 'Truth is formless, how can it be perceived?' The Master
replied, 'The mind Eye can perceive the truth. This also applies to
formless samadhi.' Ma zu asked, 'Is the truth subject to creation
and destruction?' The Master replied, 'If the truth is perceived as
subject to creation and destruction, formation and decay, it is not
real. Now listen to my gatha:

The Mind-ground holds the (flower) seeds
Which sprout when moistened by the rain.
The blossom of samadhi is formless,
How can it decay or come into being?

Upon hearing these words Ma zu awakened to the Mind Dharma.
He stayed to serve the Master for ten years during which he
gradually acquired deeper experiences of the Mind Dharma.

BIBLIOGRAPHY NUMBERS 29, 119, 150, 303, 766

ZEN

Rinzai and Koans, Soto and Dogen

The methods of Chan meditation were known in Japan not least through their use in Tendai (p. 265), but Chan did not become a separate lineage in Japan until Eisai (1141–1215) established Rinzai Zen (on the basis of Chinese Linji) and Dogen (1200–53) established Soto Zen (based on Chinese Caodong).

Rinzai and Soto reflect the split in China between Sudden (Linji) and Gradual (Caodong) Enlightenment. Linji/Rinzai taught through 'sharp shocks' such as shouts and blows with a stick, and also through *gongans*, dislocating and often seemingly absurd questions better known (from Zen) as Koans. Caodong/Soto taught the methods and process of seated meditation through which awakenings from ignorance gradually unfold. Both aim at the Enlightenment known in Chinese as *wu* ('realisation'), and in Japanese as *satori* ('catching on') or *kensho* ('seeing one's nature').

KOANS

Koans are completely fundamental to Rinzai Zen. They consist of an apparently baffling question or statement on which the pupil must concentrate until an answer suddenly breaks through. There are answers to all Koans, but never a 'correct' answer, only an answer that is appropriate to the stage reached by the learner. Two famous examples are: 'The original face, the face before you were brought into this world by your mother and father, what is it?'; and, 'In clapping both hands a sound is heard; what is the sound of one hand clapping?'

Can Koans count as a sacred text? They are supposedly never recorded or written down but are passed on by word of mouth in the encounter between teacher and learner. But that is true of many early texts (see, for example, the Vedas, p. 168), and in any case collections of Koans were made – for example, the collection of 100 Koans in *Hekiganroku* ('The Blue Cliff Record') made by Xuedou Chongxian (980–1052) and Yuanwu Keqin (1063–1135), or *Mumonkan*

('The Gateless Gate'). Of those two works, Dumoulin, the great historian of Chan and Zen Buddhism, wrote (1988, pp. 249, 252):

> To read the *Blue Cliff Record* in its given sequence . . . is to find a
> sure, albeit not easy, entrance into one of the foremost examples of
> religious world literature . . . A rich and concentrated masterpiece,
> the *Mumonkan* has also met with extraordinary success . . .
> Although the *Mumonkan* differs markedly from the *Hekiganroku*,
> both collections are considered the primary representative
> expressions of the Zen koan.

Mumonkan is the work of Wu-men Hui-kai (1183–1260) who responded to requests to give instruction by collecting forty-eight koans as they had been given to pupils by past teachers. He then added his own critical comments in prose and poetry. To give three examples (29, 36, 38, trans. Reps, pp. 117, 122f.):

> 29. Two monks were arguing about a flag. One said: 'The flag is
> moving.' The other said: 'The wind is moving.' The sixth patriarch
> [Hui-neng] happened to be passing by. He told them: 'Not the
> wind, not the flag; mind is moving.'
>
> Mumon's comment: What did he mean? If you understand this
> intimately, you will see the two monks there trying to buy iron and
> gaining gold. The sixth patriarch could not bear to see those two
> dull heads, so he made such a bargain.
>
> > Wind, flag, mind moves.
> > The same understanding.
> > When the mouth opens
> > All are wrong.

> 36. Goso said: 'When you meet a Zen master on the road you
> cannot talk to him, you cannot face him with silence. What are you
> going to do?'
>
> Mumon's comment: In such a case, if you can answer him
> intimately, your realisation will be beautiful, but if you cannot, you
> should look about without seeing anything.
>
> > Meeting a Zen master on the road,
> > Face him neither with words nor silence.

Give him an uppercut
And you will be called one who understands Zen.

38. A monk asked Joshu why Bodhidharma came to China. Joshu said: 'An oak tree in the garden.'

Mumon's comment: If one sees Joshu's answer clearly, there is no Shakyamuni Buddha before him and no future Buddha after him.

Words cannot describe everything.
The heart's message cannot be delivered in words.
If one receives words literally, he will be lost.
If he tries to explain with words, he will not attain
 enlightenment in this life.

A much later (1916) collection is *Gendai Sojizen Hyoron*. Its purpose was to attack what the author regarded as false developments in Zen, but it remains a useful and accessible introduction through the translation made by Hoffman.

DOGEN

Soto Zen was brought into Japan from China by Dogen. He had gone to learn Buddha-dharma in the Tendai monastery on Mount Hiei, but there he was assailed by 'the Great Doubt' (*daigidan*). He was taught that all appearances possess the Buddha-nature and that consequently they are 'devoid of differentiating characteristics', *shunyata*. In that case why do pupils and teachers have to struggle so hard, with such severe discipline,* to attain what they already possess? Dogen's question stands at the head of one of his earliest works, *Fukanzazengi*:

The Way is fundamentally complete and all-inclusive. So how can
it depend on practice and realisation? The Dharma vehicle runs
freely and without complication, so what need can there be for
concentrated effort on the part of humans?

He left Mount Hiei to seek in China instruction in various traditions until, under instruction from the Cao-dong master Ru Jing, he attained Enlightenment. He returned to Japan in 1227 with the intention of teaching true Dharma, but

---

* The detailed nature of that discipline has been graphically described by Holmes Welch in his invaluable book, *The Practice of Chinese Buddhism*.

when he met with opposition he withdrew to Eihei-ji in northern Japan where he founded a monastery.

He had now resolved the Great Doubt. He had been taught that all things *have* the Buddha-nature. He realised instead that all things *are* the Buddha-nature. *Wu* and *satori* are the 'realisation' of something already in existence, not the search for some future possibility. That is the real meaning of *shunyata*:

> The very impermanence of grass and trees, of woods and forests, is the Buddha-nature. The very impermanence of humans and things, of body and mind, is the Buddha-nature. All things are impermanent because they are the Buddha-nature. Because it is the Buddha-nature, supreme and complete enlightenment is impermanent. Nirvana itself, because it is impermanent, is the Buddha-nature.

Dogen emphasised that to understand this intellectually is interesting, but that to realise it in Enlightenment lies far beyond intellectual understanding. It requires constant practice to realise and manifest the Buddha-nature. Enlightenment occurs when we become what we are, nothing other than the Buddha-nature. The opportunity is always present, but not all respond to it even in identical circumstances (*Shobogenzo Zuimonki* 4.5):

> Consider those who reached enlightenment when they heard the sound of a tile striking a bamboo, or when they saw the cherry blossom in bloom. Does the bamboo sort out the wise from the dull, the enlightened from the ignorant? Does the blossom distinguish between the frivolous and the profound, the stupid and the wise? There are blossoms on the bough year after year, but not all who see them gain enlightenment; bamboos never cease to give off sounds, but not all who hear them gain enlightenment. Only after long study under a trained teacher, combined with much practice, do we grasp what we have struggled to gain – enlightenment and clarity of mind.

That study and practice are focused on 'seated meditation', *zazen*, in order 'to see all things as the Buddha did' – indeed, so characteristic is this in Dogen's instruction that his way is known as exactly that, Zazen alone. He committed his teaching to many texts, but supreme among them is *Shobogenzo*, a massive work that Dumoulin described (II, p. 72) as 'without equal in the whole of Zen literature'.

In the end, though, the truth is simple – literally 'in the end' because the verses he composed just before his death read (trans. Bowker, 2010, p. 121):

> From leaf and grass
> beneath the morning sun
> the drops of dew soon pass.
> Calm down, you autumn breath
> restless in the dry fields.
>
> The world and life and death
> to me resemble – what?
> The moon's slight print
> dropping on dew a hint
> the beak of a bird.

BIBLIOGRAPHY NUMBERS 108, 275, 298, 303, 304, 348, 441, 455, 456, 686, 873, 874, 943

TIBETAN BUDDHISM
KANGUR AND TENGYUR

Traditionally Buddhism is said to have arrived in Tibet when a king, Songsten Gampo (c.609–49), married two wives (from China and Nepal) who were devout Buddhists. Buddhism, however, did not take root until another king, Trisong Detsen (c.750–97), became a Buddhist. After this so-called First Diffusion of Buddhism in Tibet, the rulers reverted to the existing and native religion of Tibet, Bon, and for two centuries Buddhists were persecuted and driven to the margins of Tibet until the Second Diffusion with the arrival of Atisha from India in 1042.

Even from so brief a description of the settlement of Buddhism in Tibet, it can be seen how rich and varied were the sources from which the Tibetan forms of Buddhism were constructed – not just from India, China and Nepal, but also from its own native tradition of Bon. As a result Tibetan Buddhism developed in its own distinctive ways, including Vajrayana (The Diamond/Thunderbolt Vehicle), with a strong emphasis on Tantra.

From these varied sources, Tibetan Buddhists built up an immense collection of sacred texts. Their usually very careful translations of Sanskrit texts are often the only way in which those texts have survived. We have already seen (p. 236) that their sacred texts are divided into two parts: bKa'-'gyur (Kangyur, 'Translation of the Word of the Buddha') and bsTan-gyur (Tengyur, 'Translation of the Treatises').

Kangyur thus corresponds to Buddha-vacana, the words of the Buddha, and it consists of more than 600 texts in 108 volumes. It is not at all 'the Pali Canon' in Tibetan: it contains non-Pali versions of some of those texts, but mainly it contains Mahayana works, including Prajñaparamita and Ratnakuta Sutras (p. 252) as well as many Tantra texts.

Tengyur does not correspond to other collections elsewhere, although it does include works that have also been preserved elsewhere. It contains commentaries and analysis, Tantra texts and works on medicine and the arts in 224 volumes. Together, Kangur and Tengyur include nearly 5,000 texts.

Kangyur and Tengyur both include Tantra texts divided into four groups, Kriya, Carya, Yoga and Anuttarayoga. The revealed Tantras come, not from human authors, but from the Buddha or from his agents as, for example, Vajradhara, the holder of the Vajra, the Diamond/Thunderbolt Instrument of Enlightenment.

The four groups of Tantras are allocated (though somewhat artificially) to four different stages in the long progress to Enlightenment, and also to the relationships that obtain among the different deities of Tibetan Buddhism – culminating in Anuttarayoga in which the controlling metaphor of the perfect union of male and female is achieved (the *yab-yum* displayed so often in Tibetan art: compare the same controlling metaphor in *Gitagovinda*, pp. 193–6). *Hevajra Tantra*, for example, teaches that since we are bound to this world by lust, it is by lust that we can be released – but lust properly understood and controlled through the practice of sexual Yoga.

The translation of Buddhist texts could not be undertaken until a Tibetan script had been created. Once this was done, King Trisong Detsen (above) authorised the translation of a number of Chinese works – Avatamsaka Sutra (p. 261), for example, and some Agamas (p. 171) and Prajñaparamita texts. He also invited Buddhist teachers from India, including the famous Padmasambhava who came to be regarded as 'the second Buddha'.

After a debate at Samye monastery, the pro-Chinese Buddhists were expelled and a decree was issued saying that thenceforth only texts in Sanskrit were to be translated. By now, however, the increase in the number of translated texts was prolific. There was an urgent need to organise them in a more systematic way, and this work was undertaken by Bu-ston (1290–1364). By the time he was thirty-two he had written a *History of Buddhism in Tibet* (Obermiller, 1931–2), and to this he added the suggestion that the texts be classified according to Kangyur and Tengyur. On that basis, he and his pupils compiled catalogues of existing texts and translations. This was the foundation of the Tibetan Canon.

One of his decisions was that only those texts would be included that could be traced to an Indian original. That, however, meant the exclusion of many Tantric texts that had been translated into Tibetan from other sources from the time of the First Diffusion onward. One of the four great Schools of Tibetan Buddhism is known as Nyingma. Its followers (Nyingmapas) found this far too restrictive. They valued the texts in the Canon, but they valued other texts as well. In particular, they traced their own School back to Padmasambhava who, they believed, had entrusted to chosen disciples texts that are known as 'the spiritual treasures', *gter-ma* or Terma. The Terma texts were intended to be found by reincarnations of those disciples at a time when the world was ready for those teachings to be disclosed. The disciples are known as 'treasure-finders', *gter.son* or Tertons. Among the texts that have been produced or discovered in this way is *The Tibetan Book of the Dead*: on this, see further pp. 285–7.

The Nyingmapas were alone in producing their own 'supplementary Canon', but other Orders valued particular texts, especially in the production of Tantras. The Sakyapas, followers of the Sakya Order, gave highest value to *Hevajra Tantra*, while the Gelugpas, the followers of the Gelug Order, gave that high value to *Kalacakra Tantra*.

The Kagyupas, followers of the Kagyu Order, trace their lineage back to Tilopa (988–1069), also known as Prajñabhadra, who taught Naropa (1016–1100) who passed it on to Marpa (1012–96) who included among his disciples the famous Milarepa (Mi-las-ri-pa, c.1050–1135). He is believed by Kagyupas to be the only Tibetan to become a perfect Buddha during the course of a single life. His profound influence, and the importance of his autobiography as a sacred text, have been described by Lobsang Lhalungpa (p. vii):

> Never, in the thirteen centuries of Buddhist history in Tibet, has there been such a man, who not only inspired an intellectual elite and spiritual luminaries, but also captured the imagination of the common people.

The Life ends with a summary of his achievement (trans. Lhalungpa, p.197):

> In summary, after the departure of Milarepa for the Buddha realm, . . . the result of his infinite compassion and universal concern was seen in the emergence of his spiritual descendants. Those disciples who achieved Complete Enlightenment were as numerous as the stars in the night; those who achieved non-return to samsara were also many, as particles of dust on the face of the earth. Those men and women who had entered the path of liberation were too numerous to be counted. He caused the teachings of Buddha to blaze forth like bright sunshine and guided these sentient beings away from temporary and permanent miseries toward happiness and the root of happiness.

Among many disciples, Milarepa taught Gampopa (1079–1153) who wrote *The Jewel Ornament of Liberation* (trans. Guenther). It was he who organised the Six Yogas of Naropa into a systematic course of teaching.

📖 BIBLIOGRAPHY NUMBERS 167, 352, 449, 517, 659, 803, 883

TIBETAN BUDDHISM
NAROPA, *THE TIBETAN BOOK OF THE DEAD*

Naropa (1016–1100) was a key figure in the development of the Kagyu tradition. His *Na-ro-chos-drug* (*Chödrug*), the Six Yogas of Naropa, became the foundation for the teaching and training of Kagyu spiritual teachers or Lamas, the equivalent of Indian Gurus. They illustrate the detailed analysis in many Tibetan texts of the stages through which successive goals can be attained. Naropa emphasised that it is useless to understand these stages in descriptive or intellectual terms. They must produce the inner changes to which they point:

1 *Tummo* (*gTum-mo*, Heat Yoga) is the penetration of *shunyata* in real experience which generates so much heat that the yogins can continue their meditation even in extremely low temperatures; it rests on the Tantric understanding of the cosmic energies being channelled through the body (see p. 202).

2 *Gyulü* (*sGyu-lus*, Illusory Body) applies this experience to the realisation of the insubstantiality of all phenomena.

3 *Milam* (*rMi-lam*, Dream Yoga): that realisation is extended to the maintaining of this consciousness even in the dream state 'when sleep has come and sleep has not yet gone'.

4 *Osal* (*'od-gsal*, Clear Light) is the experience of the entirely different 'Clear Light' illumination that obtains when *shunyata* is completely realised and all things are seen for what they really are.

5 *Phowa* (*'pho-ba*, Ejection) means that consciousness can be detached from this body and transferred to other states – for example, to the Pure Land or to another body to avoid the process of birth again as a baby.

6 *Bardo* (*bar-do*, Intermediate State) is the condition between death and new birth, dealt with also in *The Tibetan Book of the Dead*.

BARDO THÖDOL (THE TIBETAN BOOK OF THE DEAD)

Bardo Thödol ('Liberation by Hearing in the Intermediate State') is usually referred to outside Tibet as *The Tibetan Book of the Dead*. Its purpose is to accompany those who are entering the Bardo, the states that lie between the death of one body and the birth or reappearance in another. In contrast to the assumption that no one can tell us anything about what happens after death because no one has ever come back from death, *Bardo Thödol* (and Tibetan belief in general) insists that everyone has come back from death, or at least come through death, and that consequently there is much that we know about it. Part of that knowledge is contained in *Bardo Thödol*.

It begins with the instruction that the first part of Liberation through Hearing should be read during the moments when conscious life is about to cease (unless the person involved is a yogin who has already achieved Ejection, 5 above). If life has already ceased, the reading should take place beside the dead body, or, if the corpse is not present, in some place closely associated with that person.

Bardo Thödol then gives advice and instruction on the Six Realms of rebirth (hell, ghosts, animals, humans, asuras, heavens) and on the different types of *bardo* or 'inbetween states':

1 The Bardo of life and birth.

2 The Bardo of the dream state.

3 The Bardo of meditation.

4 The Bardo of death-experience.

5 The Bardo of blissful experience of Sambhogakaya.

6 The Bardo of seeking rebirth.

For those with an accumulation of bad *karma*, torments in hell and the wrathful deities are waiting. The appearance of the wrathful deities is truly terrifying, but *Bardo Thödol* is read as a reminder that attentive Tibetan Buddhists have already visualised them in their practice of meditation. As a result they can be calm (trans. Fremantle, p. 75):

At this time the great tornado of karma, terrifying, unbearable,
whirling fiercely, will drive you from behind. Do not be afraid of it;
it is your own confused projection. Dense darkness, terrifying and
unbearable, will go before you, with terrible cries of 'Strike!' and
'Kill!' . . . In fear you will escape wherever you can, but you will be
cut off by three precipices in front of you . . . O son of noble family,
they are not really precipices, they are aggression, passion and
ignorance. Recognise this now to be the bardo of becoming, and
call the name of the Lord of Great Compassion: 'O Lord of Great
Compassion, my guru, the Three Jewels, do not let me, (name), fall
into hell.' Supplicate fervently like this; do not forget.

Those who have accumulated good *karma* will enter blissful states, but even
they are not to be desired, because they are still of a limited, conditioned nature.
What is to be desired is *buddhacitta* (p. 75):

In the case of others who have gathered merit and were virtuous
and practised dharma sincerely, all kinds of perfect enjoyment will
invite them, and they will experience all kinds of perfect bliss and
happiness . . . Whatever arises like this, whatever pleasures and
objects of desire, do not be attracted to them or yearn for them.
Offer them to the guru and the Three Jewels. Give up attachment
and longing in your heart.

For most, however, reappearance in some form is certain since they have not
passed through, or even perhaps started, the Six Yogas. *Bardo Thödol* ends with
advice to them – not least to immerse themselves in hearing, or reading if they
can, *Bardo Thödol* before the time of death arrives (p. 93):

One should read this continually and learn the word-meanings and
terms by heart; then when death is certain and the signs of death
have been recognised, if one's condition allows one should read it
aloud oneself and contemplate it, and if one is not able to do that
it should be given to a dharma-brother to read, for this reminder
will certainly liberate, there is no doubt. This teaching does not
need any practice, it is a profound instruction which liberates
just by being seen and heard and read. This profound instruction
leads great sinners on the secret path. If one does not forget its
words and terms even when being chased by the seven dogs, the

instruction liberates in the bardo of the moment before death. Even
if the buddhas of the past, present and future were to search, they
would not find a better teaching than this.

The book ends with 'The Bardo Prayer which Protects from Fear' (pp. 103f.):

> When the journey of my life has reached its end,
> and since no relatives go with me from this world
> I wander in the bardo state alone,
> may the peaceful and wrathful buddhas send out the power of their
>   compassion
> and clear away the dense darkness of ignorance.
> When parted from beloved friends, wandering alone,
> my own projections' empty forms appear,
> may the buddhas send out the power of their compassion
> so that the bardo's terrors do not come ...
>
> In all the stages of learning, high, middle and low,
> may I understand just by hearing, thinking and seeing;
> wherever I am born, may that land be blessed,
> so that all sentient beings may be happy.
> O peaceful and wrathful buddhas, may I and others
> become like you yourselves, just as you are,
> with your forms and your auspicious marks,
> your retinues, your long life and your realms.
> Samantabhadra, the peaceful and wrathful ones, infinite
>   compassion,
> the power of truth of the pure dharmata,
> and followers of tantra in one-pointed meditation:
> may their blessings fulfil this inspiration-prayer.

📖 BIBLIOGRAPHY NUMBERS 69, 700–1, 949

洪先生還有七闓之遊

惜其別作歲寒枝以

唯等珠閣之情蓋

9

CHINA

CHINESE TEXTS: KEY DATES

BCE

c.1122–722/1027–771 Western Zhou dynasty

700–255/770–256 Eastern dynasty

1000–600 *Shijing*

770–476 Spring & Autumn dynasty

c.6th cent. Laozi, *Daodejing*

551–479 Kong Fuzi (Confucius), *Liu Jing, Lunyu*

505–432 Zengzi, *Da Xue*

5th cent. Zi Si, *Zhong Yong*

475–221 Warring States dynasties

372–289 Mengzi, *Book of Mengzi*

369–286 Zhuangzi, *Nan Hua Zhen Jing*

c.313–238 Xunzi

221–210 Qin Shihuangdi, first Emperor of China

213 burning of the books

CE

25–200 Han dynasties

1st cent. Ban Gu, listed Daoist texts

175 Five Classics engraved in stone

c.300ce Guo Xiang ed. *Zhuangzi*

334–417 Hui Yuan, *Shamen bu jing wangzhe lun*

4th cent. Ge Hong listed Daoist texts

406–477 Lu Xujing, Daoist Canon organised

618–906 Tang dynasty, *Daozang*

922–953 Five Classics block-printed

960–1279 Song dynasties

c.10th cent. → Neo-Confucianism

Five Masters:

   1011–1077 Shao Yong, *Huangji Jingshi*

   1017–1073 Zhou Dunyi, *Taijitu shuo, Tong shu*

   1020–1077 Zhang Zai, *Zheng Meng*

   1032–1085 Cheng Hao

   1033–1107 Cheng Yi

1130–1200 Zhu Xi → Cheng-Zhu Harmony, *Commentary* on *Great Learning*

Previous page: 'Plum blossom' by Yan Hui illustrates the combining of text and painting, 'the host and the guest' (see p. 10); on blossom and transience see p. 346.

THE CONFUCIAN CLASSICS

LIUJING

In *An Introduction to Confucianism* (p. 47), Yao Xinzhong summarised the importance of the Confucian Classics:

> As the doctrine of *literati*, Confucianism may well be called a tradition of books, in the sense that it takes the sacred writings of the ancients as the source of values and ideals . . . Indeed, without a proper knowledge of Confucian Classics, it would be impossible for us to draw a full picture of Confucianism.

Even beyond that, it is impossible for us to understand China – now as much as in the past – without understanding the Classics on which it has been built.

There are many religious beliefs in China, but no one religion dominates to the exclusion of others. Nor do the Chinese have a single word for 'religion'. Words that come somewhere near are *dao*, meaning 'way', or *men*, meaning 'door', or perhaps more commonly *jiao*, 'disciplined teaching'. In addition, there is a word that picks up shared commitment and understanding. That is the word *jia*. *Jia* meant originally the kind of community to be found in a home or a family, and from that it came to be used of those who belong together in a shared tradition.

The three major traditions in China are known as *san-jiao*, and each of them is made up of both *jiao* and *jia*. The three are:

- Rujia+Rujiao (old spelling Jujia+Jujiao, known outside China as Confucianism).

- Daojia+Daojiao (Daoism/Taoism).

- Fojia+Fojiao (Buddhism).

There is no feeling that people must belong to only one of these to the exclusion of the others. People will draw on each of them according to the occasion or the circumstances in which they find themselves. In addition, they may turn to popular beliefs and practices without feeling that they have abandoned or betrayed their own 'religion'.

Nevertheless, for 2,000 years life in China, both individual and social, has been founded on the so-called Confucian Classics (*jing*) combined with sacred books known as *shu*. The word *jing* meant originally the thread that runs through woven material holding the whole together. Education, government, life in the family and in society rested on the foundation of those texts. Students learned them by heart and then had to pass an examination on them if they were to enter into office under the Chinese Emperor.

THE CONFUCIAN CLASSICS

The Confucian Classics came into being over a long period of time. Some of them are older than Kong Fuzi (known outside China as Confucius) who lived 551–479 BCE. Kong Fuzi lived at a time of war and conflict, and as a result he developed a practical understanding of how harmony and peace can be brought into being as much in individual life as in society. He drew on the customs of the past and he emphasised the sense of cosmic order and discipline summarised in the word 'Tian'. Tian means roughly 'Heaven', as in the Mandate of Heaven that rulers and emperors in China were supposed to obey, but in Kong Fuzi's understanding it meant seeking out and following the natural way of life, the way things are meant to be. This is summed up in a basic saying of the Chinese, *Tianren heyi*, Heaven and the human are one.

Kong Fuzi spent his life seeking a ruler who might implement his teaching and vision. He was unsuccessful, and so, at the end of his life, he retired to his home where he taught his followers and also wrote poetry and music. It was at this time that he is thought traditionally to have written or edited the Six Classics. The Six Classics (*Liujing*) are:

1 *The Book of Changes* (*I Ching* or *Yi Jing*, a book of divination with ten Wings of commentary and interpretation).

2 *The Book of Songs* (or Poetry, *Shijing*: see p. 294–7).

3 *The Book of History* (or Documents, *Shujing*, consisting originally of 100 chapters, reduced to twenty-nine after the burning of the books in the third century BCE).

4 *The Book of Rites* (*Liji*, a collection of the rituals and ceremonies from the early period of the Zhou dynasty, c.1122–255 BCE; the original 131 chapters

were shortened into an edition of forty-nine chapters: two of its chapters, *Great Learning* or *Da Xue* and *Doctrine of the Mean* or *Zhong Yong*, became Classic texts in their own right: see pp. 301–4).

5 *Spring and Autumn Annals* (*Chunqiu*, a chronological account of Lu, the home state of Kong Fuzi, in the period 722–481 BCE) whose purpose was to illustrate the nature of good government and the meaning in practice of the maxim (above), *Tianren heyi*.

6 *The Book of Music* (*Yuejing*, now lost).

According to tradition, Kong Fuzi edited 2 and 3, compiled 4 and 6, annotated 1 and wrote 5.

The Six Classics became in fact Five after the Book of Music was lost, perhaps during the 'burning of the books' under the first Emperor of China, Qin Shihuangdi (221–210 BCE), who destroyed opponents and their writings in his attempt to create a unified empire. His memorial is left in the amazing Terracotta Army of Xian.

The Five Classics (as they had become with the loss of Music) were engraved in stone in 175 CE, and made widely available in block-printed books between 922 and 953. Other texts were added, in particular the Four Books. The Four Books are:

1 *Great Learning* (see pp. 301–2).

2 *Doctrine of the Mean* (see pp. 302–4).

3 *The Analects* (*Lun Yu*) which gathers together the words of Kong Fuzi and his replies to questions, together with discussions among his followers: see pp. 298–300).

4 *The Book of Mengzi* (older spelling Mencius, 372–289 BCE, often referred to simply as *Mengzi*: see pp. 305–8).

The Confucian Classics continued to be extended in number. One of the earliest to be added was *Xiao Jing, The Book of Filial Devotion*. *Xiao*, the obligation of children to respect and care for their parents, is profoundly important in Chinese society. With the addition of the earliest Chinese dictionary, *Er Ya*, whose purpose was to clarify the correct meaning of Confucian teaching, the whole collection became the Thirteen Classics.

BIBLIOGRAPHY NUMBERS 32, 125–8, 236, 271, 390, 596, 871, 895, 999, 1030, 1036, 1039

THE BOOK OF SONGS

SHIJING

Shijing, The Book of Songs (or Poems, Odes, etc.), is a collection of poems and songs, the earliest of which may date from about 1000 BCE. The collection was put together in about 600 BCE. They came into being, therefore, during the early period of the Zhou dynasties (the dates are disputed, but traditionally 1122–722/255 BCE), and they therefore reflect the life and interests of people in that period from different levels of society. In the words of Stephen Owen (in Allen, p. xvi):

> *The Book of Songs* is a work that attempts to embrace every aspect
> of its world: the dead ancestors and the living, past history and
> present, men and women, the ruling house and the common
> people. And between each of these divisions in their world, the
> songs create relations that bind them together.

The topics thus range widely from love, war, daily life and human anxiety to commentary on good and bad government. Some are clearly ritual hymns or chants, a reminder that the Songs were transmitted orally long before they were written down. In fact it is not known when *Shijing* was first made into a text, though clearly Kong Fuzi knew it since otherwise he could not have commended it to his followers, nor could he have edited it as traditionally he is thought to have done. Of *Shijing*, Kong Fuzi said (*Analects* 2.2), 'The 300 Poems are summed up in one single phrase: "Think no evil".'

Kong Fuzi valued *Shijing* greatly. The *Analects* record his opinion (17.9,10, trans. by Leys):

> The Master said: 'Little ones, why don't you study the *Poems*? The
> *Poems* can provide you with stimulation and with observation, with
> a capacity for communion, and with a vehicle for grief. At home,

they enable you to serve your father, and abroad, to serve your lord. Also, you will learn there the names of many birds, animals, plants, and trees.'

The Master said to his son: 'Have you worked through the first and the second part of the *Poems*? Whoever goes into life without having worked through the first and the second part of the *Poems* will remain stuck, as if facing a wall.'

The tradition that Kong Fuzi edited *Shijing* is recorded in *Shiji*, a work collecting historical records dating from about 90 BCE (the title in the following quotation is *Shi*, not *Shijing*, because the word *jing*, 'classic', was not added until the work became one of the Five Classics):

In times of old *Shi* contained more than 3000 works. Kong Fuzi got rid of any duplications and then selected works that lent themselves to *li* . . . He then set the resulting 305 works to music.

Li is an impossible word to translate – though often it is translated as 'propriety'. It represents the thoughts and behaviours that are appropriate for maintaining the correct order in family, society and the cosmos. These are protected and shared in ritual, hence the translation of *li* as 'ritual propriety'. It also refers to the way in which individuals must develop in themselves the right moral attitude and motivation. Its range of reference is summarised in Schwartz (p. 67):

The word *li* on the most concrete level refers to all those 'objective' prescriptions of behaviour, whether involving rite, ceremony, manners, or general deportment, that bind human beings and the spirits together in networks of interacting roles within the family, within human society, and with the numinous realm beyond.

Kong Fuzi realised that the texts inherited from the past should be the foundation of 'the good life' for individuals and for society. He said (8.8): 'Draw inspiration from the *Poems*; steady your course with the ritual; find your fulfilment in music.'

Shijing, therefore, played a fundamental part in the long development of Confucian life and government, especially in (as Owen put it, p. xiv), 'the great Confucian project of educating the human heart back to its natural goodness'. For that to happen, a considerable work of interpretation was needed because not all the Songs seemed to be celebrating the moral perfection implied by *li*.

The Songs may thus be difficult to understand because they are full of allusions

THREE TRANSLATIONS
OF SONG 259 OF SHIJING

LOFTY IS THE SACRED MOUNTAIN, grandly it reaches to heaven; the Sacred Mountain sent down a Spirit who bore [the princes of] Fu and Shen; [the princes of] Fu and Shen became the supports of Chou [Zhou]; the states of the four [quarters] they went to [fence, be a fence to =] protect, the [states of] the four quarters they went to [wall, be a wall to =] defend.

B. Karlgren

MIGHTIEST OF ALL HEIGHTS IS the Peak
Soaring up into the sky.
The Peak sent down a Spirit
Which bore Fu and Shen.
Now Shen and Fu
Became the sure support of Zhou;
A fence to screen the homelands,
A wall to guard the four sides.

Arthur Waley

HIGH, PINE-COVERED PEAK FULL of echos,
Proud ridge-poll of Heaven, roof-tree
whence descended the whirl of spirits
begetters of Fu and Shen,
Out of the echoing height, whirling spirits of air descended.
To sires of Chou were given in vassalage, bulwarks
under the bright wings of the sun
a square kingdom against invasion,
Strong as the chamber of winds.

Ezra Pound

to people and historical events of which, apart from the Songs, we have little knowledge. In the Introduction (pp. 13–15) reference was also made to the problems of translation and to the vast difference between Karlgren's attempt at a literal translation and Ezra Pound's freedom. Somewhere between the two is the translation of Arthur Waley, now extended and annotated by Joseph Allen. The contrast can be seen, by way of example, in their versions of the opening of Song 259 (see box).

Despite the many problems of translation and interpretation, the Songs remain directly accessible. In their simplicity they often resemble the songs and chants of another world in a different age, gathered in *Carmina Gaedelica* (see p. 96). These two examples (99 and 166) are taken from Allen:

Sun in the east!
This lovely man
Is in my house,
Is in my home,
His foot is upon my doorstep.

Moon in the east!
This lovely man
Is in my bower,
Is in my bower,
His foot is upon my threshold.

——— · ———

May Heaven guard and keep you
In great security,
Make you staunch and hale;
What blessing not vouchsafed?
Give you much increase,
Send nothing but abundance.

May Heaven guard and keep you,
Cause your grain to prosper,
Send you nothing that is not good.
May you receive from Heaven in a hundred boons,
May Heaven send down to you blessings so many
That the day is not long enough for them all.

📖 BIBLIOGRAPHY NUMBERS 128, 871

THE ANALECTS

Lunyu

Lunyu is a collection of sayings and stories relating to Kong Fuzi (Master Kong, 551–479 BCE), better known outside China by a Latinised version of his name, Confucius. The collection was made over a period of about seventy-five years after Kong Fuzi's death. There is no continuous narrative; nor even a discernible organisation of the material in a thematic way. Despite this, *Lunyu* has been fundamental and indispensable during the development over 2,000 years of the Confucian way. The Confucian way was not restricted to China: it spread to Korea and Japan where its influence has been immense.

Kong Fuzi belonged to the class of teachers known as *ru* (hence *rujia/jiao*) who instructed rulers on rituals and ceremonies. He lived under the Zhou dynasty. China at that time was not the single empire that it later became. There were about 70 to 120 states during his lifetime. The Zhou king was the Son of Heaven (Tian) with a court of officials around him, but the states were largely independent, and indeed were often in conflict with each other or with the central government.

Kong Fuzi proposed a way of life and government in which the chaos of war and conflict could be overcome. He worked for the ruler of Lu, one of the semi-independent states, but his proposals were not accepted. As a result, he spent thirteen years (497–484) travelling to different places, looking for a ruler who would accept his proposals and put them into practice. He failed completely, so he returned home to teach his followers. *Lunyu* is an anthology of that teaching as his followers remembered it, and that is why it is not a systematic treatise, as can be seen, by way of illustration, in this sequence (trans. Leys, *Lunyu* 15.21–8):

> The Master said: 'A *junzi* [on the meaning of *junzi*, see p. 300] makes demands on himself; a vulgar man makes demands on others.'

The Master said: 'A *junzi* is proud without being aggressive, sociable but not partisan.'

The Master said: 'A *junzi* does not approve of a person because he expresses a certain opinion, nor does he reject an opinion because it is expressed by a certain person.'

Zigong asked: 'Is there any single word that could guide one's entire life?' The Master said: 'Should it not be reciprocity [*shu*]? What you do not wish for yourself, do not do to others.'

The Master said: 'In my dealings with people, do I ever praise anyone, and do I ever blame anyone? If I praise anyone, it is only after having tested him. The people of today are still the same people who once enabled the Three Dynasties to steer a straight course.'

The Master said: 'I can still remember that there was a time when scribes encountering a doubtful word would leave a blank space, and horse owners would have their new horses tested by an expert. Nowadays these practices are not followed any more.'

The Master said: 'Clever talk ruins virtue. Small impatiences ruin great plans.'

The Master said: 'When everyone dislikes a man, one should investigate. When everyone likes a man, one should investigate.'

In Kong Fuzi's understanding of what needed to be done, the foundation was Tian (on which see p. 292). Later Confucians tried to organise his teaching in a more systematic way, and they discerned *san gang* ('three guiding principles') and *wu chang* ('five enduring regulations'). The first of the Three Principles is that of subordination and obedience in the different levels of society. Thus a son must be obedient to his father, a younger brother to an older, a younger friend to an older, a wife to her husband, and all to those who have authority.

The Five Regulations are not laws. They are the five characteristics that Kong Fuzi emphasised as being necessary in a good life. One of them is *li*, on which see p. 295. The others are *ren*, *yi* (doing what is right no matter what the consequence), *zhi* (wisdom) and *xin* (fidelity). Of these, *ren* was of particular importance for Kong Fuzi. The Chinese character for this word is made by combining two elements, 'human' and 'two', thus suggesting that one can be human in the best sense only in relationships: 'One can only be a self in a field of selves.' *Ren* is thus the quality of generosity and altruism, the embodiment in a person of the ideal moral life.

Anyone who achieves this or who seriously aspires to it was called by Kong Fuzi *junzi*. That word is often translated as 'gentleman', but the associations of that word may be misleading. In Kong Fuzi's understanding, the Junzi are the genuine, as opposed to the social, aristocracy. They are people who constantly seek the good of others and who are self-contained at all times in calm serenity, even when they are themselves overtaken by disaster.

Kong Fuzi believed that 'aristocracy' and 'nobility' were not a matter of birth, inheritance or status. In his time it was thought that *junzi* can be attained only by leaders and rulers, but he insisted that everyone is capable of achieving the condition of Junzi. Not only are all people *capable* of achieving this: they can actually learn it by education and by putting it into practice on the way. The Classic texts exhibit exactly how this can be done, so not surprisingly they became the foundation of Chinese education until the beginning of the twentieth century.

Kong Fuzi was not without his critics during the long period of Confucian dominance in China, but that criticism became far more extreme after the fall of the Qing dynasty in 1911. Many then believed that Kong Fuzi and his ideas had held China back in the past and had led to a hierarchical and authoritarian society. Wu Zhihui, at the beginning of the twentieth century, believed passionately that only Western science could help China to recover, and as a result he attacked the past savagely (in Kwok, p. 49):

> This odorous thing, the national heritage, thrives along with
> concubinage and opium. Concubinage and opium in turn thrive
> together with status – and wealth – and consciousness. When
> national learning was at a height, all politics were rotten. This is
> because Confucius, Mencius, Lao-tzu, and Mo-tzu were products
> of the chaotic world of the Spring and Autumn and the Warring
> States. They must be thrown into the latrine for thirty years.

That rejection of the Confucian past has been endorsed in Communist China even though some of its aspects have been absorbed, not least the emphasis on obedience to authority. Despite the condemnation, Confucianism endures and is still expressed in individual and family life. The ambition to write one's life in the language of moral goodness has not been destroyed, and the insights of Kong Fuzi endure.

📖 BIBLIOGRAPHY NUMBERS **32**

GREAT LEARNING AND DOCTRINE OF THE MEAN

DA XUE **AND** *ZHONG YONG*

Da Xue and *Zhong Yong* were originally two chapters in *The Book of Rites*. In the older (Wade-Giles) system of transliteration they appear as *Ta Hsueh* and *Chung Yung*. Their brevity made them easy to memorise. Their influence as a result has been immense, not just in China but also in Korea and Japan. They are two of the Four Books (p. 293), the basic text books of Confucian education.

DA XUE

Da Xue is the learning required for those who wish to become 'great'. 'Great' may mean simply adult, or it may mean those who aspire to a good and an honourable life. Traditionally, it is thought to have been written by one of the followers of Kong Fuzi, Zengzi (505–432 BCE), though it has also been ascribed to his grandson Zi Si.

The purpose of *Da Xue* is to teach people the nature of 'the Great Way' and to show them what it means in practice. Anyone who wishes to exercise authority in the best way cannot do so by force or compulsion, still less by going to war. What are required are the inner moral strength and character of the Junzi (p. 300). *Da Xue* relates this self-development to specific needs in society.

To achieve this, *Da Xue* offers Eight Steps that will lead to the goal. The first two, the perfecting of knowledge by investigation and the sharing of it, are the root of the others. The third is to make one's thoughts and intentions sincere:

> What does 'making the thoughts sincere' mean? It is to allow no
> self-deception – as when we hate a bad smell or respond to what
> is beautiful. This is called being at peace in oneself. Therefore, the
> *junzi* must be watchful over himself when he is alone.

The fourth Step is 'rectifying the mind':

> What does 'the cultivation of the person depends on rectifying the mind' mean? We can see it like this: those who are under the control of passion will be wrong in what they do – as also when they are under the control of terror or of affectionate care or of grief and distress.

The next two Steps are the development of one's own character in order to guide and regulate one's family. The final two follow from the ability to regulate one's family. Those who know how to do that will know what is involved in good government:

> What does 'in order to govern the State well, it is necessary first to regulate the family' mean? No one can teach others who cannot teach his own family. So the ruler, without going outside his own family, learns what he needs to govern the State: filial piety [*xiao*] shows how rulers should be served; the respect a younger brother shows to an older shows how elders should be respected; the mutual support shows how the multitude should be treated.

Finally, therefore, good government will bring good order to society as well as peace and harmony to the world: 'Virtue is the root, wealth is the result.'

ZHONG YONG

Zhong Yong, Doctrine of the Mean, is thought traditionally to have been written by a grandson of Kong Fuzi, Zi Si (fifth century BCE), though it may be a compilation from earlier works. Where *Da Xue* offers guidance on good government, *Zhong Yong* is more concerned with the development of a good and moral character that will in turn lead to good government.

The word 'Mean' is not the attempt to find a compromise or middle ground between two conflicting parties of the kind to which Asquith, a former British Prime Minister, was addicted. When, for example, the government during the First World War was completely split over whether to introduce conscription, Asquith wrote, 'We seem to be on the brink of a precipice. The practical question is, shall I be able . . . to devise and build a bridge?'

For *Zhong Yong*, the 'middle way' is a matter of keeping one's balance in implementing the way of Tian (Heaven). There is a normative way to which the texts inherited from the past are a guide, and that is why the title of the work has

THE OPENING
OF ZHONG YONG

1.1. That which Tian [Heaven] gives is called human nature. Living in accordance with this nature is called the *dao* [Way]. Pursuing the Dao is called instruction [*jiao*].

1.2. The Dao may not be left even for a single moment. If it could be left it would not be the Dao. Therefore the Junzi is cautious and full of awe when he encounters the unseen and the unheard.

1.3. It is obvious what is unseen or unheard. For that reason the Junzi is vigilant when he is alone.

1.4. When passions such as pleasure, anger, sorrow or joy are not aroused, the condition is that of balance [centrality]. When those passions have been aroused and are expressed in a measured and controlled way, the condition is that of harmony. This balance is the deep root, and the condition of harmony is the universal Way of awe that exists in the world.

1.5. Wherever the conditions of balance and harmony are realised, Tian and Earth function as they should, and all things are nourished as they should be.

been translated as *Central Norm*. For this balance to be achieved there must be complete honesty and sincerity, *cheng*.

Zhong Yong encourages the endeavour of individuals to achieve this balance, because if they succeed they 'stand between Heaven and Earth' and thus become a bridge between them (see box p. 303). This creates the Trinity or Triad that became for many Confucians the ideal goal to be achieved: three realities which nevertheless constitute a single entity working in complete harmony.

The Classics were the foundation on which Chinese life was built for 2,000 years. Even so, there were opponents (and the alternatives of Daoism and Buddhism) among whom the so-called Legalists believed that human beings, far from being naturally good, are naturally inclined to evil. Instead of the Confucian belief that people can be educated into goodness they held that good government needs strong laws with punitive sanctions. It was opposition of this kind that led to the great defenders of the Confucian way.

BIBLIOGRAPHY NUMBERS 255, 297, 390, 1047

THE BOOK OF MENCIUS

MENGZI

Among those who defended and developed the Confucian way was Mengzi (372–289 BCE; Mencius is a Latinised form of the name). The book bearing his name (perhaps edited by his pupils) is usually referred to simply as *Mengzi*. It has come to be revered as one of the Four Books (p. 293), and Mengzi was described later as 'the second Kong Fuzi'. And yet for many centuries neither he nor the book had that status: it was not included among the Classics until the Song Dynasty (960–1126).

Mengzi lived in the state of Qi, not far from Lu, the home of Kong Fuzi. Like Kong Fuzi, Mengzi spent most of his working life going to rulers, hoping to find one who would put his teachings into practice. It was, however, the time of the Warring States when rulers were too preoccupied in conflict to pay much attention to a philosopher. Mengzi, therefore, decided to commit himself to teaching and in particular to refuting opponents.

Mengzi saw himself as the successor of Kong Fuzi. *Mengzi* ends with a summary of the history of the transmission of teaching from a kind of Golden Age, and in its last verse it states (7.2.38):

> From the time of Kong Fuzi until now is a little more than a
> hundred years. The distance in time from him is as little as the
> distance from the place where he lived. Given that that is so, is
> there no one to continue his teaching? It would seem so.

That is the task to which Mengzi set himself. He strongly endorsed the teaching of Kong Fuzi that human nature is essentially good – in contrast, therefore, to the Legalists and to another interpreter of Kong Fuzi, Xunzi (*c*.313–238 BCE), who held that human nature is essentially evil. In his view, Tian is impersonal, operating in the universe by a kind of natural law (cf. *karma* in India, p. 173);

MENGZI ON
HUMAN NATURE

THE PHILOSOPHER GAO ZI said: 'Human nature is like wood from a willow tree, yi [doing what is right] is like a cup or bowl. To turn human nature into yi is like shaping a cup or bowl from the wood of a willow tree.' Mengzi replied: 'When you shape a cup or bowl, can you leave the willow as it is in its own nature, or must you do violence to that nature in order to produce a cup or bowl? If you must do violence to the nature of the willow tree in order to produce a cup or bowl, it follows (on your argument) that you are doing violence to human nature in order to shape it into yi.'

Gao Zi said: 'Human nature is like fast-running water. Open the way for it to the east and it will flow to the east; open a way for it to the west and it will flow to the west. Human nature is disposed neither to good nor to evil, just as the water is disposed neither to the east nor to the west.' Mengzi replied: 'It is true that water is disposed neither to the east nor to the west, but is it disposed neither to flowing uphill nor to flowing downhill? The inclination of human nature to do good is like that of water to flow downhill. There is no one who does not have the inclination to do good, just as there is no water that does not flow downhill.

'Of course you may hit water and make it splash up into your face; you may even force water up the hill: but does that belong to the nature of water? It is the application of force that makes it happen. In the same way humans may be made to do what is not good, but that is because the same thing is being done to their human nature.'

Mengzi 6.1.1–3

rulers must therefore govern in accordance with that natural law and must if necessary direct their subjects into obedience to it. *Xunzi* 17 states:

> Tian acts with constant and undeviating rule . . . If that is reflected
> in good government, success will follow . . . Tian has its seasons,
> earth has its material resources, and humans have government.
> That is what it means to say that humans are able to form a Trinity/
> Triad [cf. *Zhong Yong* p. 304].

Mengzi, in contrast, insisted that people must resist rulers who do not follow the rule or Mandate of Heaven. He followed Kong Fuzi in affirming the basic goodness of human nature (see box).

Mengzi, however, was not naive. He did not believe that people are 'naturally good' as such. He believed, rather, that all humans are born with the four cardinal virtues within them – the virtues of *ren*, *yi*, *li* and *zhi* (for the meaning of these see the Five Regulations, p. 299). But he was clear that the virtues will not operate automatically. They are innate but not fully developed, and the major purpose of education is to develop and strengthen the virtues (6.1.6–8):

> What I mean by saying that human nature is good is this: from the
> feelings that are natural and innate, human nature is constituted
> [prepared] for the practice of what is good.
>
> If people do what is not good, you cannot blame human nature.
>
> Feelings of sympathy are common to all people. So are feelings of
> shame and dislike, approving and disapproving . . . *Ren*, *yi*, *li* and
> *zhi* are not imposed on us from without. From our origin we are
> furnished with them. That is why it is said, 'Seek and you will find
> them; neglect them and you will lose them.'

Kong Fuzi had emphasised the importance of internalising the four cardinal virtues. Mengzi agreed, but his own emphasis was on the importance of externalising them into all human relationships, especially within the family and society (7.1.15):

> Humans have an innate disposition that is not acquired by
> learning. Their innate knowledge is theirs without any thinking
> about it. Children carried in the arms know how to love their

parents, and when they grow up a little they know how to love their elder brothers. *Xiao* [filial respect] is the proper way to be human [*ren*] and respect for the elders is to act rightly [*yi*]. All that is needed is that these innate feelings should be applied to all people.

BIBLIOGRAPHY NUMBERS 656, 1031

THE DAOIST CANON

Daozang

Daoism (Daojiao and Daojia) is the second of the San-jiao, the three major traditions of Chinese thought and religion (p. 291). Daoism, particularly in its popular religious forms and in its exercises designed to align oneself with the unfolding process of the universe, is widely popular, not just in China but now throughout the world.

Like Confucianism, Daoism is concerned with the proper understanding of human nature and with the right ordering of social relationships, including family and government. The purpose of both traditions is to produce good people living at peace in themselves and in harmony with each other.

Where they disagree, however, is in their understanding of how to reach that goal. Confucianists hold that the goal can be reached by cultivating through education and practice the Four Cardinal Virtues (p. 307): if these are observed and put into effect, then life in family and society will be transformed. Daoists in contrast are clear that the goal cannot be reached through education or through any other means of imposition or control. Thus where a Confucian asks, 'What should I do?', a Daoist asks, 'What kind of person should I be?'

The immediate Daoist answer to that question is simple: I must understand what the Dao is, and I must release my life into the process of the Dao which creates and sustains all life. But that answer is not self-evidently clear. It requires a much more careful and profound understanding of the Dao (Daojia), and it requires also some guidance on what in practice I have to do to achieve that goal (Daojiao).

Not surprisingly, Daoists emphasise that the guidance and practice may be found as much in painting and art as in sacred texts, since the Dao permeates both – as Zong Bing explained in his own case (trans. de Bary, p. 254):

> Fundamentally spirit has no sign and yet it dwells in all physical
> forms and acts on all species. As truth enters into a thing, it is

reflected, like a shadow, in all its manifestations. If one can truly depict them with skill, one can truly be said to have achieved perfection. And so I live in leisure and nourish my vital power [*qi*]. I drain clean the wine-cup, play the lute, lay down the picture of scenery, face it in silence, and, while seated, travel beyond the four borders of the land, never leaving the realm where nature exerts her influence, and alone responding to the call of wilderness . . . What else need I do? I gratify my spirit, that is all. What is there that is more important than gratifying the spirit?

THE FIVE SCHOOLS AND THE QUEST FOR IMMORTALITY

There came to be a large number of different schools, sects and traditions of teaching within Daoism. In the Five Schools, for example, the Action and Karma School emphasised the importance of self-sacrificial help to others; the Ritual School developed liturgies and ceremonies to help the cleansing and cultivation of the self, especially through the chanting of sacred texts; the Talisman School offered physical means (through chants, magic, energy-producing substances and the like) in order to create an interaction and communion between human beings and the energies in the universe derived from Dao; the Divination School identified those energies in heaven, earth and humanity in order to align human life with the unfolding of the Dao, and also to predict the wisest way to live one's life in the future; the Inner Alchemy School was based on the attempts to change base metals into gold, but far beyond that it sought to change physical and mental health in order to produce a long life and perhaps even immortality.

The quest for immortality was fundamental in Daoism, and many Daoist texts are concerned with it. The Eight Immortals are exemplary figures in Daoism because they have shown how the goal can be achieved. It is not a goal that lies only beyond death: it is possible to make a start now by the proper understanding and use of Qi. Qi ('air', 'breath') is the vital energy which pervades and enables all things. The most obvious way in which to prolong one's life is to keep on breathing – or, in other words, to keep on assimilating into oneself the all-pervasive energy that sustains everything. That is why breathing exercises are so decisively important for Daoists. *Yang qi* means 'nourishing the life spirit', and that is done in many ways, including breath control, diet and the proper exercise of sexual energy.

The purpose of these exercises is to recover the scattered *yuan qi*, the primordial breath or energy. *Yuan qi* has now been dispersed throughout the universe, but its original power is reintegrated in the breathing exercises which distribute it to the whole body.

It follows that the quest for immortality takes different forms. Not surprisingly, many Daoist texts explore what it is both in meaning and practice. Some look at its foundations in the Daoist understanding of nature and the universe; others suggest the ways in which the myths and rituals of Daoists act as guidance; and others describe the different exercises that are needed.

THE DAOIST CANON

The many different forms resulted in a large number of sacred texts being produced. Each of the many Schools has its own texts – though not to the exclusion of the texts of other Schools, since many of them are shared.

The two basic texts accepted by all were *Daodejing* and *Zhuangzhu* (see following pages). A list of other recognised texts was made by Ban Gu in the first century CE, and in the fourth century Ge Hong listed all the texts that he could find. It was left to Lu Xujing (406–77) to classify and organise the texts in the first Daoist Canon. He classified them in Three Caves, and that, together with the addition of Four Supplements, has remained the basic structure of the Daoist Canon.

The Three Caves are Dong Zhen, Dong Xuan and Dong Shen. The Four Supplements are Tai Xuan (which actually includes *Daodejing* in a not particularly prominent place), Tai Ping (which includes *Tai Pingjing, Classic of the Great Peace*), Tai Jing and Zheng Yi.

The first Canon to be authorised by an emperor appeared in the Tang dynasty (618–906), and it was said to have contained at least 3,700 and perhaps as many as 7,300 scrolls. That Canon was lost in the wars and rebellions of the time. However, the recovery and building up of the Canon continued until it reached a total of about 8,000 scrolls. These are called *Daozang*.

It can be seen, therefore, that Daoism is a text-based philosophy and religion. Nevertheless, the texts themselves are clear that Daoism can be neither learnt nor understood by reading the texts. It is necessary always to receive instruction from a properly qualified person. According to *Cultivating Stillness* (Wong, p. 30): 'The person who does not receive instruction from an enlightened teacher but only looks for the Dao in books, does not recognise the Dao as supreme and precious.'

LAOZI, THE WAY AND ITS POWER

DAODEJING

Daodejing (*Tao-te Ching*), also known as *Laozi* (*Lao Tzu*) from the name of its traditional author, is a short work. It is made up of 5,000 Chinese characters, and for that reason it is sometimes called *Text of the 5000 Signs*. The claim is often made that no text outside the Bible has been so often translated. It is the fundamental text of Daoism.

Daodejing is attributed traditionally to Laozi who is greatly revered by Daoists, but very little is known historically about him. He is thought to have lived in about the sixth century BCE in the state of Chu, where he worked for the rulers of the Zhou dynasty. He is said to have met Kong Fuzi and indeed to have given him instruction. At some point he became dissatisfied with life under the Zhou and he left China, travelling to the West.

At the border he was recognised by a guard who refused to let him continue until he had set down his teaching in writing. Within a week or two he produced *Daodejing*. He then mounted a water buffalo and disappeared to the west – a scene often portrayed in Chinese painting. In India he is said to have instructed Siddhartha Gotama who subsequently attained Enlightenment and became the Buddha. *Huahujing* is a text much loved by Daoists, who claim that it contains the teaching imparted by Laozi to the Buddha – a claim passionately rejected by Chinese Buddhists.

Beyond this point the traditions divide. According to some, Laozi discovered the secret of immortality with the result that he never died. He lives now among the Immortals. However, according to others, he died in his home town of Luyi where his tomb has become a centre of reverent pilgrimage. Many Daoists came to regard Laozi as a special envoy sent into the world by Taiyi, the Supreme Unity. *Daodejing* was then believed to be a

THE OPENING OF DAODEJING

THE Dao that can be told of
   is not the eternal Dao;
The name that can be named
   is not the eternal name.
Nameless, it is the origin of Heaven and earth;
Nameable, it is the mother of all things.
Always nonexistent,
   That we may apprehend its inner secret;
Always existent,
   That we may gradually discern its outer manifestations.
These two are the same;
Only as they manifest themselves they receive different names.

Daodejing (trans. de Bary)

revelation sent down from the celestial realms long before the time of Laozi.

Daodejing is made up of eighty-one chapters divided into two parts. Part 1 (chapters 1–37) is called *Daojing*, Part 2 (38–81) is called *Dejing*. What, then, are Dao and De?

The word *dao* we have already met several times because it is the Chinese word for 'way'. The Chinese character is made up of a head (representing the person who knows) and walking. In *Daodejing*, Dao is the fundamental way in which all things happen as they do and as they should. That is because everything that exists comes from Dao as the origin of the universe and the source of life. Dao is the unproduced Producer of all that is. That phrase is used in Christianity of God as the creator of all that is, but Daoists do not understand the Dao as being any kind of personal agent. Dao is the undifferentiated reality, pre-existing Heaven and Earth, from which the energy flows forth that sustains all things in being, both animate and inanimate.

Clearly, if Dao has no differentiating characteristics, it cannot be described or defined – hence the opening line of *Daodejing*, which is so dense that it is impossible to translate. It usually appears as something like, 'The Dao that can be spoken of is not the eternal Dao', but more literally it says, 'The *dao* that is *dao*-ing is not unchanging *dao*.' The word 'Dao' appears three times as both noun and verb to show that one attempt at definition is contradicted by another. Its meaning unpacked is: 'If Dao is a process Dao cannot be a fixed and permanent Dao.' Dao is known in its effects but cannot be known in itself (*Daodejing* 25):

> Before Heaven and Earth there existed something without differenti-
> ating characteristics, complete in itself. Without either sound or form
> it is dependent on nothing and does not change. It is active everywhere
> and never fails. It acts as the mother of the universe. I do not know its
> name. I call it Dao. The best I can do to name it is to call it Great . . .
> Humans follow the ways of Earth, Earth follows the ways of Heaven,
> Heaven follows the ways of Dao, Dao follows the ways of itself.

The Chinese character for 'De' is made up of three parts, 'to go', 'straight' and 'the heart'. De is therefore to act in the right way with the right intention. An early Chinese dictionary, *Shuo wen jie* (second century CE), defined De as 'the outward effect of a person and the inward effect of the self'. De is thus the natural ability of all things to be and act as they should, and in the human case that means acting in accordance with Dao. De is Dao manifest in effect. *Daodejing* 51 shows how they are related (the reference in this passage to 10,000 things means 'everything' because at that time the language was thought to contain 10,000 nouns, the sum, therefore, of all that is):

> Dao brings all things to birth, De brings them to growth, things
> give them shape and contingent circumstances complete them.
> This means that among the 10,000 things there is not one that
> does not revere Dao or give honour to De.

How, then, can humans live in this way, going with the grain of the universe and not resisting or fighting against it? The key to the answer lies in *wuwei*. *Wuwei* means literally 'act without acting'. The usual phrase in *Daodejing* is *wuwei er wu bu wei*, 'no action but nothing does not happen'. *Wuwei* is thus living and acting but getting one's own activity out of the way so that Dao is allowed to be the action of one's life: 'The world is ruled by letting things run their course, not by interfering' (48). Or, to put it more succinctly, 'the governing of a large state should be like the cooking of a small fish.'

The result will be a quiet and accepting confidence even when the world is exploding all around: 'Seek to be empty, keep hold of quietness . . . To know the eternal truth is Enlightenment, but not to know the eternal truth is to run blindly to catastrophe' (16).

BIBLIOGRAPHY NUMBERS **261, 576**

ZHUANGZI

ZHUANGZI OR *NAN HUA ZHEN JING*

Zhuangzi is the second of the great founders of Daoism who was given by later Daoists the title Nan Hua Zhenren, 'the true person of Nan Hua'. The text attributed to him is therefore known either by his name, *Zhuangzi*, or by his title, *Nan Hua Zhen Jing*, 'The True Classic of Nan Hua'.

Very little is known of Zhuangzi, and it is unlikely that he wrote the whole work. He lived from about 369–286 BCE. According to the historian Sima Qian (145–86 BCE), he worked as a minor official in Henan Province. When he was offered a high sum to become a government official he refused, saying that the offer was like the fattening of an ox which is then led to the temple for sacrifice. It is too late then, he observed, to reflect that it would have been better to live as a humble pig, unnoticed by anyone.

Zhuangzi is made up of three parts. Chapters 1–7 are known as the Inner Book (or Chapters) and are generally thought to be the work of Zhuangzi. Chapters 8–22 are known as the Outer Book (or Chapters), and Chapters 23–33 are called the Added Book (or Miscellaneous Chapters). The text in its present form is largely the work of Guo Xiang (*c.*300CE), who arranged the material in its chapters and brought in material from other sources.

Zhuangzi shared much in common with Laozi – so much so in its fundamental ideas that some have regarded *Zhuangzi* as a commentary on *Laozi*. In particular, they had a similar understanding of Dao and De: Dao is the origin and source of all appearance, the unproduced Producer of all that is; Dao unfolds through De into the manifold and particular forms of the universe; the way to become a true and perfected person (*zhenren*) is to allow oneself to become a part of the Dao, a part of the unfolding process of what is meant to be. Chapter 12 states:

ZHUANGZI REJECTS THE FAME OF PUBLIC OFFICE

ONCE ZHUANGZI WAS FISHING in the Pu river when the king of Chu sent two of his ministers to announce that he wished to entrust to Zhuangzi the care of his entire domain. Zhuangzi held his fishing pole and, without turning his head, said: 'I have heard that Chu possesses a sacred tortoise which has been dead for three thousand years and which the king keeps wrapped up in a box and stored in his ancestral temple. Is this tortoise better off dead and with its bones venerated, or would it be better off alive with its tail dragging in the mud?' 'It would be better off alive and dragging its tail in the mud,' the two ministers replied. 'Then go away!' said Zhuangzi, 'and I will drag my tail in the mud!'

Zhuangzi (trans. de Bary)

In the great Origin there was no-thing: there was no being, no name. At the starting point there arose singularity [Oneness] which as yet had no form. Forming itself it came to life and it was called manifestation [De] . . . The shape of a form protects the essence within it, and each essential form has its own natural pattern to follow. This is its nature . . . It is like 'the union of a bird's beak and its song'. The way they work together in union is the union of Heaven and Earth. This union runs through the whole universe, below the surface, not conscious: it is De uniting all things in complete obedience.

Zhuangzi, therefore, had a strong sense of being at one with all things and thus with Dao: 'When Heaven and Earth were born, so was I, so that the 10,000 things [everything] are one with me.' The truly perfected person (*zhenren*) lives in this union by allowing Dao to be the action in his activity (*wuwei*: see p. 314). It is like a butcher who no longer has to sharpen his knife because he no longer struggles with the carcass, blunting his knife when he saws at a bone: he has learned to go with the way of the texture so that there is no resistance. The butcher says, 'My concern is the Dao which lies far beyond skill. When I began to cut up an ox all I could see was the ox. After three years I was no longer looking at the whole ox. Now I do it as it should be done and I no longer look with my eyes.'

Zhuangzi, however, saw Dao as being much more than a guide to being a good butcher, or, to put it more generally, as being a path or guide in the way to live. He saw Dao as the goal and purpose of life, the attaining of which transcends everything in life and makes death a natural incident.

Not surprisingly, much of *Zhuangzi* is made up of practical advice on how to move towards Dao in that way – or, in other words, how to enter into Enlightenment. He believed that there are two paths to follow: the first is to develop, particularly through meditation and contemplation, interior stillness; the second is to enter, again through practice, into an experienced, even ecstatic, union with all things and thus necessarily with Dao.

This brings about 'the beak and song union' which, for Zhuangzi, is the natural condition of the entire universe. Just as De manifests Dao in the external world (in mountains and valleys, in rivers and surging seas), so it does also in the internal world of the human body, in blood and bone, in breath and becoming. At death the energy of De is not destroyed; it is simply returned to Dao. This means that the *zhenren* has no fear of death because he is simply returning the gift he received in an undamaged and uncorrupted form:

> The *zhenren* does not forget his origin, nor does he struggle to find
> out where he will end. He received something as a gift and took
> delight in it. He then put it quietly on one side and returned it.

The *zhenren* who achieves this union with Dao cannot any longer have any sense of differentiation between himself and any other thing. That produced for Zhuangzi the famous image of the butterfly in the dream (2):

> On one occasion Zhuangzi dreamt that he was a butterfly, flitting
> here and there just as if he was a butterfly being itself. It did not
> know that it was Zhuangzi. Then suddenly he woke up and then
> unmistakably he was Zhuangzi. But now he does not know whether

he is Zhuangzi who dreamt that he was a butterfly, or a butterfly dreaming that he was Zhuangzi. Between Zhuangzi and the butterfly there is a relationship in distinction. This is what it means to say 'the transformation of things'.

📖 BIBLIOGRAPHY NUMBERS **214, 1050**

THE NEO-CONFUCIANISTS

THE FIVE MASTERS

When Buddhists arrived in China they brought with them beliefs that differed fundamentally from those of Confucianists (see pp. 260f.). The difficulties were epitomised in a tract written by Hui Yuan (334–417), *Shamen bu jing wangzhe lun*, 'A Monk Does Not Bow Down before a Ruler', arguing that Buddhists respect rulers but they cannot engage in rituals that give substance to the transient and insubstantial nature of human kings and emperors:

> Those who leave their home life [i.e., *bhikkhus*] have taken up
> temporary accommodation in the world. Their lives are cut loose
> from those of others. The Dharma by which they live teaches them
> that Dukkha [the suffering that arises from pain and transience,
> p. 232] comes from having a body: by cutting loose from the body
> they bring Dukkha to an end.

The refusal to bow may seem unimportant but it focused the challenge of Buddhism to traditional Confucianists' beliefs. The challenge was reinforced by the increasing popularity of Daoism, not least because of the way in which its many deities were active on behalf of ordinary people (some of the most important are described in my book *God: A Brief History*, pp. 154–7).

Confucianism retained its place in education and the organisation of government, but otherwise it seemed that it was becoming increasingly marginal. As a result, efforts were made to reaffirm Confucianism as the foundation of Chinese life. In part that was done by direct attacks on Daoist and Buddhist beliefs (Han Yu, 768–824, attacked the Buddha as an ill-educated barbarian who had no understanding of the superior ways of the Chinese), but it was also done by reconstructing Confucianism in a way that incorporated the best insights of Daoists and Buddhists.

The result was Neo-Confucianism or Li Xue ('the learning of principle'), in which an attempt was made to move on from analysing the Five Classics to building on their foundation an entirely new understanding of what 'body-mind and nature-destiny' (*shenxin xingming*) might be. Those are Buddhist questions but they were now given a Chinese answer.

In contrast to the ambition of Buddhists to move far beyond the transient concerns of this world, Neo-Confucianists insisted emphatically that Confucius had been right to insist on personal responsibility for the development of a virtuous character and for then applying it to the good of society.

Neo-Confucianism became paramount for nearly a thousand years (though not to the exclusion of Daoism and Buddhism), not just in China but also in Korea and Japan.

THE FIVE MASTERS

A critical part in the development of Neo-Confucianism was played by the School of Song Learning (*song xue*, on which see Munro), founded by the Five Masters (the Song dynasties lasted from 960 to 1279):

◆ Zhang Zai (1020–77), often considered the 'founding father' of Neo-Confucianism, was prepared to borrow from both Daoists and Buddhists. He wrote *Zheng Meng* ('Correcting Youthful Ignorance'), of which a part is known as *Xi Ming* ('Western Inscription') because it was written on the western wall of his study. The text became a fundamental point of reference in Neo-Confucianism:

> Tian [Heaven, p. 292] is my father and Earth is my mother so that
> even an insignificant creature like myself finds a home with them.
> As a result I regard the whole extension of the universe as my body,
> and I regard the principle which directs the universe as my own
> nature. All people, therefore, are my brothers and sisters, and all
> things are my friends . . . My life is obedience and service, my death
> is my peace.

◆ Zhou Dunyi (1017–73) was an equally key figure who developed the Confucian belief that humans are the highest creatures in the universe because they can understand themselves and the world around them. On the basis of that understanding he developed a Confucianist cosmology. His major works are *Taijitu shuo* ('An Explanation of the Diagram of the Great Ultimate [*Taiji*]'), and *Tong shu* ('A Systematic Interpretation of the *The Book of Changes*') in which he argued that the universe must be understood as a single entity or body.

◆ Shao Yong (1011–77) developed that cosmology further, especially in a short work *Huangji Jingshi* ('Cosmic Chronology of the Great Ultimate') claiming that the universe can be understood through mathematical understanding, to which *The Book of Changes* (*Yi Jing*, p. 292) is the key.

◆ Cheng Hao (1032–85) and Cheng Yi (1033–1107) were nephews of Zhang Zai who insisted on the self-sufficient truth of Confucianism as they and others were developing it, and they thus did not follow their uncle in regarding Daoism and Buddhism with respect. For them only Confucianism holds together in creative unity the principles derived from Heaven that are present in Nature (Tian Li, something like 'natural law') with human desires and passions. They laid out practical ways in which that can be achieved.

On those foundations, Zhu Xi (1130–1200) created a powerful synthesis of Neo-Confucian beliefs. He insisted that the Five Classics must be the foundation of present-day practices but he also gave emphasis to the Four Books (p. 293): his edition and commentaries on the Four Books became the official version of the Classics. At the same time he believed that the Cheng brothers were right to set them in the context of the principles (Li) that underlie the universe.

CHENG-ZHU HARMONY

Zhu Xi's synthesis of Neo-Confucian beliefs developed into the widely influential Cheng-Zhu Harmony or School. The achievement of Zhu Xi was to articulate the way in which the Great Ultimate, the unproduced Producer of all that is, articulates itself as much in human nature as in the natural order. Zhu Xi was once asked, 'You say that Li is received from Tian by both humans and things, but is it possible for things without awareness to be in possession of Li?' He answered, 'They are certainly in possession of Li: to give you an example, a boat can only go on water, a cart can only go on land.'

Everything, therefore, is open to rational understanding, and as a result humans, however evil or corrupt, are potentially open to change in the direction of good: the attainment of Enlightenment is possible for all. As he put it in his *Commentary* on *Great Learning* (5):

> No human mind is incapable of understanding because nothing
> in the world is without Li. That understanding, however,
> cannot be complete since it is impossible to know Li in every
> way . . . Nevertheless, those who make a complete commitment,
> no matter how long it takes, will one day suddenly find this
> understanding lying open before them. At that point they will

have a thorough understanding of the nature of the many things that there are, whether they are inside or outside, minute or massive, and whatever they think will be illuminated by complete enlightenment.

BIBLIOGRAPHY NUMBERS 196, 206, 525, 690, 1046, 1048, 1049

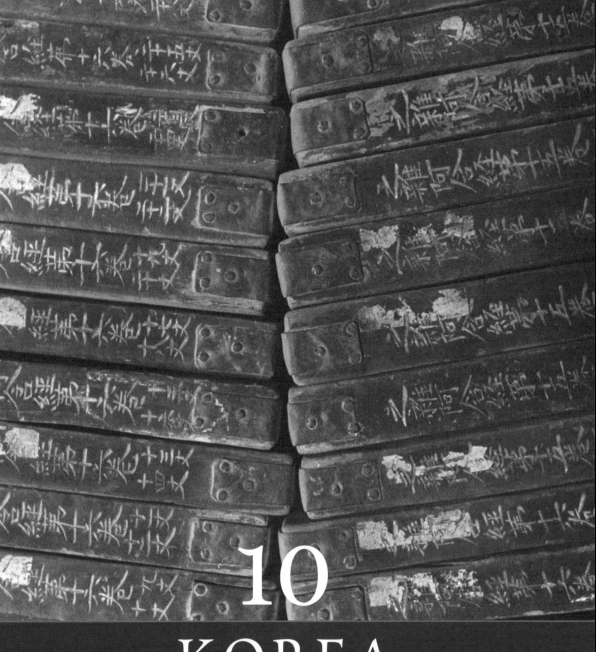

10
KOREA

KOREAN TEXTS: KEY DATES

*1st cent.*CE Buddhists arrive in Korea

372 Buddhism formally introduced into Koguryo

384 Buddhism formally introduced into Paekche

527 Buddhism formally introduced into Silla

668–935 Unification of Korea

617–86 Wonhyo, *Simmun hwajaeng non,*
YÐlban'gyong chongyo, Haedong-so

635–702 Uisang → Haedong Hwaom

918–1392 Koryo dynasty

1009–31 Hyonjong, Taejanggyong/Koryo Canon

1055–1101 Uich'on, *Kyojang Togam,*
Sokjanggyong

1158–1210 Chinul→Chogye, *Kwonsu chÐnghye*
kyÐlsa mun

13th cent. Works of Uich'on reprinted

1392–1910 Choson dynasty

Previous page: Some of the many wooden printing blocks of the Korean Tripitaka: see p. 328.

THE KOREAN CANON
Taejang Togam, Wonhyo and Chinul

Religion in Korea before the arrival of Buddhists from the first century CE onward was more ritual than text based, with a particular belief in the efficacy of shamans. Those rituals and beliefs continued to inform and influence a uniquely Korean form of Buddhism.

Buddhism was formally introduced into the Three Kingdoms into which Korea was divided, into Koguryo in 372, into Paekche in 384 and into Silla in 527. Korean rulers endorsed Buddhism not least because of the way in which its teaching of *karma* was used to point to the merit of the rulers – on the grounds that otherwise they could not have reached their position (cf., 'the divine right of emperors' in Japan, pp. 335, 341).

The status of Buddhism was enhanced when Silla became the dominant kingdom and set about unifying Korea in the years between 668 and 935. It did this under Buddhism as the 'state-protecting religion', *hoguk pulgo*, and in return Buddhism became the state religion.

For a thousand years the rulers in Korea were committed Buddhists and different forms of Buddhism were developed, each with its own sacred texts. For example, Uisang (635–702) established Haedong Hwaom, the Korean form of the Huayan School (p. 261–3), and Chan (Meditation) Buddhism became Son in the School known as the Nine Mountains of Son.

Uisang worked closely with Wonhyo (617–86) and both together made attempts to travel to China in search of instruction and Sutras, but when they were frustrated (by border guards and storms) Wonhyo realised that insight is not gained by travel but by hard study, concentration and meditation:

> If thoughts arise all kinds of dharmas [constituent properties,
> p. 253] come into being, but if thoughts are brought to cessation,
> then a tomb and a sacred place are no different from each other.

Once Wonhyo realised that appearances are different only because they are *thought* to be so, he realised instead that there cannot be anything other than the Buddha-nature or One Mind (*ilsim*). In that case, the differences between the different schools of Buddhism (for example, between Madhyamaka and Yogacara) can only be differences of emphasis or strategy, not of substance. He therefore wrote *Simmun hwajaeng non*, 'Treatise on Ten Approaches to the Reconciliation of Doctrinal Controversy'. Although not much of it has now survived, it became a foundational text for the long-running Korean attempts to reduce conflict between rival forms of Buddhism. Those attempts are so persistent and fundamental that Chung Byong-jo's overview of Buddhism in Korea is entitled, 'Korean Buddhism: Harmonising the Contradictory' (in Kim, p. 44).

Wonhyo wrote more than 100 works, but only twenty-one have survived, of which two are of particular importance: *Yŏlban'gyong chongyo*, a commentary on 'Nirvana Sutra', and *Haedong-so*, 'Awakening Faith in Mahayana'. He argued that the ultimate truth is the realisation of One Mind, but that all other Buddhist teachings and methods have validity since they all point in their own way to that truth. One Mind can take any form, from buddhas and bodhisattvas to saints and sinners, since there is nothing else for anything to be. All teachings are thus a finger pointing to the moon: they point in the right direction but they are not the moon itself.

The work of reconciliation was advanced further by collecting together recognised and authoritative Buddhist texts. The first Canon was formed under Hyonjong (ruled 1009–31) of the Koryŏ dynasty so that it is sometimes referred to as the Koryŏ Canon. Its name is Taejanggyong and it included 5,048 volumes in woodblock print. Uich'on (1055–1101), a prince who studied Huayan and Tiantai in China and published *Kyojang Togam* ('Directorate for Buddhist Scriptures'), added almost as many volumes again to create *Sokjanggyong*. Both these were destroyed during invasions in the thirteenth century, so that under the supervision of the Directorate (*Taejang Togam*) the entire Canon had to be printed again from new woodblocks (according to a list made in 1248, they amounted to 81,340 blocks).

CHINUL

On the basis of accepted texts the work of reconciliation was developed brilliantly by Chinul (1158–1210), who became known as *Pojo kuksa*, National Preceptor of Radiant Light. He argued that the way to Enlightenment, which is possible for all individuals, must be sought by combining understanding and meditation, or in other words by combining *hye* (*prajña*, wisdom) and *chong* (*samadhi*, 'composing of the mind'). By this means he drew together Kyo (with its emphasis on rigorous instruction and gradual learning) and Son (Meditation) Buddhism into an integrated form known as Chogye (from the name of the mountain where he founded a monastery).

This quest for integration did not mean that Chinul was uncritical of some forms of existing Buddhism. For example, in an early work, *Kwonsu chŏnghye kyŏlsa mun* ('Encouragement to Practice: The Harmony of Concentration and Wisdom'), he attacked severely the claim of Pure Land that most people are too ignorant to do more than chant Amitabha's name in order to attain the Pure Land paradise. Chinul argued that insight and meditation are open to all and will lead far beyond any interim paradise to the realisation of the Buddha:

> Delusion about the Mind leads to innumerable defilements in those who are sentient beings. Awakening to the Mind leads to brilliant consequences in those who are now the Buddha. Delusion and Awakening are two different conditions but they are both brought into being by the mind. If you look for the Buddha in some place other than the mind, you will never find him.

Chinul's most revered work is 'Excerpts from the Dharma Collection and Special Practice Record with Personal Notes'. Intended as a guide for students under his instruction, it is in effect a supreme summary of Chinul's understanding of Buddhism in the context of Korea. He argued that the way to Enlightenment must develop an awakening of the mind to the fact that one is already Buddha, a gradual cultivation of this insight removing all that might subvert it, followed by the awakening of complete realisation. Often summarised as 'sudden awakening, gradual cultivation', Chinul's integration of Buddhist ways became the foundation of Korean Buddhism down to the present day.

BIBLIOGRAPHY NUMBERS 168–71, 208, 271, 419, 546, 583, 1023

11
JAPAN

JAPANESE TEXTS: KEY DATES

513 Confucian scholars arrive from Korea

538 Buddhist texts sent to Japan from Korea

574–622 Shotoku

604 *Jushichijo Kempo*

607 Shotoku decreed Kami veneration

672–86 Reign of Temmu, Buddhism promoted

685 ➡ Ise rites of rebuilding

694 Copies of *Konkomyokyo* deposited in the provinces

709–87/94 Nara period, Buddhism endorsed

712 *Kojiki* transcribed by Yasumaro

720 *Nihongi* compiled

767–822 Saicho ➡ Tendai

774–835 Kukai ➡ Shingon, *Jujushinron, Hizo hoyaku*

c.8th cent. *Manyoshu* compiled

905 Compilation of *Engishiki* began

927 *Engishiki* presented to Emperor Daigo

10th cent. *Kokinshu*

11th cent. *The Tale of Genji*

1130–1200 Zhu Xi (Sushi) reforms Neo-Confucianism

1133–1212 Honen ➡ Pure Land

1185–1333 Kamakura period

13th cent. *Shinkokinshu*

1256–?1356 Watarai Ieyuki, *Ruiju Jingi Hongen*; identified Shinto Gobusho

1274, 1281 Failed Mongol invasions

1293–1354 Kitabatake Chikafusa, *Jinno shotoki*

1435–1511 Yoshida Kanetomo, *Yuiitso Shinto Myoho Yoshu*

1603–1868 Tokugawa period

1644–94 Matsuo Basho, *Nozarishi kiko*

1669–1736 Kada Azumamaro ➡ National Learning/Kokugawa

1697–1769 Kamo Mabuchi, endorsed *Manyoshu*

1730–1801 Motoori Norinaga, *Kojikiden*, endorsed *The Tale of Genji* as sacred text

1776–1843 Hirata Atsutane, *Kode taii*

18th cent. Sense of Shinto emerged

1868–1912 Meiji period

19th cent. Norito formalised

Previous page: The Kami (pp. 334, 345) are the spiritual powers in people and places, notably in Mount Fuji (Fujiyama), a 'sacred text' written in Nature itself (see pp. 346–7; cf. the Book of Nature, p. 95).

SHINTO

Kojiki and Nihongi

Japanese religion is a complex and colourful tapestry woven from many different strands (in his *Sacred Scriptures of the Japanese*, Wheeler also wrote of 'the tapestry of this omnium gatherum', p. vii). In particular, it weaves together beliefs brought to Japan from China and Korea, notably those of Buddhism and Confucianism. For more than a thousand years Buddhism was the major religion in Japan where (as happened also in Tibet) it developed its own forms and interpretations. As we have seen, it made use of earlier Buddhist texts especially from China, but it also produced many of its own.

At the same time Confucianism (or to be more precise Neo-Confucianism) supplied the dominant political and social beliefs and structures along with its own rituals. Particularly important was the interpretation of Confucianism made by Zhu Xi (1130–1200; see p. 322) in China. He was known in Japan as Shushi so that this form of Neo-Confucianism is known as Shushi-gaku. Following Kong Fuzi (Confucius), Shushi pointed the way to establish a balanced and harmonious society: it can be achieved only by the rulers developing their own interior character in appropriate ways. Where Shushi-gaku went further than Zhu Xi was in extending the 'appropriate ways' in which such development of character can be undertaken – for example, in Zen meditation or in the rigorous 'investigation of things' in order to understand their nature. *Shushin* thus became a word meaning moral and ethical behaviour.

Given the dominance of Buddhism and Neo-Confucianism in Japan for so many centuries, it might seem that the tapestry of religion in Japan was made up of foreign imports only. That perception caused great uneasiness among those Japanese who took a pride in their own land, history and customs, and at various times attempts were made to define and endorse their own native tradition.

This tradition came to be known as Shinto, but it would be a mistake to suppose that from the earliest days there was an organised and shared religion known by that name. That sense of Shinto did not emerge until the eighteenth century. Nevertheless, the word was used much earlier to refer to characteristic Japanese beliefs, particularly in the Kami.

It is impossible to define the word *kami* in any simple way, and it is usually left untranslated (for Motoori Norinaga's definition, see p. 345). It means roughly the 'enspirited nature' that gives to places, things and people their character and vitality. But it is not abstract or impersonal: the Kami are active as agents of change and can be interacted with in prayer and ritual so that the Kami are often understood as 'divine beings'. The word became familiar outside Japan in the name Kamikaze given to the suicide pilots of the Second World War: that word means 'Kami wind', i.e., the wind filled with its own 'enspirited nature', and it was originally used of the typhoons which in the thirteenth century drove off two attempts by the Mongols to invade Japan.

The pervasive Japanese belief in the Kami underlies the name Shinto. The name comes from the Chinese characters *shen* and *tao* (or in current transliteration *dao*), 'the way of the heavenly beings'. Originally, in China, *shentao* could refer to particular religions such as Daoism (or even Buddhism), but more often it meant religious beliefs in general or popular beliefs in particular. The Japanese translation of *shentao* is *kami no michi* ('the Way of the Kami').

The transition from the use of *shentao* to refer to popular or folk beliefs among the Japanese people, to Shinto as the native Japanese religion in distinction from Buddhism or Neo-Confucianism, was a gradual process reflecting the history whereby the Japanese affirmed their own distinct (and in their own view earlier and therefore superior) tradition. Each of the stages through which this was done produced its own sacred texts.

THE DEVELOPMENT OF SHINTO
STAGE 1: KOJIKI AND NIHONGI

The earliest stage of Shinto came about in response to the arrival of Buddhism from Korea in 538 CE when Song, the King of Paekche, sent tribute to Kinmei in Japan including Chinese Buddhist texts. Shotoku (574–622) welcomed Buddhism enthusiastically, seeing it as a basis on which people could be united in loyalty to the ruling family. He was called 'the father of Buddhism'. However, he also saw the importance of indigenous beliefs and rituals and he therefore issued a decree in 607 requiring the veneration of the Kami.

Those beliefs, however, were not sufficiently coherent or systematic to serve as an underlying ideology in support of the imperial family, and as a result Temmu (ruled 672–86) initiated the collection of ancient stories and traditions. The first of these, *Kojiki* ('Records of Ancient Matters'), appeared in 712. It was followed in 720 by *Nihongi* (also known as *Nihon Shoki*, 'Chronicles of Japan'), and both, as Philippi points out (p. 15, Preface 2–3), 'not only were planned and finished at almost the same time, but also, in dealing with the same subject matter, often echo, complement and elucidate each other'.

Neither of these was originally a sacred text, but both became so when they were made the foundation of the attempt in the eighteenth century to define the Japanese tradition in distinction from Buddhism and Western learning (see further p. 343). Initially they were part of the attempt by the imperial Yamato family to overcome the clan (*uji*) system of government and draw all people into a recognition of a divine Emperor (*tenno*, a term derived from Daoism, meaning 'heavenly king').

Kojiki is said to have been recited by Temmu to Hiyeda no Are who transmitted it orally to a court official, Yasumaro, who wrote the text down in 712. He used mainly Chinese characters but in a less Chinese style than *Nihongi*, and for that reason *Kojiki* was more revered in the later centuries.

Both works organise the legends and traditions to show why the imperial family should be acknowledged and obeyed. Beginning with the creation of Japan, they tell how the supreme Kami, Amaterasu o-mikami, 'heavenly-shining great kami', sent her grandson, Ninigi, to rule over the land of Nippon ('origin of the sun' or 'land of the rising sun', i.e., Japan). Those who succeed him are thus the descendants of Amaterasu, and for that reason the emperors of Japan came to be regarded as Manifest Kami (*akitsu kami*).

In *Nihongi* the word *shinto* appears only three times: once to describe how the Emperor Yomei accepted the teachings of the Buddha but also endorsed *shinto*, identified as *kami no michi*; once to describe the Emperor Kotoku who accepted the teachings of the Buddha but who had no regard for *shinto*; and once as the definition of *kamunagara* which means 'as a kami would'. It is clear, therefore, that Shinto was connected with the recognition of the Kami but was not yet at this early stage understood to be an independent and distinct religion.

📖 BIBLIOGRAPHY NUMBERS 271, 437, 555, 717, 769

THE ORGANISATION
OF JAPANESE SOCIETY

JUSHICHIJO KEMPO, *ENGISHIKI* AND NORITO

When Prince Shotoku welcomed Buddhism (p. 334), it was partly because its ideas seemed to be coherent and true – and for that reason he wrote (or delivered) commentaries on three major Buddhist Sutras, the *Lotus*, *Vimalakirti* and *Shrimala* Sutras; but it was also because of its practical importance, as he saw it, in the unifying and good governance of Japanese society. His work laid the foundations for the practical reform of Japan for many centuries.

SHOTOKU

The essence of Shotoku's vision for Japan is summarised in *Jushichijo Kempo*, 'The Seventeen Article Constitution' – though 'Constitution' is too formal a translation if it implies a document drawing up rights and obligations. It is, rather, a work of moral guidance. It is preserved in *Nihongi*.

Fundamental to his vision was his belief that Buddhism and Confucianism are not in opposition to each other (as they could be in China), but must be held together if a balanced society is to be created in which civil strife and war are eliminated: 'We are all joined to one another, whether wise or foolish, as a ring that has no end.' The aim must be to achieve a harmony (*wa*). Article 1 states:

> *Wa* is to have the highest value and the shunning of indiscriminate
> conflict is to be honoured . . . All people have biased opinions
> and there are few who are dispassionately rational. But if in the
> discussion of affairs there is a quest for balance, then 'the right
> view of things' will naturally emerge and gain acceptance. And then
> what is there that cannot be achieved?

The wise and good life advocated in *Jushichijo Kempo* is clearly based on the Five Constant Principles (*wu chang*) of Confucianism (see p. 299), just as his Three Commentaries on the Sutras (above) are based on the works of others (*Vimalakirti Sutra* shows how laypeople can attain the bodhisattva goal). But that simply illustrates the informed and reflective way in which Shotoku saw Buddhism as an opportunity to transform Japanese society through the transformation of individual lives, beginning with his own. These works of his gained the status of revered texts, which has persisted through generations.

THE DEVELOPMENT OF SHINTO
STAGE 2: ENGISHIKI AND NORITO

Following the initial development of Shinto, it still remained necessary to translate all this into practical forms of organisation and authority. The major achievement in that respect was *Engishiki* ('Procedures of the Engi Era'). It is a compilation of rules and regulations for government in fifty books. It was begun at the command of the Emperor Daigo (897–930) in 905, and it was presented to the Emperor in 927.

Engishiki represents the second major stage in the defining of the relationship between Shinto and Japan because it envisages Japan as a single community, bound together in common rituals and liturgies addressed to the Kami.

It is divided into two parts corresponding to the two major divisions of government: the first, *Jingi-kan* (the first ten books of *Engishiki*), deals with matters concerning the Kami and their relationship to the well-being of society; the second, *Dajo-kan*, deals with the secular side of government.

Books 1 and 2 are concerned with the seasonal festivals and the ways in which they are celebrated at the official shrines. The festivals are divided into three categories, great, middle and small, but there is only one 'great' festival, the enthronement festival (*daijosai*) of each new emperor. There are five 'middle' national festivals, and thirteen 'small' festivals.

Book 3 deals with festivals concerned with particular occasions, as opposed to the seasonal festivals.

Books 4 and 5 summarise the procedures to be followed at the Grand Shrine of Ise. The Inner and Outer shrines at Ise became of major importance in the later development of Shinto as Japan's national religion. Originally the Ise Shrines, dedicated to Amaterasu, were restricted to the imperial family, but later they became the shrine of the whole nation.

Book 6 gives the procedures to be followed by the Consecrated Princess at the Kamo Shrines as the emperor's representative to Amaterasu.

Book 7 gives the basic procedures to be followed at the enthronement festival, though many further details are given in subsequent books since the enthronement of the emperor involves virtually every official in Japan.

Book 8 records twenty-seven ritual prayers or chants known as 'Norito'. The meaning of the word Norito is uncertain – perhaps 'words stated with awe'. Although they are not gathered into a single work, they represent collectively the equivalent of a sacred text since they permeate the religious life of Japan.

Books 9 and 10 list the officially recognised Kami and shrines throughout Japan: there are 3,132 Kami and 2,861 shrines.

Norito are sacred words and prayers composed in formal and elegant Japanese. They are addressed to the Kami, but they also make connection with the *kami* (the enspirited power) that resides within words themselves when they are appropriately spoken. Until the Meiji period (1868 onward), Norito were composed freely by guardians of the shrines, but in that period, as a part of the attempt to organise and control Shinto as the state religion, the wording of Norito was made to conform to the wording of the twenty-seven prayers in *Engishiki*.

In general, Norito praise the particular kami addressed and make reference to the meaning and origin of the festival involved. They offer thanksgiving to the Kami and enumerate the offerings that are being presented, and they identify the people on whose behalf the offerings are made and the prayers are recited. They end with words of praise and worship (trans. Philippi):

> Before you, oh Sovereign Deity, like cormorants bending our necks low,
> As the morning sun rises in effulgent glory,
> Do we fulfill your praises.

BIBLIOGRAPHY NUMBERS 56, 316, 437, 1008

SHINGON AND SHINTO

Nanto Rokushu, Kukai
and Kitabatake Chikafusa

Shotoku's commitment to Buddhism is made explicit in *Jushichijo* 2:

> Make a wholehearted commitment to the three treasures, the
> Buddha, Dharma and Sangha, for these are the final refuge of
> beings born in the four ways, and they are the supreme focus of
> faith throughout the world. Not many people are totally evil, so
> they may be taught what to do. But if they do not go to the three
> treasures, how can their devious ways be made straight?

Later emperors endorsed Buddhism, especially after establishing their capital in
Nara from 709 to 787/94. They did so, not for the enlightenment of the people,
but for the protection and security of the state, accepting the 'nation-protecting'
qualities of sutras, bodhisattvas, buddhas and other guardian figures.

But to what kind of Buddhism should the Japanese be committed? Buddhism
takes on extremely different forms as we have seen already in Tibet and China.
During the so-called Nara period different forms of Buddhism took root in
Japan, the main lineages (brought in from Korea and China) being the Six
Sects, Nanto Rokushu: Sanron, Hosso, Kegon, Ritsu, Kusha and Jojitsu. They
were prolific in building temples and also in producing sacred texts.

Many of their Sutras were brought in from China, often adapted and
extended (following the belief in 'skill in means', p. 251), but not always so. Thus
the Heart Sutra (p. 254), known in Japan as *Hannya Shingyo*, is written with
Chinese characters but spoken or recited with Japanese pronunciation. It is
immensely popular, partly because it is short enough to be easily memorised (it
is widely used as an invocation or prayer), and partly because it is believed to
compress the teaching of the Perfection of Wisdom (p. 253), especially in its line,

shiki soku ze ku ku soku ze shiki, 'Form is not other than the undifferentiated [*ku*, the Japanese translation of *shunyata*, i.e., 'devoid of characteristics'], the undifferentiated is not other than form.'

Three other Sutras came to be known as 'the three sacred texts protecting the state': *Hokekyo* ('The Lotus Sutra'), *Ninnokyo* ('The Sutra of the Virtuous Ruler') and *Konkomyokyo* ('The Sutra of the Golden Light'). *Konkomyokyo* was written in a style of compelling beauty as an introduction to the major teachings of Mahayana Buddhism, and in order to establish the relationships between government and Buddhism. It was of particular importance in establishing Buddhism as the religion of Japan. As early as 694 it was ordered that copies should be deposited in all the provinces and that they should be read annually at the beginning of the New Year.

Other important Sutras are *Kegongyo* ('The Garland Sutra', a version of *Avatamsaka*, p. 261) and *Kako genzai inga kyo* ('The Sutra of Past to Present, Cause and Effect'), claiming that the life of the Buddha transmits merit especially to effective and good rulers. This establishes a kind of 'divine right of emperors' in contrast to the dynastic principle of succession – very useful to Temmu when he seized the throne in 672 and promoted Buddhism enthusiastically.

From 789 to 1160 the capital was Heian-kyo (modern-day Kyoto). During this period some Buddhists made an attempt to disentangle Buddhism from state control. Among them were Saicho (767–822, also known as Dengyo Daishi) and Kukai (774–835, also known as Kobo Daishi), both of whom founded Schools based on what they learnt in China but distinctively different in their Japanese form.

Saicho established Tendai on the basis of Tiantai (see p. 264). Kukai was taught in China by Hui-guo (Japanese Keika) and introduced a form of esoteric Buddhism known as Shingon or True Words (Sanskrit, *Mantrayana*). 'Esoteric' means that the teachings and practices are too obscure and difficult to understand unless explained orally by a qualified teacher. Shingon teaches that the three properties possessed by all human beings of body, speech and mind have an inner meaning. When these are learnt and expressed as Shingon teaches, they lead to ultimate wisdom and truth, and also to union with the Buddha Vairocana (Japanese, Dainichi) which leads in turn to the goal of 'becoming a Buddha in this body' (*sokushin jobutsu*). According to tradition, the Three Hidden Practices (*sanmitsu*) were first revealed by Vairocana.

Shingon regards many texts as sacred but two Sutras in particular: *Dainichikyo*, based on an eighth-century Chinese translation of the Sanskrit *Mahavairocana Sutra*, and *Kongochokyo*, 'The Diamond Peak Sutra' (Sanskrit, *Vajrashekhara Sutra*). Equally valued is Kukai's own *Jujushinron* ('The Ten Stages of Religious Consciousness') together with his response to the Emperor's request for a simpler version, *Hizo hoyaku* ('Precious Key to the Secret Treasury').

In these works he described the ten stages through which humans have advanced from living like goats or animals in their desires, through elementary education (Confucianism) and blind hopes of Heaven like a calf following its mother (Brahmanism and Daoism), through the many lineages and Schools of Buddhism until their exoteric teachings have like medicine purged the system, allowing Shingon to open the Treasury of esoteric or secret treasures.

That understanding of the way in which diversity has arisen progressively among religions and within Buddhism itself allowed Buddhists to understand Japanese religious beliefs and practices (still not an organised and shared religion, but for convenience referred to as Shinto) as a preparation for Buddhism. The Kami could be understood as manifestations of buddhas and bodhisattvas adapted to local understanding. In that sense, they would be a part of the Buddha's teaching by 'skill in means' (p. 251). This belief is summarised in the phrase *honji-suijaku*, 'original substance manifest traces' – i.e., buddhas and bodhisattvas are the original and fundamental truth, while Kami are their manifest traces in the world as the truth is accommodated to elementary understanding.

Many Japanese became increasingly angry about that understanding of the relationship and began to reverse it, saying that the buddhas and bodhisattvas were simply manifestations of Kami. One among them was Kitabatake Chikafusa (1293–1354) who wrote *Jinno shotoki* ('The Records of the Legitimate Succession of the Divine Sovereigns') to point out the unique superiority of Japan, not least in its unbroken succession of rulers coming in a direct line from Amaterasu. So he argued:

> Japan is the land of the Kami whose foundations were first laid by the
> heavenly ancestor, the Sun Goddess who directed her descendants
> to rule over it to the end of time. This is true of no other country
> except our own: nothing like it can be found in foreign lands. That is
> why it is called the land of the Kami . . . Only in this land of ours has
> the succession remained unbroken from the time when heaven and
> earth began down to the present day. There has been a single line
> of descent, and even when events have inevitably led to a collateral
> succession, the true line of descent has always been restored.

Kitabatake Chikafusa was not alone in affirming the superiority of Japan's rituals and beliefs. He was part of the next stage in defining the nature and meaning of Shinto.

📖 BIBLIOGRAPHY NUMBERS 550, 565, 633

THE DEFINING OF SHINTO

The Five Shinto Classics, Kokugaku

The next stage in the defining of Shinto as 'the religion of Japan' began in 1185 when land owners known as *daimyo* seized power with the help of a newly emerging warrior class, the Samurai. Their leader, Yoritomo Minamoto, forced the Emperor to make him Shogun (conquering general). The Shoguns held power (in different families) until the time of the Meiji restoration of imperial power in 1868.

THE DEVELOPMENT OF SHINTO STAGE 3: THE FIVE SHINTO CLASSICS

During this period, attempts of many different kinds were made to define and establish Shinto in ways that would at least rival but, even more, supersede Buddhism. An early and important example was that of Watarai Ieyuki (1256–?1356) who was a close friend of Kitabatake Chikafusa and who shared his beliefs about Shinto. He claimed that the Outer Shrine at Ise (p. 337) had preserved five sacred texts of great antiquity, recording the history and meaning of the shrine in the context of Japan as a whole. Although these were probably written or compiled for the occasion, they included earlier material. Later the five texts became known collectively as Shinto Gobusho (the Five Shinto Classics) and the claim was made that they represented a Shinto Canon equivalent to those of Buddhism and Confucianism.

The texts (using an abbreviated form of their titles) are:

◆ *Gochinza shidaiki*, a description of the Kami of Ise from the time of Amaterasu (enshrined at Ise) onward.

◆ *Gochinza denki*, an account of the origins of both shrines and of their meaning and importance.

◆ *Gochinza hongi*, a description of the enshrinement of Toyouke at Ise and of the relationship between the Outer and Inner Shrines.

◆ *Hoki hongi*, a record of the construction and form of the two shrines.

◆ *Yamoto hime no mikoto seiki*, an account of Yamoto hime and of her enshrinement at Ise, together with an exposition of fundamental Shinto beliefs.

Watarai himself produced *Ruiju Jingi Hongen* as a guide to his understanding of Shinto as the ancient and original religion of Japan. He incorporated Buddhist and Confucianist ideas and practices, but he argued that they are expressed much more effectively in Shinto ways, not least because they are available, not to an elite alone, but to ordinary people.

The beliefs focused on the Shrines at Ise were put into more general and systematic form by Yoshida Kanetomo (1435–1511). His argument that Shinto as the religion of Japan has a timeless and primordial origin led to a version of Shinto known as Yuiitso or Primal Shinto – known also from his family name as Urabe Shinto. He summarised his understanding of the relationship between Shinto and other religions in this way (*Yuiitso Shinto Myoho Yoshu*):

> Japan is the root and trunk [of well-ordered society], China
> its branches and leaves, India its flowers and fruit. Of all laws,
> Buddhism is the flower and the fruit, Confucianism the branches
> and the leaves, and Shinto the root and trunk. So all foreign
> teachings are offshoots of Shinto.

KOKUGAKU

Although the early endeavours gave increasing confidence to the assertion of Shinto as ancient and original in Japan, a certain unease developed about the authenticity of the Five Classics. As a result, Kada Azumamaro (1669–1736) gained the support of the Tokugawa Shogunate in setting up a school of what he called National Learning, Kokugawa. The initial purpose was to examine and collect together the ancient literature of Japan.

In addition to Kada, there were three other major authorities in Kokugawa: Kamo Mabuchi (1697–1769), Motoori Norinaga (1730–1801) and Hirata Atsutane (1776–1843). The problem that confronted them was that Japanese thought and literature were saturated with Chinese style and content. They therefore looked for texts that were free of that influence. It was this that led them to emphasise the fundamental importance of *Kojiki* and *Nihongi* (see pp. 334–5), giving them a kind of Canonical status.

Kamo Mabuchi claimed that he had found poems in the poetry of the eighth century, known as *Manyoshu*, that were free of foreign influence: 'They are the uncorrupted expression of our oldest heritage; they are the voice of the land of the Kami.' Nor did he simply excavate the past: he wrote poems in the same style and encouraged others to do the same, thus making poetry a kind of sacred text of a new kind (on this, see further pp. 347–9).

Motoori Norinaga reinforced the emphasis on poetry by his claim that an early (1205) anthology called *Shinkokinshu* (*New Collection of Ancient and Modern Poetry*) expressed supremely well the distinctive Japanese under-standing of human emotions. It was this that led him to claim *Genji monogatari, The Tale of Genji*, as a sacred text of Shinto. That may at first sight seem surprising since *The Tale of Genji* is a vast novel written at the beginning of the eleventh century. It had been attacked particularly by Japanese Confucianists on the grounds that it contains no educational value and exhibits a great deal of unreformed human nature.

Murusaki Shikibu, its author, disagreed and argued through Genji that it has great practical value (trans. Waley):

> Its practical value is immense. Without it what should we know
> of how people lived in the past, from the Age of the Gods down to
> the present-day? For history-books such as the *Chronicles of Japan*
> show us only one small corner of life . . . But I have a theory of my
> own about what this art of the novel is, and how it came into being.
> To begin with, it does not simply consist in the author's telling a
> story about the adventures of some other person. On the contrary,
> it happens because the storyteller's own experience of men and
> things, whether for good or ill, . . . has moved him to an emotion so
> passionate that he can no longer keep it shut up in his heart. Again
> and again something in his own life or in that around him will
> seem to the writer so important that he cannot bear to let it pass
> into oblivion. There must never come a time, he feels, when men
> do not know about it. That is my view of how this art arose. Clearly
> then, it is no part of the storyteller's craft to describe only what is
> good or beautiful . . . Anything whatsoever may become the subject
> of a novel, provided only that it happens in this mundane life and
> not in some fairyland beyond our human ken.

Motoori Norinaga seized on exactly that point. He argued that *The Tale of Genji* is not intended to be educational or instructive in matters of doctrine. It is

The library in the Haesin monastery in Taegu, South Korea, containing the largest surviving collection of the Korean Tripitaka (p. 328) printed from wooden blocks.

The Enso (empty circle) expresses Zen belief that all appearances are 'devoid of differentiating characteristics' (*shunyata*, pp. 255, 277–8). Painting the Enso (here by Ranzan, eighteenth century) illustrates *bokuseki* (p. 11). The verse states: 'The universe lingers/I bow my head'.

Bishamonten, the Indian deity Vaishravana taken into Asian Buddhism, is the protector of Buddhists and their land. This twelfth-century painted scroll (Hekija-e), 'The driving away of evil', shows Bishamonten driving away demons.

'Flowers III' by Chen Banding illustrates the integration of text and painting as 'the host and the guest': see p. 10. Bamboos came to symbolise long life and fidelity in marriage, as well as the steps to be taken to reach Enlightenment.

Sotatsu Tawaraya and Koetsu Honami (seventeenth century) combined painting and calligraphy in the new techniques of the Rimpa School. Cranes, a symbol of peace and longevity, carry the spirits of the dead to Sukhavati, the Western Paradise (see p. 267).

This calligraphy by Matsuo Basho, with painting 'accepting the invitation' (p. 10) by one of his pupils, shows how text and illustration reinforce each other with suggestive brevity: see pp. 348–9.

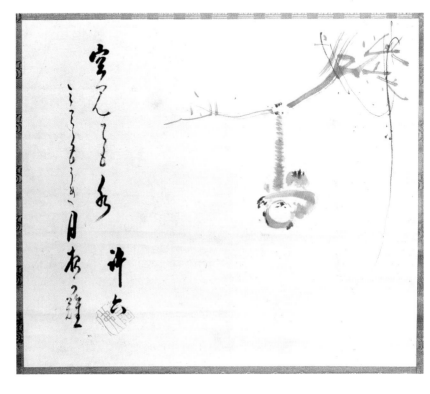

Dante's vision of Heaven (p. 111), engraved by Gustave Doré, illustrates how sacred texts can point us to the absolutes of beauty, truth and love. In complete contrast, those in authority and power who create hell on earth often destroy the sacred texts of their opponents, as in the Nazi burning of books in 1933: see pp. 353ff.

an exploration of the ways in which humans relate emotionally to each other, seeking whatever it is that moves them most deeply, the quality known in Japan as *aware* (see further p. 346). He did not pretend that the humans depicted in this extraordinary and brilliant work are without fault – far from it: there is much brutality, promiscuity and sexual exploitation. But his point remained that Shinto deals with the reality of life as people actually live it and offers them a transvaluation of experience. *The Tale of Genji* was immensely popular anyway in Japan, but Motoori Norinaga showed why it must be regarded as a sacred text.

Motoori Norinaga also devoted much of his learning and time to the definition of Japanese words and concepts. Thus, to give an example, although the word *kami* cannot be defined (p. 334), his definition is nevertheless the one most often quoted (trans. Havens):

> I do not yet well understand the meaning of the word *kami* (and
> all the old explanations are wrong), but in general, the word *kami*
> refers to, first of all, the various Kami of heaven and earth spoken
> of in the classics, and the spirits [*mitama*] enshrined in their
> shrines, and it goes without saying that it also refers to people, and
> even birds and beasts and grass and trees, ocean and mountains
> – and anything else which has superior and extraordinary power,
> provoking awe. Here, 'superb' means not only superior in nobility
> and goodness, but also awe-inspiring things of great evil and
> weirdness, anything which provokes a high degree of wonder.
> Of people, those called Kami of course include the most exalted
> lineage of emperors, who are called 'distant Kami' since they are
> so far removed from the ordinary person, and worthy of reverence.
> Then there are the human Kami, who existed long ago and also at
> present; a certain number of human Kami exist in each province,
> village, and house, each in accord with his or her station . . . In this
> way, Kami are of manifold varieties, some noble and some base,
> some strong and some weak, some good and some evil, each being
> immediately in accord with its own mind and behaviour.

📖 BIBLIOGRAPHY NUMBERS 437, 516, 557, 679, 872, 911, 928, 930, 941–2, 994

POETRY AND THE
POWER OF WORDS

Manyoshu, Kokinshu, Shinkokinshu and Basho

Motoori Norinaga's description of the Kami illustrates how they were believed to pervade places and people everywhere, giving them their character and energy. That energy is expressed also through words. In India the primordial sound became manifest in a transforming way through mantras (p. 168), a belief that Kukai expressed in Shingon, a translation of Mantrayana, the Way of Mantra.

In Japan the spirit and power of words was called originally *kotodama* and was linked especially with Norito (p. 338). It is a part of the reason why it is impossible in Japan to disentangle art and poetry from religion. Any of them (or all of them in any combination) can evoke the emotional reaction summarised in the word *aware*, the kind of feeling that people have in, for example, places of beauty or of awe-inspiring grandeur.

In such ways the Kami can be a real presence, evoking the response of *aware*. The exact meaning of that word is hard to define. In a sense it is almost an exclamation or even gasp of amazed wonder and delight. Often it is tinged with sadness at the recognition (much endorsed in Buddhism) that such intense moments are fleeting and transient. That is why the cherry blossom of spring is such a profound and controlling metaphor in Japan, not least among the Samurai (p. 342). As I wrote in *Hallowed Ground* (p. 24):

> In the words of a famous proverb, 'Among flowers it is the cherry-blossom, among men it is the Samurai: the blossom falls in full bloom, and the Samurai accepts death in the midst of life without fear.'

THE TALE OF GENJI

Motoori Norinaga recognised this transience and real presence when he characterised *The Tale of Genji* as a work of *mono no aware*. That phrase is often translated as 'the sadness of things', but that is only so provided it includes the power of 'things' to move people to transcendent delight:

> The purpose of *The Tale of Genji* is like a man who greatly desires the lotus flower: in order to plant and cultivate it, he must gather muddy and manure-saturated water. The impure mud of the illicit affairs of the *Tale* is not there to be admired, but to nurture the flower of awareness of the sorrow of human existence.

There is a sense, therefore, in which every aspect of nature can become a sacred text if it is read in the right way. Van Gogh, as an artist struggling to break the bonds of nineteenth-century realism, saw this intuitively when he wrote in a letter to his brother (in Chipp, pp. 38f.):

> If we study Japanese art, we see a man who is undoubtedly wise, philosophic and intelligent, who spends his time doing – what? In studying the distance between the earth and the moon? No. In studying Bismarck's policy? No. He studies a single blade of grass. But this blade of grass leads him to draw every plant and then the seasons, the wider aspects of the countryside, then animals, then the human figure. So he passes his life, and life is too short to do the whole. Come now, isn't it almost a true religion which the simple Japanese teach us, who live in nature as though they themselves were flowers?

That is why a sacred text in Japan does not have to be concerned intentionally or explicitly with religious beliefs and practices, and why the Kokugaku scholars could create a Canon of Shinto texts in which many of those texts seem to be about aspects of life in general: *all* life can be an epiphany of the Kami.

COLLECTIONS OF POETRY

It was on this basis that poetry was gathered into the collections that the Kokugaku scholars could claim as part of the Canon of Shinto sacred texts. The earliest of these is *Manyoshu* ('Collection of Ten Thousand Leaves'), the collection claimed by Kamo Mabuchi as 'the voice of the land of the Kami',

p. 344. It was compiled in the late eighth century and includes poems written from about 645 to 759.

Two major collections followed: *Kokinshu* ('Collection of Poems Old and New'), compiled in the early tenth century, the first of twenty-one anthologies authorised by the imperial court; and *Shinkokinshu* ('New Collection of Ancient and Modern Poetry'), compiled in the early thirteenth century. By that time the forms of Japanese poetry, culminating later in Haiku, had been greatly developed and refined. So also had the sense of what a poet's responsibility and work should be, a vocation summarised in the word *michi*.

At the heart of *michi* lay (exactly as Van Gogh recognised) the necessity for poets to immerse themselves in the essential nature of what they were writing about – a quality known as *hon'i*. This required focused concentration and meditation of a kind comparable to that practised in Buddhism, in the *shikan*, for example, of Tendai, or in the *zazen* of Dogen (p. 278).

BASHO AND HAIKU

This flowing together of Shinto and Zen is seen supremely in the poetry of Matsuo Basho (1644–94). He was born into a Samurai family and entered into court service where he became a friend of the ruler's son, Sengin. When Sengin died in 1666, Basho retired in grief to a monastery and moved increasingly into Zen. Gradually he began to express his feelings in the form of verse known at the time as *hokku*, but later, when it was further developed, as Haiku.

Haiku embodies focus and concentration in its extremely compressed form. It is made up of three lines of only seventeen syllables, five, seven, five. It also observes various conventions of content – for example, by its reference to a season of the year, *ki*. A *kigo* or 'season word' may be direct, but more often it is allusive and implied. As an example, one of Basho's verses reads (with an attempt at a five, seven, five translation):

> *Aki fukaki*
> *tonari wa nani o*
> *suru hito zo.*

> Autumn deep and deep
> my neighbour close upon me
> now what does he do?

Basho travelled constantly throughout Japan looking for the inner meaning of what he saw, and then expressing it in this highly condensed form. For example, he once passed through the town of Sukagawa, and recorded later the effect and consequence of this:

> On the edge of the town there was a large chestnut tree, and in its shade a world-renouncing monk had taken up his refuge. It occurred to me that this might be the exact place where a poem was once written about 'picking up horse-chestnuts'. I had a scrap to write on, so I scribbled this note for myself: 'The Chinese character for "chestnut" is made up of "west" and "tree". That at once suggested a link with Amida's Western Paradise [p. 267]. I saw at once why Gyogi Bosatsu always, throughout his life, used wood from this tree, both for a walking stick, and for the supporting pillars of his house. So I wrote:

> People of the world
> Never see its blossoming
> Chestnut of the eaves.

Basho's diary of his journeys, *Nozarishi kiko*, has become almost as highly valued as his Haikus. The title is taken from the first line of its first Haiku, *Nozarishi wo*, 'In a field of bones exposed to the weather'. Not surprisingly, even his last poem sees him journeying still in the mind when his body can no longer move to new places of encounter:

> Stricken on the way
> my dreams through withered fields
> go wandering still.

📖 BIBLIOGRAPHY NUMBERS 73, 151–3, 192, 421, 521, 556, 872, 928

12

CONCLUSION

SACRED TEXTS AND THE
BURNING OF BOOKS

In the summer of 2010 Terry Jones, Pastor of the Dove World Outreach Center, declared that he would observe the ninth anniversary of the 9/11 destruction of the Twin Towers in New York by burning the Quran: he named the day 'International Burn a Koran Day'. The burning was postponed until March 2011: on 1 April, twenty-two UN relief workers were killed by a mob in Afghanistan. The outrage and protest spread around the world. The burning of a text is clearly as emotionally powerful as the burning of a flag.

People have burned texts of many different kinds, particularly those containing anything of which they disapprove such as pornography. In Ray Bradbury's well-known book, *Fahrenheit 451* (1953), the protesters against the burning of books memorise them so that they will not be lost for ever. In a graphic scene, Montag says, 'Here we all are, Montag, Aristophanes and Mahatma Gandhi and Gautama Buddha and Confucius and Thomas Love Peacock and Thomas Jefferson and Mr Lincoln, if you please. We are also Matthew, Mark, Luke and John.' Among the names, those associated with sacred texts are obviously prominent.

For more than 2,000 years people have been burning books – or if not literally 'books', then codices and manuscripts in the period before printing was invented. We have already seen (p. 293) how the Emperor Qin Shihuangdi (221–210) burned any texts that seemed to him to oppose his project of creating a strong and unified empire, how the Jewish opponents of Maimonides induced the Dominicans to burn his works (p. 39), and how translations of the Bible into English were burned by Catholic bishops (p. 66), as also was Luther's translation into German (short of actual burning, the Roman Catholic Church maintained for centuries an Index of prohibited books that the faithful were forbidden to read). Other well-known examples are:

◆ The destruction by Antiochus Epiphanes (d. 164 BCE) of the Hebrew Bible when he tried to impose a Greek way of life (Hellenism) on the Jews.

◆ Diocletian's edict (303 CE), ordering the destruction of Christian books (he had already ordered the burning of Egyptian texts in 292).

◆ The destruction ordered by Theophilus of the library in Alexandria in 391.

◆ The destruction ordered by the third caliph, Uthman, of variant texts of the Quran.

◆ The burning in 1193 by Muslims of the vast Buddhist library at Nalanda.

◆ The Christian burning of the Talmud and other Jewish books from the thirteenth to the sixteenth centuries.

◆ The destruction by Mongol invaders in 1258 of the libraries in Baghdad, including the House of Wisdom.

◆ The burning at the end of the fifteenth century of Hebrew and Arabic texts by the Inquisition in Spain.

◆ Savonarola's 'Bonfire of the Vanities' in 1497.

◆ The burning of Mayan texts in the sixteenth century.

The practice of burning books has continued down to the present day. Surely the most notorious of all was the Nazi 'burning of the books' (mainly, but not exclusively, of those written by Jews) on 10 May 1933. In 1995 a memorial was constructed on the site, consisting of a window at street level under which can be seen empty bookshelves. On a plaque is carved a quotation from Heinrich Heine, 'Dort, wo man Bücher verbrennt, verbrennt man am Ende auch Menschen' ('Where they burn books in the end they also burn people').

Although many books of different kinds have been burned, most have come from the sacred texts included in this volume. Why have sacred texts so often been thrown on the fires of hatred, not least by religious believers?

Two reasons are fundamental. The first lies in the fact that sacred texts have been gathered into clearly defined collections or Canons (p. 8 and Index *ad loc.*). The texts in those collections have been of immense consequence in human history in the forming of individual lives and societies. Clearly, however, the many collections or Canons of sacred texts vary greatly from each other. The inevitable result has been that the resulting religions and civilisations are extremely different from each other. Those differences can be profoundly serious, competitive and divisive. It does not follow that religions *have* to be hostile to each other, but they frequently are.

As a result, sacred texts have often been involved in the many wars and conflicts between religions and also *within* religions. One of the dramatic weapons used in those conflicts has been 'the burning of the books' of one's opponents.

The second major reason why sacred texts have been burned lies within the texts themselves, partly because they have been so important in creating those different societies, but also more particularly because it is possible to find within them warrants and authority for actions of that kind. Sacred texts are the foundation on which the lives of individuals, of religions and of societies have been built in the past, as indeed they still are. Words from sacred texts have guided and controlled the ways in which people have lived and have created their families and societies. Those words have been woven into the brilliant tapestries of the many different civilisations of the world. They have helped to create the art, music, literature and drama which in turn have carried them from one generation to another.

Yet sacred texts have also been used to condemn those who in practice or belief disown or reject or even simply disagree with what they contain, and that condemnation may include the burning of their books. Sacred texts have created holy people and great civilisations, but they have also been used to condemn and persecute others. For that reason, to give only one example, the Bible can be very dangerous, as I pointed out in *The Complete Bible Handbook* (p. 6): on the basis of the Bible, some Christians have been murdering Jews for nearly 2,000 years, and some Jews have killed others in pursuit of a promised land. On the basis of the Bible, witches have been burned alive, homosexuals executed, children beaten, Africans shipped to slavery, women treated in law as children, animals regarded as human property, and wars justified in the name of the Prince of Peace.

At the same time, though, the Bible has supplied the reasons why those actions and attitudes have been rejected and condemned. It was in the same text endorsing slavery that William Wilberforce found the inspiration to campaign for its abolition. He wrote in his diary in 1787, 'God Almighty has set before me two great objects, the suppression of the Slave Trade and the reformation of manners.' It was in the Bible that those objectives were set before him.

What, therefore, we have to remember is that the Bible and all sacred texts are open to different understandings and changed interpretations. Obviously there are believers in all religions who passionately reject that, and who defend to the death (often literally) what they take to be the original and only meaning of the text.

But that simply does not exist. There is no 'original and single meaning' of any text, sacred or otherwise. There can only be possibilities of meaning and interpretation (on this, see the Introduction, pp. 3–5). Even if sacred texts contain timeless truths, they have to be spoken or written in a language in a particular historical and geographical context, otherwise they would be completely unintelligible. To understand a text we have to understand the language and the context.

Not surprisingly, therefore, all religions have developed the means of exegesis and interpretation so that they can build a bridge from the text in the past to its meaning and application in the present. We have already seen an example of how that was done in Islam when Muslims developed recognised and accepted ways of applying the Quran to changing circumstances (see p. 137). We can see it also repeatedly in Judaism and Christianity (to restrict the examples to the other so-called Abrahamic religions, those that acknowledge Abraham as their common ancestor). Thus the early rabbis developed the Seven and Thirteen rules (*middoth*) of interpretation that they found in Scripture itself (they are listed and described in my *Targums and Rabbinic Literature*, pp. 315–18). Or, again, Western Christians established in the Middle Ages four legitimate ways of interpretation: the literal, the allegorical, the moral and the anagogical (from the Greek, *anagoge*, that which leads to higher things, i.e., to God and Heaven). The Four Ways were summarised in two hexameters attributed to Augustine of Dacia:

> Littera gesta docet, quid credas allegoria,
> Moralis quid agas, quo tendas anagogia.*

There is, however, no agreement in any religion on how texts must or can be interpreted. Debates about the methods of exegesis and interpretation continue, and the methods themselves are still changing. This means that there can be deep and often angry divisions among believers in each religion about how to receive and use their sacred texts. What is clear, therefore, is that the burning of books will continue, at least metaphorically and often literally, unless we can begin to *share together* an understanding of what methods of exegesis and interpretation are legitimate and permissible in each tradition. If we can then participate *together* in that work of interpretation and application, there is a better chance that we can also work together effectively to change ourselves and the world in the direction of generosity and peace.

In a world of continuing religious terrorism and conflict, this is a first and urgently necessary step to take if the sacred texts themselves are to contribute,

---

* 'The literal sense teaches what happened, the allegorical what you should believe, the moral how you should behave, and the anagogical where you are going.'

not to hostility and burning, but to a better and more peaceful understanding. That cannot possibly happen while some people use a sacred text to justify their angry and destructive actions – or indeed to justify the burning of the books of other people. It is from the sacred texts themselves that those attitudes and actions have to be challenged.

Religions are concerned with matters of life and of how to live it, just as they are concerned with matters of death and of life beyond death – with everything, in fact, that humans most care about. The memories, beliefs and practices of each religion are carried and treasured in their texts. If we wish to share with each other the treasure, as well as to challenge and change the consequences of religious hatred and malice, the only chance we have is to start with the texts and to share together an entirely new enterprise of interpretation.

BIBLIOGRAPHY I

TRANSLATION SERIES

Many texts are translated in the Translation Series listed here (see also note on p. 17). For reasons of space, the individual titles are not repeated in the main part of the Bibliography (see p. 360).

Adyar Library Series

Ancient Christian Writers

Ancient Indian Tradition and Mythology

Ante-Nicene Fathers

BDK English Tripitaka [Bukkyo Dendo Kyokai]

Bibliotheca Persica

Buddhist Publication Society

Buddhist Tradition Series

Carreg Chinese Culture Series

Classics in East Asian Buddhism

Classics of Western Spirituality

E. J. W. Gibb Memorial Series

Element Classics of World Spirituality

Ethical and Religious Classics of East and West

Fathers of the Church

Gaekwad's Oriental Series (Baroda Oriental Institute)

Great Books of Islamic Civilisation

Harvard Oriental Series, organised in series (e.g., Buddhism in Translations)

Jewish Publication Society

Library of Christian Classics

Library of Classical Arabic Literature

Library of Tibetan Works and Archives

Littman Library of Jewish Civilization

Nicene and Post-Nicene Christian Fathers

Orchard Books

Pali Text Society

Persian Studies Series

Poona Oriental Series

Princeton Library of Asian Translations

Ranade Publication Series

Royal Asiatic Society of Bengal

Sacred Books of China (Legge)

Sacred Books of the Buddhists

Sacred Books of the East

Sacred Books of the Hindus

Sacred Books of the Jainas

Sikh Religion and Philosophy

Textual Sources for the Study of Religions

Tibetan Translation Series

Translation Bureau of the Library of Tibetan Works and Archives

Translations from the Asian Classics

Trubner's Oriental Series

UNESCO Collection of Great/Representative Works

Wisdom of the East

Yale Judaica

BIBLIOGRAPHY II

OF SOME ADDITIONAL TRANSLATIONS AND OF
BOOKS QUOTED OR REFERRED TO IN THE TEXT

1   Abbott, W. M., *The Documents of Vatican II*, London, Chapman, 1967.

2   Abdullah, R., *Rumi: Words of Paradise*, London, Frances Lincoln, 2006.

3   Abe, R., *The Weaving of Mantra: Kukai and the Construction of Esoteric Buddhist Discourse*, New York, Columbia University Press, 1999.

4   *Abhidharma-kosa-bhasyam*: see Pruden.

5   *Abhisamayalankara-prajñaparamita-upadesha-shastra*: see Holmes.

6   Abu Huraira, *asSahifa asSahihah*, Damascus, Arabic Academy, 1954.

7   Ackroyd, P. R., and Evans, C. F., *The Cambridge History of the Bible*, I, Cambridge, Cambridge University Press, 1975.

8   Acts of the Martyrs: see Bonhoeffer, Owen, Polycarp.

9   Adams, G., *The Structure and Meaning of Badarayana's Brahma Sutras*, Delhi, Motilal Banarsidass, 1993.

10   *AdDurrah alFakhirah*: see Heer.

11   *Adi Granth*: see Bhave, Buxi, Gopal, Gurnam, Kaur, Khushwant, Kirpal, Massey, Mohan, Pashaura, Sangat.

12   *Agni Purana*: see Dutt.

13   Agrawala, V. S., *Devi-mahatmyam: The Glorification of the Great Goddess*, Varanasi, All-India Kashiraj Trust, 1963.

14   Ajjaf, M. S., *Jewels of Guidance: Selected Commandments of the Prophet: From the Authentic Collection by Imam Muslim and Bukhari*, London, Dar al-Taqwa, 1987.

15   Aland, K., *Martin Luther's 95 Theses: with the Pertinent Documents from the History of the Reformation*, Saint Louis, Concordia, 1987.

16   AlBukhari: see Ajjaf, Asad, Brown, J., Cleary (224), El-Moughy, Khan, Torrey.

17   Alexander, A., *The Tephilloth, or Daily Prayers: According to the Order of the Polish and German Jews*, London, 1788.

18   Alexander, P. S., *Textual Sources for the Study of Judaism*, Manchester, Manchester University Press, 1984.

19   AlFaruqi, I. R., *Our Beginning in Wisdom*, Washington, American Council of Learning Societies, 1953.

20   AlGhazali: see AlFaruqi, Behari, Calverley, Faris, Field, Gairdner, Holland, MacDonald, McCarthy, McKane, Watt.

21   Ali, A. Y., *The Holy Quran*, Cairo, AlManar, 1938.

22   Ali, M., *A Manual of Hadith*, Lahore, 1951.

23 Ali, S., *The Holy Quran*, Tilford, Islam International, 1997.

24 Allchin, F. R., *Kavitavali/Tulsi Das*, London, Allen & Unwin, 1964.

25 — *The Petition to Ram: Hindi Devotional Hymns of the 17th Century*, London, Allen & Unwin, 1966.

26 Allen, J. A., *Institutes of the Christian Religion*, Philadelphia, Presbyterians Board of Christian Education, 1936.

27 Allen, J. R., ed., *The Book of Songs: Translated by Arthur Waley*, New York, Grove Press, 1996.

28 *Altaf alQuds*: see Jalbani.

29 *Altar Sutra*: see Chan (197), Luk (607), Yampolsky.

30 Alvars: see Chari, Clooney, Hooper, Hudson, Narayan (699).

31 Anacker, S., *Seven Works of Vasubandhu, The Buddhist Psychological Doctor*, Delhi, Motilal Banarsidass, 1984.

32 *Analects*: see Cleary, Dawson, Huang, Lau, Pound, Legge, Leys, Waley (986), Watson.

33 Anesaki, M., *Nichiren, the Buddhist Prophet*, Cambridge, Harvard University Press, 1916.

34 Anklesaria, B. T., *Zand-akasih, Iranian or Greater Bundahisn*, Bombay, Bode, 1956.

35 AnNawawi: see Ibrahim.

36 Appar: see Kingsbury, Ramachandran.

37 Apte, V. M., *Rigvedic Mantras in their Ritual Setting*, Poona, Decan College, 1950.

38 —*Brahma-Sutra: Shankara-bhashya*, Bombay, Popular Book Depot, 1960.

39 Aquinas: see Chenu, Foster, Pegis, *Summa Theologica*.

40 Aranyaka: see Bhattacharji, Keith.

41 Arberry, A. J., *Immortal Rose: An Anthology of Persian Lyrics*, London, Luzac, 1948.

42 —*The Koran Interpreted*, London, Allen & Unwin, 1955.

43 —*Rubaiyat: Select Translation into English Verse*, London, 1949.

44 —*Discourses of Rumi*, London, John Murray, 1961.

45 —*Tales from the Masnavi*, London, Allen & Unwin, 1961.

46 —*More Tales from the Masnavi*, London, Allen & Unwin, 1963.

47 —*Muslim Saints and Mystics: Episodes from the Tadhkirat alAwliya of Farid udDin Attar*, London, Routledge, 1966.

48 —*Mystical Poems of Rumi*, I, Chicago, Chicago University Press, 1968.

49 —*The Mystical Poems of Rumi*, II, Boulder, Westview Press, 1979.

50 Armstrong, R. J., and Brady, I. C., *Francis and Clare: The Complete Works*, London, SPCK, 1982.

51 Asad, M., *Sahih-Bukhari*, New Delhi, Kitab Bhavan, 1978; Gibraltar, Dar al-Andalus, 1981.

52 Asanga: see Griffiths, Holmes, Li Rongxi, Limaye, Nagao, Obermiller, Powers, Stcherbatsky, Tatz, Willis.

53 AshShafii: see Howard.

54 *Ashtasahasrika Sutra*: see Conze (237).

55 Ashvaghosa: see Li.

56 Aston, W. G., *Nihongi: Chronicles of Japan from the Earliest Times to A. D. 697*, London, Trubner, 1896.

57 Attar: see Arberry (47), Darbandi, Ritter, Smith.

58 AtTarjumana, A. A., and Johnson, Y., *AlMuwatta of Malik ibn Anas*, Norwich, Diwan, 1982.

59 Augsburg Confession: see Cochrane, Schaff, Tappert.

60 Augustine: see Bettenson, Chadwick, O'Donnell, Sheed.

61 *Avatamsaka Sutra*: see Chan, Chang, Cleary.

62 Ayenagar, N. S. R., *Gitagovindam: Sacred Profanities, a Study of Jayadeva's Gitagovinda*, Delhi, Penman Publishers, 2000.

63 Azami, M. M., *Studies in Hadith Methodology and Literature*, Indianapolis, Islamic Teaching Centre, 1977.

64 Badarayana: see *Brahma Sutra*.

65 Bahm, A. J., *The Bhagavad Gita, or the Wisdom of Krishna*, Bombay, Somaiya Publications, 1970.

66   Baljon, J. M. S., *A Mystical Interpretation of Prophetic Tales by an Indian Muslim: Shah Wali Allah's Ta'wil alHadith*, Leiden, Brill, 1973.

67   Bancroft, A., *The Dhammapada*, Rockport, Element, 1997.

68   Barbee, C. F., and Zahl, P. F. M., *The Collects of Thomas Cranmer*, Grand Rapids, Eerdmans, 1999.

69   *Bardo Thödol*: see Coleman, Evans-Wentz, Fremantle, Hodge, Thurman.

70   Barks, C., *The Essential Rumi*, San Francisco, Harper, 1995.

71   — and Bly, R., *Night and Sleep: Rumi*, Cambridge, Yellow Moon Press, 1981.

72   Baroody, G. M., *Crime and Punishment under Islamic Law: Being a Translation from Manar al-Sabil . . .* , London, Regency Press, 1979.

73   Basho: see Beilenson, Bly, Chamberlain, Corman, Hamill, Henderson, Keene, Lowenstein, Miner, Qiu, Sato, Stock, Stryk, Ueda, Yuasa.

74   Basil the Great: see Clarke.

75   Batchelor, S., *Verses from the Center: A Buddhist Vision of the Sublime*, New York, Riverhead, 2000.

76   Battles, F. L., *Analysis of the Institutes of the Christian Religion of John Calvin*, Grand Rapids, Baker, 1980.

77   — *Institutes of the Christian Religion (1536 edition)*, London, Collins, 1986.

78   — and McNeill, J. T., *Institutes of the Christian Religion*, London, SCM Press, 1961.

79   Bauckham, R., *Jesus and the Eyewitnesses: The Gospels as Eyewitness Testimony*, Michigan, Eerdmans, 2006.

80   Bede, the Venerable: see Colgrave.

81   Behari, B., *The Revival of Religious Sciences: A Translation of the Arabic Work Ihya Ulum udDin*, Farnham, Sufi Publishing, 1972.

82   Beilenson, P., *Japanese Haiku*, New York, Peter Pauper Press, 1956.

83   Bell, G. L., *Poems from the Divan of Hafiz*, London, Heinemann, 1928.

84   Belvalkar, S. K., *The Brahma-Sutras of Badarayana*, Poona, Bilvakunja, 1931.

85   Benedict: see Knowles, McCann.

86   Berry, L. E., *The Geneva Bible: A Facsimile of the 1560 Edition*, Peabody, Hendrickson Bibles, 2007.

87   Best, P., *The Venlo Incident*, London, Hutchinson, 1950.

88   Bethge, E., ed., *Letters and Papers from Prison*, London, SCM Press, 1967.

89   — *Bonhoeffer: An Illustrated Biography in Documents and Photographs*, London, Fount, 1979.

90   Bettenson, H., *Concerning the City of God Against the Pagans*, London, Penguin, 1972.

91   Beyer, S. V., *The Buddhist Experience: Sources and Interpretations*, Encino, Dickenson, 1974.

92   *Bhagavadgita*: see Bahm, Buitenen, Deutsch, Edgerton, Gotschalk, Johnson, Mascaro, Mitchell, Radhakrishnan, Sharma, Tsoukalas, White, D., Zaehner.

93   *Bhagavata Purana*: see Bryant, Dehejia, Tagare.

94   Bhardwaj, S. M., *Hindu Places of Pilgrimage in India: A Study in Cultural Geography*, Berkeley, University of California Press, 1993.

95   Bhattacharji, S., *Literature in the Vedic Age*, II, Calcutta, Bagchi, 1986.

96   Bhattacharya, V., *Mahayanavimsaka of Nagarjuna*, Calcutta, Visva-Bharati, 1931.

97   Bhattacharyya, S., *The Alamkara-section of the Agni-purana*, Calcutta, Firma, 1976.

98   Bhave, V., and Talib, G. S., *Commentary on Japuji, Guru Nanak's Great Composition*, Patiala, Punjabi University, 1973.

99   Bicknell, H., *Hafiz of Shiraz: Selections from his Poems*, London, Trubner, 1875.

100   Bielefeldt, C., *Dogen's Manuals of Zen Meditation*, Berkeley, University of California Press, 1988.

101   Bindley, T. H., and Green, F. W., *The Oecumenical Documents of the*

Faith: The Creed of Nicaea, . . . The Chalcedonian Definition, London, Methuen, 1950.

102 Binyon, L., *The Divine Comedy*, London, Agenda Additions, 1979.

103 Birk, S., *Dante's Divine Comedy*, San Francisco, Chronicle, 2004–5.

104 Birnbaum, B., *Daily Prayer Book*, New York, Hebrew Publishing, 1949.

105 Blackman, P., *Mishnayoth . . .*, London, 1951–63.

106 Bloom, I., *Mencius*, New York, Columbia University Press, 2009.

107 Bloomfield, M., *Hymns of the Atharva-Veda*, Oxford, Clarendon Press, 1897.

108 *Blue Cliff Record*: see *Hekiganroku*.

109 Bly, R., *Basho*, San Francisco, Mudra, 1972.

110 Blyth, R. H., *Zen and Zen Classics*, Tokyo, Hokuseido Press, 1960–70.

111 Board of Scholars, *The Brahma Purana*, Delhi, N. P. Jain, 1985–6.

112 — *The Garuda Purana*, Delhi, Motilal Banarsidass, 1978–80.

113 — *The Linga-Purana*, Delhi, Motilal Banarsidass, 1973.

114 — *The Siva-Purana*, Delhi, Motilal Banarsidass, 1969–70.

115 — *Vamana Purana*, Delhi, Parimal Publications, 2005.

116 Bock, F. G., *Engi-shiki: Procedures of the Engi Era*, Tokyo, Sophia University, 1970.

117 Bodewitz, H. W., *Jaiminiya Brahmana, I, 1–65*, Leiden, Brill, 1990.

118 —*Bodhicittasastra*: see White.

119 Bodhidharma: see Broughton.

120 *Bodhisattvabhumi*: see Asanga.

121 Boin-Webb, S., *Abhidharmasamucayya: The Compendium of the Higher Teaching*, Essex, Wisdom Books, 2001.

122 Bolland, D., *The Mahabharata in Kathakali Dance*, New Delhi, Global Vision, 2006.

123 Bonhoeffer, D., *Letters and Papers from Prison*, London, Collins, 1953.

124 Bonhoeffer: see also Bethge, de Gruchy, Robertson.

125 *Book of Filial Devotion*: see Chen, Legge.

126 *Book of History*: see Legge.

127 *Book of Rites*: see Legge.

128 *Book of Songs*: see Allen, Legge, Waley.

129 Bose, A. C., *Hymns from the Vedas*, London, Asia Publishing, 1966.

130 Bowker, J., *The Targums and Rabbinic Literature: An Introduction to Jewish Interpretations of Scripture*, Cambridge, Cambridge University Press, 1969, 2010.

131 — *Problems of Suffering in Religions of the World*, Cambridge, Cambridge University Press, 1970.

132 — *Jesus and the Pharisees*, Cambridge, Cambridge University Press, 1973, 2010.

133 — *The Religious Imagination and the Sense of God*, Oxford, Clarendon Press, 1978.

134 — *Hallowed Ground*, London, SPCK, 1993.

135 — *The Oxford Dictionary of World Religions*, Oxford, Oxford University Press, 1997.

136 — *The Complete Bible Handbook*, London, Dorling Kindersley, 1998.

137 — *God: A Brief History*, London, Dorling Kindersley, 2002.

138 — *Beliefs that Changed the World*, London, Quercus, 2007.

139 — *Before the Ending of the Day*, Toronto, Key Publishing House, 2010.

140 Bowring, R., *Murasaki Shikibu: The Tale of Genji*, Cambridge, Cambridge University Press, 1988.

141 Boyce, M., *Zoroastrians: Their Religious Beliefs and Practices*, London, Routledge, 1979.

142 — *Textual Sources for the Study of Zoroastrianism*, Manchester, Manchester University Press, 1984.

143 Boylan, M., and Clarke, W., *Dance of Life: Hafez*, Washington, Magee, 1988.

144 Bradley, I., *Abide with Me: The World of Victorian Hymns*, London, SCM Press, 1997.

145   *Brahma Sutra*: see Adams, Apte, Belvalkar, Date, Rao.

146   Brahmanas: see Bhattacharji, Bodewitz, Burnell, Caland, Eggeling, Keith.

147   Brewster, E. H., *The Life of Gotama the Buddha: Compiled Exclusively from the Pali Canon*, London, Routledge, 1956.

148   Brooks, D. R., *Auspicious Wisdom: The Texts and Traditions of Śrīvidyā Śākta Tantrism in South India*, Albany, State University of New York Press, 1992.

149   Brough, J., *Selections from Classical Sanskrit Literature*, London, Muzak, 1952.

150   Broughton, J. L., *The Bodhidharma Anthology: The Earliest Records of Zen*, Berkeley, University of California Press, 1999.

151   Brower, R. H., *Japanese Court Poetry*, Stanford, Stanford University Press, 1961.

152   — *Fujiwara Teika's Hundred-Poem Sequence of the Shoji Era, 1200*, Tokyo, Sophia University, 1978.

153   — and Miner, E., *Fujiwara Teika's Superior Poems of Our Time*, Stanford, Stanford University Press, 1967.

154   Brown, C. M., *The Devi Gita: The Song of the Goddess*, Albany, State University of New York Press, 1998.

155   — *The Triumph of the Goddess*, Albany, State University of New York Press, 1990.

156   Brown, J., *The Canonisation of al-Bukhari: The Formation and Function of the Sunni Hadith Canon*, Leiden, Brill, 2007.

157   Brownlee, J. S., 'The Jeweled Comb-Box: Motoori Norinaga's *Tamakushige*', *Monumenta Nipponica*, 43, 1988, pp. 35–61.

158   Bruce, J. P., *The Philosophy of Human Nature by Chu Hsi*, London, Probsthain, 1922.

159   Brujin, J. T. P. de, *Persian Sufi Poetry: An Introduction to the Mystical Use of Classical Poems*, Richmond, Curzon Press, 1997.

160   Bryant, E. F., *Krishna: The Beautiful Legend of God (Srimad Bhagavata Purana, Book X)*, London, Penguin, 2003.

161   Buddhaghosa: see Nanamoli, Warren.

162   Buitenen, J. A. B. van, *The Bhagavadgita in the Mahabharata: A Bilingual Edition*, Chicago, Chicago University Press, 1981.

163   — *Mahabharata: Books 1–5*, Chicago, Chicago University Press, 1973–8.

164   *Bundahishn*: see Anklesaria.

165   Burnell, A. C., *The Samavidhanabrahmana with the Commentary of Sayana, an English Translation*, London, Trubner, 1873.

166   Burns, S. L., *Before the Nation: Kokugaku and the Imagining of Community in Early Modern Japan*, Durham, Duke University Press, 2003.

167   Bu-ston: see Obermiller, Ruegg.

168   Buswell, R. E., *The Korean Approach to Zen: The Collected Works of Chinul*, Honolulu, University of Hawaii Press, 1983.

169   — *The Formation of Ch'an Ideology in China and Korea: The Vajrasamadhi-sutra, a Buddhist Apocryphon*, Princeton, Princeton University Press, 1989.

170   — *Tracing Back the Radiance: Chinul's Korean Way of Zen*, Honolulu, University of Hawaii Press, 1991.

171   — *Cultivating Original Enlightenment: Wonhyo's Exposition of the Vajrasamadhi-sutra*, Honolulu, University of Hawaii Press, 2007.

172   Buxi, L. S., *Saint-Poets of Guru Granth Sahib: History and Heritage*, Delhi, National Book Shop, 2000.

173   Caland, W., *Pañcaviṃśa Brahmana*, Calcutta, Asiatic Society of Bengal, 1931.

174   Callewaert, W. M., and Friedlander, P. G., *The Life and Work of Raidas*, Delhi, Manohar, 1992.

175   Calverley, E. E., *Worship in Islam: Being a Translation, with Commentary and Introduction, of*

176   *alGhazzali's Book of the Ihya on Worship*, London, Luzac, 1957.

176   Calvin: see Allen, Battles.

177   *Cambridge History of the Bible, The*: see Ackroyd, Greenslade, Lampe.

178   Carman, J., and Narayanan, V., *The Tamil Veda: Pillan's Interpretation of the Tiruvaymoli*, Chicago, University of Chicago Press, 1989.

179   Carmi, T., *The Penguin Book of Hebrew Verse*, London, Penguin, 1981.

180   — and Pagis, D., *Selected Poems*, London, 1976.

181   Carmichael, A., *Carmina Gaedelica: Hymns and Incantations*, Edinburgh, Floris Books, 2001.

182   *Carmina Gaedelica*: see Carmichael.

183   Carter, J. R., and Palihawadana, M., *The Dhammapada*, Oxford, Oxford University Press, 2000.

184   Carter, S. D., *Waiting for the Wind*, New York, Columbia University Press, 1989.

185   Cassian: see Chadwick, Gibson.

186   Celtic texts: see Lapidge.

187   Chadwick, H., *Augustine of Hippo: A Life*, Oxford, Oxford University Press, 2009.

188   — *The Confessions of Saint Augustine*, Oxford, Oxford University Press, 1991.

189   Chadwick, O., *Western Asceticism: Selected Translations*, London, SCM Press, 1958.

190   Chai, C., and Winberg, C., *The Humanist Way in Ancient China: Essential Works of Confucianism*, New York, Bantam Books, 1965.

191   Chalcedon: see Bindley, Neuner.

192   Chamberlain, B. H., *Japanese Poetry*, London, John Murray, 1911.

193   Chamberlain, G. W., *The Kojiki: Records of Ancient Matters*, Rutland, Tuttle, 1982.

194   Chan Wing-tsit, *Trimshika*, in Radhakrishnan and Moore, pp. 333–7.

195   — *A Source Book in Chinese Philosophy*, Princeton, Princeton University Press, 1963.

196   — *Reflections on Things at Hand: The Neo-Confucian Anthology*, New York, Columbia University Press, 1967.

197   Chang, C. C., ed., *A Treasury of Mahayana Sutras: Selections from the Maharatnakuta Sutra*, Philadelphia, Pennsylvania State University Press, 1983.

198   — *The Buddhist Teaching of Totality: The Philosophy of Hwa Yen Buddhism*, Philadelphia, Pennsylvania State University Press, 1971.

199   Chang, G. C. C., *The Hundred Thousand Songs of Milarepa*, Boulder, Shambhala, 1977.

200   Chapple, C., *The Yoga Sutras of Patanjali: An Analysis of the Sanskrit with Accompanying English Translation*, Delhi, Sri Satguru Publications, 1990.

201   Chari, S. M. S., *Philosophy and Theistic Mysticism of the Alvars*, Delhi, Motilal Banarsidass, 1997.

202   Chatterjee, K. N., *Vasubandhu's Vijnapti-matrata-siddhi*, Varanasi, Kishor Vidya Niketan, 1980.

203   Chen, I., *The Book of Filial Duty*, London, John Murray, 1908.

204   Ch'en, K., *Buddhism in China: A Historical Survey*, Princeton, Princeton University Press, 1973.

205   Cheng, H., *Nagarjuna's Twelve Gate Treatise*, Dordrecht, Reidel, 1982.

206   Cheng Hao and Cheng Yi: see Chan (196).

207   Chenu, M. D., *Toward Understanding St Thomas*, Chicago, Henry Regnery, 1964.

208   Chinul: see Buswell, Keel, Lee.

209   Chipp, H. B., ed., *Theories of Modern Art: A Source Book by Artists and Critics*, Berkeley, University of California Press, 1968.

210   Chittick, W. C., *The Sufi Path of Love: The Spiritual Teachings of Rumi*, Albany, State University of New York Press, 1983.

211   Chopra, D., and Kia, F., *The Love Poems of Rumi*, London, Rider, 1998.

212   Chrysostom, John: see *Divine Liturgy*.

213 Chu Hsi: see Zhu Xi.

214 *Chuang Tzu/Zhuangzi*: see Chan (195), Chung, Cleary, Feng, Fung, Giles, Graham, Legge, Palmer, Watson (995), Wu.

215 Chung, B., *Zhuangzi Speaks!*, Princeton, Princeton University Press, 1992.

216 Clarke, H. W., *The Divan, Written in the Fourteenth Century by . . . Hafiz-i-Shirazi Otherwise Known as Lisanu-l-Ghaib*, London, Octagon Press, 1974.

217 Clarke, W. K. L., *The Ascetic Works of St Basil*, London, SPCK, 1925.

218 Clapton, E., *Our Prayer Book Psalter: Containing Coverdale's Version from his 1535 Bible and the Prayer Book Version by Coverdale from the Great Bible, 1539–41*, London, SPCK, 1934.

219 Cleary, T., *Record of Things Heard*, Boulder, Shambhala, 1960.

220 — *The Essential Confucius: The Heart of Confucius' Teaching in Authentic I Ching Order*, San Francisco, HarperCollins, 1992.

221 — *The Blue Cliff Record*, Boulder, Shambhala, 1977.

222 — *The Flower Ornament Scripture: A Translation of the Avatamsaka Sutra*, Boulder, Shambhala, 1984.

223 — *The Essential Tao: An Initiation into the Heart of Taoism*, San Francisco, Harper, 1991.

224 — *The Wisdom of the Prophet: Sayings of Muhammad*, Boston, Shambhala, 1994.

225 — *The Dhammapada*, London, Thorsons, 1995.

226 Clooney, F. X., *Seeing Through Texts: Doing Theology among the Srivaisnavas of South India*, Albany, State University of New York Press, 1996.

227 Coburn, T., '"Scripture" in India: Towards a Typology of the Word in Hindu Life', *Journal of the American Academy of Religion*, LII, pp. 435–59.

228 Cochrane, A. C., *Reformed Confessions of the 16th Century*, London, SCM Press, 1966.

229 Cohen, B., *Mishna and Tosefta: A Comparative Study*, New York, 1935.

230 Coleman, G., and Gyurme Dorje, *The Tibetan Book of the Dead: The Great Liberation by Hearing in the Intermediate States*, London, Penguin, 2008.

231 Colgrave, B., and Mynors, R. A. B., *Bede's Ecclesiastical History of the English People*, Oxford, Clarendon Press, 1969.

232 Columbanus: see Munro, Ryan.

233 Como, M., *Sh-otoku: Ethnicity, Ritual, and Violence in the Japanese Buddhist Tradition*, Oxford, Oxford University Press, 2008.

234 Confessions: see Cochrane, Schaff, Tappert.

235 *Confessions, The*: see Chadwick, O'Donnell, Sheed.

236 Confucius: see *Analects*.

237 Conze, E., *Astasahasrika Prajñaparamita*, Calcutta, Asiatic Society, 1970.

238 — *Buddhist Scriptures*, London, Penguin, 1966.

239 — ed., *Buddhist Texts Through the Ages*, Oxford, Cassirer, 1953.

240 — *Prajñaparamita Literature*, New Delhi, Munshiram Manohal, 1978.

241 — *Buddhist Wisdom Books, Containing the Diamond Sutra and the Heart Sutra*, London, Unwin, 1988.

242 — *Perfect Wisdom: The Short Prajñaparamita Texts*, Totnes, Buddhist Publishing, 1993.

243 Cook, F. D., *How to Raise an Ox: Zen Practice as Taught in Zen Master Dogen's Shobogenzo*, Los Angeles, Center Publications, 1978.

244 Cooper, W. R., *The New Testament, Translated by William Tyndale*, London, British Library, 2000.

245 Cooperson, M., and Toorawa, S. M., *Arabic Literary Culture, 500–925*, Detroit, Thomson Gale, 2005.

246 Corman, C., *Back Roads to Far Towns: Basho's Travel Journal*, New York, White Pine Press, 1986.

247 Council of Trent: see Neuner, Schroeder.

248 Coverdale, M.: see Clapton, Pearson, Willoughby, Wormald.

249 Cowan, J., *Rumi's Divan of Shems of Tabriz*, Shaftesbury, Element, 1997.

250 Cox, J. E., *The Works of Thomas Cranmer*, II, Cambridge, Cambridge University Press, 1846.

251 Cragg, K., *Readings in the Quran*, London, Fount, 1995.

252 Cranmer: see Cox.

253 Creeds: see Bindley, Kelly, Schaff.

254 Cuntarar: see Shulman.

255 *Da Xue*: see Chai, Chan, Hughes.

256 Dalia, A. A., *Biography of Dharma Master Vasubandhu*, Berkeley, BDK, 2002.

257 Dan, J., *The Early Kabbalah*, New York, Paulist Press, 1986.

258 Danby, H., *The Mishnah*, Oxford, Clarendon Press, 1933.

259 Daniell, D., *Tyndale's New Testament, in a Modern Spelling Edition*, New Haven, Yale University Press, 1989.

260 Dante: see Binyon, Birk, De Sua, Kirkpatrick, Musa, Oelsner, Reynolds, Rossetti, Sissons.

261 *Daodejing*: see Cleary (223), Dolby, Feng, Henricks, Kwok Man-Ho, Moeller, Ryden, Waley (988).

262 Darbandi, A., and Davis, D., *The Conference of the Birds*, London, Penguin, 1984.

263 Das, N., *Couplets from Kabir*, Delhi, Motilal Banarsidass, 1991.

264 *Dasam Granth*: see Jodh Singh.

265 Dass, N., *Songs of Kabir from the Adi Granth*, Delhi, Sri Satguru, 1992.

266 Date, V. H., *Vedanta Explained: Ðamkara's Commentary on the Brahma-sutras*, Bombay, Booksellers' Publishing, 1954.

267 David, A., *The Commentary to Mishnah Aboth of Moses Maimonides*, New York, Bloch Publishing, 1968.

268 Dawood, N., *The Koran: With a Parallel Arabic Text*, London, Penguin, 2000.

269 — *The Koran*, London, Penguin, 2003.

270 Dawson, R., *The Analects*, Oxford, Oxford University Press, 1993.

271 de Bary *et al.*, *Sources of Indian/ Chinese/Japanese/Korean Tradition*, New York, Columbia University Press, 1957–97.

272 — *The Buddhist Tradition in India, China and Japan*, New York, Random House, 1992.

273 de Gruchy, J. W., *The Cambridge Companion to Dietrich Bonhoeffer*, Cambridge, Cambridge University Press, 1999.

274 De Sua, W. J., *Dante into English: A Study of the Translation of the Divine Comedy in Britain and America*, Chapel Hill, University of North Carolina Press, 1964.

275 Dehejia, H., *Slaves of the Lord: The Path of the Tamil Saints*, New Delhi, Munshiram Manoharlal, 1988.

276 Dehejia, H. V., *Celebrating Krishna: Sacred Words and Sensuous Images (The 10th Book of the Bhagavata Purana)*, Ahmedabad, Mapin, 2005.

277 Derin, S., *Love in Sufism: From Rabia to Ibn al-Farid*, Istanbul, Insan, 2008.

278 Deshpande, N. A., *The Padma-Purana*, Delhi, Motilal Banarsidass, 1988–90.

279 Deutsch, E., *The Bhagavad Gita*, New York, Holt, Reinhart and Winston, 1968.

280 — and van Buitenen, J. A. B., *A Sourcebook of Advaita Vedanta*, Honolulu, University of Hawaii Press, 1971.

281 *Devi Gita*: see Brown, Lalye.

282 Dhal, U. N., *Sivapurana, Uttarakhanda*, Delhi, Nag Publishers, 2w.

283 Dhamma, R., *The First Discourse of the Buddha*, Somerville, Wisdom Publications, 1997.

284 *Dhammacakkappavattana-sutta*: see Dhamma.

285 *Dhammapada*: see Bancroft, Carter, Cleary, Radhakrishnan (787).

286 Dharmashastra/Dharmasutras: see O'Flaherty, Kane, Olivelle.

287 Dhavamony, M. D., *Love of God according to Ðaiva Siddhantha: A Study in the Mysticism and Theology*

of Śaivism, Oxford, Clarendon Press, 1971.

288 *Diamond-cutter*: see Conze.

289 Dickinson, E., *An Introduction to the Science of the Hadith: Ibn al-Salah al-Shahrazuri,* Reading, Garnet, 2005.

290 *Digha Nikaya*: see Walshe.

291 Dimmitt, C., and van Buitenen, J. A. B., *Classical Hindu Mythology: A Reader in the Sanskrit Puranas,* Philadelphia, Temple University Press, 1978.

292 Dionysius: see Luibheid.

293 *Divine Comedy*: see Binyon, Birk, Kirkpatrick, Sissons.

294 *Divine Liturgy of Our Father among the Saints, John Chrysostom,* Oxford, Oxford University Press, 1995.

295 Dixit, K. K., *Sukhlalji's Commentary on Tattvartha Sutra of Vacaka Umasvati,* Ahmedabad, Institute of Indology, 1974.

296 Dobson, W. A. C. H., *Mencius: A New Translation,* London, Oxford University Press, 1963.

297 *Doctrine of the Mean*: see Chai, Chan, Gu, Hughes.

298 Dogen: see Bielefeldt, Cleary, Cook, Kodera, Leighton, Nishijima, Nishiyama, Wright, T.

299 Doi, A. R. I., *Shari'a: The Islamic Law,* London, Ta Ha, 1997.

300 Dolby, W., *Sir Old: The Chinese Classic of Taoism, Lao zi dao de jing,* Edinburgh, Carreg, 2003.

301 Dominic: see Tugwell.

302 Doniger: see O'Flaherty.

303 Dumoulin, H., *Zen Buddhism: A History: India and China,* New York, Macmillan, 1988.

304 — *Zen Buddhism: A History: Japan,* New York, Macmillan, 1990.

305 Durkheim, E., *The Elementary Forms of the Religious Life,* trsl. J. W. Swain, New York, Collier, 1961.

306 Dutt, A., *A Prose English Translation of the Mahabharata,* Calcutta, Dass, 1895–1905.

307 Dutt, M. N., *Agni Purana,* Varanasi, Chowkhambha, 1967.

308 Dutt, R. C., *The Great Epics of Ancient India,* Delhi, Ess Ess Publications, 1976.

309 Dutton, Y., *The Origins of Islamic Law: The Quran, the Muwatta and Madinan 'Amal,* Richmond, Curzon, 1999.

310 Edgerton, F., *The Bhagavad Gita,* Cambridge, Harvard University Press, 1944.

311 Eggeling, J., *The Satpatha-Brahmana,* Oxford, Clarendon Press, 1900.

312 Ehrman, A., *The Talmud with English Translation and Commentary,* Jerusalem, El-'Am, 1965– .

313 Ehrman, B. D., *The Apostolic Fathers,* Cambridge, Harvard University Press, 2003.

314 El-Moughy, I. H., *Al-Bukhari: A Collection of Muhammad's Authentic Traditions,* Cairo, AlAzhar, 1936.

315 Encyclicals: see Fremantle, Neuner.

316 *Engishiki*: see Bock, Como, Philippi (763), Satow.

317 *English Hexapla, Exhibiting the Six Important English Translations of the New Testament Scriptures* [Wyclif, Tyndale, Cranmer, Geneva Bible, Anglo-Rhemish, Authorised], London, Bagster, 1841.

318 Epstein, I., *et al., The Babylonian Talmud,* London, Soncino, 1935–48.

319 Evans-Wentz, W. Y., *The Tibetan Book of the Dead,* New York, Oxford University Press, 1957.

320 — *Tibet's Great Yogi Milarepa: A Biography from the Tibetan,* Oxford, Oxford University Press, 2000.

321 Fahy, B., *The Writings of St Francis of Assisi,* London, Burns and Oates, 1964.

322 Faris, N. A., *The Book of Idols: Being a Translation from the Arabic of the Kitab al-Asnam,* Princeton, Princeton University Press, 1952.

323 — *The Book of Knowledge,* Lahore, Ashraf, 1962.

324 — *The Foundations of the Articles of Faith,* Lahore, Ashraf, 1963.

325 — *The Mysteries of Almsgiving*, Beirut, 1966.

326 — *The Mysteries of Purity*, Lahore, Ashraf, 1966.

327 Farmer, H. G., *Maimonides on Listening to Music: From the Responsa*, London, Hinrischen, 1941.

328 Farrow, G. W., and Menon, I., *The Concealed Essence of the Hevajra Tantra*, Delhi, Motilal Banarsidass, 1992.

329 *Fath alBari*: see Ibn Hajar, Khattab, Murad.

330 Feng, G., and English, J., *Lao Tsu: Tao Te Ching*, New York, Vintage, 1972.

331 — *Inner Chapters of Chuang Tsu: A New Translation*, London, Wildwood House, 1974.

332 Feuerstein, G., *The Yoga-Sutra of Patanjali: A New Translation and Commentary*, Folkestone, Dawson, 1979.

333 Field, C., *The Confessions of Al Ghazzali*, London, John Murray, 1909.

334 Finn, L. M., *The Kulacudamanitantra and the Vamakesvara Tantra, with the Jayaratha Commentary*, Wiesbaden, Harrassowitz, 1986.

335 FitzGerald, E., *Salaman and Absal: Translated from the Persian of Jami*, London, Alexander Moring, 1904.

336 Flannery, A., *Vatican Council II: The Conciliar and Post-Conciliar Documents*, Leominster, Gracewing, 1992.

337 Flower, M., *The Poems of St John of the Cross*, Varroville, The Carmelite Nuns, 1983.

338 Forshall, J., and Madden, F., *The Holy Bible Containing the Old and New Testaments, with the Apocryphal Books, in the Earliest English Versions Made from the Latin Vulgate by John Wycliffe and his Followers*, Oxford, Oxford University Press, 1850.

339 Foster, K., *The Life of St Thomas Aquinas: Biographical Documents*, London, Longmans, 1959.

340 Foxe, J., *The Acts and Monuments of John Foxe*, London, Seeley, 1843.

341 Francis: see Armstrong, Fahy, Habig.

342 Francis, H. T., and Thomas, E. J., *Jataka Tales*, Cambridge, Cambridge University Press, 1916.

343 Freehof, S. B., *The Responsa Literature*, Philadelphia, Jewish Publication Society, 1955.

344 Fremantle, A., *The Papal Encyclicals in their Historical Context*, New York, Mentor-Omega Books, 1963.

345 Fremantle, F., and Trungpa, C., *The Tibetan Book of the Dead: The Great Liberation through Hearing in the Bardo*, Berkeley, Shambhala, 1975.

346 Friedlander, M., *The Guide for the Perplexed: Translated from the Original Arabic Text*, New York, Dover, 1904.

347 Frye, S., *A Drop of Nourishment for People and The Jewel Ornament*, Dharmasala, Library of Tibetan Works, 1981.

348 *Fukanzazenji*: see Cook.

349 Fung, Y., *A Tao Classic: Chuang Tzu*, Beijing, Foreign Language Press, 1989.

350 Futehally, S., *In the Dark of the Heart: Songs of Meera*, San Francisco, HarperCollins, 1995.

351 Gairdner, W. H. T., *AlGhazzali's Mishkat al-Anwar*, London, Royal Asiatic Society, 1924.

352 Gampopa: see Guenther, Gyaltsen, Holmes, Stewart.

353 Gandhi, M., *The Story of My Experiments with Truth*, Ahmedabad, Navajivan Press, 1929.

354 Gandz, S., and Klein, H., *The Code of Maimonides Book Three: The Book of Seasons*, New Haven, Yale University Press, 1961.

355 Gangadharan, N., *The Agni Purana*, Delhi, N. P. Jain, 1984– .

356 Ganguli, K. M., *The Mahabharata*, Calcutta, Roy, 1883–96.

357 Gardner, D. K., *Learning to be a Sage: By Chu Hsi*, Berkeley, University of California Press, 1990.

358 Garfiel, E., *Service of the Heart: A Guide to the Jewish Prayer Book*, Northvale, Aronson, 1989.

359 Garfield, J. L., *The Fundamental Wisdom of the Middle Way: Nagarjuna's Mulamadhyamakakarika*, Oxford, Oxford University Press, 1995.

360 Gaster, M., *The Book of Prayer and Order of Service of the Spanish and Portuguese Jews' Congregation*, London, 1901.

361 *Gathas*: see Insler.

362 Gatje, H., *The Quran and its Exegesis: Selected Texts with Classical and Modern Muslim Interpretations*, Oxford, Oneworld, 1996.

363 Geneva Bible: see Berry, Lupton, McCitterick.

364 *Genji*: see *Tale of Genji*.

365 Gershevitch, I., *The Avestan Hymn to Mithra*, Cambridge, Cambridge University Press, 1959.

366 Gibson, E. C. S., *The Works of John Cassian*, in *Select Library of the Nicene and Post-Nicene Fathers*, Series 2, vol. 11, Oxford and New York, 1894.

367 Gikatilla, J., *Sh'are Orah*: see Weinstein.

368 Giles, H. A., *Chuang Tzu: Taoist Philosopher and Chinese Mystic*, London, Unwin, 1926.

369 Giller, P., *Reading the Zohar: The Sacred Text of the Qabbalah*, Oxford, Oxford University Press, 2001.

370 *Gitagovinda*: see Ayenagar, Miller (661), Mukhopadhyay, Varma.

371 Glatzer, N. N., *Language of Faith: A Selection from the Most Expressive Jewish Prayers*, New York, Schocken Books, 1967.

372 Glunz, H. H., *History of the Vulgate in England from Alcuin to Roger Bacon*, Cambridge, Cambridge University Press, 1933.

373 Goldin, J., *The Living Talmud: The Wisdom of the Fathers and its Classical Commentaries*, New York, Harper and Row, 1960.

374 Goldman, R. P., and Sutherland, S., *The Ramayana of Valmiki*, Princeton, Princeton University Press, 1984.

375 Goldstein, D., *The Jewish Poets of Spain*, London, Penguin, 1965.

376 Gomez, L. O., *Land of Bliss: Introductions and English Translations*, Honolulu, University of Hawaii Press, 1996.

377 Gonda, J., *Vedic Literature (Samhitas and Brahmanas)*, Wiesbaden, Harrassowitz, 1975.

378 — *The Rgvidhana: English Translation with an Introduction and Notes*, Utrecht, Osthoek, 1951.

379 Goodall, D., *Hindu Scriptures*, London, Phoenix, 1996.

380 Goodman, L. E., *Rambam: Readings in the Philosophy of Moses Maimonides*, New York, Viking Press, 1976.

381 Gopal Singh, *Sri Guru-Granth Sahib: English Version*, Delhi, Kapur, 1964.

382 Gore, N. A., *The Uvasagadasao: The Seventh Anga of the Jain Canon*, Poona, Oriental Book Agency, 1953.

383 Gotschalk, R., *The Bhagavad Gita*, Delhi, Motilal Banarsidass, 1985.

384 Govinda, A., *The Psychological Attitude of Early Buddhist Philosophy: Its Systematic Representation according to Abhidhamma Tradition*, London, Rider, 1961.

385 *Govindalilamrita*: see Lopez (pp. 244–68).

386 Goyal, S. R., *A Religious History of Ancient India: Pre-Vedic, Vedic, Jain and Buddhist Religions*, Kusumanjali Prakashan, Meerut, 1984.

387 Graham, A. C., *Chuang Tzu: The Inner Chapters*, London, Allen & Unwin, 1981.

388 Graham, W., *Divine Word and Prophetic Word in Early Islam: A Reconsideration of the Sources, with Special Reference to the Divine Saying or Hadith Qudsi*, The Hague, Mouton, 1977.

389 Grant, R. M., *The Apostolic Fathers*, New York, Nelson, 1964–8.

390 *Great Learning*: see Chai, Chan, Hughes.

391 Green, A., *A Guide to the Zohar*, Stanford, Stanford University Press, 2004.

392 Greenslade, S. L., *The Cambridge History of the Bible*, III, *The West from the Reformation to the Present Day*, Cambridge, Cambridge University Press, 1963.

393 Greenup, A. W., *Sukkah, Mishna and Tosefta*, London, SPCK, 1925.

394 Gregory of Nyssa: see Malherbe.

395 Griffith, R. T. H., *The Ramayan of Valmiki*, London, Trubner, 1870–4.

396 — *Hymns of the Rigveda*, New Delhi, Munshiram Manoharlal, 1987.

397 — *The Texts of the White Yajurveda*, Varanasi, Chowkhamba Sanskrit Series, 1976.

398 — *Yusuf and Zulaikha: A Poem by Jami*, London, Routledge, 2000.

399 Griffiths, P. J., *The Realm of Awakening: A Translation and Study of the Tenth Chapter of Asanga's Mahayanasangraha*, Oxford, Oxford University Press, 1989.

400 Grimstone, L., and Sekida, K., *Two Zen Classics: Mumonkan and Hekiganroku*, New York, Weatherhill, 1977.

401 Growse, F. S., *The Ramayana of Tulasi Das*, Delhi, Motilal Banarsidass, 1978.

402 Gu, H., *The Conduct of Life, or, The Universal Order of Confucius*, London, John Murray, 1908.

403 Guenther, H. V., *The Jewel Ornament of Liberation*, London, Rider, 1959.

404 — *Buddhist Philosophy in Theory and Practice*, London, Penguin, 1972.

405 — *The Life and Teaching of Naropa*, Oxford, Oxford University Press, 1971.

406 *Guide for the Perplexed*: see Friedlander, Roth.

407 Guillaume, A., *New Light on the Life of Muhammad*, Manchester, Manchester University Press, n.d.

408 — *The Life of Muhammad: A Translation of Ishaq's Sirat Rasul Allah*, Oxford, Oxford University Press, 1967.

409 Guraya, M. Y., *Origins of Islamic Jurisprudence: With Special Reference of Muwatta Imam Malik*, Delhi, Noor Publishing House, 1992.

410 Gurnam Singh, *Sikh Musicology: Sri Guru Granth Sahib and Hymns of the Human Spirit*, New Delhi, Kanishka, 2001.

411 *Guru Granth Sahib*: see Bhave, Buxi, Gopal, Gurnam, Kaur, Khushwant, Kirpal, Massey, Mohan, Pashaura, Sangat.

412 [Guru Nanak], *Janam Sakhi, or the Biography of Guru Nanak, Founder of the Sikh Religion*, Dehra Dun, 1885.

413 Guru Nanak: see *Guru Granth Sahib*, Kohli.

414 Gutwirth, I., *The Kabbalah and Jewish Mysticism*, New York, Philosophical Library, 1987.

415 Guy, J., 'Jain Manuscript Painting', in Pal *q.v.*, pp. 89–99.

416 Gyaltsen, K. R. K., *The Jewel Ornament of Liberation: The Wish-fulfilling Gem of the Noble Teachings*, Ithaca, Snow Lion, 1998.

417 Habig, M. A., *St Francis of Assisi: Writings and Early Biographies*, Chicago, Franciscan Herald Press, 1973.

418 Hadith: see Abu Huraira, Ajjaf, Ali, Asad, Azami, Brown, Cleary, Dickinson, El-Moughy, Ibrahim, Khan, Lucas, Siddiqi, Torrey, Wensinck.

419 *Haedong Kosung Chon*: see Lee.

420 Hafiz: see Arberry, Bell, Bicknell, Boylan, Clarke, Mansfield, Robinson.

421 Haiku: see Beilenson, Bly, Chamberlain, Corman, Hamill, Henderson, Keene, Lowenstein, Miner, Qiu, Sato, Stock, Stryk, Ueda, Yuasa.

422 Hakeda, Y. S., *Kukai: Major Works*, New York, Columbia University Press, 1972.

423 HaLevi, Judah: see Carmi (179), Salaman.

424 Halevi, Z.b.S., *Tree of Life: An Introduction to the Kabbalah*, London, Rider, 1972.

425 — *The Way of Kabbalah*, London, Rider, 1976.

426 Hamill, S., *Narrow Road to the Interior*, Boston, Shambhala, 1991.

427 Hanbal, ibn: see Baroody, Ibn Duyan, Lucas.

428 Hardy, F., *Viraha-Bhakti: The Early History of Kṛṣṇa Devotion in India*, New Delhi, Oxford University Press, 2001.

429 Hardy Wallis, N., *The New Testament: Translated by William Tyndale 1534: A Reprint of the Edition of 1534*, Cambridge, Cambridge University Press, 1939.

430 Harmansen, M. K., *The Conclusive Argument from God: Shah Wali Allah of Delhi's Hujjat alBaligha*, Leiden, Brill, 1995.

431 Harris, I. C., *The Continuity of Madhyamaka and Yogacara in Indian Mahayana Buddhism*, Leiden, Brill, 1991.

432 Harvey, A., *The Way of Passion: A Celebration of Rumi*, Berkeley, Frog Ltd, 1994.

433 — *Light Upon Light: Inspirations from Rumi*, Berkeley, North Atlantic Books, 1996.

434 Hasan, A., *The Early Development of Islamic Jurisprudence*, Islamabad, Islamic Research Institute, 1970.

435 Hasan alBasri: see Cooperson.

436 Hastings, A., *A Concise Guide to the Documents of the Second Vatican Council*, London, Darton, Longman & Todd, 1968.

437 Havens, N., *Kami*, Tokyo, Institute for Japanese Culture and Classics, 1998.

438 Hazlitt, W., *Table Talk of Martin Luther*, London, Fount, 1995.

439 *Heart Sutra*: see Conze.

440 Heer, N., *The Precious Pearl: AlJami's Al-Durrah al-Fakhirah . . .* , Albany, State University of New York Press, 1979.

441 *Hekiganroku*: see Blyth, Cleary, Grimstone, Reps.

442 Henderson, H. G., *An Introduction to Haiku: An Anthology of Poems and Poets from Basho to Shiki*, New York, Doubleday, 1958.

443 Hennecke, E., *et al.*, *New Testament Apocrypha*, I, *Gospels and Related Writings*, London, Lutterworth, 1963.

444 — *New Testament Apocrypha*, II, *Apostolic and Early Church Writings*, London, Lutterworth, 1965.

445 Henricks, R. G., *Lao-Tzu: A New Translation Based on the Recently Discovered Ma-wang-tui Texts*, New York, Ballantine, 1989.

446 Hertz, J., *Authorized Daily Prayer Book*, New York, Bloch, 1961.

447 Hess, L., and Shukdev Singh, *The Bijak of Kabir*, Delhi, Motilal Banarsidass, 1986.

448 Hesychios of Sinai, 'On Watchfulness and Holiness', in Palmer, *q.v.*

449 *Hevajra Tantra*: see Farrow, Snellgrove, Willemen.

450 Hillerbrand, H., *The Reformation in its Own Words*, London, SCM Press, 1964.

451 Hill, W. D. P., *Holy Lake of the Acts of Rama*, Calcutta, Oxford University Press, 1952.

452 Hirota, D., 'On Attaining the Settled Mind: The Condition of the Nembutsu Practitioner', in Tanabe *q.v.*

453 *Historia Monachorum*: see Russell.

454 Hodge, S., and Boord, M., *The Illustrated Tibetan Book of the Dead: A New Translation with Commentary*, London, Godsfield, 2000.

455 Hoffman, Y., *The Sound of the One Hand*, London, Paladin, 1977.

456 *Hokyo-ki*: see Kodera.

457 Holland, M., *The Duties of Brotherhood in Islam*, Leicester, Islamic Foundation, 1980.

458 — *Inner Dimensions of Islamic Worship*, Leicester, Islamic Foundation, 1983.

459 Holmes, K., *et al.*, *The Ultimate Mahayana Explanatory Text on the Changeless Nature (The Uttara*

Tantra Shastra), Eskdalemuir, Kagyu Samye Ling, 1980.

460 — *Maitreya on Buddha Nature*, Forres, Altea, 1999.

461 — *Gems of Dharma, Jewels of Freedom*, Forres, Altea, 1995.

462 — *The Ornament of Clear Realization: A Commentary on the Prajñaparamita of the Maitreya Buddha (Abhisamayalankara-prajñaparamita-upadesha-shastra)*, Delhi, Sri Satguru Publications, 2001.

463 Homayounfar, K., *Love Mad: Poems of Rumi*, Leicester, Matador, 2007.

464 Hood, A. B. E., *St Patrick: His Writings and Muirchu's 'Life'*, London, Phillimore, 1978.

465 Hoogcarspel, E., *The Central Philosophy, Basic Verses/Nagarjuna*, Amsterdam, Olive Press, 2005.

466 Hooper, J. S. M., *Hymns of the Alvars*, Calcutta, Association Press, 1929.

467 Hopkins, J., and Lati Rimpoche, *The Precious Garland and the Song of the Four Mindfulnesses*, London, Allen & Unwin, 1975.

468 — *Kalachakra Tantra: A Rite of Initiation for the Stage of Generation*, Boston, Wisdom Publications, 1999.

469 Howard, E. C., *Minhaj etTalibin: A Manual of Muhammadan Law according to the School of Shafii*, London, Thacker, 1914.

470 *Hridaya*: see Conze.

471 Huang, C., *The Analects of Confucius: A Literal Translation*, Oxford, Oxford University Press, 1997.

472 Huayan: see Chan, Chang, Cleary.

473 Hudson, D. D., *Krishna's Mandala: Bhagavata Religion and Beyond*, Oxford, Oxford University Press, 2010.

474 Huey, R. N., *The Making of Shinkokinshu*, Cambridge, Harvard University Asia Center, 2002.

475 Hughes, E. R., *The Great Learning and The Mean-in-Action*, London, Dent, 1942.

476 Huineng: see Chan (195), Luk, Yampolsky.

477 *Hujjat alBaligha*: see Harmansen.

478 Hume, R. E., *Thirteen Principal Upanishads*, Oxford, Oxford University Press, 1971.

479 *I Ching*: see *Yijing*.

480 Ibn Duyan, I. M., *Crime and Punishment under Hanbali Law, Being a Translation from Manar al-Sabil . . .* , Cairo, 1961.

481 Ibn Ezra: see Carmi (179), Solis-Cohen.

482 Ibn Gabirol: see Carmi (179), Zangwill.

483 Ibn Hajar al'Asqalani, A., *Fath alBari*, Cairo, 1939/1348.

484 Ibn Hanbal: see Baroody, Ibn Duyan, Lucas.

485 Ibn Ishaq: see Guillaume.

486 Ibrahim, E., and Johnson-Davies, D., *An-Nawawi's Forty Hadith*, Cambridge, The Islamic Texts Society, 1997.

487 — *Forty Hadith Qudsi*, Cambridge, The Islamic Texts Society, 1997.

488 Ignatius: see Ivens, Munitiz.

489 *Ihya Ulum udDin*: see Faris, Holland, MacDonald, Winter.

490 Inagaki, H., *The Three Pure Land Sutras*, Berkeley, Numata Center for Buddhist Translation and Research, 2003.

491 Insler, S., *The Gathas of Zarathustra*, Leiden, Brill, 1975.

492 *Institutes*: see Battles.

493 *Ise niku sakitake no ben*: see Teeuwen.

494 Ivens, M., *Understanding the Spiritual Exercises*, Leominster, Gracewing, 1998.

495 Iyer, S. V., *The Varaha Purana*, Delhi, N. P. Jain, 1985.

496 Jacobs, L., *Jewish Mystical Testimonies*, New York, Schocken Books, 1977.

497 Jafri, S. H. M., *The Origins and Early Development of Shi'a Islam*, London, Longman, 1979.

498 Jain Agama: see Gore.

499 Jaini, J. L., *Tattvarthadhigama Sutra: A Treatise on the Essential Principles of Jainism*, Arrah, Prasada, 1923.

500   Jalbani, G. N., *Shah Walyullah's Ta'wil alHadith*, New Delhi, Kitab Bhavan, 1981.

501   — and Fry, D. B., *Lamahat and Sataat of Shah Waliullah*, London, Octagon, 1980.

502   — and Pendlebury, D., *The Sacred Knowledge of the Higher Functions of the Mind: Altaf alQuds of Shah Waliullah of Delhi*, London, Octagon Press, 1982.

503   Jami: see FitzGerald, Griffith, Heer, Rehatsek, Rogers.

504   *Janam Sakhi*: see [Guru Nanak], Vir.

505   *Japji*: see Bhave, Kirpal Singh, Sangat Singh.

506   Jataka: see Francis, Jones.

507   Jewish Prayer Book: see Alexander, A., Birnbaum, Garfiel, Gaster, Hertz, Pool, Sacks, *Siddur Lev Hadash, Service of the Heart*, Singer, Swartz.

508   Jodh Singh and Dharam Singh, *Sri Dasam Granth Sahib*, Patiala Heritage Publications, 1999.

509   John of the Cross: see Flower, Kavanaugh, Krabbenhoft, Matthew.

510   Johnson, W. J., *The Bhagavad Gita*, Oxford, Oxford University Press, 2008.

511   Johnston, E. H., *The Buddhacarita: or, Acts of the Buddha*, Calcutta, Baptist Mission Press, 1935–6.

512   Jones, J. G., *Tales and Teachings of the Buddha: The Jataka Stories in Relation to the Pali Canon*, London, Allen & Unwin, 1979.

513   Joshi, M. C., *The Samaveda: Sanskrit Text with English Translation*, New Delhi, Munshiram Monoharlal, 1980.

514   Kabbalah: see Dan, Gikatilla, Giller, Green, Gutwirth, Halevi, Lachower, Mathers, Matt, Robinson, Sassoon, Schafer, Scholem, Spector, Sperling, Weinstein.

515   Kabir: see Das, Dass, Hess, Vaudeville.

516   Kada Azumamaro: see Nosco.

517   *Kalacakra Sutra*: see Hopkins, Kilty, Wallace.

518   *Kalpacintamanih*: see Sharma.

519   *Kamakalavilasa*: see Rawson (pp. 206–9).

520   Kamali, S. A., *Al-Ghazali's Tahfut al-Falasifah*, Lahore, Pakistan Philosophical Congress, 1963.

521   Kamo Mabuchi: see Nosco.

522   Kane, P. V., *History of Dharmsastra*, Poona, Bhandarakar Oriental Institutes, 1930–62.

523   Kapleau, P., *The Three Pillars of Zen*, New York, Harper & Row, 1966.

524   Karlgren, B., *Analytic Dictionary of Chinese and Sino-Japanese*, Paris, Guenther, 1923.

525   Kasoff, I., *The Thought of Chang Tsai (1020–1077)*, Cambridge, Cambridge University Press, 1984.

526   *Kaśyapaparivarta Sutra*: see Stael-Holstein.

527   Kato, B., *et al.*, *The Threefold Lotus Sutra*, New York, Weatherhill, 1975.

528   Kaur Singh, N-G., *The Name of My Beloved: Verses of the Sikh Gurus*, San Francisco, Harper, 1995.

529   Kavanaugh, K., *John of the Cross: Doctor of Light and Love*, New York, Crossroad, 1999.

530   Kawamura, L., *Golden Zephyr*, Emeryville, Dharma Publications, 1975.

531   Keel, H., *Chinul, the Founder of the Korean Son Tradition*, Seoul, Po Chin Chai, 1984.

532   Keene, D., *The Narrow Road to Oku*, Tokyo, Kodansha International, 1996.

533   Keith, A. B., *Aitareya Aranyaka*, Oxford, Clarendon Press, 1909.

534   — *Rigveda Brahmanas: The Aitareya and Kausitaki Brahmanas of the Rigveda*, Cambridge, Harvard University Press, 1920.

535   Kellner, M., *Maimonides on Human Perfection*, Atlanta, Scholars Press, 1990.

536   — *Maimonides on the 'Decline of the Generations' and the Nature of Rabbinic Authority*, Albany, State University of New York Press, 1996.

537   Kelly, J. N. D., *Early Christian Creeds*, London, Longmans, 1950.

538   Kenner, H., *The Pound Era*, London, Pimlico, 1991.

539   Khadduri, M., *Al-Shafi'i's Risal: Treatise on the Foundations of*

Islamic Jurisprudence, Cambridge, The Islamic Texts Society, 1987.

540 Khaldi, T., *The Quran: A New Translation*, London, Penguin, 2008.

541 Khan, M. M., *Sahih alBukhari*, New Delhi, Kitab Bhavan, 1984.

542 Khatib, M. M., *The Bounteous Koran*, London, Macmillan, 1986.

543 Khattab, H., *The Isra and Miraj: The Prophet's Night-Journey and Ascent into Heaven*, London, Dar al-Taqwa, 1989.

544 Khushwant Singh, *Hymns of Guru Nanak*, New Delhi, Orient Longmans, 1969.

545 Kilty, G., *Ornament of Stainless Light: An Exposition of the Kalacakra Tantra*, Boston, Wisdom Publications, 2004.

546 Kim, J., *et al.*, eds, *Korean Cultural Heritage*, II, Seoul, Korea Foundation, 1996.

547 Kingsbury, F., and Phillips, G. E., *Hymns of the Tamil Saivite Saints*, Calcutta, Association Press, 1921.

548 Kirkpatrick, R., *The Divine Comedy*, London, Penguin, 2006–7.

549 Kirpal Singh, *Guru Nanak's Japuji: A Descriptive Bibliography*, Patiala, Punjabi University, 1990.

550 Kitabatake: see Varley.

551 Knowles, D., *The Monastic Order in England: A History of its Development from the Times of St Dunstan to the Fourth Lateran Council, 943–1216*, Cambridge, Cambridge University Press, 1949.

552 Kochumottom, T., *A Buddhist Doctrine of Experience: A New Translation and Interpretation of the Works of Vasubandhu the Yogacarin*, Delhi, Motilal Banarsidass, 1982.

553 Kodera, T. J., *Dogen's Formative Years in China: An Historical Study and Annotated Translation of the Hokyo-ki*, London, Routledge, 1980.

554 Kohli, S. S., *Travels of Guru Nanak*, Chandigarh, Panjabi University, 1969.

555 *Kojiki*: see Chamberlain, G., Philippi, Post, Robinson.

556 *Kokinshu*: see Lindberg-Wada, McCullough.

557 Kokugaku: see Burns.

558 *Kontakia*: see Lash.

559 Koran: see Ali, S., Ali, A. Y., Arberry, Cragg, Dawood, Gatje, Khaldi, Khatib, Palmer, Shakir, Watt.

560 Krabbenhoft, K., *The Poems of St John of the Cross*, New York, Harcourt Brace, 1999.

561 Kramisch, S., *Exploring India's Sacred Art*, Philadelphia, University of Pennsylvania Press, 1983.

562 Kravitz, L., and Olitzky, K. M., *Pirke Avot: A Modern Commentary on Jewish Ethics*, New York, UAHC Press, 1993.

563 Krishna Warrier, A. G., *The Sakta Upanishad*, Madras, Adyar Library and Research Center, 1967.

564 Ku: see Gu.

565 Kukai: see Abe, Hakeda, White, R., Yamamoto.

566 *Kulacudamani*: see Finn.

567 Kunst, A., and Shastri, J. L., eds, *Ancient Indian Tradition and Mythology: Puranas in Translation*, Delhi, Motilal Banarsidass, 1969– .

568 Kwok, D. W. Y., *Scientism in Chinese Thought, 1900–1950*, New Haven, Yale University Press, 1965.

569 Kwok Man-Ho, *The Tao te Ching*, Rockport, Element, 1997.

570 Lachower, F., and Tishby, I., trsl. Goldstein, D., *The Wisdom of Zohar: An Anthology of Texts*, Oxford, The Littman Library, 1989.

571 Lalye, P. G., *Studies in Devi Bhagavata*, Bombay, Popular Prakashan, 1973.

572 *Lamahat*: see Jalbani.

573 Lampe, G. W. H., ed., *The Cambridge History of the Bible*, II, *The West from the Fathers to the Reformation*, Cambridge, Cambridge University Press, 1969.

574 *Lankavatara Sutra*: see Suzuki.

575 Lao Tzu: see Laozi.

576 Laozi: see Cleary (223), Dolby, Feng, Henricks, Kwok Man-Ho, Moeller, Ryden, Waley (988).

577 Lapidge, M., and Sharpe, R., *A Bibliography of Celtic-Latin*

Literature, 400–1200, Dublin, Royal Irish Academy, 1985.

578 Larson, G. J., *Classical Samkhya: An Interpretation of its History and Meaning*, Delhi, Motilal Banarsidass, 1969.

579 Lash, E., trsl., *Kontakia: On the Life of Christ*, San Francisco, HarperCollins, n.d.

580 Lau, D. C., *Mencius*, London, Penguin, 1970.

581 — *The Analects*, London, Penguin, 1979.

582 Lee, P. H., *Lives of Eminent Korean Monks: The Haedong Kosung Chon*, Cambridge, Harvard University Press, 1969.

583 Lee, P. H., *et al.*, *Sourcebook of Korean Civilization*, Columbia University Press, 1993.

584 Legge, J., *Sacred Books of China: The Texts of Taoism*, Oxford, Oxford University Press, 1891.

585 — *The Chinese Classics*, Oxford, Clarendon Press, 1893–5.

586 Leggett, T., *Sankara on the Yoga-Sutras*, London, Routledge, 1981– .

587 Leighton, T. D., and Okumura, S., *Dogen's Pure Standards for the Zen Community: A Translation of the Eihei Shingi*, Albany, State University of New York Press, 1996.

588 — *The Wholehearted Way: A Translation of Eihei Dogen's Bendowa*, Boston, Tuttle Publishing, 1997.

589 — *Visions of Awakening Space and Time: Dogen and the Lotus Sutra*, Oxford, Oxford University Press, 2009.

590 Leys, S., *The Analects of Confucius*, New York, Norton, 1997.

591 Lhalungpa, L. P., *The Life of Milarepa: A New Translation from the Tibetan*, London, Granada, 1979.

592 Li, J., *Lives of Great Monks and Nuns*, Berkeley, Numata Center, 2002.

593 Li Rongxi, *The Life of Asvaghosa Bodhisattva*, Berkeley, BDK, 2002.

594 — *The Life of Nagarjuna Bodhisattva*, Berkeley, BDK, 2002.

595 *Life of Moses*: see Malherbe.

596 *Liji*: see Legge.

597 Limaye, S. V., *Mahayanasutralamkara by Asanga*, Delhi, Sri Satguru Publications, 2000.

598 Lindberg, C., *King Henry's Bible: MS Bodley 277, The Revised Version of the Wyclif Bible*, Stockholm, Almqvist & Wiksell, 1999–2004.

599 — *A Manual of the Wyclif Bible, Including the Psalms*, Stockholm, Stockholm University, 2007.

600 Lindberg-Wada, G., *Poetic Allusion: Aspects of the Role Played by Kokin Wakashu as a Source of Poetic Allusion in Genji monogatari*, Stockholm, Institute of Oriental Languages, 1983.

601 Lindtner, C., *Master of Wisdom: Translations and Studies*, Berkeley, Dharma Publications, 1986.

602 Lopez, D. S., ed., *Religions of India in Practice*, Princeton, Princeton University Press, 1995.

603 *Lotus Sutra*: see Kato, Leighton, Watson.

604 Lowenstein, T., *Classic Haiku: The Greatest Japanese Poetry from Basho, Buson, Issa, Shiki and Their Followers*, London, Baird, 2007.

605 Lucas, S. C., *Constructive Critics, Hadith Literature, and the Articulation of Sunni Islam: The Legacy of the Generation of Ibn Sa'd Ibn Ma'in, and Ibn Hanbal*, Leiden, Brill, 2004.

606 Luibheid, C., and Rorem, P., *Pseudo Dionysius: The Complete Works*, New York, Paulist Press, 1987.

607 Luk, C., *The Transmission of the Mind Outside the Teaching*, New York, Grove Press, 1974.

608 — *Ch'an and Zen Teaching*, 3, London, Rider, 1962.

609 *Lunyu*: see *Analects*.

610 Lupton, L., *A History of the Geneva Bible*, London, Fauconberg Press, 1966– .

611 Luther: see Aland, Hazlitt, Pelikan, Wace.

612 Lynn, R. J., *The Classic of Changes: A New Translation of the I Ching as Interpreted by Wang Bi*, New York, Columbia University Press, 1994.

613 Macdonald, D. B., 'Emotional Religion in Islam as Affected by Music and Singing, being a Translation of a Book [*Kitab Adab asSama w'alWajd*] of the Ihya Ulum ad-Din', *Journal of the Royal Asiatic Society*, 1901, pp. 195–252, 705–48; 1902, 1–28.

614 Macdonnell, A. A., *Hymns from the Rig Veda*, Oxford, Oxford University Press, 1923.

615 Macfie, J. M., *The Ramayana of Tulsidas: The Bible of Northern India*, Edinburgh, T & T Clark, 1930.

616 Machwe, P. M., *Namdev: Life and Philosophy*, Patiala, Punjabi University Press, 1968.

617 Mackey, J. P., *An Introduction to Celtic Christianity*, Edinburgh, T & T Clark, 1995.

618 Macnicol, N., *Hindu Scriptures*, London, Dent, 1938.

619 Madhva: see Rao, Sonde.

620 *Madhyamakakarika*: see Batchelor, Garfield, Hoogcarspel, Lindtner.

621 *Madhyanta-vibhaga-bhasya*: see Anacker, Stcherbatsky.

622 *Mahabharata*: see Bolland, Dutt, Ganguli, Mani, Matilal, Roy, van Buitenen.

623 *Maharatnakuta*: see Chang (197).

624 *Mahayanottaratantrasastra*: see Holmes.

625 Maimonides: see David, Farmer, Friedlander, Gandz, Goodman, Kellner, Minkin, Rosner, Roth, Silver, Stitskin, Yale Judaica Series.

626 Maitreya: see Asanga, Sponberg, Vasubandhu.

627 *Majjhima Nikaya*: see Nanamoli.

628 Malherbe, A. J., and Ferguson, E., *Gregory of Nyssa: The Life of Moses*, New York, Paulist Press, 1978.

629 Malik b. Anas: see atTarjumana, Dutton, Guraya.

630 Mani, V., *Puranic Encyclopaedia: A Comprehensive Dictionary with Special Reference to the Epic and Pauranic Literature*, Delhi, Motilal Banarsidass, 1975.

631 Mansfield, P., *The Desert is My Oasis: Poems of Hafiz*, London, Kegan Paul International, 1994.

632 *Mantiq atTair*: see Darbandi.

633 Mantrayana: see Abe, Yamamoto.

634 Manu: see O'Flaherty, Kane, Olivelle.

635 Marra, M. F., *The Poetics of Motoori Norinaga: A Hermeneutical Journey*, Honolulu, University of Hawaii Press, 2007.

636 Mascaro, J., *The Bhagavad Gita*, London, Penguin, 1962.

637 Massey, J., *The Doctrine of Ultimate Reality in Sikh Religion: A Study of Guru Nanak's Hymns in the Adi Granth*, New Delhi, Manohar Publications, 1991.

638 Masunaga, R., *A Primer of Soto Zen: A Translation of Dogen's Shobogenzo Zuimonki*, London, Routledge, 1972.

639 Mathers, S. L. M., *The Kabbalah: The Essential Texts from the Zohar*, London, Watkins, 2005.

640 Matilal, B., ed., *Moral Dilemmas in the Mahabharata*, Shimla, Indian Institute of Advanced Study, 1989.

641 Matt, D. C., *Zohar, the Book of Enlightenment*, London, SPCK, 1983.

642 — *The Essential Kabbalah: The Heart of Jewish Mysticism*, San Francisco, Harper, 1996.

643 Matthew, I., *The Impact of God: Soundings from St John of the Cross*, New York, Crossroad, 1999.

644 Maurer, W. H., *Pinnacles of India's Past: Selections from the Rigveda*, Philadelphia, Benjamins, 1986.

645 McCann, J., *The Rule of Saint Benedict*, London, Burns Oates, 1963.

646 McCarthy, R. J., *Freedom and Fulfilment: An Annotated Translation of alGhazali's al-Munqidh min al-Dalal*, Boston, Twayne, 1980.

647 McCitterick, D., *The Cambridge Geneva Bible of 1591: A Facsimile Reprint . . .*, Cambridge, Cambridge University Press, 1992.

648 McCullough, H. C., *Kokin wakashu: The First Imperial Anthology of*

Japanese Poetry, Stanford, Stanford University Press, 1985.

649 — *Brocade by Night: Kokin wakashu and the Court Style in Japanese Classical Poetry*, Stanford, Stanford University Press, 1985.

650 McGinn, B., *The Presence of God: A History of Western Christian Mysticism*, II: *The Growth of Mysticism*, London, SCM Press, 1995.

651 McKane, W., *AlGhazali's Book of Fear and Hope*, Leiden, Brill, 1962.

652 McLeod, W. H., *Textual Sources for the Study of Sikhism*, Manchester, Manchester University Press, 1984.

653 — *Guru Nanak and the Sikh Religion*, Oxford, Clarendon Press, 1968.

654 — *The B40 Janam Sakhi: An English Translation . . .* , Amritsar, Guru Nanak Dev University, 1980.

655 McManners, J., ed., *The Oxford Illustrated History of Christianity*, Oxford, Oxford University Press, 1990.

656 Mencius/Mengzi: see Bloom, Chai, Chan, Dobson, Lau, Legge, Waley.

657 Metzger, B., and Coogan, M. D., *The Oxford Companion to the Bible*, Oxford, Oxford University Press, 1993.

658 Mi-las-ri-pa: see Milarepa.

659 Milarepa: see Chang, G., Evans-Wentz, Lhalungpa.

660 Miller, B. S., *Yoga: Discipline of Freedom: The Yoga Sutra Attributed to Patanjali*, New York, Bantam Books, 1998.

661 — *Love Song of the Dark Lord*, New York, Columbia University Press, 1977.

662 Miner, E., *Japanese Poetic Diaries*, Berkeley, University of California Press, 1969.

663 — and Hiroko Odagiri, *The Monkey's Straw Raincoat and Other Poetry of the Basho School*, Princeton, Princeton University Press, 1981.

664 *Min Huna Na'alam*: see alFaruqi.

665 Minkin, J. S., *The World of Moses Maimonides, with Selections from*

His Writings, New York, Yoseloff, 1957.

666 Mirabai: see Futehally.

667 *Mishkat alAnwar*: see Gairdner.

668 *Mishkat alMasabih*: see Robson.

669 Mishnah: see Blackman, Danby, Goldin, Kravitz, Neusner, Rosenblatt.

670 *Mishqat alAnwar*: see Gairdner.

671 Mitchell, S., *The Bhagavad Gita*, London, Rider, 2000.

672 Mitchiner, J. E., *The Yuga Purana*, Calcutta, Chaudhuri, 1986.

673 Moeller, H., *Daodejing: Complete Translation and Commentary*, Chicago, Open Court, 2007.

674 Mohan Singh, *The Japu by Guru Nanak Deva: A Prose Translation . . .* , Chandhigarh, Vikas, 1979.

675 Mojaddedi, J., *The Masnavi of Jalal udDin Rumi*, Oxford, Oxford University Press, 2004.

676 *Monumenta Ignatiana*, Rome, 1934– .

677 *Moreh Nebuchim*: see Friedlander, Roth.

678 Morris, I., *The World of the Shining Prince: Court Life in Ancient Japan*, New York, Knopf, 1964.

679 Motoori Norinaga: see Brownlee, Marra, Nosco, Teeuwen.

680 Moyne, J. A., and Newman, R. J., *A Bird in the Garden of Angels: On the Life and Times and an Anthology of Rumi*, Costa Mesa, Mazda Publishers, 2007.

681 Muir, J., *Original Sanskrit Texts*, London, Trubner, 1872.

682 Mukhopadhyay, D., *In Praise of Krishna*, Delhi, B. R. Publishing, 1990.

683 *Mulamadhyamakakarika*: see *Madhyamakakarika*.

684 Muller, A. V., *The Spiritual Regulation of Peter the Great*, Seattle, University of Washington Press, 1972.

685 Muller, F. M., *Sukhavati-vyuha: Description of Sukhavati, the Land of Bliss*, Oxford, Clarendon Press, 1883.

686 *Mumonkan*: see Blyth, Grimstone, Reps.

687 Munitiz, J. A., and Endean, P., *Saint Ignatius of Loyola: Personal Writings*, London, Penguin, 1996.

688 *Munqidh min adDalal*: see McCarthy, Watt.

689 Munro, D. C., *The Life of St. Columban, by the Monk Jonas*, Felinfach, Llanerch, 1993.

690 Munro, D. J., *Images of Human Nature: A Sung Portrait*, Princeton, Princeton University Press, 1988.

691 Murad, A. H., *Selections from Fath al-Bari*, Cambridge, Muslim Academic Trust, 2000.

692 Murti, T. R. V., *The Central Philosophy of Buddhism*, London, Allen & Unwin, 1960.

693 Musa, M., *Vita Nuova*, Oxford, Oxford University Press, 2008.

694 Muslim: see Ajjaf, Siddiqi.

695 Nagao, G. M., *An Index to Asanga's Mahayanasamgraha*, Tokyo, International Institute for Buddhist Studies, 1994.

696 Nagarjuna: see Batchelor, Bhattacharya, Cheng, Frye, Garfield, Hopkins, Hoogcarspel, Kawamura, Li Rongxi, Lindtner, Murti.

697 Nanamoli, Bh., and Bodi, Bh., *The Middle Length Discourses of the Buddha*, Somerville, Wisdom Publications, 1995.

698 Narayan, K., *Storytellers, Saints, and Scoundrels: Folk Narrative in Hindu Religious Teaching*, Philadelphia, University of Pennsylvania Press, 1992.

699 Narayanan, V., *The Vernacular Veda: Revelation, Recitation, and Ritual*, Columbia, University of South Carolina Press, 1994.

700 Na-ro-chos-drug: see Guenther.

701 Naropa: see Guenther.

702 Natalio, F. M., *The Septuagint in Context: Introduction to the Greek Version of the Bible*, Leiden, Brill, 2000.

703 Nath, L. B., *The Adhyatma Ramayana: As Told in the Brahmanda Purana*, Allahabad, Panini, 1913.

704 Nayanar: see Kingsbury, Peterson, Ramachandran, Shulman.

705 Neuner, J., *The Christian Faith in the Doctrinal Documents of the Catholic Church*, London, Collins, 1983.

706 Neusner, J., *The Modern Study of the Mishnah*, Leiden, Brill, 1973.

707 — *The Tosefta*, New York, Ktav, 1977–86.

708 — *The Talmud of the Land of Israel*, Chicago, University of Chicago Press, 1982– .

709 — *The Talmud of Babylonia: An American Translation*, Chico, Scholars Press, 1984– .

710 — *The Mishnah: A New Translation*, New Haven, Yale University Press, 1988.

711 — *The Talmud Law, Theology, Narrative: A Sourcebook*, Lanham, University Press of America, 2005.

712 Nichiren: see Anesaki, Rodd, Watson, Yampolsky.

713 Nicholson, R. A., *Selected Poems from the Divani Shamsi Tabriz*, Cambridge, Cambridge University Press, 1898.

714 — *The Mathnawi of Jalaluddin Rumi*, London, Luzac, 1925–40.

715 — *Rumi, Poet and Mystic*, London, Allen & Unwin, 1952.

716 Nickelsburg, G. W. E., *Jewish Literature between the Bible and the Mishnah: A Historical and Literary Introduction*, London, SCM Press, 1981.

717 *Nihongi*: see Aston, Post.

718 Nikhilananda, Swami, *The Upanishads*, New York, Harper, 1949–59.

719 Ninety-five Theses: see Aland, Wace.

720 Nishijima, G. W., *Master Dogen's Shobogenzo*, Woking, Winter Bell, 1994.

721 Nishiyama, K., and Stevens, J., *Shobogenzo*, Sendai, 1975–83.

722 Nosco, P., *Remembering Paradise: Nativism and Nostalgia in Eighteenth-Century Japan*, Cambridge, Harvard University Press, 1990.

723 Nanamoli, Bh., *The Path of Purification: Bhadantacariya Buddhaghosa*, Berkeley, Shambhala, 1976.

724 Obermiller, E., *The Sublime Science of the Great Vehicle, Being a Manual of Buddhist Monism (Ratnagotravibhaga)*, Acta Orientealia, 1931.

725 — *History of Buddhism (Chos-hbyung)*, Leipzig, Harrassowitz, 1931–2.

726 — *The Jewelry of Scripture*, Delhi, Sri Satguru Publications, 1987.

727 O'Donnell, J. J., *Augustine: Confessions*, Oxford, Clarendon Press, 1992.

728 — *Augustine, Sinner and Saint: A New Biography*, London, Profile Books, 2005.

729 O'Donoghue, N. D., 'St Patrick's Breastplate', in Mackey.

730 Oelsner, H., *Dante's Vita Nuova: Together with the Version of Dante Gabriel Rossetti*, London, Chatto & Windus, 1908.

731 O'Flaherty, W. Doniger, *Hindu Myths: A Source Book Translated from the Sanskrit*, London, Penguin, 1975.

732 — *The Rig Veda*, London, Penguin, 1981.

733 — *Textual Sources for the Study of Religions: Hinduism*, Manchester, Manchester University Press, 1988.

734 — *The Laws of Manu*, London, Penguin, 1991.

735 Oldenberg, H., *The Grhya-Sutras*, Oxford, Clarendon Press, 1886.

736 Olivelle, P., *Samnyasa Upaniṣads: Hindu Scriptures on Asceticism and Renunciation*, New York, Oxford University Press, 1992.

737 — *The Early Upanishads: Annotated Text and Translation*, Oxford, Oxford University Press, 1998.

738 — *The Dharmasutras: The Law Codes of Ancient India*, Oxford, World's Classics, 1999.

739 — *The Law Code of Manu*, Oxford, Oxford University Press, 2004.

740 — *Manu's Code of Law: A Critical Edition and Translation of the Mānava-Dharmaśāstra*, Oxford: Oxford University Press, 2005.

741 — *Dharmasutra Parallels: Containing the Dharmasutras of Apastamba, Gautama, Baudhayana, and Vaisistha*, Delhi, Motilal Banarsidass, 2005.

742 Ostler, N., *Empires of the Word: A Language History of the World*, London, Folio Society, 2010.

743 Owen, E. C. E., *Some Authentic Acts of the Early Martyrs*, Oxford, Clarendon Press, 1927.

744 Padwick, C. E., *Muslim Devotions: A Study of Prayer-Manuals in Common Use*, London, SPCK, 1961.

745 Pagis: see Carmi.

746 Pal, P., *The Peaceful Liberators: Jain Art from India*, Los Angeles, Los Angeles County Museum of Art, 1994.

747 Palmer, E. H., *The Koran*, Oxford, Oxford University Press, 1951.

748 Palmer, G. E. H., *et al.*, trsl., *The Philokalia: The Complete Text*, London, Faber, 1979.

749 Palmer, M., *et al.*, *I Ching: The Shamanic Oracle of Change*, London, Thorsons, 1995.

750 — *The Book of Chuang Tzu*, London, Arkana, 1996.

751 Panikkar, R., *The Vedic Experience*, Los Angeles, University of California Press, 1977.

752 Papal Encyclicals: see Fremantle, Neuner.

753 Pargiter, F. E., *The Markandeya Purana*, Calcutta, The Asiatic Society, 1904.

754 Parry, T., *The Oxford Book of Welsh Verse*, Oxford, Oxford University Press, 1962.

755 Pashaura Singh, *The Guru Granth Sahib: Canon, Meaning and Authority*, Oxford, Oxford University Press, 2000.

756 Patanjali: see Chapple, Feuerstein, Leggett, Miller, Shearer, Whiteman, Yardi.

757 Patrick: see Hood, O'Donoghue.

758 Pearson, G., *Coverdale: Writings and Translations*, Cambridge, Parker Society, 1844.

759 Pegis, A. C., *et al.*, *Summa Contra Gentiles*, Notre Dame, University of Notre Dame Press, 1975.

760 Pelikan, J., *Luther's Works*, St Louis, Concordia Publishing House, 1955–86.

761 Peter the Great: see Muller.

762 Peterson, I. V., *Poems to Śiva: The Hymns of the Tamil Saints*, Delhi, Motilal Banarsidass, 1991.

763 Philippi, D. L., *Kojiki: Translated with An Introduction and Notes*, Tokyo, University of Tokyo Press, 1969.

764 — *Norito: A New Translation of the Ancient Japanese Ritual Prayers*, Tokyo, Institute for Japanese Culture and Classics, 1959.

765 Pithawalla, M. B., *Steps to Prophet Zoroaster: A Book of Daily Zoroastrian Prayers*, n.p., 1916.

766 *Platform Sutra*: see Chan, Luk (608), Yampolsky.

767 Polycarp: see Ehrman, Grant, Owen.

768 Pool, D. S., *The Traditional Prayer Book for Sabbath and Festivals*, New Jersey, Behrman House, 1960.

769 Post, W., *The Sacred Scriptures of the Japanese*, New York, Schumann, 1952.

770 Pound, E., *Confucian Analects*, London, Peter Owen, 1956.

771 Powers, J., *The Yogacara School of Buddhism*, Metuchen, Scarecrow Press, 1991.

772 — *Wisdom of Buddha: The Samdhinirmocana Sutra*, Berkeley, Dharma Publications, 1995.

773 — *Two Commentaries on the Samdhinirmocana-Sutra*, Lewiston, Mellen Press, 1992.

774 Prajñaparamita: see Conze.

775 Prayer Book, Jewish: see Alexander, Birnbaum, Garfiel, Gaster, Hertz, Pool, Sacks, *Service of the Heart*, *Siddur Lev Hadash*, Singer, Swartz.

776 Pruden, L., *Abhidharmakoshabhasyam*, Berkeley, Asian Humanities Press, 1988–90.

777 — *Karmasiddhiprakarana: The Treatise on Action by Vasubandhu*, Berkeley, Asian Humanities Press, 1988.

778 Pseudo-Dionysius: see Luibheid.

779 Puranas: see Agrawala, Bhattacharya, Board of Scholars, Bryant, Dehejia, Deshpande, Dhal, Dimmitt, Gangadharan, Goodall, Iyer, Kunst, Mani, Mitchiner, Nath, O'Flaherty, Pargiter, Shah, Shastri, Tagare, Wilson.

780 Pure Land: see Gomez, Inagaki, Muller.

781 Qabbalah: see Dan, Gikatilla, Giller, Green, Gutwirth, Halevi, Lachower, Mathers, Matt, Robinson, Sassoon, Schafer, Scholem, Spector, Sperling, Weinstein.

782 Qiu, P., *Basho and the Dao: The Zhuangzi and the Transformation of Haikai*, Honolulu, University of Hawaii Press, 2005.

783 Quran: see Ali, S., Ali, A. Y., Arberry, Cragg, Dawood, Gatje, Khaldi, Khatib, Palmer, Shakir, Watt.

784 Rabia: see Cooperson, Derin, Smith and Schimmel, Upton.

785 Radhakrishnan, S., *The Principal Upaniṣads*, London, Allen & Unwin, 1968.

786 — *The Bhagavadgita with an Introductory Essay, Sanskrit Text, English Translation and Notes*, London, Allen and Unwin, 1948.

787 — and Moore, C. A., *A Source Book in Indian Philosophy*, Princeton, Princeton University Press, 1957.

788 Rai, R. K., *Dictionaries of Tantra Sastra, or the Tantrabhidhana*, Varanasi, Prachya, 1978.

789 Raidas: see Callewaert.

790 *Ramacaritmanas*: see Allchin, Growse, Hill.

791 Ramachandran, T. N., *Tirumurai the Sixth: Appar's Thaandaka Hymns*, Dharmapuram, 1995.

792 Ramanujan, A. K., *Speaking of Siva*, London, Penguin, 1973.

793 *Ramayana*: see Allchin, Dutt, Goldman, Griffith, Growse, Macfie, Mani, Sen, Shastri.

794 Ranade, H. G., *Katayana Srauta Sutra: Rules for the Vedic Sacrifice*, Pune, Ranade, 1978.

795 Rao, S. S., *Vedantasutras with the Commentary of Śri Madhvacharya*, Madras, Adyar Library, 1936.

796 *Ratnagotravjbhaga*: see Holmes, Obermiller.

797 Rawson, P., *The Art of Tantra*, London, Thames & Hudson, 1978.

798 Redhouse, J. W., *The Mesnevi of . . . Rumi*, London, Trubner, 1881.

799 Rehatsek, E., *The Beharistan of Jami: 'Abode of Spring', a Literal Translation from the Persian*, Benares, 1887.

800 Reif, S., *Judaism and Hebrew Prayer: New Perspectives on Jewish Liturgical History*, Cambridge, Cambridge University Press, 1995.

801 Reps, P., *Zen Flesh, Zen Bones*, London, Penguin, 1991.

802 Reynolds, B., *La Vita Nuova: Poems of Youth*, London, Penguin, 1971.

803 *rGyud bzi*: see Yeshe Donden.

804 *Rig Veda*: see Vedas.

805 *Rissho ankoku ron*: see Rodd.

806 Ritsema, R., and Karcher, S., *I Ching*, Shaftesbury, Element, 1994.

807 Ritter, H., and O'Kane, J., *The Ocean of the Soul: Man, the World, and God in the Stories of Farid udDin Attar*, Leiden, Brill, 2003.

808 Robertson, E., *Selected Writings of Dietrich Bonhoeffer*, London, Fount, 1995.

809 Robinson, G. W., *The Kojiki in the Life of Japan*, Tokyo, Center for East Asian Cultural Studies, 1969.

810 Robinson, I., *Moses Cordovero's Introduction to Kabbalah: An Annotated Translation of His Or Ne'erav*, New York, Yeshiva University Press, 1994.

811 Robson, J., *Mishkat alMasabih*, Lahore, S. M. Ashraf, 1965/1973.

812 Rodd, L. R., *Nichiren: Selected Writings*, Honolulu, University Press of Hawaii, 1980.

813 Rogers, A., *The Book of Joseph and Zuleikha*, London, Nutt, 1892.

814 Romanos: see Lash.

815 Rosenblatt, S., *The Interpretation of the Bible in the Mishnah*, Baltimore, Johns Hopkins Press, 1935.

816 Rosner, F., *Moses Maimonides' Treatise on Resurrection*, New York, Ktav, 1982.

817 — *Maimonides' Introduction to his Commentary on the Mishnah*, Northvale, Aronson, 1995.

818 Rossetti, D. G., *The Divine Comedy . . . , with La Vita Nuova translated by Rossetti*, London, Agenda Editions, 1979.

819 Roth, L., *The Guide for the Perplexed by Moses Maimonides*, London, Hutchinson, 1948.

820 Roy, P. C., *The Mahabharata of Krishna-Dwaipayana Vyasa*, Calcutta, Bharata Press, 1883–95.

821 Ruegg, D. S., *The Life of Bu-ston Rin po che, with the Tibetan Text of the Bu-ston rNam thar*, Rome, Italian Institute for the Middle and Far East, 1966.

822 Rumi: see Abdullah, Arberry, Barks, Chittick, Chopra, Cowan, Harvey, Homayounfar, Mojaddedi, Moyne, Nicholson, Redhouse, Schimmel, Star, Whinfield, Wilson.

823 Rupp, E. G., and Drewery, B., *Martin Luther*, New York, Arnold, 1970.

824 Russell, N., *The Lives of the Desert Fathers: The Historia Monachorum in Aegypto*, London, Mowbray, 1980.

825 Ryan, J., *Irish Monasticism: Origins and Development*, Ithaca, Cornell University Press, 1973.

826 Ryden, E., *Daodejing/Laozi*, Oxford, Oxford University Press, 2008.

827 Sacks, J., *Hebrew Daily Prayer Book*, London, Collins, 2006.

828 Safadi, Y. H., *Islamic Calligraphy*, London, Thames & Hudson, 1978.

829 Salaman, N., *Selected Poems of Jehudah Halevi*, Philadelphia, Jewish Publication Society, 1974.

830 *Samdhinirmocana Sutra*: see Powers.

831 Samkhya: see Larson, Radhakrishnan and Moore.

832 Sangat Singh, *Japji: Rendered into English*, Delhi, Hind Pocket Books, 1987.

833 Śankara: see Shankara.

834 Sassoon, G., *The Kabbalah Decoded: A New Translation of the 'Ancient of Days' Texts of the Zohar*, London, Duckworth, 1978.

835 Sastry, R. A., *Visnusahasranama: With the Bhasya of Sri Sankaracarya*, Adyar, Adyar Library General Series, 1980.

836 *Sataat*: see Jalbani.

837 Sato, H., *Basho's Narrow Road: Spring and Autumn Passages . . .*, Berkeley, Stone Bridge Press, 1996.

838 Satow, E., and Florenz, K., *Ancient Japanese Rituals*, Yokohama, Transactions of the Asian Society of Japan, 1879–1900.

839 Schafer, P., *Mirror of His Beauty: Feminine Images of God from the Bible to the Early Kabbalah*, Princeton, Princeton University Press, 2002.

840 Schaff, P., *A History of the Creeds of Christendom, with Translations*, London, Hodder & Stoughton, 1877.

841 — *The Creeds of the Greek and Latin Churches, with Translations*, London, Hodder & Stoughton, 1877.

842 — *The Creeds of the Evangelical Protestant Churches, with Translations*, London, Hodder & Stoughton, 1877.

843 Schelling, A., and Waldman, A., *Songs of the Sons and Daughters of Buddha*, Boston, Shambhala, 1996.

844 Schimmel, A., *The Triumphal Sun: A Study of the Works of Jalaloddin Rumi*, London, East-West Publications, 1980.

845 — *As Through a Veil: Mystical Poetry in Islam*, New York, Columbia University Press, 1982.

846 — *I Am Wind, You Are Fire: The Life and Work of Rumi*, Boston, Shambhala, 1992.

847 Schmithausen, L., *Alayavijnana: On the Origin and the Early Development of a Central Concept of Yogacara Philosophy*, Tokyo, International Institute for Buddhist Studies, 1987.

848 Scholem, G. S., *Zohar: The Book of Splendor*, New York, Schocken Books, 1949.

849 — *Major Trends in Jewish Mysticism*, New York, Schocken Books, 1964.

850 — *On the Kabbalah and its Symbolism*, New York, Commentary Classic, 1965.

851 — *On the Mystical Shape of the Godhead: Basic Concepts in the Kabbalah* (ed. J. Chipman), New York, Schocken Books, 1991.

852 Schroeder, H. J., *Canons and Decrees of the Council of Trent*, Rockford, TAN Books, 1978.

853 Schwartz, B. I., *The World of Thought in Ancient China*, Cambridge, Harvard University Press, 1985.

854 Seidensticker, E., *The Tale of Genji*, New York, Knopf, 1976.

855 Sekida: see Grimstone.

856 Sen, M. K., *The Ramayana Translated from the Original of Valmiki*, Calcutta, 1952– .

857 *Service of the Heart*, London, Union of Liberal and Progressive Synagogues, 1967.

858 Shah, P., *Vishnudharmottara-Purana: Puranic Legends and Rebirths*, Delhi, Parimal, 1999.

859 Shah Wali Allah: see Baljon, Harmansen, Jalbani.

860 Shakir, M. H., *Holy Quran*, London, Muhammadi Trust, 1985.

861 Shamasastry, R., *Kautilya's Arthashastra*, Mysore, Mysore Publishing House, 1961.

862 Shankara: see Apte, Date, Leggett.

863 Sharia: see AtTarjumana, Baroody, Doi, Dutton, Guraya, Hasan, Howard, Ibn Duyan, Khadduri, Lucas.

864 Sharma, A., *The Hindu Gita: Ancient and Classical Interpretations of the Bhagavadgita*, London, Duckworth, 1986.

865 Sharma, N. N., *Kalpacintamanih Damodara Bhatta: An Ancient Treatise on Tantra, Yantra and Mantra*, Delhi, Eastern Book Linkers, 1979.

866   Shastri, H. P., *The Ramayana of Valmiki*, London, Shanti Sadan, 1959–62.

867   Shastri, J. L., ed., *Brahma Purana*, Delhi, N. P.Jain, 1985–6.

868   Shaughnessy, E. L., *I Ching: The Classic of Changes*, New York, Ballantine Books, 1998.

869   Shearer, A., *Effortless Being: The Yoga Sutras of Patanjali*, London, Unwin, 1989.

870   Sheed, F. J., *The Confessions of St. Augustine*, London, Sheed & Ward, 1944.

871   *Shijing*: see Allen, Legge, Waley.

872   *Shinkokinshu*: see Brower, Carter, Huey.

873   *Shobogenzo*: see Cook, Leighton, Nishijima, Nishiyama.

874   *Shobogenzo Zuimonko*: see Masunaga.

875   Shotoku: see Aston.

876   Shulman, D. D., *Songs of the Harsh Devotee: The Tevaram of Cuntarmurttinayan*, Philadelphia, University of Pennsylvania, 1990.

877   Siddiqi, A. H., *Sahih Muslim*, New Delhi, Kitab Bhavan, 1977.

878   *Siddur Lev Hadash*, London, Union of Liberal and Progressive Synagogues, 1995.

879   *Siddur*: see Alexander, Birnbaum, Garfiel, Gaster, Sacks, Singer, Swartz.

880   Silver, D. J., *Maimonidean Criticism and the Maimonidean Controversy, 1180–1240*, Leiden, Brill, 1965.

881   Singer, S., and Hertz, J. H., *The Authorised Daily Prayer Book of the United Hebrew Congregations of the British Empire*, London, Eyre & Spottiswoode, 1957.

882   Sissons, C. H., *Dante Alighieri: The Divine Comedy*, Oxford, Oxford University Press, 1980.

883   *Six Yogas/Doctrines*: see Guenther.

884   Smith, D. E., *India as a Secular State*, Princeton, Princeton University Press, 1963.

885   Smith, M., *The Persian Mystics: Attar*, London, John Murray, 1932.

886   Smith, M., and Schimmel, A., *Rabia the Mystic and her Fellow Saints*, Felinfach, Llanerch, 1994.

887   Snellgrove, D. L., *The Hevajra Tantra*, London, 1959, 1960.

888   — *The Hevajra Tantra: A Critical Study*, Oxford, Oxford University Press, 1959.

889   Solis-Cohen, S., *Selected Poems of Moses ibn Ezra*, Philadelphia, Jewish Publication Society, 1974.

890   Sonde, N. D., *The Commentary of Sri Madhva on Katha Upanishad*, Bombay, Prakiashan, 1990.

891   Spector, S. A., *Jewish Mysticism: An Annotated Bibliography on the Kabbalah in English*, New York, Garland, 1984.

892   Sperling, H., and Simon, M., *The Zohar*, London, Soncino Press, 1931–4.

893   *Spiritual Exercises*: see Ivens.

894   Sponberg, A., and Hardacre, H., *Maitreya: The Future Buddha*, Cambridge, Cambridge University Press, 1988.

895   *Spring and Autumn Annals*: see Legge.

896   Srauta: see Ranade.

897   *Srautakosa: Encyclopedia of Vedic Sacrificial Ritual . . .* , Poona, 1958–73.

898   *Śrividya Śakta*: see Brown.

899   Stael-Holstein, A., ed., *The Kaśyapaparivarta: A Mahayana Sutra of the Ratnakuta Class*, Shanghai, 1926.

900   Star, J., *Rumi: In the Arms of the Beloved*, New York, Putnam, 1997.

901   Stcherbatsky, T., *Madhyanta Vibhanga: Discourse on Discrimination between Middle and Extremes*, Moscow, Academy of Sciences of USSR Press, 1936.

902   Stemberger, G., *Introduction to the Talmud and Midrash*, Edinburgh, T & T Clark, 1996.

903   Stevenson, J., *Creeds, Councils and Controversies: Documents Illustrating the History of the Church AD 337–461*, London, SPCK, 1989.

904 Stewart, J. M., *The Life of Gampopa: The Incomparable Dharma Lord of Tibet*, Ithaca, Snow Lion, 1995.

905 Stitskin, L. D., *Letters of Maimonides*, New York, Yeshiva University Press, 1977.

906 Stock, D., *A Haiku Journey: Basho's The Narrow Road to the Far North and Selected Haiku*, Tokyo, Kodansha International, 1974.

907 Stoler-Miller, B. S.: see Miller.

908 Stryk, L., *Traveller, My Name: Haiku of Basho*, Norwich, Embers Handpress, 1984.

909 — *On Love and Barley: Haiku of Basho*, London, Penguin, 1985.

910 Subrahmanian, N. S., *Encyclopaedia of the Upanishads*, New Delhi, Sterling, 1985.

911 *Sugagasa no nikki*: see Marra.

912 *Sukhavativyuha*: see Gomez, Inagaki, Muller.

913 Suleiman, S. R., and Crosman, I., *The Reader in the Text: Essays on Audience and Interpretation*, New York, Columbia University Press, 1983.

914 *Summa Contra Gentiles*: see Pegis.

915 *Summa Theologica*, London, Eyre & Spottiswoode, 1964–80.

916 Suzuki, D. T., *The Lankavatara Sutra: A Mahayana Sutra*, London, Routledge, 1932.

917 — *Essays*, III, London, Luzac, 1934.

918 Swartz, M. D., *Mystical Prayer in Ancient Judaism: An Analysis of Ma'aseh Merkavah*, Tubingen, Mohr, 1992.

919 *Table Talk*: see Hazlitt.

920 *Tadhkirat alAwliya*: see Arberry, Ritter.

921 Tagare, G. V., *The Bhagavata Purana*, Delhi, Motilal Banarsidass, 1976–9.

922 — *The Brahmanda Purana*, Delhi, Motilal Banarsidass, 1983–4.

923 — *The Kurma Purana*, Delhi, Motilal Banarsidass, 1981–2.

924 — *The Narada Purana*, Delhi, Motilal Banarsidass, 1980–2.

925 — *The Skanda Purana*, Delhi, Motilal Banarsidass, 1992– .

926 — *The Vayu Purana*, Delhi, Motilal Banarsidass, 1987–8.

927 *Tahafut alFalasifah*: see Kamali.

928 *Tale of Genji*: see Bowring, Brownlee, Morris, Seidensticker.

929 Talmud: see Ehrman, A., Epstein, Neusner, Stemberger.

930 *Tamakushige*: see Brownlee.

931 Tamke, S., *Make a Joyful Noise Unto the Lord: Hymns as a Reflection of Victorian Social Attitudes*, Athens, Ohio University Press, 1978.

932 Tanabe, G. J., *Religions of Japan in Practice*, Princeton, Princeton University Press, 1999.

933 Tanner, N. P., *Decrees of the Ecumenical Councils*, London, Sheed & Ward, 1990.

934 Tantra: see Brooks, Farrow, Finn, Guenther, Hopkins, Rai, Rawson, Sharma, Snellgrove, Wallace, Willemen, Yeshe Donden.

935 *Tao te ching*: see *Daodejing*.

936 Tappert, T. G., *The Book of Concord: The Confessions of the Evangelical Lutheran Church*, Philadelphia, Fortress Press, 1959.

937 Tatia, N., *Tattvartha Sutra: That Which Is*, San Francisco, HarperCollins, 1994.

938 *Tattvartha*: see Dixit, Jaini, Tatia.

939 Tatz, M., *Asanga's Chapter on Ethics . . .*, Lewiston, Edwin Mellen Press, 1986.

940 *Ta'wil alHadith*: see Baljon, Jalbani.

941 Teeuwen, M., *Watarai Shinto: An Intellectual History of the Outer Shrine in Ise*, Leiden, Research School, 1996.

942 — *Motoori Noringa's The Two Shrines of Ise: An Essay of Split Bamboo*, Wiesbaden, Harrassowitz, 1995.

943 *Tenzo kyokun*: see Wright, T.

944 *Tevaram*: see Peterson.

945 *Theragatha/Therigatha*: see Schelling.

946 Thomas, R. S., *Autobiographies*, London, Dent, 1997.

947 — *The Penguin Book of Religious Verse*, London, Penguin, 1963.

948 Thurman, R. A. F., *The Tibetan Book of the Dead*, New York, Benton Books, 1994.

949 *Tibetan Book of the Dead*: see Coleman, Evans-Wentz, Fremantle, Hodge, Thurman.

950 *Tiruvaymoli*: see Carman, Chari, Clooney, Narayanan.

951 Torrey, C. C., *Selections from the Sahih of al-Bukhari*, Leiden, Brill, 1906.

952 *Tosefta*: see Cohen, Greenup, Neusner.

953 Trent: see Neuner, Schroeder.

954 Trilocham Singh, *et al.*, *Selections from the Sacred Writings of the Sikhs*, London, Allen & Unwin, 1960.

955 *Trimshika*: see Anacker, Chan Wing-tsit.

956 Trott, J., *A Sacrifice of Praise: An Anthology of Christian Poetry in English from Caedmon to the Mid-Twentieth Century*, Nashville, Cumberland House, 1999.

957 Tsoukalas, S., *Bhagavadgita: Exegetical and Comparative Commentary . . .* , Lewiston, Mellen Press, 2007.

958 Tugwell, S., *Early Dominicans: Selected Writings*, London, SPCK, 1982.

959 Tulsidas: see Allchin, Growse, Hill.

960 Tyndale: see Cooper, Daniell, *English Hexapla*, Hardy Wallis.

961 Ueda, M., *Basho and His Interpreters: Selected Hokku with Commentary*, Stanford, Stanford University Press, 1991.

962 Umasvati: see Dixit, Jaini, Tatia.

963 Umeroi-Diwana, M. S., *The Japu, by Guru Nana Deva*, Chandigarh, Vikas, 1979.

964 Upanishads: see Goodall, Hume, Krishna Warrier, Nikhilananda, Olivelle, Radhakrishnan, Subrahmanian.

965 Upton, C., *Doorkeeper of the Heart: Versions of Rabia al-Adawiyyah*, Putney, Threshold, 1988.

966 *Vajracchedika*: see Conze.

967 *Vamakesvara Tantra*: see Finn.

968 Van Buitenen: see Buitenen.

969 Varley, H. P., *A Chronicle of Gods and Sovereigns: Jinno shotoki of Kitabatake Chikafusa*, New York, Columbia University Press, 1980.

970 Varma, M., *The Gita Govinda of Jayadeva*, Calcutta, Writers Workshop, 1968.

971 Vasubandhu: see Anacker, Chatterjee, Chan (194), Dalia, Griffiths, Kochumottom, Pruden.

972 Vatican Councils: see Abbott, Flannery, Hastings, Neuner, Tanner, Vorgrimler.

973 Vaudeville, C., *Kabir: Introduction and Translation from the Hindi*, Oxford, Clarendon Press, 1974.

974 — *A Weaver Named Kabir*, Delhi, Oxford University Press, 1997.

975 *Vedanta Sutra*: see Adams, Date, Rao.

976 Vedas: see Bhattacharji, Bloomfield, Bose, O'Flaherty, Gonda, Goodall, Griffith, Macdonnell, Maurer, Panikkar.

977 Vir Singh, B., *Purantam Janamsakhi*, Amritsar, Khalsa Samachar, 1948.

978 *Visuddhimagga*: see Nanamoli, Warren.

979 *Vita Nuova*: see Musa, Oelsner, Reynolds, Rossetti.

980 Vorgrimler, H., *Commentary on the Documents of Vatican II*, London, 1967–9.

981 Vulgate: see Ackroyd, Glunz, Lampe, White, H., Wordsworth.

982 Wace, H., and Buchheim, C. A., *First Principles of the Reformation*, London, John Murray, 1883.

983 Waldron, W. S., *The Buddhist Unconscious: The Alayavijnana in the Context of Indian Buddhist Thought*, London, Routledge, 2003.

984 Waley, A., *The Tale of Genji*, London, Allen & Unwin, 1935.

985 — *The Book of Songs*, London, Allen & Unwin, 1937.

986 — *The Analects of Confucius*, London, Allen & Unwin, 1938.

987 — *Three Ways of Thought in Ancient China*, London, Allen & Unwin, 1939.

988 — *The Way and its Power: A Study of the Tao Te Ching and its Place*

in Chinese Thought, New York, Evergreen, 1958.

989 Wali Allah: see Baljon, Harmansen, Jalbani.

990 Wallace, V. A., *The Kalacakratantra: Translated from Sanskrit, Tibetan, and Mongolian*, New York, Columbia University Press, 2004.

991 Wallenstein, M., *Some Unpublished Piyyutim from the Cairo Genizah*, Manchester, Manchester University Press, 1956.

992 Walshe, M., *The Long Discourses of the Buddha*, Somerville, Wisdom Publications, 1995.

993 Warren, H. C., rev. Kosambi, D., *Visuddhimagga of Buddhaghosacariya*, Cambridge, Harvard University Press, 1950.

994 Watarai: see Teeuwen.

995 Watson, B., *Complete Works of Chuang Tzu*, New York, Columbia University Press, 1968; cf., *Zhuangzi: Basic Writings*, New York, Columbia University Press, 2003.

996 — *Selected Writings of Nichiren*, New York, Columbia University Press, 1990.

997 — *The Lotus Sutra*, New York, Columbia University Press, 1993.

998 — *Letters of Nichiren*, New York, Columbia University Press, 1996.

999 — *The Analects of Confucius*, New York, Columbia University Press, 2009.

1000 — *Xunzi: Basic Writings*, New York, Columbia University Press, 2003.

1001 — and Takigawa, K., *Records of the Historian: Chapters from the Shih Chi*, New York, Columbia University Press, 1969.

1002 Watt, M., *The Faith and Practice of al-Ghazali*, London, Allen & Unwin, 1953.

1003 — and Bell, R., *Introduction to the Quran*, Edinburgh, Edinburgh University Press, 1970.

1004 Weigel, G., 'The Significance of Papal Pronouncements', in Fremantle, *q.v.*

1005 Weinstein, A., *Gates of Light: Sha'are Orah*, London, HarperCollins, 1994.

1006 Welch, H., *The Practice of Chinese Buddhism, 1900–1950*, Cambridge, Harvard University Press, 1967.

1007 Wensinck, A. J., *A Handbook of Early Muhammadan Tradition*, Leiden, Brill, 1960.

1008 Wheeler, P., *The Sacred Scriptures of the Japanese*, New York, Schumann, 1952.

1009 Whinfield, E. H., *The Masnavi Abridged*, London, Octagon, 1973.

1010 White, D., *The Bhagavad Gita: A New Translation with Commentary*, New York, Lang, 1988.

1011 White, H. J., *Novum Testamentum Latine: Editio Minor*, Oxford, Oxford University Press, 1911.

1012 White, R. W., *The Role of Bodhicitta in Buddhist Enlightenment, Including a Translation into English of Bodhicitta-sastra, Benkemmitsu-nikyoron, and Sammaya-kaijo*, Lampeter, Mellen Press, 2005.

1013 Whiteman, J. H. M., *Aphorisms on Spiritual Method: The Yoga Sutras of Patanjali . . .*, Gerrards Cross, Smythe, 1993.

1014 Wilhelm, R., and Baynes, C. F., *The I Ching, or, Book of Changes*, London, Routledge, 1968.

1015 Willemen, C., *The Chinese Hevajratantra*, Leuven, Peeters, 1983.

1016 Willis, J. D., *On Knowing Reality: The Tattvartha Chapter of Asanga's Bodhisattvabhumi*, New York, Columbia University Press, 1979.

1017 Willoughby, H. R., *The Coverdale Psalter*, Chicago, Caxton Club, 1935.

1018 Wilson, C. E., *The Masnavi of . . . Rumi, Book II*, London, Probsthain, 1910.

1019 Wilson, H. H., and Franklin, M. J., *The Vishnu Purana*, London, Ganesha Publishing, 2001.

1020 Wineman, A., *Mystic Tales from the Zohar*, Philadelphia, Jewish Publication Society, 1997.

1021 Winter, T. J., *The Remembrance of Death and the Afterlife*, Cambridge, Islamic Texts Society, 1989.

1022 Wong, E., *Cultivating Stillness*, Boston, Shambhala, 1992.

1023 Wonhyo: see Buswell, Lee.

1024 Wordsworth, J., *The Oxford Critical Edition of the Vulgate New Testament*, Oxford, 1882.

1025 Wormald, F., *The Book of Psalms from the Version of Miles Coverdale, As Published in the Great Bible of 1539*, London, Haymarket Press, 1930.

1026 Wright, A. F., *Buddhism in Chinese History*, Stanford, Stanford University Press, 1959.

1027 Wright, T., *Zen Master Dogen and Kosho Uchiyama*, New York, 1983.

1028 Wu, K., *Butterfly as Companion*, New York, State University of New York Press, 1990.

1029 Wyclif(fe), J.: see *English Hexapla*, Forshall, Lindberg.

1030 *Xiao Jing*: see Chai, Chen. I.

1031 *Xunzi*: see Watson.

1032 Yamamoto, D., *History of Mantrayana in Japan*, New Delhi, Aditya Prakashan, 1987.

1033 Yampolsky, P. B., *The Platform Sutra of the Sixth Patriarch*, New York, Columbia University Press, 1967.

1034 — *Letters of Nichiren*, New York, Columbia University Press, 1996.

1035 Yampolsky: see also Watson.

1036 Yao Xinzhong, *An Introduction to Confucianism*, Cambridge, Cambridge University Press, 2000.

1037 Yardi, M. R., *The Yoga of Patanjali*, Poona, Bhandarkar Oriental Institute, 1979.

1038 Yeshe Donden, *The Ambrosia Heart Tantra*, Dharamsala, Library of Tibetan Works and Archives, 1977– .

1039 *Yijing*: see Lynn, Palmer, Ritsema, Shaughnessy, Wilhelm.

1040 *Yoga Sutra*: see Chapple, Feuerstein, Leggett, Miller, Shearer, Whiteman, Yardi.

1041 Yogacara: see Harris, Powers.

1042 Yohanan, J. D., *The Poet Sa'di: A Persian Humanist*, Lanham, University Press of America, 1987.

1043 Yuasa, N., *Basho: The Narrow Road to the North and Other Travel Sketches*, London, Penguin, 1966.

1044 Zaehner, R. C., *The Bhagavadgita with a Commentary Based on the Original Sources*, Oxford, Oxford University Press, 1969.

1045 Zangwill, I., *Selected Religious Poems of Solomon ibn Gabirol*, Philadelphia, Jewish Publication Society, 1974.

1046 Zhang Zai: see Chan, Kasoff.

1047 *Zhong Yong*: see Chai, Chan, Hughes.

1048 Zhou Dunyi: see Chan.

1049 Zhu Xi: see Bruce, Chan, Gardner.

1050 *Zhuangzi*: see Chan, Chung, Cleary, Feng, Fung, Giles, Graham, Legge, Palmer, Watson (995), Wu.

1051 Zohar: see Dan, Gikatilla, Giller, Green, Gutwirth, Halevi, Lachower, Mathers, Matt, Robinson, Sassoon, Schafer, Scholem, Spector, Sperling, Wineman.

ACKNOWLEDGEMENTS

ILLUSTRATIONS

Integrated Pictures
1. The Scroll of Torah. © Ann Ronan Picture Library/Heritage Images/Corbis.
2. 'Christ of Saint John of the Cross' by Salvador Dali. Art Gallery and Museum, Kelvingrove, Glasgow, Scotland/© Culture and Sport Glasgow (Museums)/The Bridgeman Art Library.
3. The Opening Sura of the Quran. Public domain.
4. The Faravahar. © 2003 Charles Walker/TopFoto.
5. Durga slaying Mahisa. ©TopFoto.
6. The *Guru Granth Sahib*. © Hulton-Deutsch Collection/Corbis.
7. A *siddhapratima yantra*. The Freer Gallery of Art (F1997.33).
8. The Buddha. © Luca Tettoni/Corbis.
9. 'Plum blossom'. © Seattle Art Museum/Corbis.
10. Wooden printing blocks. © John Van Hasselt/Sygma/Corbis.
11. Mount Fuji. The Bridgeman Art Library.

Plate Sections
1. Muslim scribe and a painter of miniatures. Private Collection/Photo © Bonhams, London, UK/The Bridgeman Art Library.
2. Tools used by Muslim calligraphers. Private Collection. Photography © The Museum of Fine Arts, Houston, Thomas R. DuBrock, photographer.
3. A Sikh copies the *Guru Granth Sahib*. Narinder Nanu/AFP/Getty Images.
4. A Chinese monk inscribes a sentence from the Diamond Sutra. © Wolfgang Kaehler/Corbis.
5. Japanese printmaker. © Mary Evans Picture Library/Alamy.
6. Title page of *The Golden Haggadah*. © The British Library Board.
7. Scenes in *The Golden Haggadah* from *Bereshit* (*Genesis*). © The British Library Board.
8. Maimonides' *Mishneh Torah*. The Israel Museum, Jerusalem, Israel/Extended loan from Michael and Judy Steinhardt, New York/The Bridgeman Art Library.
9. The Babylonian Talmud. The Granger Collection/TopFoto.
10. The title page of *The Gates of Light*. © 2005 TopFoto/Fortean.
11. *The Gospel according to John* in Codex Sinaiticus. The British Library/HIP/TopFoto.
12. The opening of *The Gospel according to Mark* from *The Book of Kells*. The Granger Collection/TopFoto.

13. A page of the Eusebian Canons in *The Book of Kells*. The Granger Collection/TopFoto.
14. Walton's Polyglot Bible. Private Collection/Photo © Christie's Images/The Bridgeman Art Library.
15. *The Great Bible*. Luisa Ricciarini/TopFoto.
16. Wall hanging of Islamic calligraphy. Alamy.
17. The last two verses of sura 38. Freer Gallery of Art (F1930.60).
18. A Shi'ite prayer. © Victoria and Albert Museum, London.
19. 'Incident in a Mosque' from *The Diwan of Hafiz*. Harvard Art Museums/Arthur M. Sackler Museum, Gift of Stuart Cary Welch, Jr., 1999.300.2.
20. An episode from *Ramayana*. Freer Gallery of Art (F1907.271.236).
21. Scene from *Mahabharata* depicting Arjuna with Krishna. Getty Images.
22. Scene from *Mahabharata* carved in stone. © National Geographic Society/Corbis.
23. Tantric diagram of the cakras. The Granger Collection/TopFoto.
24. Yantras used in meditation. SSPL/Getty Images.
25. The Mul Mantra. Alamy.
26. Page from a Prajñaparamita Sutra. © Corbis.
27. Page from *Avatamsaka Sutra*. © Christie's Images/Corbis.
28. Library in the Haesin monastery. © John Van Hasselt/Sygma/Corbis.
29. Enso. Private Collection.
30. Bishamonten driving away demons. © Corbis.
31. Bamboo by Chen Banding. © Artkey/Corbis.
32. Calligraphy and painting by Koetsu and Sotatsu © Sakamoto Photo Research Laboratory/Corbis.
33. Calligraphy of Matsuo Basho. Werner Forman Archive/Basho Kenshokai, Ueno.
34. *The Vision of Purgatory and Paradise* by Dante Alighieri. Classic Image/Alamy.
35. Nazi burning of books. © Austrian Archives/Corbis.

TEXT PERMISSIONS

Every effort has been made to contact copyright holders. In the event of an inadvertent omission or error, please notify the editorial department at Atlantic Books, Ormond House, 26–27 Boswell Street, London WC1N 3JZ, for a correction to be made in future printings.

'Laws Concerning the Sabbath', *Mishneh Torah*, III.1, from Gandz, S., and & Klein, H., *The Code of Maimonides Book Three: The Book of Seasons*, © Yale University Press, 1961. Reprinted by permission of Yale University Press.

Poem about a thrush by Thomas Jones, from Parry, T., *The Oxford Book of Welsh Verse*, published by Oxford University Press, 1962.

'St Patrick's Breastplate', translated by N.D. O'Donoghue, in *An Introduction to Celtic Christianity*, by J. P. Mackey, published by T & T Clark, 1995, is reprinted by kind permission of Continuum International Publishing Group.

Poems by Rumi, from *Light Upon Light: Inspirations from Rumi* by Andrew Harvey, published by North Atlantic Books, © 1996 by Andrew Harvey. Reprinted by permission of the publisher.

The Living Flame by John of the Cross, translation Sister Marjorie Flower OCD, from *The Poems of St John of the Cross*, published by The Carmelite Nuns, Varroville, in 1983. Reprinted by kind permission of The Carmelite Nuns, Varroville.

Nagarjuna's summary of the implication of *shunyata*, from, *The Fundamental Wisdom of the Middle Way: Nagarjuna's Mulamadhyamakakarika*, translated by Garfield (1995) © 1995 by Jay L. Garfield. By permission of Oxford University Press.

Verses from *Japji Sahib*, from Kaur Singh, N-G., *The Name of My Beloved: Verses of the Sikh Gurus*, published in 1995. Reprinted by permission of The International Sacred Literature Trust.

Poem by Appar, from I. V. Peterson, *Poems to Siva: The Hymns of the Tamil Saints*, published by Motilal Banarsidass in 1991, reprinted by kind permission of the publishers.

Huai Rang converts Ma zu to the Chan way, from Luk, C., *The Transmission of the Mind Outside the Teaching*, copyright © 1974 by Lu K'uan, reprinted by permission of Grove/Atlantic, Inc. and The Random House Group Ltd.

The episode of three princes and the hungry tigress, from Conze, E. (trans.), *Buddhist Scriptures*, published by Penguin Classics, 1959. Copyright © Edward Conze, 1959. Reproduced by permission of Penguin Books Ltd.

'The Heart Sutra', from Conze, E from Conze, E. (trans.), *Buddhist Scriptures*, published by Penguin Classics, 1959. Copyright © Edward Conze, 1959. Reproduced by permission of Penguin Books Ltd.

Three 'koans' (nos 29, 36 and 38) from the *Mumonkan*, from Reps, P., *Zen Flesh, Zen Bones*, published by Tuttle Publishing, 1998. Reprinted by permission of Tuttle Publishing.

A translation of the Buddhist text 'On Attaining the Settled Mind', from Tanabe, George J. (Ed.); *Religions of Japan in Practice*. ©1999 Princeton University Press. Reprinted by permission of Princeton University Press

Sayings from *Lunyu*, from *The Analects of Confucius*, translated by Simon Leys. Copyright © 1997 by Pierre Ryckmans. Used by permission of W.W. Norton & Company, Inc.

Translation of Song 259 of *Shijing*, from *Confucian Analects*, edited by Ezra Pound, translated by Ezra Pound, copyright © 1947, 1950 by Ezra Pound. Reprinted by permission of New Directions Publishing Group.

Translations of Songs 99, 166 and 259 of *Shijing*, from J.R. Allen (ed.) *The Book of Songs: Translated by Arthur Waley*, published by Grove Press, 1996. Reprinted by permission of the Arthur Waley Estate.

Passage from *Genji monogatari*, from Arthur Waley, *The Tale of Genji*, published by Allen and Unwin, 1935. Reprinted by permission of the Arthur Waley Estate.

INDEX